Benjamin Franklin
Unmasked

American Political Thought

Edited by Wilson Carey McWilliams
and Lance Banning

Benjamin Franklin Unmasked

On the Unity of His Moral, Religious, and Political Thought

Jerry Weinberger

University Press of Kansas

© 2005 by the University Press of Kansas
All rights reserved

Published by the University Press of Kansas (Lawrence, Kansas 66049),
which was organized by the Kansas Board of Regents and is operated and
funded by Emporia State University, Fort Hays State University, Kansas
State University, Pittsburg State University, the University of Kansas, and
Wichita State University

Library of Congress Cataloging-in-Publication Data
Benjamin Franklin unmasked : on the unity of his moral, religious, and
political thought / Jerry Weinberger.
    p. cm. — (American political thought)
  Includes bibliographical references and index.
  ISBN 0-7006-1396-X (alk. paper)
    1. Franklin, Benjamin, 1706–1790—Political and social views.
2. Franklin, Benjamin, 1706–1790—Religion. 3. United States—
Intellectual life—18th century. 4. United States—Politics and
government—1775–1783. 5. United States—Politics and government—
1783–1789. I. Title. II. Series.
E302.6.F8W545   2005
973.3'092—dc22
2005005623

British Library Cataloguing-in-Publication Data are available.

Printed in the United States of America
10 9 8 7 6 5 4 3 2 1

The paper used in this publication meets the minimum requirements of the
American National Standard for Permanence of Paper for Printed Library
Materials z39.48-1984.

Wilson Carey McWilliams died, suddenly and unexpectedly, on the day before I finished correcting the page proofs for this book. Carey suggested the project long ago, put up cheerfully with my procrastination, and then helped and encouraged and laughed with me along the way. The scholarly world has known no finer man. I offer this book as a tribute to his memory.

Contents

Preface   ix

Introduction: The Written Word Remains   1

1   The *Autobiography*: A Comic Moral Saga?   15

2   The *Autobiography*: Or Just a Pack of Lies?   43

3   The Philosophical Wag   67

4   Shameless Ben   100

5   The Metaphysical Follies   135

6   Dialectics and the Critique of Morality   174

7   The Political Principles of the Good Life   206

8   The Political Project of the Good Life   254

Conclusion: Will the Real Ben Franklin Please Stand Up?   287

Notes   293

Index   327

Preface

When I began this project, I had no idea that when I finished America would be in the grip of a Benjamin Franklin craze. Four impressive, admiring, and best-selling biographies of Franklin have appeared since well after I began. His face has moved from the one-hundred-dollar bill (not such a bad place) to the covers of weekly newsmagazines. As the Franklin tercentenary approaches, the hoopla is likely to increase. All this is on top of the normal stream of historical and literary studies of the manifold Franklin: self-made man, model American, natural scientist, writer, moralist, philanthropist, politician, and diplomat, to name just a few of his talents, achievements, and aspects of character. It's as if we, like the French during the American Revolution, have come to idolize Franklin as a model of virtues lost or promise still unfulfilled. Mark Twain said that Franklin's *Autobiography* makes life tough for young boys held up to its example of relentless self-discipline and hard work.[1] These boys had better not think they'll get off the hook any time soon.

Franklin's reputation did not always fly so high. There have always been those with doubts about him—those who, like John Adams, have sniffed the wispy smoke of a certain slipperiness and irony in his self-presentation and have concluded that where there is smoke there must be fire, perhaps something not so pretty, such as a liar, ambitious opportunist, nonbeliever, or phony. Some recent historians still sniff this smoke. Perhaps more powerful are the critics who take Franklin pretty much for what Franklin says he was but who don't like or really can't stand what they see. Observers from the American transcendentalists to antibourgeois thinkers such as Max Weber and of course, famously, D. H. Lawrence and, less famously, Charles Angoff, have derided Franklin as acquisitive and shallow at best and as a full-blown philistine at worst. To hear Lawrence describe Franklin, he is Friedrich Nietzsche's "last man"—a calculating, antiheroic, priggish Babbitt who not only read newspapers but purveyed them as well, in order to hector and rationalize and dull the souls of his fellow citizens.[2]

Perhaps because of the unfair drubbing Franklin took at the hands of such critics, a more balanced, appreciative, and scholarly view of Franklin has emerged since the 1960s, especially from intellectual and literary historians. Attuned to Franklin's engagements with the serious intellectual currents and thinkers of his age—men like Anthony Collins, Anthony Ashley Cooper, third Earl of Shaftesbury, John Locke, Thomas Hobbes, Bernard Mandeville, Francis Hutcheson, John Milton, Alexander Pope, John Trenchard, and Thomas Gordon—these historians could and did paint a more complicated picture of "the First American." The Franklin thus discovered was anything but shallow. However hard it is to see, Franklin wrestled with the most profound and mysterious issues that agitate the human soul: love, the meaning of life, morality, mortality, and God. Far from being a one-dimensional Babbitt, Franklin has emerged as something of a mystery: an ironic combination of simplicity and complexity who always leaves us with a puzzle. What we see with Franklin, and especially in the *Autobiography,* is an array of often conflicting and playful personae, beneath which is an elusive core.

The many-sidedness of Franklin's thought and life was given an enduring characterization in John William Ward's famous 1963 essay "Franklin: His Masks and His Character." According to Ward, Lawrence was led astray because he did not see the Franklin manifold: Franklin "contained in his own character so many divergent aspects that each observer can make the mistake of seeing one aspect as all and celebrate or despise Franklin accordingly." For all his seeming simplicity, Franklin reflected as deeply on pride and sin as did the contemporary preacher and theologian Jonathan Edwards. Franklin gets under our skin; we admire him, but "at the same time we are uneasy with the man who wears so many masks that we are never sure who is there behind them. Yet it is this very difficulty of deciding whether we admire Franklin or suspect him, that makes his character an archetype for our national experience." As David Levin argued in 1964, the *Autobiography* is a great work of art, characterized by "humorous self-criticism," in which Franklin "deliberately appearing to be more simple than he is . . . draws our attention away from the books he has read." Franklin hides himself and is "deceptively simple," but even so we have much to learn from his life that "still speaks the truth to us as an admirable representative of the Enlightenment."[3]

Just a few years after these important essays appeared, Alfred Owen Aldridge published his groundbreaking and equally important study of Franklin's religious thought: *Benjamin Franklin and Nature's God.* This work made a convincing case for the seriousness of the story Franklin tells in the *Autobiography* of his encounter with the freethinking theological currents of his time. According to Aldridge, Franklin, just as he tells us in his own story, at first broke from his Presbyterian religious background and embraced free-thinking and Enlightenment Deism.[4] He pushed this Deism—based on the natural science of the age—to a radical and ultimately atheistic and even nihilistic extreme, at which point he realized that his extreme position was morally disastrous and that nothing about God and divine providence could be deduced from the natural science he so admired. Aldridge then traces Franklin's intellectual journey from "metaphysical" and "scientific" Deism, which might as well be nihilistic atheism, to a humanistic Deism based on "the Shaftesburian assumption of moral integrity pervading the universe."[5] Far from being a spiritual bore, Franklin was as serious about religion as could be and walked to the skeptical precipice before finding a faith and morality that could make life worth living. Franklin may reveal no inner struggles—he displays no soul's *Sturm und Drang*—but about the big questions of life he did experience crisis, and he did think about them seriously and conclude decisively.

Aldridge's view of Franklin's spiritual journey still influences the best recent scholarship on Franklin's moral and religious views. Along with the kindred story about Franklin's manifold personality, elusive core, and masks, it is powerfully alive in the recent popular biographies. In his 2003 biography, Walter Isaacson follows the script to a T. Of the *Autobiography* he says:

> With a mix of wry detachment and amused self-awareness, Franklin was able to keep his creation [his younger self] at a bit of a distance, to be modestly revealing but never deeply so. Amid all the enlightening anecdotes, he included few intimations of inner torment, no struggles of the soul or reflections of the deeper spirit. More pregnant than profound, his recollections provide a cheerful look at a simple approach to life that only hints at the deeper meanings he found in serving his fellow man and thus his God.

To this argument about Franklin's elusiveness, Isaacson adds the broad story Franklin tells about his spiritual journey: At first he adopted a radical form of Deism, the "Enlightenment-era creed that reason and the study of nature (instead of divine revelation) tell us all we can know about our Creator." He then came to see that his radicalism was infused with "squirrelly" morals and came then to adopt "a virtuous, morally fortified, and pragmatic version of deism." This Franklin was moral, altruistic, theistic, and completely free of sectarian dogma.[6]

The same story appears in H. W. Brands's 2000 biography of Franklin. Brands says that Franklin was a skeptic and not a rebel, that his early Deism unsettled him with its lack of morality, and that he later came to believe that "truth, sincerity, integrity," and other virtues did indeed exist. Franklin had a moral "epiphany" when he realized that actions are not good or bad because they are commanded or forbidden but are, rather, commanded or forbidden because they are good or bad. Franklin moved from agnostic and almost atheistic immorality to pragmatic morality and pragmatic religion.[7]

Likewise, Edmund Morgan tells us that Franklin became a Deist and that when first in London he pushed that Deism to radical and "staggering," that is, immoral, results. He then rejected this hard, radical Deism, along with the metaphysics on which it was based, and adopted the morality described by Brands, as well as the view that "far from being meaningless, virtue, that is, morality, was the essence of all true religion, Christianity included." Although Franklin did not include charity in his list of the virtues, says Morgan, it "was actually the guiding principle of Franklin's life." Still, says Morgan, Franklin is in the end very hard to know "because it is so hard to distinguish his natural impulses from his principles."[8]

Even the more skeptical Gordon Wood, in his exciting new account of Franklin's political journey from mechanical upstart to gentleman, thence to British imperialist, and finally to republican patriot, adopts this general point of view. Thus, despite being a hard-boiled pragmatist and despite a tinge of opportunism and an even-stronger dose of personal interest in public affairs, Franklin was, in Wood's view, in the end devoted to public service as the highest moral obligation. Even though Franklin was a "man of many masks" and so not easy to know, the lad who once lacked religious restraints came eventually to believe that "the most acceptable service of God was the doing Good to man."[9]

This book stands squarely in the tradition of scholarship that runs from Ward, Levin, and Aldridge to recent research and to the popular biographies. In my view, this tradition establishes without doubt that Franklin was no Babbitt or Nietzschean last man and was, despite appearances to the contrary, a deeply serious thinker. But this book also, respectfully, breaks with that tradition—especially with its view of Franklin's ultimate conclusions about morality and religion. According to the traditional view, Franklin did wear his masks, so we can never be sure about his inner life; but it is clear enough that he grappled with the big questions and answered them, in favor of faith and charity, so as to live an exemplary life. Brainy boy is born poor and on his own, becomes an intellectual smart aleck and delinquent, then gets morality and religion and becomes the first American hero and exemplar of the new man for a new and promising age. This is surely a Franklin we can all come to love: We can well imagine him as a guest on the *Oprah Winfrey Show*. The problem is that he just did not exist. That Franklin is a fiction created by Franklin. I say this not to debunk the myth and rain on the parade. On the contrary, in my view, that parade has not done full justice to its hero. Franklin is, in the recent story, correctly portrayed as a fascinating, admirable, and serious man, but the story does not go all the way.

Franklin's spiritual and intellectual journey was indeed marked by a deeply serious and disturbing encounter with the big questions of life—God, the soul, morality and justice, happiness. But that journey led to a skepticism even *more radical* and more thoughtfully grounded than the one the scholarship says he rejected. This skepticism is what makes Franklin's *humanity* so impressively profound. Franklin's humanity was based on no illusions about life—on no sappy opinions about the natural goodness of human beings, on no false hopes for the future. Rather, it was based on seeing the world as it really is and not as we want it to be. Moreover, his deep skepticism was, in his view, the only means by which he or any human being could be free of pride, envy, anger, and indignation, which distort the soul, separate us from others, and give rise to folly and human wickedness.

Two things I noticed about Franklin first led me to be suspicious of the prevailing scholarly and biographical views. A brief story is in order. I am ashamed to admit that I began this book for less-than-noble motives. When I was approached about a project for this series, I chose Franklin because my university administrative position had interrupted my work on Francis Bacon and Martin Heidegger, and I was attracted to Franklin's Baconianism and rashly assumed he would be easy enough to study in the fits and starts then dictated by my duties. Moreover, I knew of Franklin's reputation for humor and looked forward to a break from the drudgery of my administrative tasks (not to mention from the dour Heidegger). I was not prepared for what I encountered. Franklin proved to be not just funny but, at least to my sensibility, hysterically funny. He had me in such stitches that my wife, hearing me in my study, often thought I was losing my marbles. And yet in reading the intellectual and literary histories, I found this comedy was either simply ignored, remarked on cursorily, or merely noted in passing as an aspect of Franklin's character or as the origin of folksy, homespun American humor.

Moreover, the literature consistently turned its eyes from a crucial aspect of Franklin's humor: its extraordinary vulgarity, scatology, and blasphemy. Franklin's humor is closer to that of Aristophanes than to that of Will Rogers. As raunchy as Franklin can be, I found that he gets even raunchier on second, third, and fourth readings, and sometimes the real joke is the opposite of what it first seemed to be. As I hope to show, Franklin's humor is radical and philosophical and is an important window to his deepest thoughts. Perhaps the scholarship, I surmised, was too enamored of its object or too concerned to defend Franklin from the arrows of his detractors to give this humor sufficient attention. But given the philosophical depth of the humor, I surmised as well that the literature might have missed the mark in an important respect.

Something else struck me about Franklin. In everything I read I discovered a massively powerful intellect lurking behind the leather-apron exterior. But Franklin does not wear his brains on his sleeve. I had expected him to be reserved and ironic and to wear his masks, as the scholarly tradition claims. But I was not prepared for how slippery and artful his writing in fact is: He pulls the rug out from under his reader, he contradicts himself, he plays games and indulges in argumentative sleights of hand. Franklin's playfulness has often been noted, especially as regards the *Autobiography*. John Updike said that the *Autobiography* is an "elastically insouciant work, full of cheerful contradictions and humorous twists—a fond look back upon an earlier self, giving an intensely ambitious young man the benefit of the older man's relaxation."[10] But as I read and reread and reread the *Autobiography* yet again, I discovered that Updike's opinion is not just an understatement but is also wide of the mark.

The more one reads the *Autobiography*, the more little things pop up that do not make sense, that do not add up, that make one start over again. Sometimes big things pop up that do not make sense, even though they seemed clear enough on the first few readings—and this despite the fact that Franklin revised the whole work several times with great care. I came to believe that the scholarly tradition, for all its careful attention to Franklin's engagement with the serious ideas of his time, went wrong in buying the broad story Franklin tells about his spiritual journey in the *Autobiography*. When, following Franklin's clues, I unraveled that story and took a bird's-eye view of it, it did not hold together. Despite all the progress made by the literature, it had, I suspected again, missed the mark in the fundamental respect. Something else was going on in the *Autobiography*, something more provocative and even disturbing than an older man's relaxed retrospection.

So I read almost every word in the *Papers* of Benjamin Franklin. Those works most relevant to my theme—his religious and moral and general political thought—I read repeatedly and slowly over the course of several years before putting pen to paper. My conclusion is this: Franklin did wear masks and practiced an amazingly elusive art of writing. Franklin *is* elusive. But the real Franklin—at least what Franklin tells us he *really* thought—is not completely hidden from our view. Franklin does not write openly. But he does write revealingly and in a manner that forces us to put two and two together and then to pursue unexpected paths and think for ourselves. We can, I think, put two and two together, and it is to that end that I offer this book. Once the sum comes into view, we can understand how Franklin could have worn so many faces and how he appeared to be so many different things to so many different people.

The real Franklin is a profound thinker who points to his most serious reflections about life in a portrait of his own path to understanding. The problem with these reflections, however, was that, unlike *Poor Richard's Almanack* and *The Way to Wealth*, they would not sell and could, and on occasion did, get him in serious trouble. This is why Franklin wore his masks, the most important of which was the picture of his spiritual journey and conversion portrayed in the *Autobiography* and still robust and in current scholarly and biographical vogue. The Franklin of the prevailing view is certainly an interesting man. But in the end, I hope to show, the real Franklin is even more interesting than anyone has yet discovered.

My topic is Franklin's moral, religious, and political thought. I hope to describe his views of the following matters: God and religion, moral virtue and morality in general, justice, equality, natural rights, love and the good life, the modern technological project, and the place and limits of reason in politics and human experience. So this book is obviously not a biography. But it has a biographical cast because, as I hope to show, Franklin presented his deepest thoughts about these matters by way of his artful account of his own life. In this regard, Franklin placed himself in the tradition of Plato, Xenophon, Augustine, and Jean-Jacques Rousseau, who philosophized by creating a written spectacle of a life: Socrates' in the cases of Plato and Xenophon and their own in the cases of Augustine and Rousseau—and Franklin. To know the most important things was, for Franklin, to answer two questions (to borrow an expression from John William Ward): Who am I? And how did I get to be me? This was not primarily because he thought *Franklin* such a big deal, but rather because in his mind the most important truths could be understood only by investigating our most immediate and concrete experiences of life—life as real people live it and not as we might see it through the dark glass of intellectual sophistication.

That is why Franklin wrote no comprehensive formal treatises. He did not believe that the deepest and most important questions could be answered by abstract, philosophical systems of the kind that become schools of thought. These systems are almost always some kind of dodge and merely obfuscate and protect us from the hard and simple facts we have to grapple with if we are to understand what it means to be human. Franklin wrote pamphlets, newspaper articles and essays, many letters, bagatelles, and even some short metaphysical tracts that he tells us he rejected. In the absence of a systematic treatise, one cannot guess beforehand where something important will turn up among these various sources. In my account, however, the *Autobiography* is the key to Franklin's thought. In that work he reveals the course of his intellectual life and tells us, from his mature perspective, how to think about the other important things he wrote. Together, these writings intimate to us how Franklin answered the fundamental and abiding questions not just of his life, or of American life, but of human life in general.

Franklin disliked high-flown theories and philosophical systems. Although we can speak of a Jeffersonian or Madisonian or Hamiltonian political theory, there is no such thing as a "Franklinian" political theory. The mere term sounds odd to our ears. So although this book is about Franklin's views of morality and religion and politics and life in general, it is not about his partisan politics in Pennsylvania, his views of the British Empire and representation, his specific take on the Revolution, his diplomacy, or his contributions to the Constitutional Convention. To the extent that this book is about these matters, my purpose will be to show how Franklin's views of such things as equality, freedom, natural rights, democracy, and the best regime show up in or cohere with his practical political activities, which, I am well aware, made up a considerable part of his life.

Since Franklin is great fun, I hope this book is fun as well. I tried to write not just for scholars and academics but for anyone interested in Benjamin Franklin. Therefore I have as far as possible engaged the relevant scholarly literature in the endnotes, so as not to disturb the interpretive flow. There are in this book a few indelicate expressions. I used them (though never beyond those of Franklin himself) and then decided to keep them, because they are the most appropriate way to express the tone as well as the gist of what Franklin, on occasion, has to say. In advance, I apologize and appeal as Franklin would to a certain excusing necessity.

My colleagues Werner J. Dannhauser, Steven Kautz, and David Leibowitz read and commented, with razor-sharpness, on previous drafts of this book. They saved me from many blunders and, on more than a few occasions, helped me see important things in Franklin that I had previously missed. I could not have written this book without their help. For it—and for their friendship—I am grateful. Fred Woodward and the editors of the American Political Thought series have been infinitely patient with missed deadlines and long delays and also provided much good advice, as did a penetrating and thoughtful anonymous reviewer and critic. I am also grateful for the sharp eye and keen advice of my excellent copyeditor, Kathy Delfosse. My wife, Diane, was heroically tolerant of my absorption in this project. It is to her that I dedicate this book, and also to the memory of my parents, Herbert and Margaret Weinberger.

Introduction:
The Written Word Remains

Tanto nomini nullum par elogium (no epitaph can be equal to so great a name). This epitaph is as appropriate to Benjamin Franklin as it is to Machiavelli, for whom it was originally written. As with "Machiavelli," mere mention of the name "Benjamin Franklin" commands immediate recognition of a comprehensive worldview, of a body of opinions about human motivation and character, moral life, politics, and the destiny of the human race. "Machiavelli": The end justifies the means; better to be feared than to be loved; the conquest of fortune, selfishness, and cold calculation; better to appear virtuous than actually to be so. "Franklin": Nothing is useful that is not honest; the bold and arduous project for arriving at moral perfection; the post office, the lending library, the matching grant, bifocals, and lightning rods; bootstrap self-improvement; a united and universal party for virtue.[1]

It may not have been such a good idea for Franklin to omit the epitaph, however. As I noted in the preface, there is considerable disagreement as to just what "Franklin" really means. The same evidence produces very differing judgments. Some, in the vein of D. H. Lawrence, take the evidence on its face and hate it. Said Lawrence of Franklin: ". . . unlovely, snuff-colored little ideal, or automaton, of a pattern American. The pattern American, this dry, moral, utilitarian little democrat, has done more to ruin the old Europe than any Russian nihilist."[2] Others find Franklin objectionable not because of who he really was, but rather because he was not who he wanted people to think he was. John Adams, Franklin's diplomatic colleague in Europe, thought him overrated and proud to a fault, a dissolute womanizer and social climber, and so much of a Francophile that he neglected American interests in favor of those of the French court. As Adams claimed to have said to the French statesman François marquis de Barbé-Marbois, Franklin had no religion and "all the atheists, deists, and libertines, as well as the philosophers and ladies, are in his train—another Voltaire, and thence."[3]

Franklin's political competitors and enemies thought him overly ambitious, a political opportunist, and an unreliable Johnny-come-lately to republican and revolutionary patriotism. To them Franklin was, in short, a hypocritical wolf in moral prig's clothing. Historians of Franklin's practical politics often incline to this skeptical point of view. And yet others, those in the interpretive tradition begun by Alfred Owen Aldridge, take the evidence pretty much on its face and like very much what they see: Franklin as the paragon American and model of morally serious pragmatism, faith, and, above all, public service.

One clear fact of Franklin's life speaks in favor of the skeptics' view: that he so obviously cultivated the *image* of the new man for a new and better age. Franklin worked hard to become a celebrity of his time. Writing from the village of Passy (near Paris) to his daughter Sarah Bache in 1779, Franklin commented that the incredible numbers of medallions, pictures, busts, and prints of his "phiz" had "made your father's face as well known as that of the moon."[4] While in France, Franklin wore his special clothes and a hairdo consciously intended to bolster his popular image as the uncorrupted American, the new man of the future.[5] At the same time, this down-to-earth and homely creature had made himself into something of a god—"i-dol-ized," as he jokingly explained to Sarah.

But Franklin did not leave matters at a self-cultivated image and celebrity among his contemporaries. He presented this image to posterity in the form of his still-famous *Autobiography*, written in four stages between 1771 and 1790. The *Autobiography* is an account of Franklin's rise. It describes the ways and means—including the maxims and aphorisms decried by Lawrence and Mark Twain—of his coming from nowhere. It is also a saga of his self-administered moral redemption—a story of how the young Franklin, through introspection and self-mastery, saved himself from freethinking and moral skepticism and the irresponsible behavior to which they led him. Once redeemed, Franklin set out on a project of moral self-perfection and a wider project of promoting virtue and progress (moral, scientific, and social) in the world. The *Autobiography*, perhaps more than anything else Franklin did or wrote, is the source of his enduring and culture-forming image as the First American and model character for a new and promising age.

Some Franklin skeptics (those who do not believe the evidence, not those who do but do not like it) think the *Autobiography* is so much self-serving, disingenuous hogwash. But against this view there is one very powerful piece of evidence: Franklin himself pours a handful of salt on the story recounted in the *Autobiography*. When, in 1784, he describes his return to writing the *Autobiography*, in which he presented his project of arriving at moral perfection, he presents the return as compliance with requests from two friends,

Abel James and Benjamin Vaughn. These requests are expressed in two letters that Franklin incorporated into the narrative. James, writing from Philadelphia, urges Franklin to proceed because "what will the world say if kind, humane and benevolent Ben Franklin should leave his friends and the world deprived of so pleasing and profitable a work, a work which would be useful and entertaining not only to a few, but to millions."[6]

If published, says James, the account of Franklin's life will lead—as the life of no other living character could—American youth of the future to industry and business, frugality and temperance. Vaughn, writing from Paris, tells Franklin that "all that has happened to you is also connected with the detail of the manners and situation of *a rising* people; and in this respect I do not think that the writings of Caesar and Tacitus can be more interesting to a true judge of human nature and society." But more important, says Vaughn, is "the chance which your life will give for the forming of future great men; and in conjunction with your *Art of Virtue*, (which you design to publish) of improving the features of private character, and consequently of aiding all happiness both public and domestic." Vaughn adds that the *Autobiography* will "not merely teach self-education, but the education of *a wise man*; and the wisest man will receive lights and improve his progress, by seeing detailed the conduct of another wise man." Vaughn goes on to ask why weaker men are to be deprived of the Franklin model "when we see our race has been blundering on in the dark, almost without a guide in this particular, from the farthest trace of time."[7]

The implication of "*almost* without a guide" is clear enough: The *Autobiography* will take its place alongside the Bible, which by itself has not been sufficient to dispel the dark. Franklin did not have to insert these letters, with their wild hyperbole. But he did. And inserting them amounts to a boast on his part that is sufficiently grand, it seems to me, that we really cannot take it seriously unless we think Franklin is in the grip of near-lunatic vainglory. Including them is a joke, and by it Franklin means to warn us not to believe everything we read. If many have swallowed it hook, line, and sinker, that cannot have bothered Franklin. But he surely wanted more-discerning readers to note the irony and think more carefully about the lesson to be learned.

Thus, most sensible professional interpreters do note the irony and conclude one of two things: Franklin wants us to think seriously about his self-deprecating moderation, so that those who imitate him will not take themselves too seriously, or he just wants to make it hard for us to know what to make of him. In either case, the interpreters agree on one thing: He was elusive. Looking on the bright side, he makes us work to appreciate his admirable moderation. Looking on the dark side, he is just a slippery customer.

Not taking either side, Gordon Wood notes that in Franklin's "personal writings . . . he assumes so many roles and personae that it is difficult to know how to read him. Is he serious? Or is he ironical? Behind all the masks we do not know who he really is." Franklin's enemies "usually disliked [him] for the very characteristics that have made him so impenetrable to us—his deep reserve, his wearing of masks, his playing of roles. He was devious and duplicitous. He could not be trusted. His loyalties were questionable. Who was he anyhow and what did he really believe in?"[8]

It is thus no wonder that modern opinion differs on how to evaluate the moral saga depicted in the *Autobiography*: Is it serious and ironically complicated and morally revealing? Or is it just Franklin's playful peeping and hiding? Or is it hogwash, insincere, boastful self-promotion or apologetics governed by Franklin's contemporary political and propagandistic concerns?[9]

To anticipate what is to come in this book, the Franklin revealed by Franklin answers, to some extent, to both his admirers and his critics. He really was at least somewhat like the frugal, hardworking, self-improving character mocked by Twain. He really was considerably like the cold and calculating democratic utilitarian detested by Lawrence. He really did like wine, women, and song—and he liked them a lot. He really was a political pragmatist, at times a partisan, and often an opportunist, as his contemporary enemies suspected and as modern critics have suggested. He really did think of himself as the model of a new and better man for a new and better world. He really did consider religion and morality with the utmost seriousness. And he really did play his moral and theological cards very close to his vest.

But as I hope to show, there is behind the masks and beneath all the personae a single, clear-sighted, *philosophical* Benjamin Franklin—a profoundly skeptical Franklin who achieved a clear view of the most important matters of life. That Franklin, however, does not strut about on the stage of the *Autobiography* or anywhere else. Despite his occasional slapstick comedy, Franklin writes ultimately with great caution and ironic reserve. Adams complained about the old conjurer's extraordinary verbal oiliness on matters of religion: "The Catholics thought him almost a Catholic. The Church of England claimed him as one of them. The Presbyterians thought him half a Presbyterian, and the Friends believed him a wet Quaker."[10] From his own hard experience, Franklin learned of the dangers to oneself that can come from the spoken word. He knew also the dangers of the written word.

As Franklin said in describing the evangelical project of his friend George Whitefield, *"litera scripta manet"* (the written word remains). Franklin tells us that Whitefield's enemies used his writings against him to great effect. Whitefield would have been better off to have written nothing, says Franklin, since unguarded comments made orally might at least have been denied or explained away.[11] Aware of the danger of the written word—that it remains for all to see and leaves one a hostage to fortune—Franklin sometimes wrote with an artful slipperiness designed both to prod his careful readers into thought and to protect himself as best he could from those who, if they were to be presented with the possibilities Franklin reveals, would not at all like what they see.

Thus, in some of his works and when addressing the really touchy subjects, Franklin wrote so as to please and instruct those who were firmly attached to conventional views and who might get mad or be corrupted when these views were challenged. To these readers he wrote in order to elevate or moderate, but within the horizon of conventional views. But then, with his artful bag of rhetorical tricks, he wrote *at the same time* to those readers with whom he could be frank, who could profit from his much more radical questioning by testing on their own the consistency and implications of their common sense and most-cherished moral intuitions, opinions, and beliefs. These readers made up no secret club (unlike the Masons, with their initiations and secret signs, whom Franklin actually mocked). They required no social connections or special instructions. All they required was the ability to read and to do so with great care, an open mind, and a natural inclination to question the obvious and the conventional. These readers would be few, but they might be found anywhere—say, behind a printing press or blacksmith's anvil.

Franklin's methods for addressing these readers included anonymous (but not unrecognizable) authorship, irony, obvious or subtle contradictions that cause us to pause and think twice in order to puzzle them out, revealing allusions, sleights of hand, and multileveled comedy.[12] The key text is, again, the *Autobiography*. As the product of Franklin's remarkable art, that key text is (to borrow a phrase from Ralph Lerner, after Timothy Wagstaff) Janus-faced.[13] At first glance, it presents the conventional, paragon-American Franklin beloved by admirers and dismissed as ugly or hypocritical by sophisticated critics. But on careful inspection, the *Autobiography* puzzles in ways that set our minds to work and that send us, on our own, down Franklin's path of questioning.

As I hope to show, all the evidence suggests that Franklin's intellectual path led him to a powerful and deep skepticism. But, always careful, Franklin never says outright the things his puzzles force us to consider. As we move along, I will develop a picture of the philosophical Franklin—but the reader should not expect an account of Franklin's didactical philosophical teaching. There is none. There is, however, something much better: the questions, lines of thought, and conclusions to which we are prodded by Franklin's artful provocations.

Two examples of Franklin's typical sleight of hand will do for now. (And we will revisit them soon.) In the *Autobiography*, Franklin tells us that the publication of his pamphlet *A Dissertation on Liberty and Necessity, Pleasure and Pain* was a moral error, in part because it defended the doctrine, presumably Deism, that he associated with the ill treatment he received at the hands of Deist friends and with his mistreatment of his close friends. In the treatise Franklin denied free will, denied the existence of vice and virtue and merit, and rejected particular providence—the doctrine that God intervenes in our moral lives and punishes vice and rewards virtue in this world or in the next. Franklin tells us in the *Autobiography* that he "doubted whether some error had not insinuated itself unperceived" into his argument in the treatise, so as to "infect all that followed, as is common in metaphysical reasonings."[14]

Elsewhere, Franklin commented twice, in a 1746 letter to Thomas Hopkinson and in a 1779 letter to Benjamin Vaughn, that he had in disgust given up metaphysical "reasoning and study" because of its uncertainty and because of the "horrible errors I led my self into when a young man, by drawing a chain of plain consequences as I thought them, from true principles."[15] These remarks by Franklin, along with his claim in the *Autobiography* later to have embraced the doctrine of particular providence, have led to the widely held view that Franklin turned from hard-boiled, metaphysical, nihilistic, and morally irresponsible Deism (or even flat-out atheism) to "humanistic (and morally responsible) Deism" based not on the evidence of nature but, rather, on the moral evidence provided by introspection and practical life.[16]

The problem is that Franklin's account of the *Dissertation* in the *Autobiography* is too slippery to support this conclusion. He never says the conclusions of the *Dissertation* are wrong. Nor does he say that the Deism the treatise supports is wrong. On the contrary, he says only that some error might have "insinuated itself unperceived" into the treatise and that the Deism was "not very useful" even "though it might be true."[17] To Vaughn, Franklin says that he disliked and then burned the *Dissertation* "as conceiving it might have an ill tendency," not because it was false. All the evidence thus suggests that the "horrible errors" into which the young Franklin was led by the *Dissertation* involved his behavior, not the treatise or its doctrine, both of which might, in his mature view, be true. Or it could even be the case that in his mature view the doctrine was true but the reasoning of the *Dissertation* was flawed—that the *Dissertation's* conclusions were true, but only on other grounds. And all these possibilities bear mightily on Franklin's claim later to have embraced the doctrine of particular providence. At the very least, both doctrines cannot be true, and Franklin leaves us more with a puzzle to solve than with a clear account of his beliefs.

And then there is the small matter of the other sleight of hand: Franklin's complete contradiction of the claim, made in Part One of the *Autobiography*, that he denied and then returned to the doctrine of particular providence. In Part Two he tells us that he *never* doubted this doctrine.[18] These two claims cannot both be true. But if both cannot be true, then the entire moral saga depicted in the *Autobiography* cannot possibly be true. The contradiction is astounding and cannot be explained away as an accident, error, or failure of memory on Franklin's part. First, how could any mentally competent person (much less a person the likes of Franklin) err about such an important moment in his spiritual life?[19] And second, if we grant no competent person could be so mistaken, it follows that any normal human being would be sufficiently in control of an autobiographical text not to make a mistake about such an absolutely crucial spiritual matter. The contradiction is no accident; Franklin means to lay an even bigger puzzle in our laps. I hope to show how we might figure it out.[20]

IT WILL BE HELPFUL for those unfamiliar with Franklin's life to recount it in a very brief, thumbnail sketch, but with emphasis on his long and varied political career. If it's not a rags-to-riches story, it's certainly a story of petit bourgeois obscurity to riches and fame.

Franklin was born in January 1706, in Boston, into a large Puritan household. After just two years of formal schooling, he was by the age of ten at work full-time at his father's trade and was then apprenticed to his brother James, a year after the latter had set up a printing business in the city. By the time Franklin was fourteen years old, he had already read widely in philosophy and theology (including the Deists Anthony Collins and the earl of Shaftesbury), at this young age exhibiting the obvious sparks of prodigious genius. In 1722, Franklin wrote the fourteen Silence Dogood essays (satirizing, among other things, the religious establishment in Boston and Cotton Mather) for James's newspaper, the *New England Courant*. On finding himself in some political and other difficulties (in part having to do with the *Courant*'s position against smallpox inoculation, which was supported by Mather) and angry with his brother for treating him badly, Franklin abandoned James and went to Philadelphia, where he secured work with a printer named Samuel Keimer and lodging with John Read, who was the father of his wife-to-be, Deborah.

In Philadelphia the ingenious young Franklin was noticed by the governor, William Keith, who encouraged him to set up his own printing business and urged him to go to London to buy the necessary equipment and supplies. Keith promised to send letters of credit for the boy, but when Franklin arrived in London he discovered that Keith (a man notoriously full of hot air) had simply fooled the young lad: There were no letters, and Franklin was on his own without connections or money. He found employment with the printer Samuel Palmer and lodging with James Ralph, the intellectual friend who, in the process of abandoning his wife, had accompanied Franklin on the trip to London. While in London, in 1725, Franklin wrote and printed his notorious metaphysical work, *A Dissertation on Liberty and Necessity, Pleasure and Pain*, a radical Deist treatise that he soon came to regret and most of whose extant copies he therefore destroyed. Despite this regret, the tract brought Franklin to the attention of London intellectuals and led to his introduction to Bernard Mandeville.

A year later Franklin returned to Philadelphia with the Quaker merchant Thomas Denham, for whom he then worked as clerk. After Denham's death, Franklin returned to work for the printer Keimer and formed a club of young intellectuals, called the Junto, for the purpose of mutual aid and improvement and for the discussion of morals, politics, and natural philosophy, as well as for drinking and dining. Franklin sustained the club for thirty years, until he left Philadelphia for England as agent for the Pennsylvania Assembly in 1757. In 1728 Franklin went into the printing business on his own, and within two years he acquired Keimer's newspaper, the *Pennsylvania Gazette*, was named official printer for Pennsylvania, fathered a bastard son, and then, as a step toward respectability, married the plodding but faithful Deborah Read.

The year 1731 marked the takeoff of Franklin's career in business, philanthropy, and public affairs. He became a Mason, began sponsoring profitable new printing partnerships, proposed the first subscription library, and, at the end of 1732, published the first *Poor Richard's Almanack*, which appeared annually until 1758 and sold, by Franklin's reckoning, a total of 250,000 copies, enough by themselves to make him a wealthy man.[21] Although Franklin was by his own account a lapsed Presbyterian, in 1735 he entered the religious and theological politics of his city, first defending in print a reformist preacher, the Reverend Samuel Hemphill, against charges of heterodoxy by the Presbyterian Synod and then in 1739 befriending (for life, as it turned out) and publishing the sermons of the revivalist Methodist preacher George Whitefield. Franklin became clerk of the Pennsylvania Assembly and organized the first fire company of Pennsylvania, and in 1737 he became postmaster of Philadelphia.

Four years later he invented the Franklin stove, and then in 1743 he proposed the formation of the American Philosophical Society and heard Archibald Spencer's lectures on electricity. Franklin began his remarkable career as a natural scientist after receiving, from Peter Collinson of the Royal Society of London, a glass tube and a pamphlet about recent German experiments with electricity. Franklin's proposed experiment on electricity, which showed how to prove that lightning and electricity were the same (and resulted in the invention of the lightning rod) earned him the Copley Medal of the Royal Society of London, honorary degrees from Harvard and Yale, and membership in the Royal Society in 1756. That was the upside of his electrical studies. The downside occurred when, in the course of his practical investigations, he nearly lost his life when zapped while electrocuting a turkey.

At roughly the same time that he began his studies of electricity, Franklin began his political career as well. In 1747 he published the essay "Plain Truth," which argued for stronger defenses against French and Spanish privateers (during King George's War), and the next year he organized a militia and a lottery to fund the building of defensive batteries. Franklin got his Union Fire Company to subscribe to that lottery by some subtle management of the company's Quaker members. In the course of his efforts for defense, Franklin became noticed—and feared as a democratic rabble rouser—by the colony's proprietor, Thomas Penn. Franklin retired from business—a rich and independent man—in 1748 and was elected to the Common Council of Philadelphia. He became a justice of the peace in 1749. In February 1751 the Pennsylvania Assembly passed Franklin's matching-grant bill to establish the Pennsylvania Hospital, and later that year Franklin was elected to the assembly, where he served until 1764.

Franklin had been thinking about colonial union for the sake of defense and relations with the Indians at least from 1751, when he proposed voluntary union of the colonies—and commented about the boundless potential for growth in America—in a letter to his business partner James Parker. Later in that same year Franklin wrote his famous essay "Observations Concerning the Increase of Mankind, Peopling of Countries, etc." eventually published in 1754, in which he outlined his theory of population growth and made, at the end of the piece, an infamous remark about the danger of immigration by Germans, whom he labeled "Palatine Boors." In 1754 Franklin attended the Albany Congress of colonial representatives to consider relations with the Iroquois and matters of defense against the French. At the congress Franklin proposed the ultimately rejected Albany Plan for the union of the colonies, this time to be imposed by Parliament. The next year, with the French and Indian War going on, he took on the arduous and ultimately expensive task of providing transport to General Edward Braddock for his attack on Fort Duquesne. That same year, 1755, Franklin proposed a successful militia bill, became a colonel in the militia (a position he had refused in 1748), and took on the dangerous task of building border forts and defenses.

In 1757 Franklin was appointed by the assembly to serve as its agent in

London. He was to argue the case for taxing the property of the proprietors, Richard and Thomas Penn, whose opposition to paying taxes had been a long-standing bone of contention among the Quaker Party and the assembly, the governor, and the proprietors. The issue was, of course, the funding of defense. Franklin stayed in London until 1762, and while there, he hobnobbed with intellectuals, philosophers, and natural scientists (including David Hume, Joseph Priestly, and Adam Smith), became Dr. Franklin (by way of an honorary doctorate from the University of St. Andrews), published an important essay on the importance of Canada for Great Britain—an essay that expressed his understanding of America as a fundamental pillar of the British Empire—and obtained a compromise decision from the Privy Council on the Supply Act of 1759, which provided for taxing proprietary land.[22] He also invented the glass harmonica, for which Mozart and Beethoven composed.

After returning to Philadelphia in late 1762, Franklin soon became embroiled in politics, and especially in the scheme to replace proprietary with royal government—a scheme that Franklin had long had on his mind before he left for England and that he had pursued doggedly and unsuccessfully for years. Still a member of the assembly (his friends had ensured his reelection each year during his absence in England), Franklin wrote in favor of the change to royal government in the pamphlet *Cool Thoughts* and then drafted a petition to the king for such a change, which, despite a poor showing in gathering signatures, was adopted by the assembly in 1764. In the course of the petition drive, however, Franklin lost the support of influential members of the Quaker Party (as well as of broader public opinion), who feared that royal government would diminish the liberties enjoyed under proprietary government. A countering petition drive by the supporters of the proprietors proved much more successful than Franklin's. In the election in October, Franklin lost his seat in the assembly. He was besieged by his enemies' charges of hidden ambition, fiscal misconduct while in England, and, especially, prejudice against Germans for having called them "Palatine Boors" in the essay "Observations Concerning the Increase of Mankind, Peopling of Countries, etc.,"[23] which was used by Franklin's enemies to mobilize the Germans against his reelection. Despite the loss of his seat, Franklin's Quaker Party won, and he was returned to London (again without his wife, Deborah) by the assembly as its agent; there, he continued to scheme on behalf of royal government until 1768.

Franklin remained in London from 1765 until May 1775. During this period, he argued successfully (and famously) in the House of Commons for the repeal of the Stamp Act, although not before nominating a personal friend to be the stamp distributor in Pennsylvania and thus fueling rumors of his support for the act, rumors that motivated a protesting mob in Philadelphia to threaten his house and poor Deborah. During the Stamp Act crisis, Franklin clearly misjudged the depth and breadth of colonial opposition. Even so, in his speech to the Commons, he argued that the Americans objected not to external taxation—taxes on imported goods—but only to internal taxation. After the repeal of the Stamp Act in March 1766, Franklin's support of "external taxation" came back to haunt him the next year with the passage of the Townshend Acts, which Franklin actually supported and tried to sell to his boycotting constituents. He pressed for reconciliation between England and the colonies and denied that the Americans' intention was independence, and as late as January 1768 he could tell his son that there was talk in London of his being appointed undersecretary to Lord Hillsborough, just that month appointed secretary of state for the colonies.[24]

By the following August, however, Hillsborough had informed Franklin that there was no ministerial support for royal government in Pennsylvania (and here ended the scheme), and relations between Franklin and the secretary became strained because of Hillsborough's hard line regarding the colonies and opposition to a land-company scheme, promoted by Franklin, for the sale of land in the Ohio Valley. By 1770, Franklin had become the agent not just for Pennsylvania but also for Georgia, New Jersey, and Massachusetts. But in January 1771, Hillsborough refused to accept Franklin's credentials as agent for Massachusetts, and that summer Franklin traveled in Ireland and Scotland (where he visited Hume) and wrote Part One of the *Autobiography*.

The years between 1771 and Franklin's return from England to America in 1775 were marked by increasing turbulence, not just between the two countries but for Franklin himself. The turbulence was not on account of Deborah, whose pleas for his return Franklin ignored and whose death, in 1774, seems not to have ruffled his feathers. Perhaps her death paled, in his mind, in comparison to the event that did ruffle his feathers: the single most painful humiliation of his life—the famous Hutchinson letters affair.

In 1772 Franklin had obtained letters, written during the Stamp Act crisis, sent by the governor and lieutenant governor of Massachusetts, Thomas Hutchinson and Andrew Oliver, respectively, to friends, including Thomas Whatley, subminister to First Minister George Grenville, that made it clear that some of Grenville's harsh policies toward the colonies had been suggested by Hutchinson and Oliver. With the harebrained intention of easing colonial passions by deflecting blame from Parliament to the governor and lieutenant governor, Franklin sent the letters to the speaker of the Massachusetts House, Thomas Cushing, who subsequently published them, supposedly against Franklin's wishes. A clamor and petition to the Crown for ousting Hutchinson and Oliver ensued. Franklin, in December 1773, admitted in public to having sent the letters to Cushing, and on the following January 29 (just nine days after the Boston Tea Party), at the final hearing by the Privy Council of the petition to remove Hutchinson and Oliver, Solicitor General Alexander Wedderburn delivered an hour-long diatribe attacking Franklin's behavior and character in the matter of the letters.[25]

The Cockpit (the meeting room, named for Henry VIII's cockpit) was jammed with thirty-five privy councilors and an audience (those lucky enough to gain admittance) that had anticipated fireworks—an audience that included Jeremy Bentham, Priestly, and Edmund Burke. Wedderburn called Franklin a thief and a scoundrel and a violator of private correspondence moved by the "coolest and most deliberate malice." Wedderburn made a vicious joke, based on a line from Plautus, that elicited laughter from the crowd. Franklin held his tongue but later described the scene as a bullbaiting, with himself as the bull.[26] Hume, among other of Franklin's friends, was shocked at his behavior, thinking it betrayed Franklin as a "very factious man."[27]

Two days after the ordeal in the Cockpit, Franklin was fired from his position as deputy postmaster general for North America. This was clearly the end of Franklin's hopes for political office in London, hopes that had been rekindled after Hillsborough's departure from ministerial office in August 1772.[28] Even so, Franklin stayed in London, offered to pay for the tea destroyed in Boston, and argued against the Coercive Acts. In the summer of 1774, Franklin worked with Lord Chatham (William Pitt) on a plan for reconciliation that was hooted down in the House of Lords, and on March 20, 1775, fearing arrest, Franklin left for America. Two days after his arrival, he was elected by the Pennsylvania Assembly as delegate to the Second Continental Congress.

While in Congress, Franklin drafted and worked for Articles of Confederation and served on the committee to write the Declaration of Independence. In July 1776 he served as delegate to and president of the Pennsylvania state convention, where he helped draft the radical unicameral Pennsylvania State Constitution, and two months later he was elected by Congress to serve as commissioner to France (along with Arthur Lee and Silas Deane and later the informal hangers-on William Lee and Ralph Izard).

Franklin was in France from December 1776 until September 1785, when he returned to Philadelphia and a locally triumphant reception. His tasks—and those of his colleagues, including John Adams, who replaced Deane in 1778—were to secure a treaty with France and, of course, desperately needed supplies and troops. Adored by the French—or as Franklin himself said, "i-dol-ized" by them—Franklin was famously successful and in January

1778 secured the first of a series of huge grants and engaged in the complex diplomacy (teasing France into support by intimations of reconciliation with England) that resulted in the commercial and military treaties with France signed in February 1778.

The commission was not without its internal strains and intrigues, the most notable being the conflict between Franklin and Adams. Adams was mortified when he and the other commissioners were recalled by Congress in September 1778, leaving Franklin to work in peace. The two men disagreed about the importance of France and about how to secure American interests in a future peace settlement with England.[29] In 1780 Franklin accused Adams (now back as commissioner to work out the peace with England) to Congress of having offended the French Court and especially the French foreign minister, Charles Gravier de Vergennes. In late 1781 Franklin was appointed—along with John Jay, Henry Laurens, and Thomas Jefferson—to join Adams as commissioners to negotiate the peace with England. And in early 1782 Franklin began the secret negotiations with England, behind Vergennes's back, that led eventually to the treaty that was signed in September 1783.

The following year Franklin wrote Part Two of the *Autobiography*. He had long desired to be relieved of his continuing diplomatic duties, and he got word in May 1785 that he could return to America, being replaced as minister plenipotentiary by Jefferson. Franklin's diplomatic achievement—not always appreciated at home, where the Lees and Izard worked against him in Congress—was without doubt the crown of his political career. He was, to use the words of Gordon Wood, "the greatest diplomat America has ever had."[30] During Franklin's time in France, he continued printing—including French translations of the American state constitutions—and also continued his involvement in natural philosophy. He also engaged in notorious flirtations with the ladies of aristocratic Paris, including the married Madame Anne-Louise Brillon de Jouy and the widow Madame Anne-Catherine Helvétius. He proposed marriage to Madame Helvétius; had she said yes, Franklin never would have returned to America.[31]

But she did not, and so on his return Franklin was elected to the Supreme Executive Council of Pennsylvania and then became its president, and he was elected to the office again in 1786 and 1787. Then, at the age of eighty-one, he became president of the Pennsylvania Society for Promoting the Abolition of Slavery. He served as Pennsylvania delegate to the Constitutional Convention and, though not in general a significant player in the proceedings, intervened in two crucial issues: the debate about limiting the suffrage to freeholders, which he opposed, and (reversing his prior unicameralism) the Connecticut compromise providing for equal representation of the states in an upper house. In 1788 he started Part Three of the *Autobiography* and stepped down as president of the Supreme Executive Council, and during that year he suffered the indignity of asking in vain for Congress to pay him his unpaid salary (this from the man who proposed in the convention that offices not be paid). In his remaining months of life, Franklin worked for abolition and started Part Four of the *Autobiography*. On April 17, 1790, he died, at the age of eighty-four.

1 • The *Autobiography*:
A Comic Moral Saga?

Franklin's *Autobiography* is addressed to his son, William, on the supposition that it will be agreeable to the son to know the circumstances of his father's life. But it is also addressed more generally to posterity:

> Having emerged from the poverty and obscurity in which I was born and bred, to a state of affluence and some degree of reputation in the world, and having gone so far through life with a considerable share of felicity, the conducing means I made use of, which, with the blessing of God, so well succeeded, my posterity may like to know, as they may find some of them suitable to their own situations, and therefore fit to be imitated.[1]

When Franklin speaks of the "means [he] made use of," we are unprepared for what is to follow, despite his comments in the sequel that in offering himself as a model he is giving fair quarter to vanity and that it is not absurd to thank God for vanity as one of the comforts of life. What follows in the *Autobiography* is not just an account of how to get rich and become famous. It is, rather, no less than a moral saga, an account of self-administered moral and religious redemption. At first corrupted by modern philosophy and religious freethinking, Franklin came to think "that vice and virtue were empty distinctions, no such things existing," and also came to "want" religion.[2] Franklin's nihilism led him to harm others and to corrupt his friends, who then, not surprisingly, harmed him. Shocked and chastened by his own behavior, Franklin next became convinced of morality—convinced that "*truth, sincerity and integrity*" were of the "utmost importance to the felicity of life"—and soon after, by 1728, came to the religion that he had earlier scorned. Once redeemed, Franklin set out on what he calls his "bold and arduous project of arriving at moral perfection."

That project would involve writing a book, to show others how he perfected himself, to be called "The Art of Virtue." As it turned out, that book was never written, but only because it was tied to an even nobler end: "A *great and extensive project* that required the whole man to execute."[3] This greater project, one of whose principles was to be "that the most acceptable service of God is doing good to man," would involve the creation of a "united party for virtue, by forming the virtuous and good men of all nations into a regular body" to work for the common human good. Franklin tells us that he did not finish this project because his circumstances and later public and private occupations caused him continually to postpone it. He continued to think that it was both a practical and useful idea, was never discouraged by its magnitude, and "always thought that one man of tolerable abilities may work great changes, and accomplish great affairs among mankind, if he first forms a good plan, and, cutting off all amusements or other employments that would divert his attention, makes the execution of that plan his sole study and business."[4]

The moral saga makes up over half of the *Autobiography* and covers the time from Franklin's birth until 1732, when he published his first *Poor Richard's Almanack*. The rest of the *Autobiography* covers the following twenty-five years of Franklin's business, philanthropic, scientific, and political career until 1757, when as agent for the Pennsylvania Assembly he went to London to mediate the dispute between the assembly and the proprietors. The text breaks off for the simple reason that Franklin himself broke off, not from writing, but from life.

Although it is formally incomplete, however, the *Autobiography* is thematically complete, since we see the hero's fall and redemption, we see the upward trajectory of the life of public service that ensued, and we are told by Franklin at the very beginning, and speaking as an older man, that his life has been so happy and successful that he would live it again exactly as it actually transpired. The essentials of the exemplary life are thus presented for us to see.

Before we take an extended look, it will be necessary to sketch out the moral saga in some detail. For the sake of convenience, I will divide the story into its distinctive stages in the order that Franklin presents them, and for further convenience I will provide titles, not used by Franklin, that convey the central message of each stage. In addition to the stages, there is one "interlude" in which Franklin explains why he returns to writing Part Two after a long interruption.

Stage One: A Pretty Good Boy

After addressing his son and posterity, and after some brief remarks about his forebears, Franklin turns to some details of his early life.[5] Although his older brothers were all apprenticed to tradesmen, the precocious and early-reading Ben was sent to grammar school (Boston Latin School, a preparatory school for Harvard), where he excelled, for not quite one year. Unable to manage the expense of a college education, Franklin's father removed him from the grammar school and sent him to another school for writing and arithmetic. There young Ben learned "fair writing pretty soon" but failed in arithmetic. When he was ten, his father removed him from that school and took him home to assist in the family business, and by the age of twelve he was apprenticed to his brother James, who had opened a printing business.

As he describes this stage, Franklin started out his moral life well enough, having a father who excelled in judgment and prudence and who, in his conversation, tried to improve the minds of his children and turn their "attention to what was good, just, and prudent in the conduct of life."[6] When Franklin, already a leader, and his playmates purloined some building stones to make a little fishing wharf in a pond and were found out, Franklin pled in his own defense the "usefulness of the work." But his father "convinced" him "that nothing was useful which was not honest."[7] The bookish lad read his father's books on polemical divinity, but Franklin says he has since regretted that reading because, since he was not bound for the clergy, he could better have spent his time with "more proper books." He read as well John Bunyan, Daniel Defoe's *Essay on Projects*, and Mather's *Essays to Do Good*.

As we soon learn, however, there was another reason Franklin regretted the time spent reading his father's books of polemical divinity: They played their part in what Franklin soon describes as his adolescent fall from morality and religion. His father's lesson thus did not stick for long, and it was not until Franklin was between twenty and twenty-two years old, just prior to his "public appearance in business," that he redeemed himself and returned to religion and his father's teaching.

Stage Two: Disagreeable Disputation

In the second stage,[8] Franklin explains that "by reading my father's books of dispute about religion" he "caught" the habit of disputatious argument that aimed at confutation. He used this form of argument with his bookish friend John Collins. Franklin tells us, in hindsight, that the habit was a bad one, "making people often extremely disagreeable in company, by the contradiction that is necessary to bring it into practice, and thence, besides souring and spoiling the conversation, is productive of disgusts and perhaps enmities where you may have occasion for friendship." In addition to having picked up and practiced this bad habit, Franklin learned from his father, who came across some argumentative letters between Franklin and Collins, that he needed to improve his writing as well.

Stage Three: Socratic Method Number One

After discussing his efforts to improve his writing, which kept him from attending "public worship," Franklin tells us that at "about 16 years of age," as the result of adopting a vegetarian diet, he was able to save money and to buy books and that he "read about this time Locke on Human Understanding and the Art of Thinking by Messrs du Port Royal." (Franklin refers here to the *Port Royal Logic*, the popular and influential book on logic, metaphysics, and epistemology written by Antoine Arnauld and Pierre Nicole in 1662 and named for the Jansenist abbey of Port Royal.)[9] In the course of improving his language, he came upon an English grammar that included a "specimen of a dispute in the Socratic method." After that, says Franklin, he secured a copy of Xenophon's *Memorabilia*, which had many examples of the Socratic method of disputation. "I was," says Franklin, "charmed with it, adopted it, dropt my abrupt contradiction, and put on the humble enquirer and doubter." And

> being then, from reading Shaftsbury & Collins, become a real doubter in many points of our religious doctrine, I found this method safest for myself and very embarrassing to those against whom I used it, therefore I took delight in it, practiced it continually, and grew very artful and expert in drawing people even of superior knowledge into concessions the consequences of which they did not foresee, entangling them in difficulties out of which they could not extricate themselves, and so obtaining victories that neither myself nor my cause always deserved.

This mode of discourse, which I will call Franklin's Socratic method number one, he continued "some few years."

Stage Four: Socratic Method Number Two

Although Franklin continued Socratic method number one for "some few years," he "gradually left it,"[10] until he retained

> only the habit of expressing myself in terms of modest diffidence, never using when I advanced any thing that may possibly be disputed, the words, *certainly*, *undoubtedly*, or any others that give the air of positive-

ness to an opinion; but rather say, *I conceive,* or *I apprehend* a thing to be so and so, *it appears to me, or I should think it so for such and such reasons,* or *I imagine* it to be so, or *it is so if I am not mistaken.*

This method I will call Franklin's Socratic method number two.

This second Socratic method, says Franklin, has been to his advantage throughout his life whenever he wanted to inculcate his opinions and persuade people into measures he promoted. Since "the chief ends of conversation are to *inform* or be *informed,* to *please* or to *persuade,*" a "positive dogmatical manner in advancing your sentiments" provokes contradiction, prevents candid attention, and defeats the purposes of giving or receiving information or pleasure. Franklin notes that if you want the benefit of others' information and yet express yourself "as firmly fixed in your present opinions," then modest and sensible men will "leave you undisturbed in the possession of your error." Thus you cannot please your hearers or persuade those you want on your side. Franklin says that proof of his argument is provided by Alexander Pope, and to show it he quotes from Pope lines of poetry that we'll consider in detail in chapter 6.

Stage Five: The Five Moral Errata

After describing his writing of the Silence Dogood essays for James's paper, the *New England Courant,* and admitting his disclosure, after "my small fund of sense for such performances was pretty well exhausted," of his secret authorship (and describing James's displeasure at the consequent improvement in Ben's reputation among the "brother's acquaintance"), Franklin explains the tension between himself and James and his father's general preference for Ben when their disputes were brought before him.[11] According to Ben, James had a passionate nature and had often beaten him—"harsh and tyrannical treatment" that might have been a "means of impressing me with that aversion to arbitrary power that has stuck to me through my whole life."[12] He then explains that when the paper took a position that angered the assembly and his brother was jailed, he took over the paper and then, with his barbs against the rulers, earned a reputation as a "young genius that had a turn for libeling and satire." James was released from prison on the condition that he no longer print the paper, and so the scheme was cooked up that Benjamin should be the publisher, with the further twist (so that it would not seem that James was continuing to publish by way of his apprentice) that Benjamin would be released from his indentures of apprenticeship and new indentures would be signed that would be kept secret.

Erratum Number One: Brother James

A fresh dispute having arisen with his brother, Franklin asserted his freedom, "presuming that he would not venture to produce the new indentures."[13] Says Franklin, "it was not fair in me to take this advantage, and this I therefore reckon one of the first errata of my life: But the unfairness of it weighed little with me, when under the impressions of the resentment, for the blows his passion too often urged him to bestow upon me. Though he was otherwise not an ill-natured man: Perhaps I was too saucy and provoking." When James got wind of Ben's plan to leave him, he prevented his employment at any other printing firm in the city, and so Ben thought of going to New York to find work:

And I was the rather inclined to leave Boston, when I reflected that I had already made my self a little obnoxious, to the governing party; and from the arbitrary proceedings of the Assembly in my brother's case it was likely I might if I stayed soon bring myself into scrapes; and farther that my indiscreet disputations about religion began to make me pointed at with horror by good people, as an infidel or atheist; I determined on the point.

Franklin sneaked out of town at night and made his way first to New York and then to Philadelphia. At this time, we know, he was seventeen years old.[14]

Erratum Number Two: Mr. Vernon

After describing his adventures on the trip to Philadelphia, his arrival there, his first employment with the eccentric printer Samuel Keimer, his acquaintance with and encouragement by Governor William Keith, and his improving circumstances and triumphant visit to his family in Boston, Franklin tells of an event that transpired on the journey home from Boston.[15] Along the way to Philadelphia, he visited his brother John, in Newport, Rhode Island, where a friend of John's, one Mr. Vernon, asked Franklin to recover thirty-five pounds owed to Vernon by a person in Pennsylvania, which Franklin agreed to do and which "afterwards occasioned me a good deal of uneasiness." In New York he teamed up with his old intellectual friend Collins, who had now become a serious drinker and gambler and had lost all of his money. On the way to Philadelphia Franklin got the money owed to Vernon, and in Philadelphia Collins depended on Franklin to pay his lodging and boarding, which Franklin did with Vernon's money. Franklin and Collins then quarreled, and Collins left with a promise, never fulfilled, to pay the debt to Franklin. "The breaking into this money of Vernon's," says Franklin, "was one of the first great errata of my life."[16]

Erratum Number Three: Deborah

Franklin then relates (as I described more fully in the introduction) Governor Keith's promise to set him up in business and Keith's sending Franklin to London for equipment, his ongoing employment with Keimer, and his continued worry that Vernon might ask for his money. Franklin describes his conversion, upon seeing small fish removed from bigger fish, from vegetarianism back to meat-eating. He recounts his continued "disputations" with Keimer, in which "I used to work him so with my Socratic method, and had trapanned him so often by questions apparently so distant from any point we had in hand, and yet by degrees led to the point, and brought him into difficulties and contradictions, that at last he grew ridiculously cautious, and would hardly answer me the most common question, without asking first, *What do you intend to infer from that?*" This led to their "collaboration" in founding a new sect in which the clearly insane Keimer was to propound the doctrines and Franklin was to confound all those who opposed them, followed by Franklin's "diversion" at Keimer's expense—to half-starve the normally gluttonous man by convincing him to practice vegetarianism for three months—which ended in the hilarious event of Keimer's premature devouring of an entire roast pig.[17]

Franklin then tells us of his courtship of Deborah Read and of her mother's view that it would be prudent for them to postpone marriage until after Franklin's return from London and his settlement in business (which in fact she may have doubted he would accomplish), and he then describes his "chief acquaintances" at the time.[18] Two of them, James Ralph and Collins, who had been "unsettled" by Franklin, were particularly "lax in their principles of religion" and later made him suffer for it.

Then follows the account of Franklin's trip to London, which begins with the tale of the trick played on Franklin by Governor Keith, who never provided the letters of credit and introduction he had promised.[19] While in London, Franklin says, he and Ralph, who borrowed constantly from Franklin, spent a lot of money "going to plays and other places of amusement." In the process, Franklin spent all of his money, Ralph forgot his wife and child, and Franklin "by degrees [forgot his] engagements with Miss Read, to whom I never wrote more than one letter, and that to let her know I was not likely soon to return. This was another of the great errata of my life, which I should wish to correct if I were to live it over again."[20]

Erratum Number Four: The Dissertation on Liberty and Necessity, Pleasure and Pain

In the very next paragraph,[21] Franklin tells us that while at work as a printer for Samuel Palmer, he typeset William Wollaston's *Religion of Nature*

Delineated and found some of its reasoning poor, and so "I wrote a little metaphysical piece, in which I made remarks on them. It was entitled *A Dissertation on Liberty and Necessity, Pleasure and Pain*—I inscribed it to my Friend Ralph." Franklin printed a small number of copies, and the piece caused Palmer to consider him "a young man of some ingenuity, though he seriously expostulated with me upon the principles of my pamphlet which to him appeared abominable. My printing of this pamphlet was another erratum." Even so, Franklin then tells us that the pamphlet fell into the hands of a surgeon, William Lyons, "who took great notice of me" and took Franklin "to the Horns a pale Alehouse in——Lane, Cheapside, and introduced me to Dr. Mandeville, author of the Fable of the Bees who had a club there, of which he was the soul, being a most facetious entertaining companion." Lyons also introduced Franklin to a Dr. Henry Pemberton, who promised to secure the lad a meeting with Sir Isaac Newton. This never panned out, although Franklin was "extremely desirous" that it should.

Erratum Number Five (the Last): Mrs. T.

In the sequel, Franklin tells us that one Mrs. T. lived in their house[22] and that Ralph and she became intimate and together moved to another place. Ralph then left her, became a teacher in a village in Berkshire, changed his name to Franklin so as to avoid the shame of having taken such a job, and sent a letter to Franklin "recommending Mrs. T to my care." Ralph sent Franklin an epic poem he was writing, which led Franklin to recommend that he give up poetry. Meanwhile, on account of Ralph, Mrs. T. had lost her friends and business and often asked Franklin for money to help her out of her difficulties. "I grew fond of her company, and being at this time under no religious restraints, and presuming on my importance to her, I attempted familiarities, (another erratum) which she repulsed with a proper resentment, and acquainted him [Ralph] with my behavior." A breach between Ralph and Franklin ensued, and Ralph then told Franklin that the latter's behavior had "cancelled all the obligations" Ralph had owed to Franklin, so that Franklin found that he was never to expect repayment of the money he had loaned to his friend.

Stage Six: Moral Reformation

After recounting the fifth and final erratum, Franklin tells of his work, his lodging with an old, pious, and self-denying Catholic woman, his feats of swimming, his burgeoning association and partnership with the Quaker merchant Thomas Denham, and his voyage back to Philadelphia and the journal he wrote while on that journey.[23] The "most important part" of the journal was "the Plan to be found in it which I formed at Sea, for regulating my future conduct in life. It is all the more remarkable, as being formed when I was so young, and yet being pretty much faithfully adhered to quite through to old age."[24] He then tells of his work with Denham, Denham's death, his return to work for Keimer, his continuing unease at the "debt owed to Vernon," a proposal by Hugh Meredith (another drinker) that he and Franklin set up their own printing business, and the last days of Franklin's work for Keimer, during which time Franklin met friends who "were afterwards of great use" to him and who continued their regard for him as long as he lived.[25]

At this point, Franklin interrupts the narrative—before he enters "upon my public appearance in business"—to account for the condition of his "principles and morals" at that time—presumably by the time he wrote the journal while at sea in 1726, with its plan for the conduct of his future life.[26] His purpose in recounting these facts is to tell his son (and of course posterity) how these principles and morals "influenced the future events of my life." Franklin does not just report his moral condition at the time; rather, he recounts briefly the course of his religious and moral life from the beginning until his business debut.

Although his parents had given him early "religious impressions" and had brought him up piously, he "was scarce 15 when, after doubting by turns of several points as I found them disputed in the different books [presumably his father's] I read, I began to doubt of revelation itself." Franklin got hold of some books against Deism, which were said to be "the substance of the sermons preached at [Robert] Boyle's [endowed] lectures." Their effect on him was just the opposite of their intention: The deistic arguments that were quoted in order to be refuted appeared to Franklin stronger than the refutations, and "in short I soon became a thorough Deist." His arguments perverted some others, especially Collins and Ralph, "but each of them having afterwards wronged me greatly without the least compunction, and recollecting Keith's conduct toward me, (who was another freethinker) and my own toward Vernon and Miss Read which at times gave me great trouble, I began to suspect that this doctrine though it might be true, was not very useful." His "London Pamphlet" (the *Dissertation*), which had for its motto lines from Dryden "and from the attributes of God, his infinite wisdom, goodness, and power concluded that nothing could possibly be wrong in the world, and that vice and virtue were empty distinctions, no such things existing," then appeared less clever than he had once thought it, and he "doubted whether some error had not insinuated itself unperceived, into my argument, so as to infect all that followed, as is common in metaphysical reasonings."

He "grew convinced that *truth, sincerity and integrity* in dealings between man and man, were of the utmost importance to the felicity of life, and I had formed written resolutions, (which still remain in my Journal book) to practice them ever while I lived." Despite this moral change of heart, "revelation had indeed no weight with me as such; but I entertained an opinion, that though certain actions might not be bad *because* they were forbidden by it, or good *because* it commanded them; yet probably those actions might be forbidden *because* they were bad for us, or commanded *because* they were beneficial to us, in their own natures, all the circumstances of things considered." Franklin then goes on to say:

This persuasion, with the kind hand of Providence, or some guardian Angel, or accidental favorable circumstances and situations, or all together, preserved me (through this dangerous time of youth and the hazardous situations I was sometimes in among strangers, remote from the eye and advice of my father,) without any *willful* gross immorality or injustice that might have been expected from my want of religion.—I say *willful*, because the instances I have mentioned, had something of *necessity* in them, from my youth, inexperience, and the knavery of others.—I had therefore a tolerable character to begin the world with, I valued it properly, and determined to preserve it.

Stage Seven: Two Errata Corrected

After recounting his moral and religious history, Franklin then tells of his leaving Keimer and beginning his business with Meredith, his founding of the club of young intellectuals called the Junto and the character of its members, and the appearance of his first successful papers and his growing business and reputation among the members of the assembly, including Mr. Andrew Hamilton, whose patronage Franklin enjoyed until his death.[27] Now Franklin can make some amends.

To Vernon
Then says Franklin, "Mr. Vernon about this time put me in mind of the debt I owed him:—but did not press me.—I wrote him an ingenuous letter of acknowledgments, craved his forbearance a little longer which he allowed me, and as soon as I was able I paid the principal with interest and many thanks.—So that *erratum* was in some degree corrected."[28]

Franklin then describes his further success in business and his failure to make a profitable nuptial match with a niece of his co-boarders, the God-freys. (Thomas Godfrey was a glazier and a member of the Junto.)[29] In this failed affair, Franklin tells us that he learned that as a mere printer he was "not to expect money with a wife unless with such a one, as I should not otherwise think agreeable." In the meantime, "that hard-to-be-governed passion of youth, had hurried me frequently into intrigues with low women that fell in my way, which were attended with some expense and great inconvenience, besides a continual risk to my health by a distemper which of all things I dreaded, though by great good luck I escaped it." And then in the very next paragraph he tells of his amends to Deborah.

To Deborah

Franklin tells us that he had renewed his acquaintance with Miss Read's family and that he pitied poor Deborah, who had been married to but abandoned by a previous husband, whose subsequent death was not certain.[30] Franklin felt that his "giddiness and inconstancy when in London" were in a great degree the cause of her unhappiness, "though the mother was good enough to think the fault more her own than mine, as she had prevented our marrying before I went thither, and persuaded the other match in my absence." Despite the complications of the situation, Franklin and Deborah "ventured however, over all these difficulties, and I took her to wife Sept. 1, 1730. None of the inconveniences happened that we had apprehended, she proved a good and faithful helpmate, assisted me much by attending the shop, we throve together, and have ever mutually endeavored to make each other happy.—Thus I corrected that great *erratum* as well as I could."

Stage Eight: First Public Project

After relating the correction of the erratum concerning Deborah, Franklin ends Part One with a brief mention of the Junto's common library,[31] which lasted for one year, and he then describes briefly his "first project of a public nature" for a subscription library. At this point, Part One breaks off and Franklin explains, in a note, that the "affairs of the revolution" caused the interruption. In the note he comments that what has been written so far was done "with the intention expressed in the beginning and therefore contains several little family anecdotes of no importance to others. What follows was written many years after in compliance with the advice contained in these letters, and accordingly intended for the public." In speaking of "these letters," Franklin refers to the two letters from friends, Abel James and Benjamin Vaughn, which he inserted in the text at the beginning of Part Two.

Interlude: The Letters

James had seen a draft of Part One of the *Autobiography* and Franklin's outline of the whole work yet to be completed. He sent the letter that Franklin reproduced in the *Autobiography*, along with the outline, to Franklin, who then showed them to Vaughn, who was in Paris. Vaughn then wrote his letter to Franklin, based on what he read in James's letter and the outline. In the letters, both men warmly urge Franklin both to finish and publish the *Autobiography*, on account of the moral example it will afford for coming generations.[32]

Stage Nine: Back to Good Works

At the beginning of Part Two, Franklin again describes his return to writing the *Autobiography* in 1784 as compliance with requests expressed in the preceding letters.[33] Franklin begins Part Two by commenting that distance from his papers—he is in Passy—has so far kept him from complying sooner with his friends' requests, but since he does not know when he will return home, and having at the time some leisure, he returns to the task. Not having a copy of Part One in Passy, Franklin begins where he recollects that he left off: at the account of the means he used to establish the Philadelphia Public Library. Franklin's memory could not have served him better—that is in fact exactly where he left off, and what follows is a fuller account of the founding of the new, public library after the Junto library had "for some time contented us." The new library afforded him "the means of improvement by constant study." He worked hard at the printing business and with Deborah's help made enough to buy their first luxuries—plate and china—which was followed in the course of years by an increase of wealth to "several hundred pounds in value."

Stage Ten: Religious Correction and the Bold and Arduous Project

Following the comment about his increasing material prosperity, Franklin returns abruptly to his religious history, this time telling a somewhat different story, and then relates his "bold and arduous project of arriving at moral perfection."[34] Franklin says that he was religiously educated as a Presbyterian, although he found the "dogmas" of "the eternal decrees of God, election, reprobation, etc." to be unintelligible and others of the dogmas to be doubtful, and that early in his life he absented himself from public Presbyterian worship (Sunday was his day of study). Even so,

> I never was without some religious principles; I never doubted, for instance, the existence of the Deity, that he made the world, and governed it by his Providence; that the most acceptable service of God was the doing good to man; that our souls are immortal; and that all crime will be punished and virtue rewarded either here or hereafter; these I esteemed the essentials of every religion, and being to be found in all the religions we had in our country I respected them all, though with different degrees of respect as I found them more or less mixed with other articles which without any tendency to inspire, promote or confirm morality, served principally to divide us and make us unfriendly to one another.[35]

This evenhanded attitude and his view that the worst religions have some good effects, says Franklin, induced him to "avoid all discourse that might tend to lessen the good opinion another might have of his own religion," and he never refused his "mite" for any sect that needed a building for public worship. He even maintained his annual subscription for the Presbyterian church in Philadelphia, though he seldom attended and, upon being persuaded on one occasion to attend for five weeks in a row, found the sermons so dogmatic and bereft of admonitions to good works that he never attended the minister's preaching again.

Then says Franklin,

> I had some years before composed a little liturgy or form of prayer for my own private use, viz, in 1728, entitled, *Articles of Belief and Acts of Religion*. I returned to the use of this, and went no more to the public assemblies.—My conduct might be blameable, but I leave it without attempting farther to excuse it, my present purpose being to relate facts, and not to make apologies for them.[36]

Franklin tells us that about this time—that is, at about the time he wrote the *Articles of Belief and Acts of Religion*—he "conceived the bold and arduous project of arriving at moral perfection." The description of this project (to whose details we will return) takes up the rest of Part Two.[37] Franklin provides his famous list of the thirteen virtues (temperance, silence, order, resolution, frugality, industry, sincerity, justice, moderation, cleanliness, tranquility, chastity, humility) and the equally famous system he devised to attain these virtues.

For now, it is important to note two things. First, Franklin says he avoided in his moral scheme "any of the distinguishing tenets of any particular sect," in order that his "method" should be useful to people of all religions. He also proposed to write "a little comment on each virtue, in which I would have shown the advantages of possessing it, and the mischiefs attending its opposite vice." He should have called the book "The Art of Virtue," because

> it would have shown the *means and manner* of obtaining virtue; which would have distinguished it from the mere exhortation to be good, that does not instruct and indicate the means; but is like the Apostle's man of verbal charity, who only, without showing to the naked and the hungry *how* or where they might get clothes or victuals, exhorted them to be fed and clothed. *James* II, 15, 16.[38]

He never wrote "The Art of Virtue," he says, because he was diverted first by private and then by public business. Because that book was connected in his mind "with a *great and extensive project* that required the whole man to execute, and which an unforeseen succession of employs prevented my attending to, it has hitherto remained unfinished." It was his intention in the book, says Franklin, "to explain and enforce [give strength to] this doctrine, that vicious actions are not hurtful because they are forbidden, but forbidden because they are hurtful, the nature of man alone considered: That it was therefore every ones interest to be virtuous, who wished to be happy even in this world." In other words, Franklin would have "explained and enforced" the doctrine that his father had taught him in his youth and to which he had now completely returned: "that nothing was useful which was not honest."

The second important thing to note is Franklin's story about how the last virtue, humility, came to be added to his list, which originally contained but twelve items. This addition was occasioned by a "Quaker Friend," who informed Franklin that he "was generally thought proud" and that his pride "showed itself frequently in conversation; that [he] was not content with being in the right when discussing any point, but was overbearing and rather insolent; of which [the Quaker] convinced [Franklin] by mentioning several instances." At this admonition, Franklin added humility to his list of virtues. He did not succeed in achieving this virtue, although he "had a good deal with regard to the *appearance* of it." He made it a rule to forbear all direct contradiction to the sentiments of others, and all positive assertion of my own. I even forbid myself agreeable to the old laws of our Junto, the use of every word or expression in the language that imported a fixed opinion; such as *certainly, undoubtedly,* etc. and I adopted instead of them, *I conceive, I apprehend,* or *I imagine* a thing to be so or so, or it so appears to me at present.[39]

Franklin says that "when another asserted something that I thought an error, I denied my self the pleasure of contradicting him abruptly, and of showing immediately some absurdity in his proposition; and in answering I began by observing that in certain cases or circumstances his opinion would be right, but that in the present case there *appeared* or *seemed* to me some difference, etc."

Franklin comments that the new method of conversation served him well—he had readier reception and less contradiction to his own views and had less mortification when others proved him wrong—and that though at first against his natural inclination, this method of argumentation became so easy and habitual that "perhaps for these fifty years past no one has ever heard a dogmatical expression escape [him]." Franklin concludes the discussion with a comment on how difficult it is to subdue the "natural" passion of pride.[40]

Stage Eleven: The Great and Extensive Project

Here begins Part Three.[41] The time of writing is 1788, and Franklin tells us that he cannot expect help from his papers since many had been lost in the war. Even so, he has accidentally preserved a paper from 1731, called "Observations on My Reading History in Library," which shows the "first rise" in his mind of the *"great and extensive project"* with which Part Two ended. Following a brief account of how partisanship operates in history to the detriment of the "good of mankind," Franklin then quotes from the piece that

there seems to me at present to be great occasion for raising an united party for virtue, by forming the virtuous and good men of all nations into a regular body, to be governed by suitable good and wise rules, which good and wise men may probably be more unanimous in their obedience to, than common people are to common laws. I at present think, that whoever attempts this aright, and is well qualified, cannot fail of pleasing God, and of meeting with success.

Franklin then tells us that although most of his notes about the project have been lost, he finds one purporting to be the substance of a creed, "containing as I thought the essentials of every known religion, and being free of every thing that might shock the professors of any religion." The creed has six principles:

> That there is one God who made all things.
> That he governs the world by his providence.—
> That he ought to be worshiped by adoration, prayer, and thanksgiving.
> But that the most acceptable service of God is doing good to man.
> That the soul is immortal.
> And that God will certainly reward virtue and punish vice either here
>   or hereafter.

Franklin goes on to describe how he would have the sect begin first with young, single men, who would swear to the creed and learn the practice of virtue from the model earlier described, who would associate in secret until their numbers had become "considerable," and who would help promote each others' interests in business and life. "For distinction we should be called the Society of the *free and easy*; Free, as being by the general practice and habit of the virtues, free from the domination of vice, and particularly by the practice of industry and frugality, free from debt, which exposes a man to confinement and a species of slavery to his creditors." Making no comment on what he meant by "easy," Franklin says this is all he remembers of the project, and that his circumstances and later public and private occupations caused him continually to postpone it (and with it, we should recall, the book to be called "The Art of Virtue"), "so that it has been omitted till I have no longer strength or activity left sufficient for such an enterprise," though he still thinks it was practical and would have been very useful by "forming a great number of good citizens."

Franklin says he was never discouraged by the magnitude of the project, as he has "always thought that one man of tolerable abilities may work great changes, and accomplish great affairs among mankind, if he first forms a good plan, and, cutting off all amusements or other employments that would divert his attention, makes the execution of that same plan his sole study and business."

Stage Twelve: Public Instruction and Public Religion

Franklin next tells us that in 1732 he first published *Poor Richard's Almanack,* which he continued to publish for twenty-five years.[42] He "reaped considerable profit from it," since he sold almost ten thousand copies each

year. He observes that it was so popular he thought it an appropriate "vehi-
cle for conveying instruction among the common people" and that to that
end he included proverbs that would inculcate "industry and frugality as the
means of procuring wealth and thereby securing virtue, it being more difficult for a man in want to act always honestly, as (to use here one of those
proverbs) *it is hard for an empty sack to stand upright.*"
     He also used his newspaper (the *Pennsylvania Gazette*) as a

> means of communicating instruction, and in that view frequently
> reprinted in it extracts from the Spectator and other moral writers, and
> sometimes published little pieces of my own which had been first com-
> posed for reading in our Junto. Of these are a Socratic Dialogue tending
> to prove, that, whatever might be his parts and abilities, a vicious man
> could not properly be called a man of sense. And a discourse on self de-
> nial, showing that virtue was not secure, till its practice became a habi-
> tude, and was free from the opposition of contrary inclinations.—These
> may be found in the Papers about the beginning of 1735.[43]

After commenting that he never printed libel or personal abuse, Franklin
also tells a story about the affair of the "Presbyterian Preacher named
Hemphill."[44] He tells us that he liked the revivalist Samuel Hemphill because his sermons favored the practice of virtue and good works and contained little dogma. When Hemphill was brought before the Presbyterian
Synod on charges of heterodoxy, Franklin says,

> I became his zealous partisan, and contributed all I could to raise a party
> in his favor . . . and lent him my pen and wrote for him two or three
> pamphlets, and one piece in the Gazette of April 1735. Those pam-
> phlets, as is generally the case with controversial writings, though ea-
> gerly read at the time, were soon out of vogue, and I question whether a
> single copy of them now exists.

In the midst of the controversy, Hemphill was exposed as a plagiarist, and
his support soon dwindled. Franklin stuck by him, so he says, because he
"rather approved his giving us good sermons composed by others, than bad
ones of his own manufacture; though the latter was the practice of our common teachers." At the end of the affair, Franklin quit the Presbyterian con-
gregation, never to return, although he continued for many years to pay his
subscription to support its ministers.
     In the next few pages, Franklin describes his study of languages, his recon-
ciliation with his dying brother James and his agreement to set up James's

son in the printing business (which he did and which made "ample amends" for the services James was deprived of when Franklin ran off to Philadel-phia), the death of his own son (Frankie) from smallpox, matters relating to the Junto, his promotion to clerk of the assembly, his appointment as deputy postmaster, and his turn to public affairs (the city watch and the fire com-pany).[45] Then follows the second story about public religion, that concern-ing the Reverend George Whitefield.[46]

Reverend Whitefield, Franklin says, "arrived among us" in 1739. Franklin admired him because he drew followers from "all sects and denominations" and because he caused those with no care for religion to become religious. The crowds were so big that a large building was erected for use by White-field and by "any preacher of any religious persuasion who might desire to say something to the people of Philadelphia, the design in building not be-ing to accommodate any particular sect, but the inhabitants in general, so that even if the Mufti of Constantinople were to send a missionary to preach Mahometanism to us, he would find a pulpit at his service." Franklin de-scribes the captivating eloquence that Whitefield used in support of the project for building an orphanage in Georgia and tells of the man's rhetori-cal power even over Franklin's reluctant purse. Whitefield's enemies accused him of purloining the funds, but Franklin assures us that he knew him well, "being employed in printing his sermons and journals, etc.," and that in Franklin's view Whitefield was thoroughly honest.

Franklin then says that his testimony on this matter should have special weight, "as we had no religious connection. He used indeed sometimes to pray for my conversion, but never had the satisfaction of believing that his prayers were heard. Ours was a mere civil friendship, sincere on both sides, and lasted to his death." To show "something of the terms" on which they stood, Franklin tells a story about his offering Whitefield his home as lodg-ing. "He replied, that if I made that kind offer for Christ's sake, I should not miss of a reward.—And I returned, *Don't let me be mistaken; it was not for Christ's sake, but for your sake.*" Franklin then reports the comic remark of a mutual friend: "that knowing it to be the custom of the saints, when they re-ceived any favor, to shift the burden of the obligation from off their own shoulders, and place it in heaven, I had contrived to fix it on earth."

Franklin concludes his reminiscences with further remarks about White-field's extraordinary rhetorical skill and power. At one point, Franklin used some practical mathematics to estimate the size of one of Whitefield's audi-ences. He concluded that the crowd was thirty thousand people—a discov-ery that led Franklin to believe newspaper accounts of Whitefield's great audiences and also to credit the ancient histories that report generals "ha-ranguing whole armies, of which I had sometimes doubted."

Franklin closes the account of Reverend Whitefield with some comments about why his legacy was not greater that it might have been. Whitefield's written words were effectively used against him by his enemies, whereas unguarded comments made orally might have been qualified or even denied. Critics attacked Whitefield's writings so violently and with such an appearance of reason that the number of his votaries was diminished:

So that I am of opinion, if he had never written any thing he would have left behind him a much more numerous and important sect. And his reputation might in that case have been still growing, even after his death; as there being nothing of his writing on which to found a censure, and give him a lower character, his Proselites would be left at liberty to feign for him as great a variety of excellencies, as their enthusiastic admiration might wish him to have possessed.

With this remarkable comment about Whitefield's excellences, the moral saga comes to an end. What follows is then the story of Franklin's continuing success in business and politics, beginning with education and military affairs and ending with the mission to London. It is not quite right to think of the moral saga as having come to an end, however. For clearly, as Franklin says at the outset of the *Autobiography* and implies throughout, all of his life's successes and his tireless commitment to good works for his fellow citizens and for mankind, detailed in the remaining text, can be attributed to his discovery of morality and religion and his discovery of the method for *becoming* moral, as opposed to merely knowing that morality exists and knowing what it is. Although Franklin claims that he was forced by circumstances never to pursue "the great and extensive project" for the worldwide party of virtue, the course of the life that follows in the *Autobiography* seems to make clear, in the words of a recent scholar, that "it was precisely the execution of this design, expressed through the products of an unusually diverse and accomplished career, to which Franklin devoted his abundant vitality in the first half of the eighteenth century."[47]

DESPITE HAVING BEEN WRITTEN in four separate parts, the *Autobiography*'s thematic unity and flow are clear. And Franklin leaves no doubt that he wants us to see the story of his redemption and turn to morality and good works as the very axis of his exemplary life. Lest there be any doubt, we need only consider the hyperbolic letters—which speak of the redeemed Franklin as if he were a new Jesus—that Franklin ordered to be inserted at the beginning of Part Two.

The message of the *Autobiography* is thus really very simple: A smart and good boy becomes so corrupted by philosophy that he thinks virtue and vice

do not exist, lacks religion, and harms his friends and himself. He then discovers that truth, sincerity, and integrity in dealings between man and man
are of the utmost importance to happiness in life. He then comes back to religion, whose essentials dictate that the most acceptable service of God is
doing good to man. He soon after discovers the virtues that make one happy
and make it *possible* to do good to man. He likewise discovers the method by
which one can attain these virtues, and so be happy and actually be *able* to
do good to man. The never-written "Art of Virtue," we have to remember,
was "connected in" Franklin's mind to the great and extensive project for
the good of mankind. (The very greatness and extensiveness of the charitable project prevented his writing that book, but some of its essentials were
published in the *Autobiography*. Not only do we get the list of virtues and the
manual for achieving them, but we get them embedded in the most impressive testimonial of its practical result.) And then Franklin *does* good to
mankind, tirelessly. In the course of this life, the fallen, once-good little boy
becomes a benefactor of all mankind and an example for the ages to come.

Lest we doubt Vaughn's implied comparison of Franklin's *Autobiography* to
the Bible, Franklin himself suggests that the example of his life is an *improvement* on the Bible. His "Art of Virtue" was to supply what the apostle
James had said is lacking in merely "verbal charity." But Franklin's version of
the apostle's words makes a subtle but important change. (And here is the
first small but revealing "mistake" that we note.) The apostle blames merely
verbal charity for just telling the poor to "be warmed and filled" (2:16) and
for not *giving* the poor the things needed for the body. Says James (2:17): "So
Faith by itself, if it has no works, is dead." In Franklin's version of what
James said, the apostle blames verbal charity for just telling the poor to be
"warm and filled" and for not showing the poor "*how* or where they might
get" (my emphasis on "get") those needed things.

In Franklin's version, charity is not giving to others but, rather, showing
them how to get for themselves. Applying this lesson to the virtues instead
of to food and clothes, the Bible would have Franklin merely "give" the
virtues to others, merely tell others what the virtues are and exhort his hearers to practice them. But Franklin will tell others what the virtues are *and*
show them how to "get" them for themselves—how actually to become virtuous and to do so on their own.

Franklin suggests that the Bible's notion of good works is not quite right.
According to the apostle, good works consist in giving one's own clothes to
the poor. According to Franklin, good works consist in showing the poor
how to get their own clothes. All are thus better off: The virtuous keep the
clothes they have, and the poor get the clothes they lack. These deficiencies
in the Bible—a wrong notion of good works and no directions for actually

becoming able to perform these works—would have been supplied by the missing "Art of Virtue." But the *Autobiography* will do just fine: It presents the virtues and the method for attaining them, it shows the advantages of possessing the virtues and the mischiefs that attend the vices, and it shows in concrete detail what good works really are and how the virtuous man performs them for his own good and the good of mankind. As Franklin said of his refusal to profit from his inventions, "*as we enjoy great advantages from the inventions of others, we should be glad of an opportunity to serve others by any invention of ours, and this we should do freely and generously.*"[48] In the *Autobiography* we read over and over again that good works done to others result in good works done to oneself.

James and Vaughn were impressed, although the Franklin they admired is, on reflection, a priggish and superficial man. But, as I have said, Franklin does not mean for us to take this story at face value. Though many did (including the surprisingly ham-fisted Lawrence), Franklin is none the worse for wear. Most of those who now admire both Franklin and the *Autobiography* know perfectly well that Franklin wrote his story with at least some of his tongue in his cheek. True, he presents the moral saga as the passion play for the modern age to come, but the story presents an ideal and, with moderating irony, does not claim to portray a real man. How else are we to understand the charming humor and self-deprecation with which he presents the tale?

He begins by admitting that he could be accused of vanity in telling this tale, and even tells us that vanity has its uses as a "comfort" to life.[49] If telling the tale involves the *comfort* of vanity, then, at the very least, even the most perfect striving for virtue must end in some disappointment. Franklin admits that he succeeded in achieving not the virtue of humility but only its appearance, and that if he had achieved humility completely, he "should probably be proud of my humility."[50] He tells the charming story of how the hard work of attaining virtue tempted him to lower his sights, so that

> something that pretended to be reason was every now and then suggesting to me, that such extreme nicety as I exacted of my self might be a kind of foppery in morals, which if it were known would make me ridiculous; that a perfect character might be attended with the inconvenience of being envied and hated; and that a benevolent man should allow a few faults in himself, to keep his friends in countenance.[51]

He tells the appealing story of his conversion to and then from vegetarianism. He resumed eating flesh when, upon smelling frying fish and seeing small fish gutted from a large one, he concluded that if fish eat fish there was no reason that he should not do so as well. Of the story he then remarks: "So convenient a thing it is to be a *reasonable creature*, since it enables one to find or make a reason for every thing one has a mind to do."[52] And he tells the equally attractive story of the matching grant by which he tricked—by getting all involved to pledge money they did not expect to have to pay— the unwilling to contribute to the hospital in Philadelphia: This was, he says, the political maneuver that gave him at the time the most pleasure, and he says further that "in after-thinking of it, I more easily excused myself for having made some use of cunning."[53] The *Autobiography* simply abounds with Franklin's ironic, self-deprecating good humor and wit.

Moreover, one could argue that Franklin does not just provide comic and ironic *relief* in the course of the *Autobiography*, but that the whole work, as structured by the moral saga, is in fact a comedy. Although one might think Franklin bold to compare himself to Jesus, the apostle James, and the Bible, and not to the advantage of Jesus, James, or the Bible, the comparison is obvious playfulness on Franklin's part. Franklin makes it clear that he did not believe in the divinity of Jesus. As he says, the Reverend Whitefield's prayers for his conversion were never answered. Franklin does not really claim to be better than an immaculate Jesus. In this same vein, the entire story contrasts the stirring moral saga of fall and redemption with the good-natured and homely but benevolent utilitarianism of the morality and religion to which that redemption led.

Nothing could be further from the stern morality of the Gospels (not to mention that of the Presbyterians with whom Franklin sparred) than Franklin's view that God's will is that men practice the virtues for the sake of happiness—their own and that of others—that good works are as good for oneself as they are for others, and that such works and not faith alone are what earns divine rewards. Virtue is not charity in the sense of sacrifice, says Franklin, but free and generous benevolence that works to everyone's advantage both in this world and in the next. If the poor are shown how to get food and clothing on their own, rather than being simply given what we have, then all will be better off. Apparently, the redeemed Franklin returned to, and this time came firmly to believe, his father's principle: Nothing is *useful* which is not honest.

The *Autobiography* is thus a religious and moral comedy in the following sense: At this level of irony, Franklin presents the saga in order to defend religion and morality as, in his view, they can best be defended. Or, better still, he presents the saga so as to display the only really defensible forms of morality and religion. This involves taking morality and religion down a peg or two from what people commonly expect them to be. The comic disproportion between the saga of fall and redemption and the homely lesson to be learned rests on our expectation that the saga, concerning as it does fall and redemption, should bespeak noble sacrifice, something selfless and grand that we admire and that makes our hearts soar. It is much more inspiring to see someone give his coat to another than to watch him tell the other how to sew. In Franklin's contrary view, so it would seem, we are much better off to see that genuine redemption consists in striving for good works that are, by virtue of their true goodness, good for everyone, oneself included.

But we need to be taught this fact; we need to be sobered up with ironic comedy in order to be as good as we can be. Franklin's purpose is not to debunk claims of morality but, rather, to tease moral seriousness for the sake of morality. This is the point, I would suggest, of the charming and comic story about the power of the Reverend Whitefield's rhetoric. Franklin liked Whitefield because his zeal was interdenominational and also because the established clergy took "a dislike to him." The bulk of Franklin's account concerns Whitefield's project for an orphanage in Georgia (a "good work" of the sort that, according to Franklin's discussion of the Hemphill case, would have mattered little to the Presbyterian clergy, with whom Franklin had been warring politically during the later 1730s).[54] Whitefield did not just preach good works, however. He also had "an extraordinary influence" on his hearers and had great power over the hearts and purses of his audiences, on one occasion including even Franklin.

The children of Georgia needed the orphanage because the settlement of Georgia had begun with unfit settlers, insolvent debtors, and "many of indolent and idle habits, taken out of the goals [*sic*]." Being unable to stand the hardships of a new settlement, many died and left indigent children. The sight of their miserable condition "inspired the benevolent heart" of Whitefield, who then "preached up this charity." Franklin liked the general idea, but he thought—sensibly—that since Georgia was bereft of workmen and materials, it would be better to build the orphanage in Philadelphia and bring the children to it, rather than to build it in Georgia with workmen and materials sent from Philadelphia "at a great expense." Thus Franklin advised the reverend. But Whitefield "was resolute in his first project" and rejected Franklin's counsel. And so Franklin "thereupon refused to contribute."[55]

Soon afterward, however, Franklin and his Junto friend Thomas Hopkinson went to one of Whitefield's sermons. Both agreed on the imprudence of the project. Knowing that a collection would be held, Franklin resolved not to give, even though he had in his pocket some coppers, paper money, three or four silver dollars, and five gold pistoles. But, says Franklin, as Whitefield "proceeded I began to soften, and concluded to give the coppers. Another stroke of his oratory made me ashamed of that, and determined me to give the silver; and he finished so admirably, that I emptied my pocket wholly into the collector's dish, gold and all." Hopkinson, with more foresight, had emptied his pockets before coming to listen. But toward the end of the ser-mon, he too was so moved to give that he asked to borrow money from a neighbor standing nearby. That neighbor turned out to be the only person in the crowd "who had the firmness not to be affected by the preacher." Good luck for Hopkinson, since the neighbor answered the request: "At any other time, friend Hopkinson, I would lend to thee freely; but not now, for thee seems to be out of thy right senses."[56]

According to the neighbor, Whitefield sent his listeners, certainly Hopkin-son and by clear implication Franklin as well, "out of their right senses." But is the neighbor (who is of course the artful Franklin writing to us) correct as regards Franklin? And if so, just *how* was Franklin out of his right senses?

We can answer both questions by puzzling out the sensible explanations for Franklin's behavior and then seeing what senseless ones might remain. At least for Franklin and his Junto friend, one sensible explanation might be that the preacher's eloquence caused them to forget the fact of the greater expense. The story tells against any forgetting, at least in Franklin's case. We normally do not forget things gradually: One either remembers something or does not, and there is no in-between. But Franklin gave up his money in stages, and for this to be so there must have been resistance at each stage to the reverend's appeal precisely by Franklin's memory—by his knowledge of the useless expense.

Another explanation might be that Whitefield's eloquence convinced them that they should give, despite the great and needless expense, because the project would not otherwise be accomplished at all. But the neighbor's characterization of the two as out of their right senses tells also against this explanation. This is not a senseless reason for giving. On the contrary, one could make a plausible, if not necessarily persuasive, case for it. It makes some sense to think: better the needless expense than no orphanage at all. One might, it is true, do something sensible but for reasons that lack any sense. Perhaps this is what happened to Franklin.

But we can still, given the evidence we have, better surmise the following: Franklin could well have been ashamed to give nothing in the face of all the charitable rhetoric, which would explain the coppers and then the silver. It really could have appeared mean-spirited to be so blatantly tightfisted amid all the good feeling. Then, between the silver and the gold, Franklin could have thought something like the following: "The really sensible thing to do would be to redouble my efforts to convince the reverend to build in Philadelphia. (This would be more charitable, as well, since it would leave money for other charity.) But I can see from the reverend's passion and the crowd's reaction that it will be impossible to change his mind, as I thought might happen from my first refusal to give. So here's the real dough."

And this conclusion could have been arrived at progressively: first the small donations out of simple decorum, and then the big one based on the sensible conclusion that the reverend *really* would not budge and that a needlessly expensive orphanage is better than none at all. The neighbor may have judged Franklin to be out of his senses, but we can, if we just try, make sense out of what he did.

Can we, then, account for Franklin's giving on grounds that would *not* be sensible in Franklin's view? We can. If Franklin thought it was foolish to build the charity in Georgia because it was imprudent, and so foolishly imprudent as to prevent a donation, then the purely senseless thing for him to do, under the reverend's spell, would have been for him to give the gold not *in spite* of the needless expense but *because* of that needless expense. This would have been to give not just for the project's utility (although of course that would be required, since utterly useless sacrifice is absurd) but *also and primarily* for the sake of its nobility—for the sake of the difficulty and expense and sacrifice involved.

As Franklin has the neighbor say, under the preacher's spell, Hopkinson and (by clear implication) Franklin were out of their right senses. It really would have been sensible, and more prudent, to try again to change the preacher's mind. And it would have been more prudent for the public not to waste its money either, and to get two orphanages instead of one. For Franklin, it is no crime for faith, virtue, and good works to be more than less useful, and useful for oneself and others, as indeed real good works are and nothing else is. If good works help others help themselves, and if they provide for warmth and clothing, hospitals and universities, clean streets, safety from fires and lightning, scientific progress, material prosperity, and more rather than fewer orphanages, are they somehow less than noble? To think so, as enthusiastic moralists do, is to be out of one's senses.

Lawrence presents the practical Franklin as if Franklin had a disease and did not know it. Lawrence, one could well say, is simply deaf to the comedy of the *Autobiography:* He entirely misses the comic contrast between the saga of fall and redemption and the homeliness of the lessons portrayed. This comedy is absolutely central to Franklin's moral teaching for the ages: that God and morality are real and can really work in our hearts and in this world only when we understand them for what they are, without the distortions caused by rigid and sectarian doctrine as regards God and by dreams of nobility as regards morality.

To Lawrence, Franklin would perhaps respond: "I know perfectly well that my story will irk the likes of you. That's in part why I wrote it. When I say that moral virtue is good and profitable for all involved, it makes you want to throw up because you want, instead, grand and noble sacrifice. So tell me: Just where does all this noble sacrifice get anybody, and doesn't it simply cause a lot of trouble? What's wrong with moral virtue that helps everyone involved?" In the *Autobiography*, we might say, the first level of Franklin's ironic comedy discloses the genuine moral dignity of what the misguided (or even deranged) disparage as "merely" useful things.

Moreover, the Franklin of the *Autobiography* is no "snuff-colored . . . automaton." Despite its cheery tone and comic defense of useful moral virtue and practical piety, the *Autobiography* shows that Franklin came to his pragmatic morality and religion as the consequence of a personal crisis of faith. He teetered on the edge of the nihilistic abyss and then, with a moral epiphany, recovered an understanding of morality and God that could and did make his life worth living. But that personal crisis did not just happen. It had causes—the skeptical Enlightenment intellectual currents that corrupted the faith and decency of Ben Franklin and, one might argue, were the dark cloud on the horizon of progress. It is not unreasonable, I think, to see the *Autobiography* as a Franklinian warning about a danger of the dawning modern age: the possible death of God. How else are we to explain Franklin's crisis, the lessons he drew from it for himself and for society, and his obvious concern, expressed throughout the story, to see religion healthy and effective in public life?

So if the *Autobiography* is a moral and religious comedy—as disclosed through Franklin's irony—then it seems, ultimately, a comedy with an absolutely serious end in view. There seems little doubt that whatever warts the real Franklin may have had—and the *Autobiography* displays quite a few—he really did devote his life to public service, statesmanship, and philanthropy. And he really did propose his art of virtue as a model of moral training for men who, in the new world Franklin saw dawning, would be pretty much on their own. As Edmund Morgan said, although Franklin did not include charity in his list of the virtues, it certainly seems that charity "was actually the guiding principle of Franklin's life."[57]

It is not really surprising that charity was not included in Franklin's list of virtues. With the exception of sincerity and justice, Franklin's listed virtues are perfections of the self. But for Franklin, the perfections of the self make one capable of rendering the most acceptable service to God: "doing good to man." Franklin's virtues establish strength of soul, self-reliance, and civility—all of which are the means to do God's work on this earth. But although God will punish vice and reward virtue in this world or the next, virtue on this earth is sensible in the eyes of Franklin's God: The divine reward is a bonus that accrues to those with the good sense to help others and at the same time help themselves. Thus as a consequence of its ironic comic charm, the *Autobiography* seems intended as a kind of new gospel.

THE AUTOBIOGRAPHY IS A GOSPEL for new times. But it also merely seems to be new and genuine good news, because it is presented through the first layer of Franklin's irony, and the first layer is not the last. We have to distinguish two quite different ironic strategies. One is intended to warn of pride and to moderate the excesses of moral enthusiasm for the sake of morality—to disclose the genuine dignity of homely, utilitarian virtue, of doing good to man, oneself included. We get to this lesson by seeing how Franklin's first irony pierces the plain surface of the text, which if taken at face value gives us the unlikable prig so admired by James and Vaughn. But despite its critical thrust, the first ironic layer stands thoroughly within the horizon of conventional moral opinion: We are meant to see realistically and thus admire the dignity and purity of public service, however sensible it might be. Even if we are freed from the deranging spell of noble sacrifice, our admiration for realistic public service and doing good to man still depends on the remaining effects of that very same spell.

To see how, let us think about the matter with Franklinian simplicity: Suppose Franklin became rich by honest means but, had circumstances required, was willing to do so by crooked ones if no one were to find out. And suppose he talked others into public service for their sake and for his but, had circumstances required, was willing to do so for his benefit alone. And suppose that he engaged in public service for others' sake and for his but, had circumstances required, was willing to do so for his sake alone. And then suppose that in a real moral pinch and when circumstances did require, Franklin had said to himself something like "other people can stick their necks out; I'm watching out for mine" and suppose also that nobody observed what he then did. Would we then admire him as a moral hero? Even as a utilitarian moral hero? No, obviously we would not—and the one thing missing and thus required for our admiration would be the element of sacrifice, the nobility of subordinating one's own interest to that of others and for the others' sake.

So despite our admiring agreement with Franklin's equating of honesty and utility, we cannot really believe that honesty is *always* the most useful policy—simply because it is not, especially in a pinch, as Franklin knew perfectly well. Rather, what we really think is that honesty is useful or somehow good for us *even when* and indeed *because* it redounds in no way to our interests as we commonly understand them—that is, *even when* and indeed *because* we subordinate or sacrifice our interests to others'. It is on that ground and no other that we can really admire the dignity of Franklin's "doing good to man."

Franklin's first ironic layer consists of broad exaggeration, admissions of vanity, revelation of obvious warts, and a comic narrative frame, which all combine to moderate the image of moral perfection and to present morality, especially public service and "doing good to man," on a realistic human scale. For the sake of morality, it sobers up the likes of Lawrence. But this picture harbors a fundamental contradiction. On the one hand, in order to see it, we have to agree that admiring noble sacrifice is to be out of one's right senses. But on the other hand, to admire that very picture we have to grant that virtue at its peak in fact consists in noble sacrifice. Lawrence's precious nobility gets sneaked in through the back door. Franklin's irony has to open the back door if sensible morality is not just to make sense but also to be something we really admire.

At the very least, then, the contradiction in Franklin's new gospel makes us wonder if there is not much more to be learned before we can know what moral virtue, properly understood, really is. In following up this contradiction, we make our way to Franklin's second ironic layer. Here the exaggerations and comic admissions give way to narrative contradictions and problems that are much harder to discern. We now meet with a different ironic strategy that means to hide and also reveal something Franklin did not want all to see. Once disclosed, however, the contradictions and problems undermine fundamental aspects of the moral saga and then lead us to surprising lines of thinking about morality and religion. At this point, then, we're standing on a floor with a trapdoor. We have to work much more patiently to pierce the next ironic veil. But once we do, it's a dizzying ride to the heart of what Franklin wants us to consider. Hold on to your hats.

2 • The *Autobiography:*
Or Just a Pack of Lies?

If the *Autobiography* is Franklin's gospel for the new age to come, then it is not so hard to understand his lifelong friendship with the Reverend Whitefield (Stage Twelve, as I've identified the stages in chapter 1).[1] It seems plausible, then, that Franklin was interested in and drawn to the reverend at least in part because in their different ways and with different conceptions of faith, they were apparently engaged in similar projects: to create and then leave behind a "numerous and important [and growing] sect"[2] of virtuous and charitable men that will bring light and morality to the world. What else are we to make of the great and extensive project for a party of virtue? Even if Franklin did not himself get that party practically under way, he tells us enough about how we might set it up for ourselves. He describes the kind of man to enlist in that party, and he describes the kind of man to be produced by that party: Benjamin Franklin.

Now, if the comparison to Whitefield is plausible, as I think Franklin wants us to see, then a small problem pops up. Franklin says that Whitefield's sect was diminished and failed to grow because Whitefield made his legacy hostage to the written word. His "writing and printing from time to time gave great advantage to his enemies."[3] If he had written nothing, these enemies would have been denied this advantage, because "unguarded expressions and even erroneous opinions," if merely spoken, could have been explained away. But there was another advantage as well: His followers could then have made up for him "as great a variety of excellencies, as their enthusiastic admiration might wish him to have possessed."[4] We cannot conclude that Franklin here speaks of conscious lies told by the followers. Franklin could well mean simply that in the absence of Whitefield's writings, his followers would have been freer to have their enthusiastic admiration lead them to imagine his excellences, thinking them to be real. That these excellences were not real would then be known by Franklin and by us, but not by them. But this is not to say that the followers could *not* consciously have made up the excellences, in which case they could have engaged in well-meaning, pious fraud. Franklin presents the matter so that we cannot be sure. It is hard not to think here of the example of Jesus who, unlike Whitefield and Franklin and Moses, wrote nothing.

If Franklin and Whitefield are alike in their aim to found a new sect, Franklin's comments about Whitefield's mistake are telling. If it was a mistake for Whitefield to write, then Franklin must have had good reasons for thinking that his own writing was, in his case, not a mistake. If so, then his own writing did not leave unguarded expressions and erroneous opinions as hostages to his enemies.[5] It is difficult—though not impossible—to conclude that Franklin thought his writing included no erroneous opinions that could later be used against him. Franklin says explicitly and on two occasions that after he gave up his disagreeable and direct disputation, he remained open throughout his life to being corrected in the course of conversation. Thus, at least in describing this safer mode of communication (conversation), he thought his opinions might possibly be erroneous.

It seems reasonable for us to think the same as regards his writing. The explanation for Franklin's writing seems, on the surface of things, more likely to be this: At least as regards religion, Franklin's doctrine consists, in his opinion, of the essentials of "every known religion" and is free of "every thing that might shock the professors of any religion."[6] If his opinion is wrong, and these principles in some way do shock those who profess some particular religion, Franklin pronounces himself open to being corrected, so even if he cannot posthumously concede a point to a reading critic, the critic could imagine that he would. It seems, then, that the latitudinarian and undogmatic Franklin has overcome the problem of the written word as regards erroneous opinions.

What then, of unguarded expressions? Let's first be clear about what such a thing must be. It cannot be the expression of an erroneous opinion one thinks is true, which *could* shock simply because it is wrong. If this is what we mean, then all expressions of opinion would be unguarded. And at least in the present case, Franklin seems to have taken care of honest opinions that *may* shock precisely by his latitudinarian and undogmatic stance. When we refer to "unguarded expressions," we surely mean instead a slip of the tongue that reveals an opinion that one knows will shock, or else a careless indifference to what one knows will shock, or a naïve ignorance of what one should know will shock others.

If Franklin wrote, then he must have thought that he included no unguarded expressions, either because he expressed no opinions he knew or should have known would shock others, or because he expressed such opinions so as to hide them from those he knew would be shocked. And if he did the latter, he would then also have written with an eye to discovery by those who would be shocked and so always provided for sufficient cover and plausible deniability. In any of these ways, he could have accomplished in writing what Whitefield could only do with the spoken word.

At this point, we do not know which of these possibilities of "no unguarded expressions" might obtain. There is no doubt, however, that the possibilities have been placed before us on the table, so to speak, by Franklin's comments about Whitefield. In fact, Franklin says something at least a little bit shocking about the Whitefield case: that if Whitefield had written nothing, then his followers might consciously or unconsciously have feigned for him excellences that he did not have. If they consciously feigned such excellences for him, then Franklin seems to recommend such craftiness to those who would found a sect, and this at least suggests that Franklin might have thought Jesus was a well-meaning fraud.

On the one hand, it must seem shocking to the religious in general and to Christians in particular to hear Franklin say that a sect can be founded either on a pious fraud or on sincere but merely imagined attributions of excellences. And either assertion must at least give ammunition to those who scoff at Christianity and religion in general. This hardly seems consistent with Franklin's professed resolution to "avoid all discourse that might tend to lessen the good opinion another might have of his own religion."[7] Also, Franklin had already made it clear—to his friend Whitefield no less, who prayed in vain for his "conversion"—that he does not believe in the divinity of Jesus. In this respect, he has already indicated his opinion that those who do believe in the divine Jesus have merely imagined, even if sincerely, his excellences.

But on the other hand, even if these opinions are shocking, Franklin has softened the blow by voicing others that are not. He has related his moral epiphany and conversion to religion, with its principles of good works, and to particular providence, with its divine rewards and punishments. In this respect, Franklin could even explain how a pious fraud might be justifiable and not a threat to religion, at least so long as the fraud is not discovered: If some fibs about Jesus bring men to God and to the service of God by good works, then more power to the fibs.

It thus seems reasonable to conclude, again from the surface of things, something like the following: Franklin thinks it would be better if people believed in the religion he espouses; and if they don't, he thinks it would be better if they agreed with his religious principles, even if he does not agree with theirs insofar as they involve such "distinguishing" things as the divinity of Jesus. And the enthusiastic and pious Christian Whitefield was his lifelong good friend and companion in charity. If Whitefield could be his friend, so too might most other Christians. So at least those Christians who have the least bit of tolerance and charity will be shocked but not necessarily angry at what Franklin says because, after all, he clearly means well. And those who will be shocked and angry (the intolerant and uncharitable) can do with a little nudge in the direction of thinking less of their own religion.

It's thus not simply outrageous, again on the surface of things, for Franklin in effect to recommend to Whitefield a pious fraud that would allow his admirers to imagine of him excellences that he did not have. Moreover, it's not simply outrageous that we are thus led to see the following: that what *would* have been good for Whitefield, for founding his numerous and growing sect, *was,* with proper alteration, in fact good for Franklin for founding his own numerous and growing sect.

In the first layer of irony, the comic frame of the *Autobiography* makes it clear, for anyone with interpretive eyes to see, that Franklin exaggerates the excellences he had and perhaps even claims some he never had at all. In this case, the little fraud works only because it is quickly and easily revealed. The effect is to make the real excellences show up more vividly as merely human, but as nevertheless exuding genuine moral dignity. The real excellences are thus ultimately described with humorous self-deprecation and as being in service to a utilitarian and homely idea of charity understood as Franklinian good works. The little exposed fraud illuminates the excellences, and they then justify it. But from this point on, the fibs and frauds get considerably more substantial. We're now standing on the trapdoor.

At the outset of the *Autobiography,* after telling his son that he wishes to share with posterity both the means of his rise "to a state of affluence and some degree of reputation" and the fact of his going through life with "a considerable share of felicity," Franklin continues his opening comments by saying that

> that felicity, when I reflected on it, has induced me sometimes to say, that were it offered to my choice, I should have no objection to a repetition of the same life from its beginning, only asking the advantage authors have in a second edition to correct some faults of the first. So would I if I might, besides correcting the faults, change some sinister accidents and events of it for others more favorable.

But even if he were denied the chance to alter the second life, Franklin tells us he would still live it again. (In other words, he would commit those faults and sinister accidents and events again.) "However, since such a repetition is not to be expected, the thing most like living one's life over again, seems to be a *recollection* of that life; and to make that recollection as durable as possible, the putting it down in writing."[8]

Lives cannot be relived and do not endure. Only a life presented in the written word can endure. Franklin would live his life again, even if it had to be exactly as it was; but he would also, if he could, relive it as authors do and correct its errors. But since he cannot live again, the next best thing is to do so as a real author, who as such has the liberty in writing but not in real re-living to make changes and "corrections." In other words: Here is my life— so good and so happy that I would live it again exactly as it was, and thus I offer it for others to emulate.

But what Franklin is offering is an author's enduring artful product, not a real life. And this product is subject to the author's post hoc alterations. With this clever sleight of hand, Franklin warns us at the outset that we should not believe everything he says about his own exemplary life. We do not have to guess at this fact or compare his claims with the historical record. Franklin uses a method akin to a fib (the clever sleight of hand) in order to tell us the truth about his telling of lies. So at the very least, it seems reasonable to suspect some other perhaps more important but less obvious lie—and maybe more than one.

According to the moral saga, Franklin's early reading led him to a Deism that corrupted his friends (particularly Collins and Ralph) and to disputa-tions that led people to call him an atheist or an infidel (see chapter 1, Stage Six).[9] While in London, he published his *Dissertation on Liberty and Necessity, Pleasure and Pain*, which argued that "nothing could possibly be wrong in the world, and that vice and virtue were empty distinctions, no such things exist-ing." Reflecting on the harm done to his friends and to himself, Franklin be-gan to doubt "this doctrine"—evidently the Deism—on the grounds of its ill consequences as opposed to its possible truth. Then he suspected that his pamphlet on liberty and necessity might have contained an error. And then he discovered morality, next rediscovered religion (as related in chapter 1, Stage Ten),[10] embarked on the "bold and arduous project of arriving at moral perfection" (also Stage Ten), and finally thought up the "great and extensive project" for a worldwide party of virtue (Stage Eleven).[11]

At the time he discovered morality, he still lacked religion. Franklin never tells us that he was an atheist. At the most, we know that as a result of his refutations, he came while in Boston to be *thought of* as an atheist or infi-del. And his "want of religion" does not necessarily mean that he was simply an atheist. Indeed, if the "essentials of every known religion" consist in the six principles of the creed for the party of virtue (God, providence, worship, service to God as service to man, immortal soul, reward and punishment for virtue and vice), then one could lack religion for not believing in all six and still believe, for instance, that there is a God of some kind.

One thing, however, seems certain: According to the saga, as the result of his philosophizing Franklin did at one time lack religion as defined by the six essential principles. In addition to Franklin's bald statement of the fact, his want of religion is evident in the teaching of the *Dissertation* as he reports it: If Franklin both argued and believed that nothing can be wrong with the world and that virtue and vice do not exist, then it is impossible for him to have believed at that time in particular providence—that God rewards virtue and punishes vice both in this world and in the next.

But at the beginning of Stage Ten, in introducing the "bold and arduous project of arriving at moral perfection," Franklin flatly contradicts the picture of his earlier want of religion. It is not an obvious problem for him to begin describing this stage by asserting that he was never "without some religious principles." As we saw, his former want of religion could be consistent with his believing in some kind of God. What follows immediately, however, is indeed a very big problem: his statement that he "never doubted, for instance, the existence of the Deity, that he made the world, and governed it by his Providence; that the most acceptable service of God was the doing good to man; that our souls are immortal; *and that all crime will be punished and virtue rewarded either here or hereafter*; these I esteemed the essentials of every religion" (my emphasis).[12]

Here we have five of the six essential principles of the creed later described for his project, excepting only the principle that God ought to be worshiped by adoration, prayer, and thanksgiving.[13] And as regards this exception, Franklin begins his list of the principles he never doubted with "for instance," which clearly suggests there were more, and then in the next breath he says that although he seldom attended public worship, he "had still an opinion of its propriety, and of its utility when rightly conducted," and when he came finally to be disgusted by the public worship as it was conducted, he "returned" to the use of the 1728 *Articles of Belief and Acts of Religion*.[14] Franklin clearly intends for us to understand that he never doubted the six principles of the creed for the party of virtue—and that creed includes God's particular providence, including punishment for vice and reward for virtue.

Now, the contradiction here is hard to see and thus easy to overlook. Franklin places Stage Ten at some textual distance from the earlier account of his Deism, the *Dissertation*, and his moral reform and want of religion in Stage Six.[15] And his remarks about what he never doubted are more in the vein of recapitulation and as an introduction to the account of how he came to avoid public worship. And in addition, the story of the fall and redemption is so prominent and dramatic and so tied (although ambiguously, as it turns out on close inspection) to the moral errata that it overshadows Franklin's claim never to have doubted. And so, to my knowledge, this flat contradiction has remained unnoticed by everyone who has written on Franklin's religion and especially on the story of Franklin's fall and redemption. But that it has not been noticed does not make the contradiction disappear.[16]

It might be argued that Franklin simply forgot, when writing Part Two, what he had written on this topic in Part One. We know, however, that Franklin's memory was prodigious. For example, even without a copy of his earlier text at hand, he picks up Part Two at exactly the right spot.[17] But these facts, though relevant, are beside the really important points. First, it beggars belief that Franklin could for even a moment forget the central dramatic theme, the moral saga of fall and redemption that spans Parts One and Two and the first pages of Part Three. Second, it even more powerfully beggars belief that Franklin could forget that he once lacked religion.

But perhaps Franklin merely failed to notice the inconsistency when he was revising. We know that he revised Parts One and Two several times between the summer of 1788 and 1790. It was not until May 1789 that Franklin's letters complain of pain, caused by his illness, and of the resulting opium-induced oblivion that gave him "little time . . . to write anything," and Part Four, written after November 12, 1789, is perfectly lucid, as are the letters and other pieces Franklin wrote literally in his final days.[18] Franklin thus had ample opportunity to correct this (impossible) "mistake" during revision. But he did not.

There is no reasonable way to make the contradiction go away. It is just not possible to explain the contradiction as a lapse in memory or a careless slip of the pen that went unnoticed by Franklin in the process of revision.

Why so? For the reasons already discussed, but also because the implications for the saga are enormous. If the claim in Stage Ten, that Franklin never doubted particular providence, is true, then the story of religious redemption is not. And this makes the entire religious saga a really big lie and not just a matter of some ironic self-deprecation.

Perhaps we can keep the trapdoor from springing. Perhaps, we could speculate, this saga is a really big but nevertheless pious fraud, concocted by one who always had religion and then written down by him so as to inspire the wayward to join the growing sect to come. But if so, why does Franklin expose this fraud by leaving the evidence, however difficult it is to see, of the contradiction? Perhaps, we could still speculate, because to those who do see it, the *piety* of the fraud will justify it—and this could be said to be in keeping with the self-deprecating humor of the *Autobiography*. The big fraud, then, would in this case be the high point of the pious and moral comedy.

These pious explanations are plausible, although just barely. But they cannot outweigh the following telling facts that send us through the trapdoor in the floor of the first ironic layer: Franklin told a big lie about the saga and then exposed that lie—so we are sure that he has lied—and if he told such a lie he could be lying about other important matters as well. (And we would especially suspect this if we really believe that nothing is useful that is not honest.) One then easily wonders if perhaps Franklin is lying not about lacking religion and then getting it back but, rather, about ever having religion at all. And if he lied about ever having religion, then he also lied about never having been "without some religious principles." One could even suspect that he was simply an atheist. And then comes the crucial and telling question: Why, if Franklin's purposes were pious, would he even put such thoughts as these in our minds?

Note the important difference: When Franklin makes his startling assertion about Whitefield's followers' freedom to feign excellences the reverend did not have and reminds us that Jesus was not divine (an opinion that Franklin openly avows), Franklin has his own charitable religion as a fixed position for retreat. Neither Whitefield nor his followers are themselves accused of lying. But Franklin reveals his *own* lie, which feigns an excellence he did not have (the fall and subsequent redemption). Unlike the remark about Whitefield, Franklin's exposure of his fib in the end opens a can of suspicions that serve no pious purpose. Franklin never says anything straightforwardly and makes it difficult to see the contradiction. It is very hard to explain why one who always had religion would so deliberately, even if so slyly, leave such a big fly in the redemptive ointment and thereby raise the inescapable suspicion about his piety.

So much for the first fib. There is another lurking close by, although in this case it emerges not from a flat contradiction but through oddness and obscurity of expression that set us on a series of startling thoughts and conclusions.

When Franklin tells us of his moral reformation (Stage Six), he describes his path to Deism and his corruption of others (Collins and Ralph). He then tells us that his reflection on the harms he had committed (against Vernon and Deborah) and suffered from others (Collins, in the Vernon affair; Ralph, in the Mrs. T. affair; and Keith, who never sent the letter of credit) led him to think that the doctrine (clearly implying Deism) that virtue and vice do not exist was not very useful. He then thought the London pamphlet, the *Dissertation*, which espoused that doctrine, not so clever and perhaps infected by an error that had insinuated itself into the argument unperceived. Reflection on the practical effects of the doctrine (which might still be true) thus led him to doubts about the argument of the *Dissertation*. He then grew to his view that "truth, sincerity and integrity" were of the utmost importance for happiness, and he then formed written resolutions about them. And then, although he still lacked religion, he came to his opinion about good and bad, commanded and forbidden, "all the circumstances of things considered."[19] He then remarks:

> And this persuasion, with the kind hand of Providence, or some guardian Angel, or accidental favourable circumstances and situations, or all together, preserved me (through this dangerous time of youth and the hazardous situations I was sometimes in among strangers, remote from the eye and advice of my father,) without any *willful* gross immorality or injustice that might have been expected from my want of religion.—I say *willful*, because the instances I have mentioned, had something of *necessity* in them, from my youth, inexperience, and the knavery of others.—I therefore had a tolerable character to begin the world with, I valued it properly, and determined to preserve it.[20]

The narrative at this point is very compressed, and we have to think it through before we can say, quite sensibly, the following: Franklin's persuasion about morality, which followed from his reflection on the errata and his consequent suspicion about Deism and then led to his doubt about the argument of the *Dissertation*, along with any or all of providence or a guardian angel or favorable circumstances, protected him from willful gross immorality from the time between his reflections on the errata and his coming back to religion. Prior to his reflections, only providence or a guardian angel or favorable circumstances (good luck) kept him from willful gross immorality. And he does not mean here even to be considering the errata, because they were not willful, having "something of *necessity* in them."

However, we should not yet count our interpretive chickens. The clarity comes with the introduction of a new distinction: willful gross immorality, on the one hand, and errors *excused* by "something of *necessity*," on the other. Why, after all, would Franklin raise the issue unless necessity—and so lack of willfulness—excuses errors? Franklin's expression here seems unremarkable—"something of *necessity*"—unless we think about it more than once. If the mentioned errata were not willful because they were excused by "something of *necessity*," rather than by the fact that they were really no big deal (and a moment's reflection on the errata shows them to be pretty small potatoes), then it would follow that much bigger immoralities would be excused by "everything of necessity"—bigger immoralities would be excused by more pressing necessities. One would certainly think that if a little necessity ("something of *necessity*") excuses, then more necessity would excuse even more.

This thought is supported by an important fact: Although Franklin clearly says that the errata were not willful and although we might conclude that they were petty, Franklin, notably, does *not* say they were petty and even speaks of them as if they were gross, singling out only the issue of willfulness. And he does not here mention the one erratum that really was serious: running out on one's indentures was not a petty matter at the time.[21] Yet he tells us here that he committed *no* willful gross immoralities, thus drawing our attention to the unmentioned matter of James, which thus must also have been excused by necessity. The upshot is clear: "something of *necessity*," by ruling out willfulness, excused the mentioned errata that Franklin might have thought gross immorality and injustice, but that we can surmise were no big deal, and also the gross immorality and injustice of the unmentioned erratum that really was a big deal.

Since most of the errata were in fact small matters (the sins against Deborah, Vernon, and Mrs. T. were hardly theft, rape, or murder), we could think in terms of proportion and then reason from youth, inexperience, and the knavery of others to all other circumstances that might count as necessities (stupidity, wrong opinions, weak will, strong passions, extreme need, big loss, big gain, and so on) excusing gross immorality and injustice. And why not, since the more serious case of James was excused by the fact that Franklin was younger, more inexperienced, and subjected to his brother's beatings?[22] Here the more serious offense is excused by more powerful necessities. Again the upshot is clear: If just "something of *necessity*" excuses the rather minor gross immoralities Franklin reveals, then more necessity would excuse much worse.

These reasonable conclusions shine a very odd light on Franklin's opinion "that though certain actions might not be bad *because* they were forbidden by it [revelation], or good *because* it commanded them; yet probably those actions might be forbidden *because* they were bad for us; or commanded *because* they were beneficial to us, in their natures, *all* the circumstances of things considered" (my emphasis on "all"). The Bible does not say, "Thou shalt not steal, all the circumstances of things considered"; the commandment means that one should not steal regardless of the circumstances or consequences. And here Franklin speaks not just of three necessities (such as youth, inexperience, and the knavery of others) but of all circumstances, which would include all necessities and more, of things considered.

Franklin's qualifying final clause is a blockbuster when we put all the clues and hints together. If all circumstances matter, including all necessities, and if bigger necessities excuse bigger immoralities, then we might well conclude that virtue is useful for happiness in our dealings with men who believe in virtue, but not under all circumstances—such as in a real pinch with a lot to lose or a lot to gain. The errata were not very big deals. But what should we have expected if there had been a really big benefit to be gained (not just a roll in the hay with Mrs. T.) or a really big loss to be suffered, such as the loss of one's life or limbs? Loss of life or limbs would be worse than beatings by one's brother. If youthful inexperience excuses an attempted roll in the hay, would not the press of a big loss or a big gain excuse something much worse?

Franklin opens yet another line of thinking on the matter of necessities or causes that excuse immorality. One could read Franklin's moral reformation, and his remark about all circumstances, to mean something like the following: It shows Franklin's conviction to be the moral equivalent of the most serious and austere piety. Although he did not believe in revelation, he came to think that revelation, were it to exist, would require men to do the right thing, which is good ("beneficial") for them, *regardless* of the consequences and *regardless* of the rewards and punishments that might be involved. It is for men to do the right thing for the sake of doing the right thing, and for God to worry about what only God can know: "all the circumstances of things considered" until the end of days.

The most serious and austere piety requires this, because a judging God cannot really love one who is righteous only for the rewards to come in this world or in the next and at the hands of God. Or, if that God loves the sinner but not the sin, then he cannot but think the righteousness performed only for rewards a sin and thus deserving of punishment. Divine rewards and punishments and the justice they provide may come, and we probably believe that they must come (more on that later), but they cannot be the motive of or the end of righteousness, which properly understood is nothing but righteousness. Franklin certainly knew of this from reading Shaftesbury, if not from his experience with sincere believers.[23] (No seriously pious man will say that he acts righteously only for the sake of the divine rewards.) And it is Franklin, after all, who in this context discusses his opinion about good and bad in terms of revelation, which he does not do later in describing what he would "explain and enforce" in his "Art of Virtue." There, he would defend the opinion "the nature of man alone considered."[24]

So we have to consider revelation seriously, and on this serious reading we could conclude that Franklin's conviction about the "utmost" importance of truth, sincerity, and integrity was accompanied by the belief that—just as with revelation rightly understood—the "utmost" is to be taken with absolute seriousness. Franklin's conviction thus means that truth, sincerity, and integrity are good for us, and loved by God if he exists, regardless of the outcome, regardless of all circumstances considered, including divine rewards and punishments if they exist. The power of this moral belief, then, kept Franklin from the immorality that might be "expected" from one who lacks religion—but only as might be expected by one who understands religion, incorrectly, to be a matter of rewards and punishments alone.

But we cannot reason to this righteous conclusion without ignoring Franklin's careful presentation. Everything turns on two small details: an unraveling "with" and "or." Before coming to his persuasion, which followed on the errata, it must have been providence or an angel (the same thing, one would think) or just good luck that kept Franklin from inexcusable (willful gross) immorality and injustice. Youth, inexperience, and the knavery of others might then have excused the errata, but by themselves they would not have excused rape or murder (although we could wonder why not, given the implications of the case of James).

But *after* his persuasion and before coming to religion, why would Franklin need providence as well ("*with* the kind hand of Providence," my emphasis), and why might he depend not on that persuasion along with providence but on something else by itself ("*or* some guardian Angel, *or* accidental favourable circumstances and situations," my emphasis), and why would he need everything ("*or* all together," my emphasis)? Why would he need these if in his persuasion he took the "utmost" with absolute seriousness? Only because the persuasion, as interpreted by the righteous opinion, was not enough. What was needed besides good circumstances provided by luck or an angel or providence? It can only be the *rewards and punishments* meted out by God with his particular providence.

So if Franklin came to his moral reformation before his religious one, and even if he really (contradicting the moral saga) never doubted particular providence, according to this context, that providence can *only* have concerned rewards and punishments for virtue and vice. (And that is the clear meaning of what he never doubted and the creed for the party of virtue.)[25] These rewards and punishments are doubtless strong necessities—the strongest that can be imagined. But by the righteous interpretation of Franklin's opinion, which Franklin clearly wants us to consider, taking the divine rewards and punishments as *necessary* for righteousness would make a mockery of those rewards and punishments, which should not matter to the righteous and do not matter first and foremost to God. If these necessities eventually saved Franklin from willful gross immorality, then he did not entertain the opinion about good and bad and revelation according to its righteous interpretation. And if he did bow merely to the rewards and punishments meted out by God, he would by his own ironic admission not have really deserved those rewards at all.

If all that matters for religion is the fact of divine rewards and punishments and if religion is not true, then the same must be true for morality on this earth: All that matters are the secular rewards and punishments that might follow from our behavior. Then the utmost importance of truth, sincerity, and integrity becomes a matter of empirical fact and calculation, and "all the circumstances" are not those things that we disregard for the sake of righteousness but those outcomes we consider most as regards "the felicity of life." Then happiness does not consist in virtue; rather, virtue is a means to happiness. And if happiness does not consist in virtue, then virtue may not always be the sole means to happiness.

Here we're back, then, to the interpretation that "all the circumstances of things" can be seen as "necessities" (big gains or big losses) that excuse the things people call "willful gross immorality." Without the rewards and punishments of revealed particular providence, Franklin implies, he would have engaged in immorality of any size to gain a big benefit or avoid a big loss. And there would be no blame to be leveled because, after all, *all* the circumstances and necessities can be considered, and, according to the evidence we have here, they excuse immoralities when virtue costs too much or when vice promises a really big reward.

These conclusions leave us where we were before the purported moral reformation. If there is no blame because all the circumstances of things can be considered and excuse all immorality, then there really are no such things as vice and virtue. Then Franklin's opinion about good and bad, which followed his purported conviction about truth, sincerity, and integrity, would really be the very same position as presented in the pamphlet. And so the moral reformation as reflected in the persuasion *never happened at all.*

From this line of thinking, it is plausible to conclude that the moral saga is as much a fraud as the religious saga. And if the moral saga is a fraud, then how could Franklin eventually have been saved from gross immorality by his religion, since that religion would have required him to believe in particular providence solely in terms of rewards and punishments? Franklin helps us think (with Shaftesbury) that such a claim of salvation would have made him unrighteous in the eyes of God. So how could he really have been saved by God from willful gross immorality? Only if he did come to think, along with God, that virtue *consists* in the noble subordination of one's fundamental (big) interests to others or to some noble cause. (Lawrence sneaks in again.) But Franklin never says this in the *Autobiography,* or anywhere else for that matter, and we can see now that his silence on this point is a real problem.

The genuinely pious man might at this point respond as follows: Were Franklin to bow to God only for the rewards and so not deserve them, it would show simply that he is a sinner and besmirched by evil, which all of us are, including those who strive for righteousness. God shows us righteousness. And then we do our best, and God provides the rewards and punishments knowing that as sinners they will matter to us to some extent—an extent the righteous strive as hard as they can to minimize.

But as Franklin presents the case, even righteousness that is indifferent to all circumstances is beneficial *to* us. Righteousness is surely, then, a great good. This seems to be a perfectly reasonable thing to say; would the righteous man deny it? But at the same time, righteousness is indifferent to consequences and is at its peak when it consists in sacrifice and the subordination of one's basic interests to another's. We wonder, then, if the righteous man, who reminds us of our sin and who must agree with Franklin as to righteousness being a good, is in something of a pickle: If righteousness is good for us regardless of all the consequences, and if we then, as sinners, weaken and want the good consequences that God can give, is not the difference here between greater and lesser (that is, sin-tainted) goods that are nevertheless *both* goods for us? And how can righteousness be both a benefit and a greater good for us and at the same time also the sacrifice of our essential good for the sake of another?

The point is not that the righteous man really acts secretly for the sake of the rewards. He tries not to, but as a sinner he cannot fully succeed. Rather, the point is that he simply does not realize that he cannot but think of both righteousness and rewards as goods for him, with the former (righteousness) being better than the latter (sin-tainted). It is not that he secretly acts for the lesser rewards but that the distinction between the good of righteousness (which requires us not to care for consequences) and the good of reward (those very consequences), both being goods, may just not make any sense.

As usual, Franklin leaves room for himself to wiggle and leaves us with the task of picking up on his clues and thinking things through for ourselves. But there is no doubt that he puts the disturbing thoughts to work in our minds. And when we follow them up, we find ourselves in a quite different ironic layer beneath the surface of the text. In this layer, we encounter a different Franklin altogether—not the moral and religious realist but the profound skeptic about religion and morality.

Moreover, his moves here are really very subtle. He raises the claim of righteousness in our minds, only then to make us think that it may not really have been his youthful opinion and that his opinion was really the one professed in the *Dissertation*, and he then intimates a confusion that may lurk in the thoughts of the righteous. And at the same time, he tells us that he came to doubt the argument—but not necessarily the "truth"—of the *Dissertation*'s doctrine that virtue and vice (and thus righteousness) do not exist. So we are led to wonder if he came to see the truth of the doctrine *on other grounds*. At the very least we have to wonder: What moral purpose could Franklin serve by putting such thoughts in our minds?

There is one more contradiction that certainly looks like another lie. It's not a blockbuster, but it's interesting nevertheless.

When Franklin describes his early methods of disputation, we get the following story (Stages Two, Three, and Four).[26] From reading his father's books of disputes about religion, he picked up the habit of disputatious argument aimed at confutation. He used such arguments with his friend Collins, who we know was corrupted by Franklin's arguments in favor of Deism and who later harmed Franklin. We do not know for sure if these very first disputations "perverted" Collins in religion and morals, because Franklin does not tell us whether, at the time of his very first disputatious confutations, he himself was a Deist. The evidence certainly suggests that the subject was religion, and we know that the disputations produced "disgusts and perhaps enmities where [one] may have occasion for friendship."

At any rate, by the time Franklin was "scarce fifteen" he *had* become a thorough Deist, and by sixteen, after reading Shaftesbury and Anthony Collins (the deistic writer), he had "become a real doubter in many points of our religious doctrine." He then read Locke and the *Port Royal Logic* and discovered Xenophon and then adopted the Socratic method number one, which involved playing the "humble enquirer and doubter" and engaging his interlocutors in dialectical refutations—confuting them by entangling them in the difficult and unforeseen consequences of their own opinions. As one who doubted much religious doctrine, says Franklin, "I found this method safest for myself and very embarrassing to those against whom I used it." Franklin tells us that he stayed with this method for some few years, which at the very least means that he was at his Socratic refutations just a year later, when he left James.

Now, in the story about James (Stage Five, Erratum Number One), we learn that the erratum was occasioned by two factors: Franklin's resentment of the ill-treatment he suffered at the hands of his brother and the political problem that had emerged between his brother and the Massachusetts Assembly.[27] When James prevented his employment in any other printing houses in Boston, Franklin then embarked on a different course to which, it turns out, he was already inclined for different reasons than just escaping his brother. He was "the rather inclined," in fact, not just to seek new employment in Boston but to leave the city because he "reflected that I had already made myself a little obnoxious, to the governing party" and feared that "from the arbitrary proceedings of the Assembly in my brother's case it was likely I might if I stayed soon bring myself into scrapes." The political problem afforded the means—the secret indentures—that enabled Franklin to run out on his apprenticeship.

But the political problem was not, it turns out, the *determining* reason for his flight from Boston. Even this prior inclination was not by itself enough to precipitate Franklin's departure from town. That departure was "determined" by another fact: "that my indiscrete disputations about religion began to make me pointed at with horror by good people, as an infidel or atheist." The crucial point to note here is that it was absolutely time to leave when the good people, not just irritated partisans who found him a little obnoxious, came to view him with horror because of his religious and theological refutations.[28]

The Socratic refutations, in which Franklin played the humble doubter and dissembled his own offensive views, were safer than the blunt contradictions that aroused anger and indignation. But they were not absolutely safe, since they produced embarrassment in his interlocutors. And it seems very likely that the "indiscreet disputations about religion" included the Socratic refutations. However safer they might have been in providing humble self-protection, it was surely somewhat indiscreet to lead interlocutors into embarrassing religious refutations based on the implications of their *own* opinions.

Moreover, since these humble Socratic refutations followed on Franklin's confrontational refutations, with their consequent enmities and disgusts, could not the "good people" and the refuted alike have thought something like this: "Don't trust that Franklin, who now wears the mask of humble doubter. We've *heard* the loudmouth under that mask—and he was an atheist or infidel loudmouth. Only now he's even worse: a liar and poseur (see, atheists are liars too) who not only makes people angry and disgusted (anger and disgust are good things to direct at atheists and infidels), but makes them embarrassed for themselves and their own beliefs."

At the very least, we know that Franklin's confrontational and his ironic Socratic refutations concerned religion and that the former and most likely both together got him in such theological hot water as to cause people to conclude that he was an atheist and to make him (among other reasons, of course) determine to go on the lam. At least in another town, we can surmise, the Socratic refutations would in fact be safer, since there would be no public memory of his confrontational refutations. Even so, Franklin says that after continuing the Socratic refutations for some few years, he "gradually left" them until he "retained" only the habit of expressing himself in "terms of modest diffidence" in any matter that might possibly be disputed, and eschewing terms like "certainly," "undoubtedly," or any others that imply positiveness and using instead such expressions as "I conceive," "I apprehend," "it appears to me," "I should think it so for such and such reasons," "I imagine it to be so," or "it is so if I am not mistaken." This latter and retained method, Socratic method number two, was throughout his life useful both for inculcating his opinions in others and persuading them and for leaving himself open to having his own errors corrected.[29]

But in the later story about adding the thirteenth virtue to Franklin's list in the project for achieving moral perfection (Stage Ten), Franklin tells a different and apparently contradictory story.[30] There we learn that after his conversion to morality and religion, and even later, while discovering the virtues and the means to attain them, Franklin was still obnoxiously disputatious.

When describing the project for moral perfection, Franklin tells us that his list of virtues originally consisted of the first twelve and that he added the last, humility, at the admonition of a "Quaker Friend" who informed Franklin that he was "generally thought proud" and that his pride "showed itself frequently in conversation" because Franklin "was not content with being in the right when discussing any point, but was overbearing and rather insolent."

The Quaker convinced Franklin of the charge "by mentioning several instances." And as a result, Franklin determined to cure himself of the vice or folly and added humility to his list. He did not succeed in attaining it, but "had a good deal with regard to the *appearance* of it." Franklin made it a rule to forbear all contradiction to the sentiments of others and even forbade himself the use of every word or expression that "imported a fixed opinion; such as *certainly, undoubtedly,* etc. and I adopted instead of them, *I conceive, I apprehend,* or *I imagine* a thing to be so or so, or it appears to me at present." He even denied himself the pleasure of contradicting an error abruptly or immediately and rather "in answering . . . began by observing that in certain cases or circumstances his opinion would be right, but in the present case there *appeared* or *seemed* to me some difference, etc." Franklin found the advantage of this method and more success in convincing and less mortification when he was found in error. Despite rubbing against his grain, the method eventually became so habitual that "perhaps for the fifty years past no one has ever heard a dogmatical expression escape me."[31]

If we measure the "fifty years past" from Franklin's dating of Part Two at 1784, he would have mastered the humble method by 1734, after he first got the idea for the great and extensive project for the party of virtue, which we learn in Stage Eleven occurred to him first on May 9, 1731.[32] Now, this humble method provoked by the Quaker Friend sure looks like Socratic method number two, which consisted in Franklin's expressing himself only in reserved terms and eschewing aggressively positive terms.

There appears to be a flat contradiction as to how Franklin came to his habit of speaking with modest diffidence. According to the story about adding the virtue of humility (Stage Ten), Franklin took up the diffident method at the behest of the Quaker Friend and even after conceiving of the party of virtue. But in the account of Socratic method number two (Stage

Four), Franklin had been practicing his diffident method since the time he discovered and adopted Socratic method number one at the age of sixteen (Stage Three). We know this because he tells us that he practiced Socratic method number one—with its dialectical and embarrassing refutations—for some few years and gradually left it until he *retained* only the habit of expressing himself diffidently.

In other words, from the age of fifteen he practiced this diffidence, at first with the aggressive dialectical refutations and then later without them. He retained the diffidence, as what we have called Socratic method number two, which means he did not later take it up from scratch. But according to the story of the Quaker Friend, he *did* take it up from scratch. And, arguably, not just after "some few" years: Twelve years, it seems to me, is more than just a few. Why this contradiction, and what are we to make of it? If it's a fib, why would Franklin lie about this matter?

It is not, in fact, another lie, however much it looks like one. In the first lie, we are simply unable to resolve the contradiction and must either ignore one of its terms or be driven to surprising suspicions. In the second, we are driven to surprising suspicions by pregnant expressions and odd obscurity. In this case, however, it is possible to resolve the matter based on the evidence we have, although resolving the dilemma proves telling. According to Franklin, his first and youthful disputation produced enmity and disgust, and his Socratic, humble-inquirer refutations produced embarrassment. The habit of disputatious confutation was a bad one because the enmity and disgusts precluded "occasion for friendship."[33] What, then, are we to think of the Socratic refutations in this regard?

We know that they produced embarrassment, but we hear nothing of their having produced friendship. As regards "many points of our religious doctrine," three possible results of the Socratic refutations come to mind. The first is that an attempted refutation simply fails, that the interlocutor is not drawn into unforeseen and inescapable difficulties. In this case, one could well think friendship could prevail between the humble doubter and the unshaken believer.

The second possibility is that the refutation succeeds to the extent that the believer is confuted but not to the extent that he is thereby convinced. This is the case in which embarrassment makes sense: The believer would be embarrassed because he could not defend what he thinks is in principle defensible or what he "knows" to be true in his own heart. He would be embarrassed because he would blame himself and, blinded by Franklin's mantle of the humble inquirer, would not blame Franklin. Or perhaps he might both be embarrassed and, under the right conditions, doubt Franklin's humble disguise, blame him, and become angry with him as well.

The third possibility is that the believer is not just refuted but is convinced that what he once thought true, is not. There may be some slight twinge of embarrassment at having been so mistaken, but one could expect friendship to result from having been shown the truth: "Thanks, Ben, for releasing me from this important error." As we saw, Franklin admits only the second possibility and is not definite as between mere embarrassment and embarrassment accompanied by anger.

Now in the case of the Quaker, we have reason to believe that something else is going on. First, the Quaker comments on Franklin's way of discussing *any* point, not just points of religion. And Franklin makes no mention of religion in this context, as he did so explicitly in the other. Furthermore, we have good reason to think that, in fact, the issues at stake are not religious ones. For the Quaker Friend convinced Franklin that general opinion held him to be proud, when right, and that his pride often appeared in conversation, "by mentioning several instances." Perhaps these were instances of which the Quaker Friend was told (and which he believed) and not instances involving the Quaker Friend himself. But in either case, the point is that Franklin was "not content with being in the *right* [my emphasis] when discussing any point, but was overbearing and rather insolent."[34] At least if the Quaker Friend is a believer, it is hard to see how he could concede that Franklin was "right," even if overbearing and insolent, in a religious refutation regarding any essential point of his broad-minded religion. And the same holds for the generality of believers, which would include Presbyterians, whose opinion he reports.

The same difficulty applies to the "general" opinion that Franklin was thought proud. First of all, Franklin *gradually* left off his Socratic refutations, which it is safe to say means that they became fewer and fewer, although one could, rather, say that he gradually abandoned them by leaving off the last confuting steps in his refutations. If they became fewer and fewer, then it would seem less likely that a resulting bad reputation would have become general. The same could be said if he just stopped pushing to the very end in the conversations—that would seem not even to provoke the charge of pride. And these arguments are in a way beside the point: Had Franklin been engaging in his Socratic refutations, it is hard to see why the charge would be being "proud" and "overbearing and rather insolent." At the very least, one would think the humble inquirer guise, when it worked, would have prevented this particular charge. And at the worst, from those defeated and both embarrassed and angry at Franklin, the charge would have been, as before, that the man was an atheist or infidel.

All the evidence points to the following conclusions, which entail no contradictions, with one small but still telling exception: Franklin's overbearing and rather insolent lack of contentment with merely being in the right did not pertain to his discussing "any" point, as the Quaker says. In the case of the Quaker, the instances mentioned did not include religion—or if they did they did not include refutations of "our religious doctrine" (in the case of Presbyterians) or more spare but essential principles (in the case of the Quakers). Nor would the instances that produced the general opinion of pride have had to do with refuting those doctrines.

The story thus emerges as follows: Assuming nothing else about any moral or religious reformation, Franklin first engaged in obnoxious disputations about religion, in the course of which he became a thorough Deist and, after reading Shaftesbury and Collins, a real doubter in many religious doctrines. Armed with such doubt, he then read Xenophon and engaged in his newly discovered Socratic refutations, covered as far as possible by the guise of humble doubter and inquirer. The guise did not in the end work, and the boy had to flee the good people of Boston, who openly called him an atheist or infidel. In Philadelphia he continued the Socratic refutations for a few years, although he gradually abandoned them, and the cover apparently worked this time and he suffered no need to run again. By the time he abandoned the "humble doubter" refutations completely—when, we do not exactly know—he *retained* only the habit of modest diffidence. But he practiced this diffidence only in matters of religion, or at least in matters of religion that touched on fundamental points. In every other respect, Franklin remained a prideful, overbearing, and insolent conversationalist until advised against the vice by the Quaker Friend.

We can thus confidently surmise the following: Franklin's eventual diffidence in matters of religion was more fundamental than the diffidence in all other matters. He could get along without the latter, although perhaps with less success in life than otherwise might have transpired. But he could not do without the former without the risk of much greater troubles—he still bore the risk of earning a reputation that could get him run out of town. At some point in his life, Franklin came to think that taking this risk in refuting religion was no longer necessary, for one of three possible reasons: (1) He had learned what he needed to know; (2) he thought the risk no longer worth what he might yet discover; (3) after his redemption, he came to see the truth of what he had once thought himself to have refuted. But as regards the last possibility, why does Franklin still point his careful readers to the radical alternative that he became and remained an atheist? It can only be because he wanted us to take this more shocking possibility with absolute seriousness.

The question arises as to why Franklin makes us work so hard to see the precise details of his practice of rhetorical diffidence. In the religious and moral sagas, the broad focus is on the harms Franklin did to others, the harms the perverted did to him, and the supposed shock he suffered when reflecting on these harms. But when we notice the apparent contradiction as regards his modest diffidence and when we think our way through to the noncontradictory solution, we see a completely different aspect of Franklin's want of religion and his refutations: not the harms done to others or the harms he suffered at the hands of those he corrupted, but the harms he suffered and risked suffering at the hands of the good who were not corrupted. As we shall see, the lesson about this danger from the good was one he never forgot.[35]

Moreover, we begin to suspect a subtle difference between the Deists and Deism, on the one hand, and Franklin's "want of religion," on the other. There were doubtless sincere and believing Deists—those who believed in a God and the Creation but did not believe in miracles, revelation, and particular providence. And there were probably among the Deists covert atheists. Both were, of course, quite obnoxious to orthodox Christians and especially to the Calvinist Presbyterians. But the Deists were by and large an upper-crust crowd, benevolent supporters of enlightenment, and their Deism was primarily a subject of theological books and postprandial discussion. They did not run around obnoxiously shoving their freethinking in Everyman's face, and so although Deism was abhorred by the orthodox and was often derided as atheism, Deists were not seriously persecuted. William Keith—the freethinker who harmed Franklin—was, after all, the governor of Pennsylvania. If the puzzle of Franklin's rhetorical method discloses the danger to himself from the good, a danger so pressing that he had to skip town, then the situation of Franklin's "want of religion" or freethinking appears somewhat different from the situation of the Deists.

Before he took up the technique of Socratic refutation, Franklin *was* obnoxiously shoving his heterodoxy in people's faces. And even with it, despite the guise of humble doubter, he was still taking the irritating offensive, so to speak. He made disguised sorties among the orthodox believers, whom he confounded and embarrassed by hoisting them on the petard of their own opinions. And he kept at this offensive even after being run out of town. Had Franklin kept up this aggressive posture for too long, even with his humble disguise, we could at least doubt that he would have succeeded in business, society, public service, and politics as he did—even in more tolerant Pennsylvania. Perhaps we can ascribe Franklin's aggressiveness simply to his youth and inexperience. But strong evidence tells against jumping to this easy conclusion.

Franklin continued the Socratic refutations even after learning the lesson of how dangerous the good people could be. Moreover, the extraordinary contradictions (indeed, the lies) in the *Autobiography* at the very least suggest that Franklin may never have rejected what he learned or concluded from his obnoxious and his Socratic refutations. If so, then we may have to account for those refutations as having occasioned perhaps the most important discovery of his life—so important that he endured the risks involved. This is not what we should expect from some error of brash youth and inexperience. We know the youthful and dialectical Franklin primarily from the mature perspective of the *Autobiography*. For all we know, the story may be pure invention. But that possibility doesn't matter. What does matter is that the mature Franklin has presented, to his careful readers, his picture of the young Franklin on the path to this most important discovery.

We can draw a revealing comparison between Franklin's methods of discourse as he describes them in the *Autobiography* and the method we see at work in the *Autobiography*. According to the description of his retained modest diffidence (Socratic method number two), Franklin used it "whenever I advanced any thing that may possibly be disputed," and we know that he applied this first and foremost to matters of religion.[36] To *us*, however, Franklin speaks positively about his lacking and never having lacked religion, and when he says he never doubted religion he speaks positively about the principles he espoused: He never doubted those principles and he "esteemed" them common to all religions. Here we see juxtaposed two positive but patently contradictory assertions about religion. The effect is to render ambiguous his genuine opinion about a religious matter that might be disputed. But the effect is not quite the same as if he had simply spoken with his modest diffidence. In this case (the flat contradiction) we are driven to consider some shocking opinions about religion.

In the story about his moral reformation, Franklin does use the language of modest diffidence, especially the words "probably" and "might be."[37] But even here, we are driven by Franklin's clues to consider some shocking opinions about morality. It thus happens that Franklin has not completely abandoned his youthful aggressiveness, if only because we are set to thinking critically on our own.

In Stage Ten, just before relating the story of the Quaker Friend, Franklin describes his plan to write his book to be called "The Art of Virtue," in which he would lay out the principles of his project for the achievement of moral perfection.[38] In this book he would "explain and enforce this doctrine, that vicious actions are not hurtful because they are forbidden, but forbidden because they are hurtful, the nature of man alone considered: that it was therefore every ones interest to be virtuous, who wished to be happy even in this world." Here he abandons his diffidence (no "probably" or "might be"). But here he tells us that, "connected in [his] mind with a great and extensive project that required the whole man to execute, and which an unforeseen succession of employs prevented my attending to, it [the book] has hitherto remained unfinished."

He never got around to "explain[ing] and enforc[ing]" his doctrine of bad and forbidden as regards man alone. In discussing the principle as regards God (in Stage Six), Franklin uses the voice of modest diffidence. Thus, at the very least, we could say that the principle as regards religion was a matter of dispute at the time he wrote the *Autobiography*.

And no wonder: If he had not explained and enforced the opinion as regards man alone—and especially if he thought it impossible—then it would have been even more difficult, if not impossible, for him to explain and enforce it as regards God. Franklin's description of the principle in Stage Six provides no solid evidence that he ever came again to believe in morality. On the contrary, it is entirely possible that he always thought virtue and vice do not exist. If so, and if Franklin were correct in his view, then it would seem to follow that the doctrine of divine rewards and punishments makes no sense at all.

POOR RICHARD TELLS US that fish and company smell after three days. The surface and the first ironic layer of the *Autobiography* smell of roses—or perhaps first of that exotic flower, the orchid, and then of the more familiar and likable rose. But as we penetrate to the second ironic layer, the *Autobiography* smells fishy indeed. It may not be easy at first to catch the whiff, but the clues for doing so are embedded in the text and cannot be dismissed as unimportant slips or mistakes. Franklin cannot have forgotten about such fundamental experiences of his life as the religious reformation as told in the saga, and so we cannot dismiss the flat contradiction (and its disturbing implications) of his claiming both to have disbelieved and never to have doubted particular providence. We cannot simply dismiss the disturbing line of thought provoked by the odd and obscure account of the moral reformation. And we cannot dismiss what is needed to explain the apparent conundrum of his coming to the rhetorical method of modest diffidence.

The three sets of clues taken together reveal an altogether different path of Franklin's thinking: Whereas the surface and the first ironic layer show a journey from morality to philosophy and skepticism and then back to morality and religion, the second ironic layer shows a path from morality to philosophy and then back to an *ironic* morality and religion—that is, to a public display of conventional morality and piety that masks a deep and persistent and, we can surmise, well-grounded skepticism. Franklin gives himself much room to wiggle and implants his clues in a sea of conventional and practical moral wisdom and piety. But had Franklin thought his moral and religious reformations truly good for him as well as for everyone else, he would *not* have inserted the clues that so powerfully force us to suspect the contrary.[39] And he would have taken the time required to write and publish "The Art of Virtue." Could it have been less important than the reams of other things he found time to write?

We'll come back to the *Autobiography* and the trail of other Franklin writings to which it points. Even though Franklin wrote the *Autobiography* with a laser-beam eye on a selected few of his earlier and youthful writings, we cannot say that he wrote those earlier pieces and any others with an eye to later writing the *Autobiography*. Although not outside the bounds of possibility, to say this would be a purely speculative stretch. But no stretch is involved if we examine these writings, so clearly picked out by the *Autobiography*, to see if they contain indications or even specific details of the skepticism indicated by the second ironic layer of the later work.

But first, it is important to note that the *Autobiography* is not Franklin's only comic work. He wrote many comic pieces, many of them at the time of or after the supposed moral epiphany and return to religion and public service, and it will be helpful (and a lot of fun) to examine them before we proceed with the trail marked out by the *Autobiography*. They are, I hope to show, subtle and philosophic: As funny as they are on the surface, a careful reading finds clues and sleights of hand that point to surprising and radical lines of thinking and critique. So in chapters 3 and 4 we turn to Franklin's other comic writings. The guiding question is: Does the humor serve the practical morality and piety of the saga, or does it, beneath the comic surface, undermine the conventional assumptions of the saga? This much I'll say right now—if you've presently got one hand on your hat, you'd better keep the other on your side.

3 • The Philosophical Wag

Franklin's humor marks him off from all the American Founders and indeed from most political philosophers of the entire Western tradition. Even if not to all sensibilities, at least to some, Franklin is very, very funny. I found that if I read Franklin every day for a week, it was hard not to have a chuckle every day. If one were to read Franklin for a month, it would be hard not to laugh long and loud at least once a week. And if one were to read Franklin for a year, it would be impossible not, on several occasions, to laugh until one cried. He never lets up with advancing years, refusing, at least in print, to succumb to the angry crabbiness of old age.

Moreover, there is nothing that Franklin does not in some way make fun of. He is, to put it bluntly, shameless, although almost always cautiously so. This is not to say that Franklin was a frivolous man. He was, of course, just the opposite, taking on throughout his life enormous and world-historic responsibilities and engaging in the most serious, pressing, and often dangerous practical and political affairs of his nascent country. But he cannot be accounted a fully serious man, for whom at least some things are beyond mockery. Franklin's humor went far beyond just taking established power down a peg or two, and far beyond what is often described as his good-natured, civil, and above all tolerant moderation.[1]

In his introduction to the 1905 edition of the *Writings of Benjamin Franklin*, Albert Henry Smyth, a man of more delicate sensibilities than are current today, divined the hard edge of Franklin's sense of humor and character. After discussing briefly Franklin's satire in the Silence Dogood essays and in *Poor Richard* and the columns of the *Pennsylvania Gazette*, Smyth, an enthusiastic admirer of Franklin, comments (and it deserves quotation in full):

> Unfortunately, it is impossible without offence to quote many of his briefer paragraphs. We may track him through thirty years of the

Gazette by the smudgy trail he leaves behind him. His humor is coarse and his mood of mind Rabelaisian. His "salt imagination" delights in greasy jests and tales of bawdry. He came of a grimy race of hard-handed blacksmiths, and they set their mark on him. With all his astonishing quickness and acuteness of intellect and his marvelous faculty of adaptation, he remained to the end of life the proletarian, taking an unclean pleasure in rude speech and coarse innuendo. He out-Smolletts Smollett in his letters to young women at home and experienced matrons abroad. Among the manuscripts in the Library of Congress, and in the columns of his newspaper and the introduction to "Poor Richard," are productions of his pen, the printing of which would not be tolerated by the public sentiment of the present age. It is no use blinking the fact that Franklin's animal instincts and passions were strong and rank, that they led him to the commission of many deplorable *errata* in his life, and that the taint of an irremediable vulgarity is upon much of his conduct. As is said of Angelo in the play, "I am sorry, one so learned and wise, should slip so grossly."[2]

Smyth is correct to sense the extraordinary vulgarity of some of Franklin's humor. But he is surely wrong—and perhaps moved to error by his obvious snobbery—to say that Franklin's vulgarity springs from unbridled animal spirits. Franklin indeed had such spirits, but to say that they animated his humor is to miss its cool and collected reason. Franklin's humor, indeed his comic genius, reveals and springs from his deepest thoughts about human nature and experience. One could say that his humor is philosophical and that as such it always points beyond itself and to some sober revelation, however much it makes us laugh and, sometimes, turn red in the face.

Bedlam for Believers

From the outset of his printing career, Franklin took delight in publishing tidbits and hoaxes depicting bizarre human behavior, as if to present a kind of circus freak show in print. Sometimes he just lets a brief picture stand by itself, as if to say "just have a look at *this!*"[3] The first such item (in 1729) was a mean-spirited wisecrack that appeared in his "account" of a fiddler and his wife overturned in a canoe: "And sometime last week, we are informed, that one Piles a Fiddler, with his Wife, were overset in a Canoo near Newtown Creek. The good man, 'tis said, prudently secured his fiddle, and let his wife go to the bottom."[4] Soon after followed more subtle pieces depicting religious madness and extreme credulity, divine inspiration, bizarre punish-

ments, and astounding reversals of fortune. In all of them there is more going on than at first meets the eye, with much sleight of hand and pulling of
the rug. For this reason they have to be read with care, but also for another:
They often concern and make fun of religion.

In October 1730 Franklin published a hoax pretending to recount a witch
trial at Mount Holly.[5] Some three hundred people came to watch "an experiment or two tried on some persons accused of witchcraft. It seems the accused
had been charged with making their neighbours sheep dance in an uncommon manner, and with causing hogs to speak, and sing Psalms, etc. to the
great terror and amazement of the King's good and peaceable subjects in this
province."[6] The accusers were convinced that if the accused were to be
weighed in a scale against a Bible, the Bible would be heavier, and that if
they were to be tied and placed in the river, they would float. These would be
signs that the accused were indeed witches. The accused agreed to the trial
on the condition that two of the most zealous accusers be tried with them.

And so the trial was set, for two men and two women, one of each sex of
the accused and one of each sex of the accusers. First came the scales. After
a careful search to make sure that no one had anything weighty on his or her
person, a "grave tall man" carrying "a huge great Bible" read a chapter out of
the book of Moses and placed the book in the scale opposite the accused,
and "to the great surprise of the spectators, flesh and bones came down
plump, and outweighed that great good Book by abundance. After the same
manner, the others were served, and their lumps of mortality severally were
too heavy for *Moses* and all the Prophets and Apostles."

Then both the accusers and the mob, not satisfied with the first trial, de-
manded the trial by water. When bound, tied to ropes for safety, and placed on
the water, all floated, except for the very "thin and spare" male accuser who
"with some difficulty began to sink at last." When a sailor jumped on the back
of the accused man, both went to the bottom, but the accused, though bound,
popped up before the sailor. When told that she floated, the woman accuser
asked to be dunked a second time, whereupon she floated again, at which she
declared that she had been bewitched by the accused to make her so light and
"that she would be ducked again a hundred times, but she would duck the
devil out of her." The accused man, surprised at his floating, became less convinced of his innocence and said, "If I am a witch, it is more than I know."

[The] more thinking part of the spectators were of opinion, that any
person so bound and placed in the water (unless they were mere skin
and bones) would swim [float] till their breath was gone, and their lungs
filled with water. But it being the general belief of the populace, that
the womens shifts, and the garters with which they were bound helped

to support them; it is said they are to be tried again the next warm weather, naked.

Just several months later, Franklin published the following gem:

We hear from the Jersey side, that a man near Sahauken being disordered in his senses, protested to his wife that he would kill her immediately, if she did not put her tongue into his mouth; She through fear complying, he bit off a large piece of it; and taking it between his fingers threw it into the fire with these words, *Let this be for a Burnt-Offering*.[7]

Franklin was still at it as late as the early 1740s, during his rise to public prominence and after his involvement in the controversy involving the Reverend Hemphill and after befriending and helping the evangelical Reverend Whitefield. In March 1742 he published the following short piece in the *Gazette*, about Benjamin Lay, here portrayed as an eccentric and unbalanced Quaker:

On Monday about noon, being in the time of the general meeting of Friends, Benjamin Lay, the Pythagorean-cynical-christian philosopher, bore a public testimony against the vanity of tea-drinking, by devoting to destruction in the market-place, a large parcel of valuable china, etc. belonging to his deceased wife. He mounted a stall on which he had placed the box of ware; and when the people were gathered round him, began to break it piecemeal with a hammer; but was interrupted by the populace, who overthrew him and his box, to the ground, and scrambling for the sacrifice, carried off as much of it whole as they could get. Several would have purchased the china of him before he attempted to destroy it, but he refused to take any price for it.[8]

And perhaps the most bizarre was a piece that appeared in the *Gazette* the following October:

About two weeks ago, one John Leek, of Cohansie in West-New-Jersey, after twelve months deliberation, made himself an eunuch (as it is said) for the Kingdom of Heaven's Sake, having made such a construction upon Mat. xix.12. He is now under Dr. Johnson's Hands, and in a fair way of doing well.[9]

These stories make us spectators at bedlam: the ridiculous believers in dancing sheep, in talking and psalm-singing hogs, and in trials by scales and water; the deranged man who makes a sacrifice to God of his wife's roasted tongue; the crackpot who makes a sacrifice of his dead wife's good china; the lunatic interpreter of the Scriptures who cuts off his own testicles to gain access to the kingdom of heaven. We cannot but laugh at the benighted irrationality on display, and our delight outweighs any guilt we might feel from laughing at the small cruelties involved. But these stories are, I think, much funnier to those inclined toward unbelief than to believers, or at least enthusiastic believers, since all, in one way or another, ridicule faith and inspiration.

When we are told, for instance, that the lumps of mortality were too heavy for Moses and all the prophets and apostles, we are surely invited to think, or to be confirmed in our opinion, that the miracles and events recounted in the Bible—monstrous plagues, parting waters, rocks that when struck spurt water, burning bushes, piles of foreskins, strolls across water, loaves and fishes, resurrections from the dead, and so forth—are no less incredible than the dancing sheep and talking hogs or trials by scales and water. It was Jesus who said, according to Matthew 19:12, that there are men who have made themselves eunuchs for the sake of the kingdom of heaven. Was he not perhaps just as deranged as the tongue-roasting husband or the self-made pious castrato?

These comic pieces tell against Franklin's claim in the *Autobiography* about his tolerance. There, Franklin claims that, on discovering that the principles of his religion were to be found in "all the religions we had in our country," he respected them all, "though with different degrees of respect as I found them more or less mixed with other articles which without any tendency to inspire, promote or confirm morality, served principally to divide us and make us unfriendly to one another." Despite this varying respect, he says, he was even so induced to "avoid all discourse that might tend to lessen the good opinion another might have of his own religion."[10] It is hard to believe that the comic pieces about religion were not intended precisely to make others have a lesser opinion of their own religions.

Moreover, the stories have an effect—ridiculing religion—that Franklin warned against on more than one occasion: in *Poor Richard* in 1751, in a famous letter to an anonymous friend (thought to be Tom Paine) in 1757, and in the *Gazette* itself in 1730, at the very time he started publishing the believe-it-or-not stories and hoaxes.[11] The upshot of the warning is that to ridicule religion is to risk unchaining a tiger: men freed from religion and its salutary moral restraints. As Franklin puts it in *Poor Richard*, "talking against religion is unchaining a tiger; the beast let loose may worry his deliverer."

One way of explaining this apparent contradiction between Franklin's blasphemous humor and his warning about the tiger seems obvious and well evidenced by what Franklin says, for instance, in the course of his public defense of the Reverend Hemphill in *Defense of Observations* in 1735. Franklin was, it would be said, a Deist who denied miracles, doubted the divinity of Jesus, and denied original sin, which he denounced as a bugbear invented by priests to scare people out of their wits.[12] And so although in general he encouraged the organized faiths, he went on with his humorous attacks in order to dampen dangerous religious enthusiasm and belief in miracles. Hence the stories, with their ridicule and doubts cast upon miracles old and new. But this attack was above all well-intentioned. As a Deist, Franklin understood Christianity to contain a rational moral doctrine, stressing especially charity and good works, and he honestly professed belief in the religion of reason and nature, in the general and particular providence of God, and in toleration for all religions that were themselves tolerant.[13]

On this account, Franklin's blasphemies served his deistic faith, and so they were in full accord with the *Autobiography*'s moral and religious saga morally and piously understood. There is another fly in the ointment, however, and it's stuck in the original 1730 warning, in the *Gazette*, about talking against religion.

Perhaps They Are Not So Crazy After All

The 1730 warning was part of the "response" by one Philoclerus to a previously published spoof entitled "Letter of the Drum." The "Letter" is an anonymous and hilarious account of a man's conversion from unbelief to belief in spirits, and his subsequent experience of a "staggering" (wavering) of that conversion.[14] "I know well," the staggering man begins, "that the age in which we live, abounds in *Spinosists, Hobbists,* and *most impious free-thinkers,* who despise *revelation,* and treat the *most sacred truths* with ridicule and contempt." These scoffers deny the existence of the Devil and of spirits in general, and even go so far as to say the story of Saul and the witch of Endor is a fake and that "no credit is to be given to the so well-attested one of the *Drummer* of *Tedsworth.*" The correspondent was convinced by "some of these unbelieving gentlemen" and was not afraid of demons and hobgoblins. But then something happens that makes him so fearful of them that he pins his curtains shut every night and sleeps with his bedclothes over his head.

The occasion for this newfound fear was not some event he experienced but a story told to him by a "Reverend Gentleman, of a certain house's being haunted with the D—l of a drummer, not a whit less obstreperous than the *Tedsworthian* Tympanist." It seems the Reverend Gentleman was meeting with colleagues to discuss measures for preventing the spread of atheism, and when they went to bed that night (in two groups of two sharing separate rooms), the Reverend and his bedmate were terrified by the beating of a drum that disturbed no one else in the house. The undisturbed others were at first skeptical of the Reverend's story, but they came to believe him when the story was confirmed by the Reverend's bedmate. The next night, the same Reverend's bedmate was seized violently by the big toe and was released only at the renewed banging of the drum. The toe-seizer turned out to be a skeptical colleague who was playing a trick but who was then so terrified by the drum that he refused to go back to his room and insisted on sharing the bed, where all lay sweating and almost dead with fear.

The honest Reverend's relation of this story convinced the former Spinosist-Hobbist that the Devil had indeed been at work. He knows that many will doubt and raise objections to the story, as did one person who said that, according to all the German divines, the Devil plays his tricks after midnight and not in the earlier hours in which the drum was beaten. The new believer "almost staggered" when that same man related a story about a drunken preacher who was called from a tavern for a funeral. When in the course of the service he recited the words "I heard a voice from heaven," he was interrupted by his drinking companion, who said: "By G——that's a d——'d lie, for I have been drinking with you all day at Mother——'s, and if you had heard the voice, I should have heard it too, for my ears are as good as yours." In the light of all this skeptical evidence, asks our staggering new believer of the *Gazette*, should he still believe the Reverend?

Just four days after this spoof appeared, Franklin wrote the "reply" from Philoclerus.[15] Until now, Philoclerus has seen nothing in the *Gazette* to give offense to church or state. But the "odd Letter of the drum," says Philoclerus, is another story. Whoever the writer is and despite his "seeming reflection on *Spinosists, Hobbists, and most impious freethinkers*, his design is apparent, to bring the dispensers of religion among us into contempt, and to weaken our belief of the divine writings." Such a design is unworthy of an honest man and good subject "even though he was of no religion at all." Philoclerus will not try to persuade the obviously nonreligious satirist by any appeal to "the truth of our religion" and requests him simply to consider that it has always been taught by the wise that religion is necessary for the well-ordering and well-being of society. Thus, even if there were no truth at all in religion, "yet, in consideration of the inestimable service done to mankind by the clergy, as they are the teachers and supporters of virtue and morality, without which no society could long subsist, prudent men should be very cautious how they say or write anything that might bring them [the clergy] into contempt, and thereby weaken their hands and render their labours in-effectual." If the writer of the parody has any sense, he will not write such a thing again.

At this point, Franklin has Philoclerus make an unexpected argumenta-tive move: He returns to the issue of the anonymous writer's sincerity, as if more proof were needed that he is in fact an unbelieving wag. If the writer really believed the Reverend's story, then Philoclerus cannot see why the story of the drunken preacher should have shaken his faith. "For though one man's ears may be as good as another's when both are awake and in com-pany, it does not thence follow that one man may not sleep sounder than another when in bed." This is, of course, a completely reasonable argument that a genuine believer could make in defense of the banging drum's reality.

But why does Franklin have Philoclerus return to the matter, as if anyone reading the obviously satirical "Letter" could possibly not know it was a joke? Any believer would see the joke immediately (and not like it), and any nonbeliever thinking it sincere would have to be a hopeless blockhead. As Philoclerus had said, the author's antireligious "design is apparent." The an-swer is that Franklin here shows not that the wag is a wag—which anybody with eyes can see—but that he is a wag because he refuses to believe the miracle from the outset, apart from any reasonable evidence that might es-tablish that the honest Reverend is really honest and not just a liar or a drunkard or otherwise deranged.

This subtle demonstration sets the stage for the next surprising move: Philoclerus, adopting a tone of cool rationality, makes the following and also perfectly lucid argument:

> Besides, as far as we know, *there is nothing impossible in the thing it self:* We cannot be certain there are no spirits existing; it is rather highly proba-ble that there are: But we are sure that if spirits do exist, we are very ig-norant of their natures, and know neither their motives nor methods of acting, nor can we tell by what means they may render themselves per-ceptible to our senses.

Why does Philoclerus say it is probable that spirits exist? Because even those who study animals conclude that mind and will affect the body. Indeed, the anatomists and philosophers report that the brain and the body are con-nected and that the brain forms sounds and images based on the striking of air and light on the sensory organs. A blow upon the eye creates the sense of light when no light is in fact present, and no one but the person whose eye is struck can see that light. Given these facts, says Philoclerus, how can we be so sure that a spirit could not likewise affect a man's eyes and cause him to have a vision that others cannot see? And, says Philoclerus, might not the same principle apply to "the auditory nerves," so that one person might hear a drum beating even though no one else heard it?

These are not the arguments of a raving lunatic, and, as Philoclerus says, there are reasonable men who are convinced that spirits exist and are able sometimes to communicate with us. Philoclerus closes with a knock to the wag's dogmatic solar plexus. Indeed, he says, the writer should cease to be staggered and should continue to believe the story of the drum, and for three reasons: because it is not absolutely impossible that spirits exist; because the Reverends were sober, learned, and possessed of good sense; and because both attested to the drum and would not have told a falsehood such as this "since they could expect nothing but to be ridiculed for their pains, both by him [the waggish writer] *and every other unthinking skeptic in the country*" (my emphasis).

Franklin's comic moves in these pieces are wonderfully deft. We are charmed by the satirical and debunking account of the Reverend Gentleman's divine experience, only to have a powerful case made that the wag relating the tale, not the Reverend Gentleman, is the unthinking one. The wag is exposed as a dogmatic skeptic no less in the grip of his own mere faith than those he smugly ridicules. We wonder if what applies to the writer might not also apply to the Spinosists, Hobbists, and impious freethinkers who despise and ridicule the most sacred truths. In fact, it certainly does apply to Hobbes. Franklin does not mention Hobbes very often. But it is clear from Philoclerus's argument that Franklin knew Hobbes's work extremely well. Philoclerus's defense of the Reverend Gentleman's experience of the miracle of the drum is clearly directed at the nub of Hobbes's argument against spirits or "powers invisible" in chapter 12 ("Of Religion") of the *Leviathan*.

According to Hobbes, belief in spirits springs from men's fear of unknown causes, especially the unknown causes of their good and bad fortune, about which they live in perpetual anxiety. Since this fear must have an object, and since the object cannot be seen, "there is nothing to accuse, either of their good, or evil fortune, but some *Power*, or *Agent* invisible." And as to the ontological character of these invisible agents,

they could not by natural cognition, fall upon any other conceit, but that it was the same as the soul of man; and that the soul of man, was of the same substance, with that which appeareth in a dream, to one that sleepeth; or in a looking-glass, to one that is awake; which, men not knowing that such apparitions are nothing else but the creatures of the fancy, think to be real, and external substances, and therefore call them ghosts . . . and thought them spirits.[16]

Franklin's Philoclerus responds precisely to this Hobbesian argument. Here's the response, again, verbatim:

Those who have contemplated the nature of animals seem to be convinced that spirit can act upon matter, for they ascribe the motion of the body to the will and power of the mind. Anatomists also tell us, that there are nerves of communication from all parts of the body to the brain: And philosophers assure us, that the vibrations of the air striking on the auditory nerves, give to the brain the sensation of what we call sound; and that the rays of light striking on the optic nerves, communicate a motion to the brain which forms there the image of that thing from which those rays were reflected.

We find, says Philoclerus, that a blow on the eye creates a sense of light, which no one else can see, where there is none (what Hobbes calls an apparition). And then he concludes:

Now, how can we be assured that it is not in the power of a spirit *without* the body to operate in a like manner on the nerves of sight, and give them the same vibrations as when a certain object appears before the eye (though no such object is really present) and accordingly make a particular man see the apparition of any person or thing at pleasure, when no one else in company can see it?

Thus could a person hear a spirit or the voice of God, and thus could a person become inspired.

Philoclerus with a stroke shows that Hobbes's argument cuts no ice at all. Hobbes does not prove the impossibility of spirits; rather, he shows that if one begins with materialistic presuppositions (that spirit and mind do not exist), one ends up with a materialistic conclusion: that there are no spirits. Hobbes says that the notion of an "incorporeal spirit" is but unintelligible speech. At the very least, it seems, Philoclerus can respond that the interactions of the mind, spirit, and matter, which we do indeed experience, are beyond our powers fully to comprehend. And so too, and as comes as no surprise, would be God and his revelation and the Devil and his drum. Philoclerus could respond intelligibly that perhaps God is some kind of body that is akin to mind, but that that kind of body and the kinship are beyond our merely human comprehension. Hobbes's dogmatic materialism in no way demonstrably refutes the evidence as presented in the miracle of the drum—especially the experience as reported by an honest and learned man (not some obvious lunatic, drunk, or fraud) who would not lie since he knew that he would be ridiculed by "every other unthinking skeptic in the country."

Hobbes, we know, says that making up tales about miracles can increase the power of the liar over believers, and we know that the Reverend Gentleman was meeting with his colleagues to discuss measures for preventing the spread of atheism.[17] So the Reverend could have had reason to make up the story if his aim had been to shore up the believers against the skeptics. But if the Reverend did not make it up, because to do so would bring ridicule at his lying from the skeptics, does not ridicule also follow from the unthinking skeptics even if he is telling the truth? And if his aim was to lie in order to shore up the believers, why then worry about the ridicule from the skeptics?

Here we see Franklin's final comic twist. The Reverend's refusal to lie, out of fear of the skeptics' ridicule, can only make sense if his thinking were as follows: The skeptics' ridicule at his telling a lie would be worse than their ridicule at his telling the truth *only* if the lie were exposed to the believers. But at least in this case, so long as all the witnesses stuck to the story, there is no way to expose for sure that the story is a lie. There is no statement or implication that a lie was in fact exposed. Thus, in this case, the Reverend suffered no more ridicule than he might have expected from telling a lie; and he managed, at least until the staggering, to convert an unbelieving skeptic. And at the least, the staggering believer was set up for the argument of Philoclerus.

The Reverend wins. He shores up the believers and converts a skeptic. And even if the story were a lie and were to be exposed, that fact would not entirely free the skeptics (including ourselves, if we incline in that direction) from the charge of being unthinking. Philoclerus makes a strong case for the following: If the story were in this case exposed as a lie, we cannot prove that it still could not possibly have been true. Were the lie to be found out, the very most we could be sure of is that the Reverend is a liar, not that the lie could not have been true.

With the "Letter of the Drum," Franklin's comedy unfolds so as to show that acceptance of miracles is not wholly outside the bounds of sanity: Reasonable people believe in them, and it is possible to clear away, by reason, objections brought by reason against a specific case. In this light, even the hilarious story of the witch trial displays a certain ambiguity. Is it not reasonable to have two trials rather than one, so that if one does not reveal the truth another does? The accused male floater, at first convinced of his innocence, came to have second thoughts about the matter. And if witches are possible, is it not possible for there to be one that does not know it of himself? Again, if there really are witches, is it not possible for such a one to bewitch the female accuser who floated? The "more rational" spectators did not know, but merely opined, that all human beings but the skinny would float. Now, perhaps this opinion was a quite reasonable inference from their own experiences in the water. But it is possible that the women floaters—both accused and accuser—floated because of their shifts and garters. The perfectly reasonable way to find out would be to perform the trial again, with the women stark naked.

And then finally, just how do people float if the rational spectators are correct in their opinion? If all but the skinny float, how do people drown? The rational know how: They swim until their breath is gone and their lungs fill with water, and only then do they sink. Could not, then, the following test have been devised: Let the accused and the accusers swim until exhausted and until they sink, and then see if they float. To be sure of the results, it would be necessary that nobody be plucked out of the water at the last second, and so it would be necessary to let both the accusers and the accused drown. This would be a misfortune for the accusers and the accused, although all would die and go to God as nonwitches, and the accusers would face God as martyrs to the test, since they knew they weren't witches and thus wouldn't float and yet got in the water anyway. On the criterion that witches will float, this trial would have established that the accused were not, in fact, witches. Even the insane behavior of those who believe in talking and psalm-singing pigs and dancing sheep has at least a comic patina of experimental reasonableness.

So how is the "Letter of the Drum" a fly in the ointment of the conventional understanding of the religious and moral saga? Because it tells powerfully against the argument that Franklin's ridicule of religion was a well-meant service to a mature and morally responsible Deism. The "Letter" leaves little doubt, I think, that at the very least, Franklin thought it is not so easy to disprove the existence of spirits and the reality of miracles, and that among the forms of human credulity is the rationalistic conviction—the mere belief—that spirits and miracles are impossible. The rationalist and materialist Hobbes is as much a believer as is the Reverend Gentlemen. If Franklin had been any kind of Deist, it is hard to see how he could have written so forcefully in favor of the one thing that Deists of every stripe could not abide: miraculous interference by God (or the Devil) in the regular courses of nature. If his Deism had been grounded in "the Shaftesburian supposition of moral integrity pervading the universe," rather than on metaphysics or natural science to prove the existence and nature of God, it would still no less have been able to tolerate, as Deism, miraculous interventions by God in the physical order of that universe.[18]

It is true that Franklin says on more than one occasion, and in accord with Deism, that beholding the rational order of the world is enough to cause belief in a creator God who leaves the creation alone. But Franklin's humor leads us to consider that if a God is powerful enough to create the world so as to leave it alone, he is certainly powerful enough to make a pig talk or sing psalms, to make a sheep dance, or to talk to us with his voice from heaven, even if it is for an end known more to him than to us.[19]

We can thus hazard the following suggestions: Franklin did indeed ridicule religion. But it is not so easy to explain this ridicule away as service to his Deism and its practical morality. Moreover, his ridicule was accompanied by the knowledge that the "*most impious free-thinkers, who despise revelation, and treat the most sacred truths with ridicule and contempt*," can themselves be described as dogmatic believers. We are forced to wonder, therefore, about the ground of Franklin's ridicule. If it was not Deism, and not Spinosist-Hobbist freethinking, what might it have been?

Credulity and Doubt

Franklin's humorous spoofs of religion show that, as regards credulity, there is no easy dichotomy between the absurd and the rational. Indeed, for Franklin it is only the reasonable creature—man—who can be so deluded and believe in such fantastic things and events, as we know from his comment in the *Autobiography* about his abandonment of vegetarianism: "So convenient a thing it is to be a *reasonable creature*, since it enables one to find or make a reason for every thing one has a mind to do."[20]

Even the world of science, Franklin knew, can be moved to delusions by hope and reason gone awry, as in the case of Franz Mesmer's so-called animal magnetism (a natural cosmic fluid that could be transferred from doctor to patients deficient in it). In a letter to the physician La Sabliere de la Condamine, Franklin ascribed the delusion and the quackery based on it to "there being so many disorders which cure themselves and such a disposition in mankind to deceive themselves and one another on these occasions." Which is not to say that delusions cannot be used fruitfully. There are, says Franklin, in every rich city a lot of hypochondriacs. If they could be convinced to give up gulping medicines for the sake of being cured by the doctor's finger or an iron rod, "they may possibly find good effects though they mistake the cause."[21]

Franklin's humor discloses a complex interaction between reason and belief—even between reason and fantastic credulity. Faith and credulity can grow from reason, reason can support faith and credulity, and rationalistic skepticism can itself be a form of dogmatic belief. The interaction can cut both ways: Just as skeptics can be dogged by their own faith, as is revealed by the wag's story of the miraculous drum, so too believers are dogged by doubts.

One powerful example of the latter occurred in the report, published in 1729–1730, of "The Trial and Reprieve of Prouse and Mitchel."[22] Escaped convicts James Prouse and James Mitchel were arrested for burglary. Prouse was guilty and Mitchel was not, but both were condemned to hang. Mitchel, having declared his innocence throughout, was directed to apply to the governor for mercy. At the time of the executions

> a numerous crowd of people was gathered near the prison, to see these unhappy young men brought forth to suffer. While their irons were taken off, and their arms were binding [sic], *Prouse* cried immoderately; but *Mitchel* (who had himself all along behaved with unusual fortitude) endeavored in a friendly tender manner to comfort him: Do not cry, Jemmy; (says he) in an hour or two it will be over with us, and we shall both be easy.

As the two were then driven to the "fatal tree"—along with a coffin for each—Prouse was extremely dejected whereas "*Mitchel* seemed to support himself with a becoming manly constancy."

Upon their arrival at the bough of doom, both were asked to speak. Prouse—prevailed upon to speak with difficulty—merely said that he had written his confession and had acknowledged the burglary, but that the man who testified against him was the one who put him up to the theft, and that he, Prouse, had harmed no man before. Mitchel "being desired to speak, replied with a sober composed countenance, *What would you have me to say? I am innocent of the fact*." When told that he had been found guilty by twelve honest men, Mitchel "only answered, *I am innocent; and it will appear so before God*; and sat down." And then comes the punch line, so to speak, of the story:

> Then they were both bid to stand up, and the ropes were ordered to be thrown over the beam; when the sheriff took a paper out of his pocket and began to read. The poor wretches, whose souls were at that time filled with the immediate terrors of approaching death, having nothing else before their eyes, and being without the least apprehension or hope of a reprieve, took but little notice of what was read; or it seems imagined it to be some previous matter of form, as a warrant for their execution or the like, 'till they heard the words PITY and MERCY [*And Whereas the said* James Prouse *and* James Mitchel *have been recommended to me as*

proper objects of pity and mercy.] Immediately *Mitchel* fell into the most violent agony; and having only said, God bless the Governor, he swooned away in the cart. Suitable means were used to recover him; and when he came a little to himself, he added: *I have been a great sinner; I have been guilty of almost every crime; Sabbath-breaking in particular, which led me into ill company; but theft I was never guilty of.* God bless the Governor; and God Almighty's name be praised; and then swooned again. *Prouse* likewise seemed to be overwhelmed with joy, but did not swoon. All the way back to the prison, *Mitchel* leaned on his coffin, being unable to support himself, and shed tears in abundance. He who went out to die with a large share of resolution and fortitude, returned in the most dispirited manner imaginable; being utterly over-powered by the force of that sudden turn of excessive joy, for which he had been in no way prepared. The concern that appeared in every face while these criminals were leading to execution, and the joy that diffused it self through the whole multitude, so visible in their countenances upon the mention of a reprieve, seems to be a pleasing instance, and no small argument of the general laudable humanity even of our common people, who were unanimous in their loud acclamations of God bless the Governor for his Mercy.

This story is comic because it has a happy ending and is based on a trick, however cruel, of the near execution and because it depicts such a curious and bizarre example of human behavior: the strange reversal from stout courage in the face of death to utter dispiritedness in the face of reprieve.

But as Franklin presents the story, it is, I think, possible to make further sense of it. More than just a curious picture of an inexplicable twist of human character, the story turns out to have a teaching about religious faith and doubt. Along with the account of the story, Franklin printed, "with little or no alteration from their own words," the "declarations" of Prouse and Mitchel given the night before the "execution." "Little or no alteration" means that, whatever the characters actually said or wrote, what we read is exactly what *Franklin* wants us to read. In his written account, Prouse admits candidly to having fallen under the influence of evil men rather than following the dictates of his master and, "having not the fear of God before my eyes," to having been "deservedly brought to this wretched and shameful end." He deserves death, says Prouse, but only because he was seduced to this one crime, but no other, by one John Greyer. Regarding Mitchel, says Prouse, "as I hope to receive mercy at the great Tribunal, he the said *James Mitchel* is entirely innocent, and knew nothing of the fact until apprehended and taken."

Mitchel, on the other hand, says nothing in his statement about the fear of God or divine mercy or justice; he only recounts how he became involved in the affair by accident and says he had the stolen money on his person only because Prouse asked him to change a fifteen-shilling note—the loot, as it turned out, but unbeknownst to Mitchel. Both men are believers, at least to the extent that they are willing to declare that they will die as Protestants. But in their respective statements, the guilty Prouse speaks much more fully of his fear of God and his failure to keep it before his eyes, of evil and his sin, and of his hopes for mercy from the great tribunal in the sky. Mitchel, on the other hand, knowing himself to be innocent, says nothing about God and sin and mercy, commenting only and perfunctorily that he will "die a Protestant." This near silence is perhaps because he knows himself to be innocent. But it is very surprising that, contrary to what one might well expect, Mitchel does not even swear by God—that is, by divine wrath—in his assertion of his innocence. After all, an oath is, for believers, the most powerful evidence one can bring to bear on one's own behalf, and even tepid believers or even nonbelievers would be likely to swear by God.

Now, as regards references to divine judgment, sin, punishment, and mercy, the two statements are almost the mirror opposites of the events recounted in the story of the faked executions. According to the story of the "execution," Prouse cried immoderately but when finally cajoled to speak made no mention of God and referred only to his statement of the night before. Mitchel, on the other hand, displayed uncommon composure, tried to comfort Prouse, and in his oral statement pronounced his innocence and declared that "it will appear so before God." After the last-minute reprieve, Prouse was overwhelmed with joy but did not swoon and said nothing, whereas the supercomposed Mitchel "fell into the most violent agony," said, "God bless the Governor," and then was transported to a hysterical swoon; upon awakening, he admitted to being a sinner, criminal, Sabbath-breaker, and keeper of bad company but not a thief and said, "God bless the Governor; and God Almighty's name be praised" before swooning yet again.

There is, I think, a plausible construction of the written "statements" and the contrasting story of the "execution" that makes sense of the strange twists and turns and contradictory events. Prouse, the stronger and hopeful and loquacious believer in his statement of the night before the execution, blubbers the next day when faced by the noose and fails then to mention or call upon God, and then is overwhelmed (but not to the point of swooning) with speechless joy. Mitchel, the weaker and laconic believer of the night before the execution, shows remarkable courage on execution day and finally mentions God, not to swear by him but simply to say that God will see his innocence, and then, on hearing of the pardon, falls into paroxysmal swoons and ranting about his manifold sins.

We can make sense of all this if we follow Franklin's subtle clues and connect the dots he presents. Prouse, as Franklin has him explain in his statement, was guilty and hoped for divine mercy. But he *was* guilty, after all, and knew it, and so he could not be assured of deserving or receiving that mercy: Hope for something does not involve certain conviction that it will transpire.[23] We can guess, however, that although he said he merely hoped for divine mercy, as a staunch believer he really trusted in his heart that that mercy would come. Having had the night to ponder that divine punishment may, in fact, ensue, his hope and trust could well have wavered, and so we cannot be surprised at his immoderate tears in the face of death and his overwhelming (though not paroxysmal) joy at being granted a reprieve, which he had not even requested, from the governor. He had good reason to be terrified, since divine punishment might well have been very much worse than the mere rope on this earth. And he had good reason to be overwhelmed with joy—so much so as to become speechless—since he had just discovered that he had indeed received the divine mercy he first hoped for and trusted in, then doubted, and then got and had also recovered more time to atone on his own for his sins. Thus Prouse was a guilty believer in divine judgment, punishment, and reward and had doubts about as well as hope and trust in divine mercy, and his behavior is consistent with this frame of mind.

Mitchel, on the other hand, was innocent and knew it, and at the time of writing the statement, he was just enough of a believer to say that he would die a Protestant. He was so convinced of his innocence that he was, it seems, sure of divine salvation after death and saw no reason to swear by God to persuade those who had already found him guilty. He had no need to hope for divine mercy, knowing that he deserved divine reward. Even after a night to reflect on his impending doom, he again fails to swear by God and merely states that God will see his innocence. He does not count on divine intervention in this life and seems convinced of God's justice in the afterlife soon to come: hence his steely, courageous resolve, his silence about evil, sin, and redemption, his "do not cry, Jemmy; . . . we shall both be easy," and the cool and certain "I am innocent; and it will appear so before God." So what can explain the cool man's hysteria at being saved at the very last minute?

The following would seem to make the most sense: Prouse was a convinced believer and thus, knowing he was guilty, was torn between hope in and doubts about God's mercy. Mitchel's belief was, however, more forced than utterly secure, more a willful attempt to believe than an internal certainty of

God's existence and love. He knows that he is a Protestant, but he does not know much about God. Mitchel's doubt concerned the existence of God himself. Thus, his faith, such as it was, was at first supported by his impressive courage, and his unconquered doubt was broken only by the reprieve: There *really is* a God who has saved him from undeserved death and to whose arms he will fly when he finally does meet death. Only then his swoons, his hysteria, his ranting about his own sin and guilt and innocence, and then his praise to Almighty God.

The violence of his response matched the power of this discovery. Prouse was a staunch believer from the outset and was moved by real fear of divine justice. He learned that he had received the mercy for which he had hoped and trusted but which he also doubted would be forthcoming. With Mitchel, on the other hand, we witness a transition from forced belief, belief still shadowed by real doubt, to a shocking and real event that leads to a full conversion. He learned that there *is* a God and discovered in his heart that God was caring for *him*. His hysteria is the moment of true conversion, the moving of the spirit within him. Thus, his reaction was more violent than that of Prouse, even though Prouse had more to fear. And so Mitchel's opinion about divine care differs considerably from the opinion of the common people who witnessed the whole affair.

As Franklin reports the matter, Mitchel between swoons cried, "God bless the Governor" (twice) and "God Almighty's name be praised," while the common people cried, "God bless the Governor for his Mercy." The common people saw the governor as the cause of the mercy and asked God to bless him for it. For Mitchel, God should be praised because he is the ultimate and immediate cause of his salvation, which required no mercy from God, who knew of his innocence. The governor should be blessed, but only because the governor, who granted *his* own "mercy," was but God's tool. And to judge from his behavior, Mitchel now knows this with all his heart and all his soul.

As touching as is the story of the two saved convicts, we have enough information from Franklin to detach ourselves from its pathos and see the two poor wretches almost as laboratory mice. The story then looks like an experiment: Take two normal human beings and the normal combinations and degrees of faith and doubt (as regards God, what we do and do not deserve, and, obviously, what happens to us when we die), apply the nasty fake execution, and behold the results. Though both results make perfect sense, the case of Mitchel is certainly the most interesting and in tune with Franklin's other comic pieces in the *Gazette*.

As in those other pieces, Mitchel's reaction is extreme—almost as if he had been zapped by electricity (as Franklin did to many an experimental turkey and, by accident, once to himself). One can well imagine that

Mitchel might have subsequently (had he been let out of jail) become a crusader against the vanity of tea drinking or a smasher of fine china or an accuser of witches or a tongue- or testicle-sacrificer. And we can distill a hypothesis from the experiment: that the most bizarre forms of human enthusiasm, almost always associated with religion, emerge not simply from dogmatic belief but, rather, from the tension between belief and doubt when that tension is stretched to the limit—as was surely the case with Prouse and even more with Mitchel as he found himself suddenly snatched away from the maw of death. It certainly appears that, according to Franklin, faith, hope, reason, and doubt are forever at work in the human mind and that's why we can be so crazy.

Is Justice Just a Joke?

Except for the wife of the deranged tongue-roaster, Franklin's comic stories have no serious casualties (and even she did not lose her entire tongue). Anger, such as it is, is displayed in ridiculous or self-directed forms. Even so, however, Franklin, as well as any of his well-informed readers, knew that witches had indeed been burned as well as doused. And the case of Prouse provides an important indication that serious anger and indignation are not far removed from the bizarre behavior described in Franklin's comic vignettes. The Prouse story is especially illuminating in this regard precisely because the anger and indignation involved are divine, not human: Prouse was genuinely concerned, indeed very frightened, about his own guilt as he stood, hoping for divine mercy, in the face of divine justice—that is, in the face of divine wrath and punishment. In the whole of the comic context, Franklin reminds us that the bizarre behavior depicted in fact takes one of two forms: either the paroxysms that accompany sudden conversion to belief (and even the experience of the spirit of God moving within) or the sometimes ridiculous but often quite dangerous madness of those who believe they know and are called by God to administer divine justice and wrath on this earth.

In 1747, about seventeen years after the publication of the witch hoax and "The Trial and Reprieve of Prouse and Mitchel," Franklin again considered the theme of divine anger and earthly justice in another comic piece, the famous "Speech of Miss Polly Baker."[24] This hilarious canard was taken seriously in Europe—both as describing a real event and as sincere and heartfelt—until Franklin admitted to the Abbé Guillaume-Thomas-François de Raynal around 1778 that it was his hoax. John Adams was not fooled and described the piece "as one of Franklin's many 'Outrages to Morality and Decorum.'"[25] Nor was the sourpuss Adams wrong on this

count, for as funny as it is, the speech really does pack a radical and outrageous punch. The canard begins with a description of the piece to follow as
the speech of a Miss Polly Baker, obviously a whore, delivered at her fifth
prosecution in Connecticut for having given birth to a bastard child. The effect of the speech is then said to have been so powerful as to have "influenced the court to dispense with her punishment, and induced one of her
judges to marry her the next day."

In her speech, Polly asks that her fine be remitted because she is poor and
because this is the fifth time she has been dragged before the court for having been mother to bastards. Twice before she paid heavy fines, and twice
before she was "brought to public punishment" because she could not pay
the fine. But in addition to the plea for simple mercy, Polly goes on to argue
that the law is "unreasonable in itself, and particularly severe with regard to
me, who have always lived an inoffensive life in the neighborhood where I
was born, and defy my enemies (if I have any) to say I ever wronged man,
woman, or child." She has brought five fine children into the world and has
raised them well, at no one else's expense, has committed no adultery, "nor
enticed any innocent youth."

No one has any cause for complaint about her conduct, says Polly, except
perhaps the minister of justice, who has had to forego a wedding fee. But she
is not to blame even for that small offense. After all, she is not against marriage and would have to have been stupid to prefer her condition to the
"honourable state of wedlock." No one can say that she ever refused an offer
of marriage. In fact, the only one she ever got, and to which she "readily
consented," was when she was still a virgin. It came from a man, now a mag-
istrate of the county, who got her pregnant and then forsook her, so that "I
unhappily lost my own honour, by trusting to his." Polly says she had hoped
that the man—known by all present—would have appeared on her behalf. If
so, she would not have mentioned his perfidy. But since he did not show, she
complains that it is "unjust and unequal" that he, the scoundrel, should
have risen to honor and power in the same government that punishes her
misfortunes with "stripes and infamy." Polly then goes on to say:

> I shall be told, 'tis like, that were there no Act of Assembly in the case,
> the precepts of religion are violated by my transgressions. If mine, then,
> is a religious offense, leave it, gentlemen, to religious punishments. You
> have already excluded me from all the comforts of your church com-
> munion: is not that sufficient? You believe I have offended heaven, and
> must suffer eternal fire: Will not that be sufficient? What need is there,
> then, of your additional fines and whippings? I own, I do not think as
> you do; for, if I thought, what you call a sin, was really such, I would not

presumptuously commit it. But how can it be believed, that heaven is angry at my having children, when, to the little done by me towards it, God has been pleased to add his divine skill and admirable workmanship in the formation of their bodies, and crowned it by furnishing them with rational and immortal souls? Forgive me gentlemen, if I talk a little extravagantly on these matters; I am no Divine.

Polly closes by asking her judges to reflect on the terrible consequences of the law, which produces abortion and infanticide by women terrified of punishment and public shame. The gentlemen should repeal the law against illegitimacy, she says, and they should also think of all the cheapskate men who, for fear of the cost, avoid marriage and thus leave so many children unborn, which is "little better than murder." They should each year have to pay a fine double the one for fornication. After all, what are women to do? They are by custom not allowed to solicit men or force themselves on husbands, and the law does nothing to help them but, rather, punishes them when they do their duty. Yes, says Polly, it is a duty—"the first and great command of nature, and nature's God, *Increase and multiply*." This duty she has steadily performed, at the cost of lost public esteem and public disgrace and punishment. Instead of a whipping, closes Polly, she ought "to have a statue erected to my memory."

Now, there is no doubt that this canard has a serious edge. It really does move its reader to consider the hard plight of women, for whom both custom and law often made life difficult. But in the typical Franklin manner, its comic touches really seem to prevail. The whole piece, as serious as one might take it to be, is framed by two very funny twists: the improbable marriage that followed the very next day and the image of a statue of the county's best fornicator. The first thing that comes to mind at the end is just how Polly's statue would look: Polly with her flock of bastards? Or, better still, Polly with her flock and swelled with another soon to arrive? And what would be the inscription? "Polly Baker: Our Own Most Extraordinary Whore and Servant of God"? To use Adams's terms, the piece is an outrage to morality in justifying and then ennobling fornication as service to divine law, and it is an outrage to decorum in being funny about such a matter at the same time. But then, again in Franklin's way, the piece turns out to be far more subversive of morality and decorum than first meets the eye. Had Adams read more carefully, he would have been even angrier with Franklin than he was.

When Polly turns extravagant theologian, her argument rests on the distinction between religious and civil offences. Her position is this: If fornication is a sin, an angry God will punish me, and there is no need for you to add your punishments to God's eternal fire. No need to pile it on. But in fact, to my mind, it is not a sin. God tells us to be fruitful and multiply, and no one has been harmed by my having bred five illegitimate children. If I thought fornication was a sin, I certainly would not have done it. If you think, on the contrary, that fornication is a sin, we will find out who is right in the world beyond, and no one will be the worse for waiting to see.

Now, Polly could have said in her defense only that fornication is in fact innocent and harms no one and that if she had thought it was a sin she would never have done it. In rhetoric, however, two arguments are better than one—and hence the added argument about piling on punishment. Now these two arguments are different, and, considered carefully, they provoke two sets of different thoughts and questions.

Let's first think about the difference between punishments determined by acts of assembly and those determined by precepts of religion—the issue of piling on. Even if fornication was a sin (which it is not, she says) or if she had committed adultery (which is a sin, she says), why add human punishments to the divine fire? Is not the divine fire quite sufficient? This makes us wonder if those who propose acts of assembly have some doubt about whether God or the divine fire exist or about whether, if they do exist, somehow God cannot be trusted to use the fire correctly.

What if there is no divine fire waiting for Polly? Then, we could ask, is not virtue at its best its *own* reward, and even besmirched if one behaves virtuously for some other end? Surely Polly's self-righteous judges would smugly grant this high moral principle. But if so, then why is Polly's vice not its own punishment? Simple logic would require this conclusion. When Polly fornicates, she might not know it, but she is just besmirching her own soul and laying waste her own true happiness. And if it is true that Polly's vice is its own punishment, then regardless of divine matters, why pile more punishments on the one she has inflicted on herself? Is not the self-punishment enough for the harm Polly might have done to someone else? So again, why the piling on in this world? Do the outraged virtuous folks perhaps think, deep down in some murky part of their souls, that adultery and fornication are good things that Polly gets but they do not, and they are angry because they miss out?

Now let's think about the other argument: that were fornication in fact a sin, Polly "would not presumptuously commit it." Polly's simple point here is really very powerful. It is something like this: "Do you really think that I would commit fornication if I knew that it is a sin deserving of and sure to be punished by the *eternal fire*? What kind of fool do you think I am?" Committing fornication even knowing that it is a sin is what the believer thinks makes the sinner deserving of punishment. But Polly is a believer also, so let's look at her point of view.

If she knew fornication was a sin and did it anyway, then she would deserve punishment, according to believers' common sense. But this common sense does not make much sense when we think of the eternal fire. It's simply true, as Polly implies, that no one in her right mind would commit adultery or fornication while knowing that eternal fire will certainly follow. But if she was not in her right mind, then she certainly would not be a sinner, even if her acts were sins—she would be crazy and the proper object of our pity but not our blame. Or perhaps, as at Mount Holly, she is a witch and doesn't know it. This must mean that she is in the grip of the Devil, and again, the Devil is to blame for that, not Polly.

But Polly's point makes further sense even when we don't think about sure knowledge of the divine fire, if only because, as with Prouse, people sometimes weaken and have "not the fear of God before [their] eyes." However, does one *willingly* forget about the divine fire? This is really no more plausible than that Polly would lift her skirts knowing about that fire. It is the same as to say: "He knew the bridge over the volcano was out, but he forgot this time and fell into the molten lava." The forgetting could be traced to poor memory, or strong natural passions, or even to the Devil, but again, we have to pity and not blame in these instances.

But let's forget about the eternal fire. In everyday life and moral experience, it is taken as common knowledge that we do things we know we should not, and afterward we regret them and reproach ourselves both for the consequences we and others suffer and for the weakness or stupidity that led us to do what we "should have known better" than to do (including not resisting the Devil).

But that we reproach ourselves for our "weakness" or "stupidity" would seem to suggest that at the time we did the bad thing we were weak or stupid—somehow not in possession of what we knew. But do people will themselves to be weak or stupid, knowing what it will mean? This simply does not make any sense, at least on the morally high-minded assumption that virtue and vice *are* rewards and punishments in themselves and not just means to other ends. Suppose Polly commits adultery because she desires the husband of a friend. In this case, she harms her friend, not for the sake of harming the friend but because she puts her own interest ahead of her friend's, regardless of the cost. Now, if she simply thinks that such selfishness is really good and is unaware of the fact that it is in fact morally bad and harmful to others and herself, then, again, she is simply ignorant, and we should pity her but cast no blame, on the same argument we saw above. And if she knows the selfishness is morally bad for others and for herself and still acts selfishly, then we are back to the issues of stupidity, forgetfulness, weakness, or strong natural passions. Can she be blamed for these?

But what if a righteous judge were to say: "Stop with these sophisms. You knew that fornication is a sin and thought you could get away with God not seeing you, or you thought that you could atone for it and earn God's forgiveness, and so you did it, and for this you deserve the fire." Even here, however, we might better describe this response as depicting Polly as being torn between different opinions: that fornication is a sin, but not one so serious that God pays much attention to it; or that it is a sin, but not so big a one that she cannot atone for it. Again, Polly might be wrong in these opinions, but it is very hard to think that she wanted to be wrong or to be torn between them as she is. So again, do we blame her, or do we pity her?

So let's go back to her first point. What if she were to say: "I know that fornication is a sin, I know that God will find me out, and I know *as I do it* that I will for sure be condemned to eternal anguish in the eternal fire, and still I do it. And I'm in complete possession of all my marbles." We really face only two alternatives here. We could say that lunatics always think they are sane and all others are mad, or we could say, perhaps with a shrug, that such is the nature of evil.

But it's not clear that we're really making any sense when we say "Polly is evil." Let's come down to earth and forget about the eternal fire. Suppose that Polly debauches another woman's husband and simply thinks it is good for her, and suppose also that she refers to the piling on to show her judges that they think the same thing but do not admit it. That is, Polly thinks something like: "I like to debauch other women's husbands and my only regret is that I got caught—I'll do much better next time." Well, we would say, that's proof that Polly is evil. But how did she get that way? We do think that, if she is morally evil, she freely chose the path of evil. Otherwise, it is hard to see how she is evil and not just a danger to married women in the same way that a poisonous snake is a danger to barefooted hikers. The snake, we would say, is a danger, and we might well also say (against good ecological sense) that we should kill these snakes whenever we find them. But we don't morally blame the snake for being a snake.

So let's think about how Polly became evil by freely choosing the path of evil. Perhaps she chose the path of evil because she honestly thought, mistakenly, that it was good, not evil. That doesn't do the trick, as we saw above. She had to have chosen the evil knowing it to be good for her and knowing it to be evil. But then, why did she choose the evil? What kind of person chooses to become evil? To become evil, to *choose to become* evil, Polly had to have been before the choice—evil! But then that rather makes her, like a snake, not "evil" as we think of it in our common sense. It looks as if our common sense does not really make any sense.

The example of Polly as like a snake raises another consideration. In raising the issue of piling human punishments onto those of God, Franklin actually forces us to think not just about the human punishments but about
the divine ones as well. By comparison to the eternal fire, surely the human
punishments are nothing. But then, assuming that fornication is a sin and
that Polly committed no adultery, what are we to make of God's dishing out
eternal fire for this? Would eternal fire be a reasonable punishment for Polly
even if she had also committed adultery? It really does seem a bit much. In
fact, eternal fire, one might argue, is too much for any sin one can imagine
and clearly not in tune with the principle of an eye for an eye, the basic
(biblical) principle of justice that the punishment should fit the crime.[26] Is
it not indeed shocking to think that God would do such a thing? And is it
not even more shocking to think God would do this if, in fact, it turned out
that Polly was just out of her mind? Or even just mistaken? Or torn between
contradicting opinions? It is shocking, in all these instances.[27] It could make
sense, however, if Polly was just like a snake but the example of her turning
on the eternal spit was intended to deter other snake-like women (on the assumption that snakes, like dogs and people, can be trained by force not to
bite) from debauching other women's husbands.

As regards an eye for an eye, Polly does not see what thin ice she is on.
Let's grant that Polly is simply ignorant, mad, stupid, weak, or in the grip of
strong natural passions, and we'll forget about evil. Or let's say that she is
just bad. Let's then say that God condemns her to eternal fire because he
does not like fornication and adultery and wants to deter people from committing them and the only thing that really will deter them is the threat and
punishment of the divine fire; that is, we will just forget about the principle
of an eye for an eye. By the logic of Polly's argument, punishments should
deter: "Do you think I would do this at the cost of the fire?" But if so, then
what is necessary for deterrence will determine what the punishment should
be, not justice more traditionally understood.

If so, however, then just as God might use eternal fire, far beyond the dictates of justice, to deter adultery or fornication, so too might the community
on this earth use whatever will be effective to deter behavior that is deemed
harmful to the public good. The cold logic of Polly's argument actually puts
her at considerable risk: If her fornication is harmful to society, then society
can and should use whatever means necessary to keep her from raising her
skirts, regardless of whether she is insane, ignorant, weak, in the grip of natural passions, or just a snake. It is really a good thing for Polly that she was
such a charming, humorous, and persuasive speaker. These cold, utilitarian
implications would not have sat well with John Adams. And he surely

would have been suspicious of the disturbing light shone by the entire piece on morality and on human and divine justice. As Franklin puts the simple words in Polly's simple mouth, he also puts all these complex and disturbing thoughts into our minds.[28]

Franklin makes a related argument in another comic piece, published pseudonymously in 1758, "A Letter from Father Abraham, to His Beloved Son."[29] Despite the topic—the attainment and character of genuine virtue—and the sanctimonious tone, the piece is another of Franklin's spoofs because of what is planted in its conclusion. In summing up the need for moral virtue and the ways and means of acquiring it, Franklin as Father Abraham warns his son Isaac against letting small acts of dishonesty open the way for greater ones and the eventual habit of knavery. When this happens, "farewell all peace of mind, and inward satisfaction; all esteem, confidence, and reputation among mankind. And indeed if *outward* reputation could be preserved, what pleasure can it afford to a man that must *inwardly* despise himself, whose own baseness will, in spite of his endeavors to forget it, be ever presenting itself to his view."

And then comes the whopper: "If you have a *Sir-Reverence* [a turd] in your breeches, what signifies it if you *appear* to others neat and clean and genteel, when you *know* and *feel* yourself to be b——t [beshat]." Father Abraham makes no apology for the coarseness of the comparison, for "none can be too much so for a defiled and foul conscience." And one should not expect to be able to keep this conscience concealed, for not everyone can be fooled: "Some body or other will *smell* you out" (my emphasis, but Franklin's joke here is clear enough).[30] We are reminded here of the saying in *Poor Richard's Almanack* of 1751: "He that is conscious of a stink in his breeches, is jealous of every wrinkle in another's nose."[31] The issue in the scatological example is, on a moment's reflection, not how one might appear neat and clean and genteel despite packing a load in one's pants but how one must inevitably smell to oneself and, especially, to others.

Now, what on earth could be Franklin's intention in this funny but (one has to admit) disgusting joke? The first and most obvious effect is to puncture the seriousness of the previous account of virtue and how to attain it. No matter how little Father Abraham may feel the need for an apology, the example surely takes virtue down a peg or two in presenting it as the opposite of the ridiculous figure of an otherwise neat, clean, and genteel man with a stinking bulge in his pants. After all, if vice—rascality and really meant having a turd in one's pants, it would be more than just impossible to hide behind apparent virtue, as Father Abraham argues. Vice would be utterly repulsive to anyone in his senses (pun intended), that is, to anyone in his right mind.

This example is more direct than the example of Polly, because here vice is clearly depicted as having, literally, a terrible natural consequence—it is its own punishment—in addition to its being a kind of harm to others (who must suffer the offensive stink). As Father Abraham presents his case, the vicious do not just suddenly defecate in their pants. Rather, the load is the result of smaller "acts of dishonesty" or, to follow the trope, perhaps small passings of gas that eventually become habitual and greater and then, before the knave knows what has happened, result in the disgusting package. The wicked are presented here as foolish, since they do not see the self-destructive consequences of their acts.

Franklin, in the voice of Father Abraham, starts his letter by saying that men do not generally err in their conduct through ignorance; rather, they err through "inattention to their own faults" or because of strong passions and bad habits. Until that inattention is cured and the passions reduced, advice about conduct is received as a reproach rather than as something to be accepted gratefully. Suppose, continues Franklin, that the son has had, from parents and others, an education sufficient to have provided a good conscience. Franklin then suggests that in order for the lad to have a *"clear* sight and *constant* sense" of his errors, he should set aside a portion of each day as a time for self-reflection and the measurement of his actions by the "rule of rectitude implanted by God in your breast." If the lad by this measure acknowledges his faults to God and begs for pardon and for the strength to guard against them in the future, he will find his faults continually diminishing and his stock of virtue and consequently of favor with God and man continuously increasing. Franklin then repeats the point that self-examination is the key to steady virtue and quotes *"Pythagoras"* from "his truly *Golden Verses"* (no such text exists) to illustrate his point.[32] And so that no means toward the lad's virtue should be kept secret and so that the lad does not have to depend on self-examination alone, old Father Abraham adds "a *golden extract* from a *favorite* OLD BOOK." This extract has never been identified, and it is clearly written by Franklin himself.[33]

The extract consists of advice to the young lad on how to choose a disinterested friend to remind him of "such misconduct as must necessarily escape your severest inquiry." Since enemies abound for everyone in every walk of life, he should be careful not to offend, hate, or envy other men, so as not to increase the enemies life provides "by the common course of human nature" and so as to procure as many friends as necessary. We also have enemies within ourselves, since our natural characters are subject to being altered by "many external objects and accidents." It is vain, says Franklin, "for a passionate man to say, *I am pardonable* because *it is natural to me,* when we can perhaps point out to him an example in his next neighbor, who was *once* affected in the very same manner" but who has changed for the better. Nothing is ever well said or well done in a passion, but our passions can be conquered or improved, unless they are allowed to persist into old age.

But since our strongest natural passions "are seldom perceived by us," it is necessary that the lad have a monitor. We need such a monitor because we are poor judges of ourselves, because many vices and follies resemble their opposites and thus require great prudence to discern. It is therefore necessary for anyone who wishes to be wise to *"take particular notice"* of his own actions and thoughts and intentions with "great care and circumspection." But "lest all this diligence should be insufficient, as partiality to himself will certainly render it," it is "very requisite" to choose a friend or monitor to whom should be given the greatest freedom to point out failings and suggest reme- dies. The monitor must himself be discreet and virtuous and not one to "play the spaniel." One must find such a person and attain his confidence. Most men see things in others that they cannot see in themselves, and the happi- est person is one who "can attain to a reasonable freedom from sin and folly, even by the help of *old age,* that great mortifier and extinguisher of our lusts and passions." Then follows the disgusting reference to the Sir-Reverence as proof that one cannot merely wish to appear virtuous, since a vicious reality will always be smelled out.

Now, the ostensible lesson of the essay is that we are not slaves of our pas- sions and can thus be held responsible and blameworthy for our vices. One cannot claim that the devil of one's nature made one do some vicious deed, because there is the evidence of a person with that same devil who has over- come its sway. This is, of course, a common and conventional argument that is absolutely essential to our common intuitions about morality. But every- thing in the essay in fact adds up to just the opposite. Two things are *neces- sary:* that we have a monitor, because we seldom see our own natures; and that anyone who wishes to be morally wise engage in very careful self-exam- ination. One thing is *certain:* that partiality to oneself will make that self-ex- amination insufficient. The avoidance of that certainty depends, then, on finding an honest monitor from among the vast number of enemies who naturally surround us in every walk of life. Father Abraham argues that men err more through inattention to their own faults than through ignorance of their duty.[34]

But as the "extract" that Father Abraham "quotes" makes clear, such inat- tention is itself a form of ignorance:

The strongest of our natural passions are seldom perceived by us; a chol- eric man does not always discover when he is angry, nor an envious man when he is invidious; at most they think they commit no great faults.

Therefore it is necessary that you should have a MONITOR. Most men are very indifferent judges of themselves, and often think they do well when they sin; and imagine they commit only small errors, when they are guilty of crimes. It is in human life as in the arts and sciences; their plainest doctrines are easily comprehended, but the finest points cannot be discovered without the closest attention; of these parts only the wise and skillful in the art or science, can be deemed competent judges. Many vices and follies resemble their opposite virtues and prudence; they border upon, and seem to mix with each other; and therefore the exact line of division betwixt them is hard to ascertain.[35]

The conclusion we have to draw could not be clearer: Vice is ignorance. And virtue is not just knowledge of general precepts (which is important enough); it is also the subtlest art and science of fine points that are confusing and hard to see. But if vice is ignorance and moral knowledge requires such a difficult art and science, then for that reason alone there is no moral free will, because knowing what is right will be beyond most people's capacities, and those who do have the capacity will have it out of pure luck.

But even for those lucky enough to have the intellectual capacity, our natural preference for ourselves makes us *necessarily* and *certainly* dependent on finding a good monitor from among the good and the prudent, and the good and prudent themselves have to be "jealous and fearful" of themselves, lest they "run away too hastily with a likelihood instead of truth; and abound too much" in their own understandings.[36] It is, in short, sheer luck that we know our duties, sheer luck that we know ourselves, and sheer luck that we overcome our passions, since doing so depends on knowing ourselves—both what our passions are and what our vices and virtues are—and on the remote possibility of finding a good monitor from among the vast sea of enemies that surrounds us. Still, could we not say, with moral common sense, that those lucky few who do know what is right nevertheless sometimes do the wrong thing out of wickedness? But as we saw with Polly, Franklin indicates that if we think through the logic of our own opinions, "wickedness" is disclosed as a condition, like being a snake or a rat, and not a choice. Thus, in "A Letter from Father Abraham," the reasons for moral error are inattention, which is really ignorance, or "strong passions" or "bad habits." The ignorance is not chosen. And the passions are conditions: We cannot choose our passions.

What then, about the bad habits, which would seem to be freely acquired? Father Abraham says in his closing that the knave who remains undiscovered by mere men may "even . . . approve his own actions" that are "discovered and detested" by God. Now, this clearly suggests that at the time of the small acts of vice, the lad might well have thought the acts were good, or at least not sinful. Here we are back to the issues raised by Polly. The lad could simply have been mistaken and not thought of the deeds as sinful, or he might have thought them sinful in general but not in his particular case, or he might have thought that they were sinful but necessary and that God would understand and forgive. In each case, the lad would have been acting according to what he thought to be good at the time and so, as Franklin says, worthy of the lad's own approval (as little boys often think of their farts). The poor lad would come to smell like shit by repeated small acts of doing what he thought at the time to be good and worthy of approval. His bad habit of farting would be an acquired one, but acquired only by his trying to do his best. Now that is surely a stroke of bad luck.

Franklin's comedy here forces us to consider the virtue praised prior to the scatological shock. That virtue is the source of "peace of mind, and inner satisfaction; all esteem, confidence, and reputation among mankind." On the one hand, the inner satisfaction and external esteem could be understood to derive from the nobility of virtue—virtue's goodness in itself apart from any gains and rewards, and perhaps even consisting in the sacrifice of one's own good to that of someone else or for some higher end. But on the other hand, the example of the turd shows vividly that vice is its own punishment—a loss that consists in one's becoming repulsive to oneself and others. From this point of view, then, virtue as the opposite of vice would be its own reward, so that we could look at the inner satisfaction and external esteem as goods or gains accruing to oneself. From this point of view, it is clearly in one's interest to possess virtue: Who wants to suffer turbulence of mind and inner dissatisfaction, and who despises the esteem, confidence, and reputation of his fellow men?

One could argue that virtue is good in itself *and* its own reward *and* deserving of other rewards. Indeed, this is what most people think. But still, the scatological shock does put the spotlight on consequences and rewards to ourselves and at least suggests the following thoughts: First, if virtue is good in itself despite *any* of its consequences, then, considered strictly, although it would be nice if virtue made one smell like a rose, one's consequent smell should not matter. Or to state the issue more forcefully: If virtue consists most fully in sacrifice to another, then if the virtuous man and another had to divide the two smells, roses for one and shit for the other, then the virtuous man would choose the latter—but doing so with nothing really in his pants. In both cases, the virtuous man smells like shit but is really clean, and no matter how hard he scrubs he still smells bad, even to himself, for all his efforts. (One thinks of Plato's *Republic*, in which the virtuous man, considered apart from any possible gain, is described as having a reputation for vice and as suffering for it.) He is clean and he knows it, but to *have* his inner satisfaction at the nobility of his cleanliness (attained by choosing to stink so his friend can smell like roses), he stinks in everyone else's nose, including his own.

Are we not disturbed by such a thought? And what can Franklin mean by hinting that the noble and clean but stinking man also smells the stink himself? Perhaps something like this: If virtue is fullest in noble sacrifice, and so much so that the virtuous man chooses to stink, has he just preferred the good of inner satisfaction with his nobility to the lesser good of a sweet smell? Or to take one further step and forget about the satisfaction: Has he just preferred the cause of the satisfaction, *his* nobility, to the lesser good of a sweet smell? And is it noble to prefer the greater to the lesser good for oneself? Doesn't this then turn the noble into shit? Franklin's comic scatology, it seems to me, at least suggests that when we admire the sacrificial nobility of our virtue, and when we praise the inner satisfaction and external esteem bestowed upon us for that virtue, we may in fact be so confused as to think roses and shit smell the same.

Father Abraham raises two other smaller but still disturbing issues. First, the scatological joke casts some doubt, it seems to me, on just how vulnerable the vicious really are to discovery. Precisely because the Sir-Reverence is so obvious—so sure to cause wrinkles in people's noses—the example appears, when we stop laughing, well more than over the top. Anyone with the slightest experience of real life thus has to think about how, in fact, just a touch of rascality, used on those rare occasions when it might be deemed necessary (and so not practiced as a habit), can be useful and remain undiscovered. And as anyone familiar with political life has to know, a big dose of rascality can be seen and not only go unpunished but even be admired. Second, there is a problem, it seems to me, with Father Abraham's closing words:

But, again, suppose it possible for a knave to preserve a fair character among men, and even to approve his own actions, what is that to the certainty of his being discovered and detested by the all-seeing eye of *that righteous* BEING, who made and governs the world, whose just hand never fails to do right and to punish iniquity, and whose approbation, favor, and friendship, is worth the universe?[37]

Now this appeal to divine justice clearly regards virtue in terms of gain and reward. Here, however, the stakes are much bigger. On this earth the vicious forego the goods of "all peace of mind, and inward satisfaction; all esteem, confidence, and reputation among mankind." Before God, the vicious forego the very universe itself. And, of course, this is looking on the bright side of things. As Polly points out, the vicious do not just lose the universe; they gain the eternal fire. But why would the all-seeing righteous judge detest and punish such a wretch as the poor smelly boy? Why the piling on? Perhaps because the judge is not just all-seeing but also all-smelling—perhaps for the sole reason that the poor wretch simply stinks to high heaven. According to this line of thinking, however, it is not clear how divine punishment of the young wretch would be different from divine punishment of a skunk for the offense of being a skunk.[38]

THERE IS A CLEAR THEMATIC COURSE discernible in Franklin's humor. We are at first led to join the Spinosist-Hobbist scoffers in guffawing at the lunacy of religious fanaticism—these jackass believers will swallow *anything*. But then the tables are turned on the scoffers and even on the rationalistic and sincere Deists. It's not so easy to disprove the most unbelievable things the believers believe, especially the miracle of divine inspiration. The materialistic scoffers are dogmatists and believers themselves. Then, rather than leaving matters at this standoff, and rather than establishing a position with some metaphysical countertheory, Franklin gets us to think our way into the heads and hearts of the believers and to see the tensions within what they hope for and what they think—especially as regards morality and human and divine justice.

With Polly and Father Abraham's poor smelly boy, we're led into some very surprising territory: It is not at all clear that we know what we are talking about when we praise virtue and blame vice or when we reward virtue and punish vice or when we condemn evil. If indeed we *are* confused about these matters, then it would seem to follow that we do not really know what we are talking about when we praise the Franklin of the moral and perhaps even the religious saga. Franklin's humor, at least so far as we have seen, points in the direction of a skepticism quite different from that of the Spinosists and Hobbists. It does not just mock; rather, it forces us to think comically and critically about assumptions so close to our faces that, for the most part, we barely see them.

The Father Abraham talking to his son is a far cry from the sanctimonious workaholic Father Abraham haranguing the foolish crowd with the sayings of Poor Richard in the final edition of the *Almanack* (in what was later published separately as *The Way to Wealth*). Both were first published in the same year, 1758. In *The Way to Wealth*, Father Abraham fails to mention what Poor Richard said in 1736—that "force shits upon reason's back." And when he quotes Richard, from that same year, to the effect that "*he that lives upon hope will die fasting*," there is a subtle change from the original: "He that lives upon hope, dies farting."[39] There is nothing important to be learned from the haranguing Father Abraham, however rich his words made Benjamin Franklin.

At this point, the primary question remains: Just how deep is Franklin's skeptical humor? If it's correct that Franklin's comedy was aimed at our most fundamental moral intuitions, then we should not be surprised to discover that nothing is too dignified to be beyond his comic barb. It's important to keep in mind that Franklin's comedy spanned, in varying degrees of intensity, the whole of his life. Thus, we cannot attribute it simply to the young, philosophical smart aleck. Rather, the comedy followed the unfolding course of his public service, scientific investigations, and manifold political engagements. Indeed, that comedy was directed at the very objects of his several endeavors.

4 • Shameless Ben

Franklin's humor is always multilayered and subtler than it appears—and always more shocking. It swoops from amusing satire to parody, then to obscenity and scatology, and sometimes to blasphemy. At the same time, however, it makes fun of scoffers and blasphemers, and then, in almost the same breath, it makes us wonder about the nature of divine and worldly justice. In the reply to the "Letter of the Drum," Philoclerus, commenting on the supposed "wit and humor which some persons of reputed taste pretend to discern in it," says that he sees no humor in it at all. To Philoclerus, "true wit and humor cannot be employed in ridiculing things serious and sacred."[1] Satire would presumably be more than acceptable to Philoclerus, since it consists in exposing the vain pretensions of men and revealing the folly of their vices.

But to a man like Philoclerus, there are some things so serious as to be simply beyond ridicule. Franklin has his character make this point because in fact most human beings are, to one degree or another, very much like Philoclerus. Most comedy, in fact, is motivated and thus restrained by some moral concern or indignation. To my knowledge, for instance, the comedian Lenny Bruce, who never shrank from obscenity, never ridiculed freedom of expression, which he revered as much as Philoclerus reveres God and religion. For most humor, especially satire, shamelessness is limited by shame. With Philoclerus's remark, Franklin indicates to us what we surely by now suspect: For all of his grace and charm and wit, and for all of his seriousness and the moral bite of his satire, Franklin is shameless.

There is nothing he was unwilling to mock at least to some degree: He mocked not just human justice but also divine; not just religious cranks and nuts but ordinary individuals torn between faith and doubt; not just those who believe in miracles but also the Spinosists, Hobbists, and the most impious freethinkers. And Franklin's humor was not just confined to abstract themes, such as religion, virtue, and justice. He also made fun of very concrete matters that were, to one degree or another, close to his own heart. Was anything beyond his comic wit?

Not the Family and His Poor Wife Deborah

Perhaps the most notorious of Franklin's comic spoofs is the *Old Mistress Apologue*. Even though Franklin was careful to preserve this piece and left three versions, one in his own hand, to his grandson, the now-famous essay, written in 1745, did not see the full light of day until the twentieth century, appearing before then only in obscure or aborted or private printings because it was considered so risqué. Smyth knew of it but, out of shame and indignation, did not print it. The essay was first widely printed in its entirety in Phillips Russel's 1926 biography of Franklin; fifteen years later, it appeared as part of a volume delivered to the 250,000 members of the Book-of-the-Month Club (a club, by the way, that one can well imagine Franklin founding). It is not altogether clear whether this fast rise to respectability was due to rapidly changing values or to a sudden failure to see what the essay was really about.[2]

The *Apologue* was written in the form of a brief letter to an anonymous friend in need of advice about managing his sexual desire.[3] Franklin starts out by saying, "I know of no medicine fit to diminish the violent natural inclinations you mention; and if I did, I think I should not communicate it to you." Marriage, continues Franklin, is "the proper remedy" and the most natural condition for a man in general and the one that will afford his correspondent "solid happiness."

The friend should not postpone marriage, because the advantages of doing so are slight and uncertain in comparison with the advantages of married life:

It is the man and woman united that make the complete human being. Separate, she wants his force of body and strength of reason; he, her softness, sensibility and acute discernment. Together they are more likely to succeed in the world. A single man has not nearly the value he would have in that state of union. He is an incomplete animal. He resembles the odd half of a pair of scissors. If you get a prudent healthy wife, your industry in your profession, with her good economy, will be a fortune sufficient.

However, should the friend not be persuaded to marry and yet continue to be moved by sexual desire, Franklin, referring to what must be a prior communication, repeats his advice that the friend should prefer old to young women.

To explain this surprising advice, Franklin provides eight reasons:

1. Being more experienced, old women make better conversation than do the young.
2. As women cease to be handsome, they "study to be good. To maintain their influence over men, they supply the diminution of beauty by an augmentation of utility. They learn to do a 1000 services small and great, and are the most tender and useful of all friends when you are sick. Thus they continue amiable. And hence there is hardly such a thing to be found as an old woman who is not a good woman."
3. There is no danger of children, "which irregularly [illegitimately] produced may be attended with much inconvenience."
4. Old women are more discreet in conducting an intrigue and are therefore safer for one's reputation. And, as regards the woman's reputation if the affair is revealed, people will be more inclined to excuse an old woman who kindly takes care of a younger man, forms his manners with good counsel, and "prevent[s] his ruining his health and fortune among mercenary Prostitutes."
5. In all upright animals flaccidity proceeds from top to bottom—face first, then neck, then breast and arms—"the lower parts continuing to the last as plump as ever: so that covering all above with a basket, and regarding only what is below the Girdle, it is impossible of two women to know an old from a young one. And as in the dark all cats are gray, the pleasure of corporal enjoyment with an old woman is at least equal, and frequently superior, every knack being by practice capable of improvement."
6. It is less sinful, unlike the debauching of a virgin.
7. The "compunction is less"; making a young girl miserable would fill a man with regret, which cannot happen with making an old woman happy.
8. Old women are "*so grateful.*"

Now, the last reason is the one most remembered by posterity. Ask any ten people likely to know of the *Apologue* and, if indeed they do know, most will say: "Oh yes, the one where old ladies are said to be so grateful." I have actually performed this questioning experiment (in the locker room of my athletic club). It's no wonder it remains the most familiar line: It is funny and charming in its appeal to common decency—gratitude, after all, is a virtue associated with love and beneficence and akin to justice but without the compulsion or harshness of justice. The line is tender and it picks up the other sweet things said about old women earlier on. When, for a further experiment, I asked a professional woman in her early sixties to read the *Apologue* and then report her first impression, she said it was racy, to be sure, but really very sweet and kindhearted.[4]

These experiments suggest the rhetorical effectiveness of the *Apologue*. To be sure, it is a recommendation of what Smyth would call fornication. But it begins with a praise of married life and then proceeds to discuss the moral and intellectual superiority of old women when compared to the young. It bows to the concept of legitimacy, praises old women's discretion, and warns of the dangers of prostitution. Then follows the most risqué argument—that old women are just as good if not better than young women at sex—and then a quick ending with the three morally uplifting reasons: less sin and unhappiness, less consequent compunction, and, of course, gratitude for a gift bestowed. Franklin's irony is subtle: He makes a racy case for fornication, moralizes it, and in the process softens and naturalizes that morality and exposes conventional hypocrisy.

But a second, more careful look helps explain why Smyth got so hot under the collar. This very brief piece (it's just a few paragraphs long) is, just beneath the surface, brimming with unexpected implications and interesting lines of thought. First, there is not a single mention of love in the piece, whether in the discussion of marriage or in the discussion of affairs with old ladies. The term "affection" is used once, but only in Franklin's closing salutation to the young correspondent ("your affectionate Friend"). Marriage is praised for its solid happiness, to be sure, but that happiness is described solely in terms of economic success in the world. Even the "amours" with old ladies are praised in terms of utility: The old ladies provide a thousand services and are tender and useful friends when their young lovers are sick.

Second, the depiction of sex itself is enough to make Mercutio (that ugly, obscene, cynical foil to Romeo) nod in agreement.[5] As regards sex, women are all alike with bags over their heads, and in this regard they are likened to animals, cats, that are all gray in the dark. We cannot miss the obvious corollary that what goes for the difference between young and old women, who have suffered a "diminution of beauty," surely goes for the difference between beautiful and ugly young women. With remarks like these, Franklin describes sexual desire completely apart from the longing of romance and the hopes that accompany our attraction to the beautiful. Marriage is for commerce; amours are for a thousand services; sex is for physical pleasure ("corporal enjoyment"). And sex, on the woman's part, is a knack performed best by old ladies, who are experienced even if ugly. At best one might say that Franklin here gives solace to the legions of men stuck with ugly young women: Good looks are more trouble than they're worth. It seems to me better to conclude that this picture, at least for the romantic, is not a pretty sight.

But we've not yet seen the whole picture. Recall that at the outset of the piece, Franklin says he knows of "no medicine fit to diminish the violent natural inclinations" the friend had mentioned and that if he did know of such a fit medicine he thinks he "should not communicate it to you." The remark at first seems clear enough: Franklin seems to mean that if he knew of some method simply to suppress or expunge the urge for sex—say, castration or some drug like saltpeter—he would not tell his friend about it because it is unnatural and bad to suppress or expunge the urge for sex. This understanding of Franklin's remark is plausible.

But second thought reveals some ambiguity. Why does Franklin refer to the unknown substance (or operation) and marriage with synonymous terms: the former he calls a "medicine" and the latter he calls a "remedy"? Franklin clearly implies that expunging the urge for sex would be like the amputation of one's hand to get rid of a strong itch that can with pleasure be scratched. Would we call the amputation of one's hand to get rid of such an itch a "medicine"? The "proper" ("fit") "remedy" ("medicine"), Franklin says, is marriage, or if not marriage, then amours with old ladies. But as proper remedies for the violent natural inclinations, do not marriage and amours with old ladies *diminish*, in the sense of relieving and taming, but not eliminate, those inclinations?

This meaning of the remedy seems in fact what Franklin has in mind. In detailing the specific advantages of marriage, he does not even mention sex (although from the context sex is clearly involved); and in detailing the advantages of old ladies, the superior "corporal enjoyment" is but one of eight advantages. He thus makes an obvious point: One who goes without regular sex is the one most racked by the "violent natural inclinations" and the one most likely to do stupid things to satisfy it, such as consorting with possibly diseased whores or taking risks with pretty young girls.

According to this more plausible reading, the "medicine fit to diminish the violent natural inclinations" could be an *equivalent alternative* to marriage and sex with old ladies—an alternative that like marriage and sex with old ladies diminishes, manages, and tames the inclination but does not eliminate it. Why, then, does Franklin say that he "should not communicate it"? But this question provokes another: How can Franklin know that he "should not communicate it" unless he in fact knows what it is? So why *not* recommend it? On this reading, the reason for Franklin's reluctance to recommend the fit medicine cannot be that it has unacceptable side effects. Why, then, call it "fit"? The only reason that comes to mind is that the method is too shocking or vulgar to recommend out loud. What might it be?

A medicine that preserves and yet diminishes the inclinations, that has no poisonous side effects, results in no illegitimate children, involves no debauching of others, and makes no others miserable: masturbation. In other words, if one is not concerned to have an unpaid partner in commerce (a wife or old mistress), or a tender nurse when sick, then one's hand is almost and perhaps as good as a hooded woman's private parts.

There is yet another and surprising step to the joke. At the same time that Franklin seems to divorce beauty from sexual desire and pleasure, with a sleight of hand he pulls that debunking rug out from under us. Were the young friend to take up masturbation as his medicine, it is doubtful that his head would at the time be filled with images of ugly or old women. That is why Franklin qualifies his recommendation of sex with old ladies: It's easy to forget that one premise of his reasoning is that old ladies are like cats, which are *in the dark* all gray. So old ladies win out over masturbation after all: The trick is for the couple to do it in the dark, during which time the man's pleasure of corporal enjoyment is not spoiled by what he sees and can be enhanced by what he might imagine. In this case, masturbation and dalliance with old ladies are equal, as regards imagined beauty; but the old ladies provide the added benefits of different friction and a practiced knack.

Franklin's humorous account of sex begins with charming and moralizing naughtiness, then moves to cold and calculating indifference to beauty, from thence to an indirect and subtle recommendation of masturbation as mechanical relief, and then back to beauty, but only as imagined, not real. Franklin does not assert that beauty does not exist; beauty is, of course, what young men want and old ladies lose. It would be better, indeed, if one could have all the benefits of old women and still have them be beautiful, or have beautiful young girls without the attending troubles (illegitimate children, youthful indiscretion on the woman's part, the ruination by debauchery of the young woman, and the feeling of compunction for making the young woman miserable). So although Franklin hints in a reductionist direction, it would be wrong to conclude that he is telling us that sex is but mechanical relief and that we humans are no different than the shameless monkeys in the zoo.

But Franklin does suggest that given the limitations of real life, *imagined* beauty is what a prudent man must settle for, as if something about the tie between real beauty and sex were itself imaginary. Somehow, he seems to suggest, we expect more from that tie than circumstances can allow, as if the beauty of our lover will by itself make us happy and thus protect us from the inevitable troubles that can be avoided only by turning to old ladies.

The beauty is real. The erotic drive is real. The happiness they jointly promise is not.

It is hard not to recognize the ironic self-reference of the Apologue and hard not to think that Franklin had the Apologue in mind when, in the Autobiography, he describes his marriage to the plodding but useful Deborah Read as a stroke of good luck that saved him from the "hard-to-be-governed passion of youth," which had "hurried me frequently into intrigues with low women that fell in my way, which were attended with some expense and great inconvenience, besides a continual risk to my health by a distemper which of all things I dreaded." Deborah proved, says Franklin "a good and faithful helpmate" who assisted him much by attending the shop, and together they thrived and "mutually endeavored to make each other happy."[6] Franklin says they "endeavored" to make each other happy, not that they actually were.

He went into the marriage with Deborah with no romantic excitement but, rather, with a sigh of relief at his good luck in having avoided the clap (or worse) and with the secure knowledge that he would avoid it in the future. But Franklin was not indifferent to beauty or to the link between beauty and sexual desire. That we know from too many facts, including his admitted recourse to young whores, his obvious attractions to smart and beautiful young girls, and his later desire for the beautiful Madame Helvétius. It does seem reasonable to suggest that for Franklin, beauty, as we experience it in erotic life, always promises more in the way of happiness than it can ever deliver. And as a consequence, we would expect him to pursue his amours with a philosophical reserve.[7]

This same theme appears again in Franklin's 1767 letter to Margaret Stevenson, with whom he lived in London and in whose house Deborah, it should be noted, never set foot, since she never visited London. (Franklin had a lifelong intellectual and flirtatious relationship with Margaret's young daughter, Polly.) In the letter, Franklin requests that Mrs. Stevenson—away on a visit—return sooner and by herself, rather than later and fetched by Franklin. This should not lead Mrs. Stevenson to think Franklin cannot do without her, as regards "good order and comfort." Says Franklin:

> You are really mistaken in your fancy that I should, by your absence, become more sensible of your usefulness to me, and the necessity of having you always near me; for in truth I find such a satisfaction in being a little more my own master, going any where and doing any thing just when and how I please without the advice or control of any body's wisdom but my own small as it is, that I value my own liberty above all the advantage of others services, and begin to think I should be still happier

if Nanny and the cat would follow their mistress, and leave me to the enjoyment of an empty house, in which I should never be disturbed by questions of whether I intend to dine at home, and what I would have for dinner; or by a mewing request to be let in or let out. This happiness however is perhaps too great to be conferred on any but saints and holy hermits. Sinners like me I might have said us, are condemned to live together and tease one another, so concluding you will be sentenced to come home tomorrow, I add no more but that I am as ever your affectionate friend and humble servant.[8]

As we move from *Old Mistress Apologue*, to the remarks about Deborah in the *Autobiography*, and to the letter to Mrs. Stevenson, we witness Franklin's comic reflection on himself as a sexual and romantic being. Indeed, from this point of view, the addressee of *Old Mistress Apologue*, who has never been identified, could very easily have been Franklin himself. But we also see fleeting reflections on sex and beauty as such. We human beings are not simply driven to sex and attracted by beauty. We expect them together to promise happiness. But wisdom discloses, it seems, that this happiness is really just a tease. It would be hard, I suggest, for Franklin, holding such a view, to have been a passionate and romantic lover. Everything we know about him suggests that he was not and that he approached his amours with detachment. But we have at least some reason now to think that perhaps his romantic reserve was more than just temperament and sprang, rather, from his reflections about human nature.

We can, I think, hazard some preliminary conclusions. At least in the case of sex and beauty—and so too for romance and love—Franklin presents a contrast between his wisdom and most people's false expectations. We expect the happiness promised by youthful beauty to last. But it does not. In speaking of affairs with young girls, Franklin assumes that marriage does not ensue and that the affair does not last. He tells his young correspondent how to manage "all [his] amours"—using the plural, not the singular. Expected happiness, promised by youthful beauty, is marred by trouble. The expectant eye thus wanders. But Franklin clearly also implies that affairs with old ladies do not last either. Perhaps that is because old ladies often die soon or get too old "to do a 1000 services small and great" and to be "the most tender and useful [friend] when you are sick," before the young lover has grown older. Or perhaps, being young, the man still has an itch for youthful beauty and must learn the lesson of its dangers and the safety and utility of old ladies more than once.

Even a lucky marriage to a beautiful woman has its problems, however. For beautiful young wives, too, suffer diminution of their beauty. Time alone assures that the difference between young wives and old mistresses disappears. Yet Franklin tells us that young women keep their men by the "influence" of beauty. But even to get to the waning of that influence would require that the marriage to a young and beautiful woman survives the troubles that arise from the clearly inferred deficiencies of the young and beautiful wife: less knowledge of the world, a mind stocked with fewer observations, weaker capacity for improving conversation, less goodness, less utility and fewer services, and a poorer companion when one is sick.

Franklin describes marriage as a "proper remedy." And so despite its provision of a solid happiness that consists primarily of economic success and good fortune, marriage is, at first or at least eventually, but a medicine (like castor oil) for beauty-smitten passion. Wisdom would thus have young men be resigned to family life with an ugly wife or to affairs with old ladies. Both married and unmarried young men must understand that they will wind up with old ladies, so long as they stick with what reason recommends. But then, the joke about the alternative medicine (masturbation) and old ladies in the dark suggests that it is not necessary to give up on beauty altogether. And so the wise solution to the young man's problem—affairs with old ladies—can at least count on imagined as opposed to real beauty. And this applies (if the lights are out) just as easily to sex with an old wife (and also, we should note, to an old wife's sex with her old husband). In these cases, the mutual exchange of good works depends on replacing one delusion (that real happiness can follow from real beauty) with another (that the ugly partner is beautiful).

We are thus left with no assurance from Franklin that good sense can be made to rule in erotic life. If ordinary men can delude themselves into thinking, if even for a brief time, that their ugly partner is beautiful, then it seems equally possible that these same men could still fall prey to the delusion of beauty as such and try, despite the risks, to secure their enduring happiness in a pair of beautiful arms. And this is not to mention another alternative that is clearly compatible with Franklin's advice: to have fun with young girls (although that always entails some risk), then get a useful even if homely wife and with her help become wealthy, then become famous, and then abandon the wife and use the wealth and fame to get access to young and beautiful women. If young men can be convinced to have their affairs with old ladies, is it impossible for young ladies to become convinced to have affairs with old men—especially if the men are rich and famous? Long experience suggests that it certainly is not impossible. It could be argued that such was the course that Franklin chose for himself. His famous reserve suggests, however, that he pursued the young and the beautiful with an old but clear head.

From the comic evidence of the *Apologue*, it is almost impossible to think that Franklin thought the family a sacred institution. But this obvious conclusion is not the most important lesson to be drawn from the bawdy joke, written well after his supposed moral and religious "conversions," fifteen years after he married Deborah, and three years prior to his retirement from business. The more important lesson, I think, is rather that the joke makes it hard to be charmed by the utility described in the good sexual works exchanged between young men and old ladies or between old men and old ladies. The young and old men and the old wives would in truth rather be elsewhere. The final joke is that as described in *Apologue*, the only *real* winners are the old ladies in affairs with young men!

If young and old men and young and old women know clearheadedly what *really* to expect from beauty and have the means to pursue and secure it, there is no good reason, presented in the *Apologue*, why they should not pursue it—and with as many beauties as means and powers can secure. Thus, although bourgeois marriage (and this is what Franklin is talking about in this joke) is certainly useful for most men, it is not easy to see why we should admire it or think it possesses some special dignity, however down-to-earth that dignity might be. The really final joke of the *Apologue* is that in the guise of a naughty defense of bourgeois marriage, Franklin in fact presents an argument in defense of the aristocratic tryst. From this point of view, anyone with money, a clear head, and the power to attract the beautiful will think of bourgeois marriage as a safe haven for losers. Perhaps this reading is wrong on its face. For it is reasonable to wonder if the morally and religiously redeemed Franklin, the defender of humble good works as the only service to his God, could have written such a joke.

In a wonderful and hilarious letter to Madame Helvétius, Franklin, begging for her hand (and more) in marriage, recounts that after being rebuffed by the lady for the sake of her dead husband, he fell asleep and dreamed that he had been transported to the Elysian fields.[9] Asking to be taken to the home of the philosophers, he came into the neighborhood of Socrates and the dead Monsieur Helvétius. Franklin says he met Helvétius and told him of his wife's steadfast fidelity, whereupon Helvétius replied that although he had thought of his former felicity for a while, "it is necessary to forget it in order to be happy here." He has thus remarried, to a woman less beautiful but with as much good sense and spirit and who loves him "infinitely," so much that she has gone to hunt the best nectar and ambrosia in order to regale him that evening. Madame Helvétius is more faithful than is her former husband, says Franklin. And who is the unfaithful Helvétius's new wife? None other than "Madame F——, my old American friend." (Now, *who* could that be?)

When Franklin cried out to her in rebuke, she replied "coldly" that she had been his wife for nearly fifty years and that he should be content with that, and that she had a new connection that would last to eternity. At which point, says Franklin, "offended by this refusal of my Euridice, I suddenly decided to leave these ungrateful spirits, to return to the good earth, to see again the sunshine and you. Here I am! Let us revenge ourselves." Franklin, who had much to be ashamed of in his treatment of Deborah, was not so ashamed as to refrain from making fun of her memory in the pursuit of another woman.[10]

Not the Revolution

According to Smyth, "the moment after [Franklin] had seen the serious side of anything he saw the comic side of it." For that reason, "it is said that Jefferson explained that Franklin was not asked to write the Declaration of Independence because he could not have refrained from putting a joke in it."[11] This remark of Smyth's is supported by Franklin's extraordinary fraud at the expense of those who suffered so terribly during the revolutionary struggle.

While in Passy, Franklin wrote and published in 1782 what he claimed was an article from the *Boston Independent Chronicle*.[12] The article presented an extract from a report by a Captain Samuel Gerrish, of the New England militia, of the capture of a ship carrying a huge cargo of over one thousand scalps taken from American frontier inhabitants by the Seneca Indians and sent by them to the governor of Canada. Rather than simply reporting the fact of the scalps, Franklin presents an "invoice," contained in a letter to the governor of Canada on behalf of the Indians, in which the contents of each of eight large packages are described in grotesque detail. Suffice it to say that the invoice depicts the "scalps, cured, dried, hooped and painted, with all the Indian triumphal marks" that indicate age (by hair color), sex (hoop color), occupation, and manner of death. Of one crate of scalps the invoice says, "most of the farmers appear by the hair to have been young or middle-aged men; there being but 67 very gray heads among them all; which makes the service [the excellent work of the scalping Seneca] more essential."

The invoice is then followed by a letter, purported to be from Chief Conejogatchie to the governor, asking the latter to "send these scalps over the water to the great King, that he may regard them and be refreshed; and that he may see our faithfulness in destroying his enemies, and be convinced that his presents have not been made to ungrateful people." This astounding salutation is then followed by a warning about the increasing power of the "great King's" enemies, who "have driven us out of our country for taking part in your quarrel," a plea to the king to provide them with a new country, and a further plea for cheaper prices for the goods the poor Indians must buy from the king's traders.

The hoax continues with the report that although it had first been proposed that the scalps be buried, it was then suggested by one Lieutenant Fitzgerald, then on his way to Ireland, that he take the scalps to England and on some dark night hang them all on the trees in St. James's Park, so that they could be seen by the king and queen, with the hoped-for result that "Muley Ishmael" should have some "compunction of conscience." This proposed, the scalps "were accordingly delivered to Fitz, and he has brought them safe hither" and will be taken by him to Boston. Then follows another report a few days later from Boston that Fitzgerald had arrived in Boston with the scalps and that "thousands of people are flocking to see them this morning, and all mouths are full of execrations."[13] Then, before adding a "letter" to the English ambassador from John Paul Jones (protesting the ambassador's having called Jones a pirate), the report continues, with cool matter-of-factness, to state that "fixing them to the trees is not approved. It is now proposed to make them up in decent little packets, seal and direct them; one to the King, containing a sample of every sort for his museum; one to the Queen, with some of women and little children: the rest to be distributed among both Houses of Parliament; a double quantity to the Bishops."

Now, even if Franklin believed this hoax to be true in "substance" if not in "form," because the number of Americans scalped during the Revolution actually exceeded what is mentioned in the invoice, as he later remarked to John Adams, the fact remains that the piece is a deliberate hoax.[14] On the one hand, hoaxes can be exposed and are in themselves hard for the incredulous to believe—and this one is surely pretty hard to swallow. Thus, it could have helped the British as much as or even more than the American cause: Behold the preposterous lies these colonials tell!

On the other hand, to the extent that the hoax is believed by overly serious and credulous men, that fact in itself says as much, to the incredulous, about the follies of human credulity as it does about the real horrors of the war. Moreover, the piece has a subtle but quite evident comic edge. The horrific "invoice" sets the stage for the comical image of the king taking his "refreshment" from the sight of the multicolored scalps, as if they were not much different, at least to the king, from a good bottle of Claret. Then follows the image of the American gawkers. And then the absurd project first for hanging them like leaves on the trees in St. James's Park and then sending them as nicely wrapped gifts for the king, the queen, members of Parliament, and—a double dose—the bishops.

And this is not to mention the countervailing pathos of the Indian chief's letter. The butchery has gone both ways: The Indians are poor and getting poorer because of the war and have been expelled from their country by the Americans, who have "also got great and sharp claws." One could read the chief's letter—and even see the scalps—as a mark of the chief's good faith and gratitude to an ally and friend. That the chief sees the scalps—so revolting to us—as a refreshing gift simply springs from his different conceptions of the spoils and trophies or triumphs of war. We know, in fact, that Franklin would have considered this last statement true. As he remarks of the Indians at the opening of "Remarks Concerning the Savages of North-America," written not even a year later, "Savages we call them, because their manners differ from ours, which we think the perfection of civility; they think the same of theirs."[15]

Franklin could and did see even the Revolution and its horrors not in terms of righteous indignation and the justice of his cause but in the light of the credulity and folly of all mankind, each and every tribe of which thinks its ways the perfection of humankind.[16]

Not His Beloved Natural Science

Franklin was a thoroughgoing Baconian and partisan of the technological conquest of nature. I will return to this important matter later, but for now suffice it to say that experimental natural science was, for Franklin, among the activities in life he most enjoyed and the human endeavor that would most change the world for the relief of the human estate—more than politics, more than empire, more than philanthropy, more than anything else. Its material promise was, in his eyes, limitless. Even so, he could and did laugh at the standard of utility at work in Baconian science. Hence the hilarious proposal "To the Royal Academy of *****."[17]

Franklin begins the proposal by commenting that the academy had proposed a mathematical prize question, rather than a physical one, because it could not at the time think of a physical question that promised more utility. Franklin has a suggestion for such a question that might do the trick. To set the stage for the discussion to come, I will relate a brief personal story. I once asked a distinguished friend what it was like to dine at a state dinner. "Wonderful," he replied, "you squeeze your bum together and try hard not to offend your tuxedoed and rhinestone-studded tablemates."

Well, Baconian science to the rescue, in the form of Ben Franklin's proposal. Franklin proceeds as follows: It is well known that digestion produces great quantities of wind in the bowels and that permitting it to escape is usually offensive to company because of its fetid smell. Thus, the well-bred forcibly restrain the efforts of nature to produce this discharge, so as to avoid giving offense, and as a result suffer "great present pain" and "future diseases," such as colics, ruptures, and tympanies, that are often harmful and sometimes fatal. Now, were it not for the "odiously offensive smell," people would not mind discharging their wind in public any more than they mind blowing their noses. So, "his prize question therefore should be, *to discover some drug wholesome and not disagreeable, to be mixed with our common food, or sauces, that shall render the natural discharges of wind from our bodies, not only inoffensive, but agreeable as perfumes.*"

Then follows an even more hilarious account of why such a project is not chimerical and is, on the contrary, based on real experimental evidence. We already know some means for varying the smell. One who eats meat with lots of onions will "afford a stink that no company can tolerate," whereas one who dines only on vegetables "shall have that breath so pure as to be insensible to the most delicate noses; and if he can manage so as to avoid the report, he may any where give vent to his griefs, unnoticed." But since few will be vegetarians, it is worth experimenting to see if something such as powder of lime might transform the air in our bowels, just as quicklime corrects the fetid air of a privy. After all, he notes, a small pill of turpentine changes the disagreeable smell of asparagus-laced urine to the pleasant odor of violets.

The discoverer of the gas pill will receive immortal honor, which is proved by the fact that other philosophers have achieved fame with much less useful discoveries: Are there twenty men in Europe happier because of what they have learned from Aristotle? What are Descartes' vortices compared to the whirlwinds in men's bowels? What is Newton's mutual attraction of matter by comparison to matter's mutual repulsion, with its cruel distensions? Can the pleasure of a few philosophers when they gaze on the seven threads of light separated by the Newtonian prism compare with "the ease and comfort every man living might feel seven times a day, by discharging freely the wind from his bowels? Especially if it be converted into a perfume."

So many thus pleased by the delight of smell! Such benevolence! "The generous soul, who now endeavors to find out whether the friends he entertains like best Claret or Burgundy, Champagne or Madeira, would then enquire also whether they chose musk or lily, rose or bergamot, and provide accordingly." The freedom of "*ex-pressing* one's *scent-iments*" is infinitely more important to human happiness than is the freedom of the press or the freedom of abusing one another, for which the English are so ready to fight and die. Indeed, "this invention, if completed, would be, as *Bacon* expresses it, *bringing philosophy home to mens business and bosoms.*"[18] By comparison to the universal utility of such a project, says Franklin, the science of all the philosophers mentioned and the mathematical question posed by the academy are "all together, scarcely worth a FART-HING."

It would take a pretty stuffy sourpuss not to laugh at this joke. Bringing philosophy home to our business and bosoms? Guess again. Imagine the spectacle of well-dressed, elegant diners (perhaps at a state dinner) eating foie gras, drinking fine wines, and gassing each other, often loudly, with anal perfumes.

But funny as it is, the essay has its serious side. Franklin juxtaposes the two virtues of natural philosophy: discovery and contemplation of the truths of nature, and the experimental conquest of that nature for the relief of man's estate. These two virtues are not necessarily at odds. As Bacon argues, what we can *do* with material nature reveals what that nature really is. Bacon even argues at one point that the discovery of the world as it actually is, and not as we hope it to be, is better than all the uses to which such discovery can be put, even though that utility is, in fact, the most potent form of generosity or benevolence.[19] Even with this argument for the superiority of understanding over use, however, it is still clear that for Bacon there is no understanding of nature without bending the latent courses of nature to useful purposes. For Bacon, utility is the means by which we discover truth.

With this hilarious spoof, Franklin suggests the following corollaries of Baconian natural science: We should have no illusions about the natural phenomena disclosed by Baconian science, nor should we have any about the object of scientific benevolence—about the dignity of the creature to whose interests the courses of nature will be bent. The latent possibilities of fart gas are no less dignified or important than the general laws of motion or the courses of the stars and planets. There is no superior realm of nature. And we, the beneficiaries of natural science, are, among other things, flesh and blood and brains surrounding an alimentary canal, and we are thus as likely to want mellifluous gas as we are to sacrifice for such things as freedom of the press. Indeed, sweet farts could be thought superior to sacrifice for a free press. The ills of this world might be traced to our enthusiasm for such supposedly high principles. The truth about the world may be that the goods of sweet flatus and fine wine are real, whereas our high principles are, in fact, illusions. The principles may be chimerical, the benevolence of transforming our farts may be chimerical, but not so the sweet smell of those farts.

Not Even the Freemasons

To show that not even the Masons were safe from Franklin's wit, I refer not to a piece of comic writing but, rather, to an actual event, one about whose meaning Franklin left some written clues. Franklin was, as is well known, a longtime Mason, having been accepted into membership in 1731. This comes as no surprise given his Baconianism and commitment to general enlightenment and his ideas for a secret society of the friends of virtue and progress. However, in June 1737 Franklin became involved in an affair that caused him considerable public embarrassment and that casts some doubt on the seriousness of his dedication to Masonic principles. In the June 16 edition of the *Pennsylvania Gazette*, Franklin reported that a few days earlier some people pretending to be Freemasons "got together in a cellar with a young man who was desirous of being made one, and in the ceremony, 'tis said, they threw some burning spirits upon him either accidentally or to terrify him." The young man "died this morning. The Coroners inquest are now sitting on the body."[20] Now, in publishing this brief note, Franklin said much less than he actually knew. In February 1738 Franklin was forced to defend his conduct in the affair, and he had to do so again two months later to his own parents.

What had actually happened was that three of Franklin's friends, Evan Jones, John Tackerbury, and John Remington, had played a practical joke on Jones's apparently slow-witted apprentice, Daniel Rees, who wanted to become a Mason.[21] The three pranksters cooked up a phony rite of initiation, which consisted of teaching the boy some ridiculous "signs, words, and ceremonies," having him pledge an oath to the devil, making him drink a "violent purge," and having him kiss Tackerbury's exposed posterior. The joke proved so amusing that the three devised a further spurious rite to raise the lad to another degree of Masonry. At this second farce, another gentleman, Sullivan, dressed up in a cowhide to impersonate the Devil, and Jones lit a bowl of brandy, whose flame was to render the scene frightening. Jones then raised the bowl and approached the hapless lad in order to frighten him still more and, either by accident or on purpose, threw the brandy on the lad, to lethal effect.

At some point between the first and second initiations, Franklin met Jones and Remington, along with John Danby and Harmanus Alrihs, on other business, at which occasion Jones and Remington told Franklin and the two others of their first initiation prank and showed them the oath they had made the boy read, at least at first to Franklin's hearty amusement. Franklin testified for the prosecution in the subsequent trial, in which Jones and Remington were found guilty of manslaughter. But in an article in the *Mercury*, one "C. D.," commenting on the trial, attacked Franklin for having read the blasphemous oath and for being

pleased to express his approbation thereof by a most hearty laughter, and in friendship desired to have the further perusal of it; which in several companies he diverted himself with the reading of, and being informed how D. R. had been initiated in the garden, he candidly saluted him by the name of *Brother*, and to encourage him in it gave him a sign, as they term it, and congratulated him on being admitted to the *Brotherhood*, and desired to have notice to be present at the diversion of snap-dragon [the second, and fatal, initiation].[22]

To this Franklin replied in print that he had indeed laughed heartily when he heard of the "ridiculous signs, words and ceremonies, of which [Rees] was very fond." But, says Franklin, neither he nor Danby nor Alrihs thought the purge, the rump kissing, or the diabolical oath funny. Franklin says that when the boy came in and Jones told him that Franklin was a Mason and that he should make Franklin a sign, he, Franklin, turned his head "to avoid seeing him make his pretended sign, and looked out of the window to the garden." That he wanted to see the snap-dragon was false. Indeed, says Franklin, he tried to follow the boy down the stairs to warn him of what was still to come but lost sight of him and never saw him again. Of the oath, Franklin says

I did desire R——n when he had read it to let me see it; and finding it a piece of a very extraordinary nature, I told him I was desirous to shew it to some of my acquaintance, and so put it in my pocket. I communicated it to one, who mentioned it to others, and so many people flocked to my house for a sight of it, that it grew troublesome, and therefore when the mayor sent for it, I was glad of the opportunity to be discharged from it . . . and I may call every one to whom I read that paper, to witness, that I always accompanied it with expressions of detestation.[23]

To this apology Franklin appended the sworn oaths of Danby and Alrihs that the proceedings related by Jones and Remington "were not countenanced or encouraged by any person present, but the contrary. And that Benjamin Franklin in particular *did speak against it*, and did neither approve of what had been *already* done (as related by the Doctor and R——n) nor desire to be present at what was proposed to be *farther* done with the said Daniel R——s, as is falsely insinuated in Mr. Bradford's last *Mercury*."[24]

Now, Franklin was clearly skating on very thin ice in publishing this defensive piece, and he also reveals as much against his case as for it. First, Franklin admits that at first he laughed heartily at the "signs, words and ceremonies." So at least to that extent, he found the burlesque at the expense of the poor boy *and the Masonic rites* to be very funny. Danby and Alrihs, by simply not mentioning this fact, do not explicitly deny it, saying only that

Franklin spoke against what had been done and did not desire to be present at the next and fatal hoax. Given the scatological bent of Franklin's sense of humor, it is not easy to grant him the benefit of doubt as regards the purge and the rump kissing.

But if we do grant him that doubt—and also rightly grant that he certainly did not want or like the tragic end of the hoax—there remains the matter of the obscene and blasphemous oath. Danby and Alrihs stipulate only to what happened at the intervening meeting and say nothing about what followed: Franklin's having shared the ridiculous and blasphemous oath with his friends and, quite plausibly, having made sport of it. The oath was, after all, part of the "signs, words and ceremonies" that Franklin admitted to having thought worthy of hearty laughter. No one came forward to his call for witnesses to his having denounced the oath as detestable, and Franklin simply ignored a second article by one "C. D." saying that Franklin's supposed condemnations of the oath were insincere and that if, as he claimed, he had thought the poor lad, the son of a respected acquaintance, was so imposed on, he should have gone to the boy and his father to warn them of what was to come.[25]

Franklin's parents got wind of the affair and wrote to him to express their concern about his lack of religious orthodoxy and, apparently, about his association with the Masons, who, they thought, were given to such ruthless pranks. Franklin replied to them that

> since it is no more in a man's power *to think* than *to look* like another, methinks all that should be expected from me is to keep my mind open to conviction, to hear patiently and examine attentively whatever is offered me for that end; and if after all I continue in the same errors, I believe your usual charity will induce you rather to pity and excuse than blame me.[26]

And as regards the Masons, Franklin admits that his mother may have grounds to dislike them for their refusal to admit women but says that she should believe him when he assures her that "they are in general a very harmless sort of people; and have no principles or practices that are inconsistent with religion or good manners."

But this reply to his parents is widely beside the point. If we grant that the Masonic principles are consistent with religion and good manners, the fact is that Franklin was willing to laugh at spoofs of them, at least as much as he admitted or, as surely seems likely, to the further degree indicated by laughing at the oath. Which is worse: mocking the Masons whose principles are corrosive of religion (or at least of orthodoxy) and good manners, or mocking the Masons whose principles are consistent with religion and good manners?

The point here is not what Franklin actually did or said in this sad and bizarre affair. The point is that what was said of him by others—that he delighted in the vulgar satire of the Masonic rites—is sufficiently confirmed by his *own* published words: the admission of his early laughter at the affair; his own publishing of the incomplete sworn testimony of Danby and Alrihs, which makes no mention of the oath; and the silence that greeted his own published public call to witnesses as regards his sport with the oath. And then there is the unpublished but completely misdirecting letter to his parents, which if read carefully makes his mockery of the Masons all the worse, since the letter defends the Masons as being in tune with piety and good manners. The almost-lifelong Mason Franklin was unashamed to laugh at the society dedicated to universal enlightenment, rational religion, and benevolence.

Not Benjamin Franklin

There is some reason, it seems to me, to be suspicious of the charges made by Franklin's enemies and detractors that he was given to vanity. He was a prodigious genius, a successful entrepreneur and inventor, a scientific star, a successful diplomat in the most important foreign affairs of his country (at least in some popular eyes), and, literally, the most famous American in the world of his time. One can well imagine that he thought himself superior to everyone around him not out of vanity, but because he really was.

Even so, Franklin was not reluctant to mock himself. In 1731, after he had become a Mason and after his common-law marriage to Deborah Read—that is, at the beginning of his rise to responsibility, respectability, and success—Franklin published a brief note in the *Gazette* at his own expense.[27] It seems that on "Thursday last, a certain p——r," whose name he omitted, was walking well clothed and carefully over some barrels of tar on the wharf, when the top of one gave way, and one of his legs plunged in over the knee. "Whether he was upon the catch at that time, we cannot say, but 'tis certain he caught a *Tartar*." As we know from Franklin's later published "Drinker's Dictionary," to be "upon the catch" or "catch'd" meant to be drunk. "T'was observed he sprung out again right briskly, verifying the common saying, As *nimble as a Bee in a Tarbarrel*. You must know there are several kinds of Bees: 'tis true he was no *Honey Bee*, nor yet a *Humble Bee*, but a *Boo bee* he may be allowed to be, Namely B.F." The proud printer was not above a drunken and ridiculous escapade, nor was he too proud to reveal this to the public.

On a later occasion, Franklin was more reluctant to disclose his own folly in public but was not reluctant to do so in private correspondence. In 1749, while engaged in his experiments on electricity, Franklin lightheartedly proposed to Peter Collinson a final experiment to close out that year and to correspond with a philosopher's picnic.[28] Chagrined that no practical use for electricity had yet been discovered, Franklin proposed, tongue in cheek, that "a turkey is to be killed for our dinners by the electrical shock; and roasted by the electrical jack, before a fire kindled by the electrified bottle; when the healths of all the famous electricians in England, France and Germany, are to be drank in electrified bumpers, under the discharge of guns from the electrical battery."

Franklin in fact did experiment with the electrocution of turkeys (on the assumption that birds killed "in this manner eat uncommonly tender"), which led eventually to an experiment that he described as one he desired never to repeat.[29] This was the famous episode in which, in trying to electrocute the bird, Franklin carelessly touched the wrong wire and almost wound up himself a dead duck. In describing this to an unknown correspondent (although probably his brother John), Franklin asked that the episode be communicated to James Bowdoin as a caution—as Franklin did later to Peter Collinson of the Royal Society—but that he should not make it more public, "for I am ashamed to have been guilty of so notorious a blunder; a match for that of the Irishman, sister told me of, who to divert his wife poured the bottle of gun powder on the live coal; or that of the other, who being about to steal powder, made a hole in the cask with a hot iron. Yours &c."[30]

Franklin's near brush with death was without question an accident and was due to his momentary lack of proper attention. But he did not hesitate to describe it, doubtless with a chuckle, as an act of manifest stupidity.

Franklin made fun of himself as a lover, gourmand, and bon vivant, as can be seen in some of the charming bagatelles. In the piece entitled "Bilked for Breakfast," Franklin describes to one Madame de La Freté the comic scene of his cold and sore-footed morning walk to the home of Madame Helvétius, where he expected the company of Madame de La Freté and where he anticipated a big breakfast, including, perhaps, tea, coffee, chocolate, ham, and other good things.[31] To his surprise on his arrival, Franklin found no guests and no food, and from Madame Helvétius he received only an explanation for why she had not expected poor Ben. He complains to Madame de La Freté that he left disconsolate and that, instead of the "half a dozen of your sweet, affectionate, substantial, and heartily applied kisses" that he had hoped for, he was left with "only the shadow of one given by Madame Helvétius, willingly enough, it is true, but the lightest and most superficial kiss that can possibly be imagined."

In the "Dialogue between the Gout and Mr. Franklin," the gout (addressed by Franklin as Madame Gout) takes Franklin to task for the quantity
of meat and drink he has consumed and for his indolent lack of exercise.[32]
Says Madame Gout, "Why, instead of gaining an appetite for breakfast by
salutary exercise, you amuse yourself with books, pamphlets, or newspapers,
which commonly are not worth the reading. Yet you eat an inordinate
breakfast, four dishes of tea with cream, and one or two buttered toasts, with
slices of hung beef, which I fancy are not things the most easily digested."
All this is followed by more leisure, and were it not for the intervention of
Madame Gout, all this food and indolence would destroy his constitution
with dangerous maladies and humors.

The moaning Franklin asks Madame Gout to give him any instruction she
pleases, if only she will stop her "corrections." Yet to the charge that he is indolent, Franklin protests that he does take exercise: He often goes out to dine
and returns in his carriage. This does no good, says Madame Gout, since moving by carriage is not the same as moving by one's own feet. And when
Franklin protests that perhaps only ten times a year he finds some lame excuse not to exercise, Madame Gout says that this happens, rather, "one hundred and ninety-nine times" in a year. Not once has he walked in Monsieur
Brillon's garden, preferring to sit, talk, and play chess. Franklin finally con-
fesses that he is "convinced now of the justness of Poor Richard's remark, that
'Our debts and our sins are always greater than we think for.'" Franklin should
burn his carriage, says Madame Gout, or at least he should allow its use by the
poor old men and women who work in the vineyards and grounds of Passy.

Franklin, says Madame Gout, should be grateful that she has saved him
from palsy, dropsy, and apoplexy, and when Franklin thanks her for her past
services and reminds her that he has not sought out any physician or quack
to run after her, she replies that the quacks can only kill him and not her,
and the physicians agree with her that the gout is, for such a one as Franklin,
a remedy and not a disease. When Franklin promises that he will exercise
and live temperately if only she will release him from his torment, Madame
Gout says that she knows Franklin all too well: When he returns to good
health, he will soon return to his old habits and his "fine promises will be
forgotten like the forms of the last year's clouds." But not to worry, says
Madame Gout, she will be back, because she is Franklin's "*real friend*."

Franklin even made fun of his role in an episode that occasioned his most
morally serious publication: *Narrative of the Late Massacres*, published during
Franklin's brief return to America from November 1762 to November
1764.[33] This pamphlet denounced the murderous behavior of a mob called
the Paxton Boys. The events described occurred between December 1763
and March 1764 and concerned Indian predations on the western frontier of

Pennsylvania. In early December a lower-class mob from Paxton and Donegal, angered at what they thought neglect of their defense by the Anglican and Quaker establishments located on the East Coast and out of harm's way, took matters into their own hands by killing six peaceful Indians at Conestoga Manor in Lancaster County. Some weeks later an even-larger mob murdered fourteen Conestoga Indians who had been given protection in Lancaster.

Despite proclamations from the new governor, John Penn, urging all authorities to apprehend the murderers, the affair became embroiled in the political situation of the time, with the Anglican Proprietary Party and the Quaker Party, including Franklin, in vocal opposition to the attacks on the Indians and the Presbyterians, Lutherans, and poorer urban and border-dwelling inhabitants much less sympathetic to the Indians—and it even endangered general civil peace as the Paxton men threatened to march on Philadelphia to kill Indians under protection in the city. Franklin played an important role on the pro-Indian side, publishing the pamphlet, organizing a militia to enforce the riot act passed by the governor in response to the threat in early February, advising the governor (who, panicked by events, sought Franklin's aid), and joining a delegation that persuaded the mob against moving on the city.

In the pamphlet, Franklin appealed to humanitarian and Christian values to condemn the cruelties inflicted on the defenseless Indians, most of whom were women and children. Franklin, who in even the most serious of matters usually could not resist a joke, kept his tongue entirely out of his cheek on this occasion. The piece is, in fact, completely over the top, at least for Franklin, as regards its unrelenting high moral dudgeon. Franklin first argues, soberly, that we should judge others by what they do and not simply by who they are. Although some Indians have been enemies, others have not. And among all people, including, he says, the ancient heathens and the more recent Turks, it is disgraceful to murder those who have surrendered and laid down their arms. Franklin challenges those who fear the peaceful Indians to give evidence to support their fear, and he charges that the murderers are mere cowards. But the piece also includes the following:

Oh ye unhappy Perpetrators of this horrid Wickedness! Reflect a Moment on the Mischief ye have done, the Disgrace ye have brought on your Country, on your Religion, and your Bible, on your Families and Children! . . . Think of the mild and good Government you have so audaciously insulted; the Laws of your King, your Country, and your GOD, that you have broken; the infamous Death that hangs over your Heads:—For JUSTICE, though slow, will come at last. . . . Let us rouze ourselves, for Shame, and redeem the Honour of our Province from the Contempt of its Neighbors; let all good Men join heartily and unanimously in Support of the Laws . . . that JUSTICE may be done, the Wicked punished, and the Innocent protected; otherwise we can, as a People, expect no Blessing from Heaven, there will be no Security for our Persons or Properties; Anarchy and Confusion will prevail over all, and Violence, without Judgment, dispose of every Thing.[34]

Now, the affair had another dimension that Franklin spoke of later to his friend John Fothergill, a London Quaker. Franklin had been at odds with the Proprietary Party and the Penns over the taxation of proprietary lands, the authority of the assembly, and ultimately the very government of the colony. Franklin wanted to eliminate proprietary rule and bring the colony under the direct government of the Crown. It was no small pleasure to him, then, to see John Penn—the new governor and the nephew of Thomas Penn, with whom Franklin had wrangled for so long while in England—now coming to him for aid, advice, and even protection.[35] Franklin wrote of this to Fothergill and in the course of his letter reveals a very different take on the matter of the massacres.[36]

Franklin begins his letter to Fothergill with a reflection not on the wickedness of the mob but on the stupidity and worthlessness of most human beings. He starts by asking Fothergill, "By the way, *When do you intend to live?* i.e., to enjoy life." By this he means, says Franklin, that he wonders when his friend will go back to the study of nature "in the vegetable creation" and surround himself with ingenious friends and enjoy their conversations and his scientific experiments and give up his work as a physician.

To be hurried about perpetually from one sick chamber to another, is not living. Do you please yourself with the fancy that you are doing Good? You are mistaken. Half the lives you save are not worth saving, as being useless; and almost the other half ought not to be saved, as being mischievous. Does your conscience never hint to you the impiety of being in constant warfare against the plans of Providence?

Disease, continues Franklin, was sent to punish vice and to recommend virtue, and the good doctor uses his art to thwart the "intentions of nature" and "make men safe in their excesses." His good friend is like a "first minister" who, out of benevolence, pardons every criminal who applies to him—this, however tongue-in-cheek, from the Franklin who, in his 1751 "Appeal for the Hospital," argued so forcefully that Christian doctrine requires the charitable care and cure of the sick.[37]

Franklin clearly has the massacres in mind, since the letter goes on to comment on the wonders—the peculiar twists of fortune—involved in the situation. In England the Quakers are blamed for causing the war by their aggressions against the Indians. Can Fothergill believe that in Pennsylvania the Quakers are accused of befriending the Indians, providing them arms, and egging them on to attack the frontiersmen? Would Fothergill believe that in Pennsylvania thousands believe this accusation, that Quakers fear for their lives and do not trust in the government to protect them, and that the mob is being used, by that very government, to "awe the assembly into Proprietary measures"? Even so, the wonders never cease, because Franklin, no friend of the proprietary family, has come to the aid of "his nephew" by drawing his "pen in the cause" to "render the rioters unpopular" and by establishing an association under arms, and even by carrying a musket himself. And still more wonders:

> And, would you think it, this Proprietary Governor did me the honor, on an alarm, to run to my house at midnight, with his counselors at his heels, for advice, and made it his head quarters for some time: And within four and twenty hours, your old friend was a common soldier, a counselor, a kind of dictator, an ambassador to the country mob, and on their returning home, *Nobody*, again. All this has happened in a few weeks!

Franklin continues that even more wonders are to be seen in the fact that the governor, despite having been served well in the affair by the assembly, turned against that body by dealing with the rioters by himself, so that all hopes of happiness under proprietary government have now been lost and that everything in the country, that once was so peaceful, is now running fast toward anarchy and confusion. The only hope, he concludes, is direct government by the Crown.

Franklin's intention in this letter is clearly very serious: In writing to Fothergill he was enlisting the support of London Quakers for his scheme to bring Pennsylvania under royal government.[38] But it is impossible not to hear a drastic change in Franklin's tone: Gone are the high moral dudgeon, the soaring and flowery rhetoric, and the calling upon divine justice for the wicked mob. On the contrary, the line of reasoning is not from the mob's behavior to the certainty of its eventual punishment by God but, rather, from that behavior to the uselessness and viciousness of *most* human beings, who deserve the diseases they get. It is far better for Fothergill to attend to philosophy than to tend to the sick. The miserable fate of the Indians and the rioting of the mob are presented as much as the occasion for Franklin's comical rise from common soldier to dictator and ambassador and then down again, as they are as dangers to peace, order, and good government.

Franklin and Fothergill were good friends and fellow natural philosophers. And so, although Franklin supplies Fothergill with exaggerations in order to highlight the political situation in Pennsylvania, he also signals to his friend not to take the exaggerations with complete moral seriousness. In the *Narrative of the Late Massacres*, Franklin's tone is adjusted to the rhetorical task at hand: to turn public opinion as quickly as possible toward support for the governor and for the governor's temporary defense of Franklin's partisan allies in Philadelphia, allies who were definitely at risk of physical harm. In the letter to Fothergill, the philosophical "promoter of useful projects," Franklin presents the Indians' misery as but another example of human viciousness and stupidity and a circumstance for reflecting on the odd ways of divine providence.[39]

On the one hand, divine providence sends disease in order to afflict stupid and useless and wicked men, who make up the vast majority of all men. But on the other hand, that same divine providence requires our charitable care for and curing of those same sick human beings (as Franklin notes in "Compassion and Regard for the Sick").[40] That charity keeps Fothergill busy and distracted from better activities and makes him not much different from the first minister who floods America with pardoned criminals. The joke here is as much on divine providence as it is on Franklin's rise and fall and political schemes. It is a strange divine providence whose command that we charitably care for and cure the sick is, at the same time, a command that we be impious.

Not Divine Providence

From the time Franklin returned to Philadelphia from his first trip to England until the end of his life, he professed a belief in divine providence. As he reports in the *Autobiography*, when he was reflecting on the united party for virtue, he jotted down some thoughts on an appropriate religious creed for the party, a creed that at once contained the essential points of all religions and was free of everything that "might shock the professors of any religion."[41] These essential points included the assertion that God made everything and "governs the world by his Providence" and that God rewards virtue and punishes vice either in this world or the next. In a letter to Ezra Stiles, one of the very last letters Franklin wrote, just a few weeks before his death, he repeated essentially these same points: that there is a God who governs by his providence and rewards virtue and punishes vice. As is clear from the letter to Fothergill, Franklin was not above casting comic doubt even on these barest and most fundamental principles of religion, the principles of particular providence and rewards and punishments for virtue and vice. Thus we see the odd conundrum of charity for the sick.[42]

But Franklin was also not above making fun of general providence: the notion that although God does not intervene in the course of nature (that is, there are no miracles) and does not mete out rewards and punishments, there is still a divine design visible in the universe, with the corollary that this world is the best of all possible worlds, as regards the whole of the world and as regards the lives we lead in that world. This was the rationalistic and freethinking view of general providence so dear to the Deism of his time, to which Franklin says he was drawn in his youth and of which he was suspected throughout his life.

Two spoofs of general providence—one early and the other fairly late—are especially charming. In 1734 Franklin published a piece in the *Gazette* now known as the "Parody and Reply to a Religious Meditation."[43] In response to the Reverend Joshua Smith's "Meditation on the Vanity and Brevity of Human Life," which Franklin had published in August 1734, Franklin published his own immediate reply, under the pseudonym "S. M." "S. M." objects to the gloomy and splenetic folks who always see the dark side of things and says that, in fact, "the world is a very good world, and if we behave ourselves well, we shall doubtless do very well in it." Job was wrong to complain, for if our days are both few and full of trouble, then all would be just fine since our troubles would be few as well. "S. M." sees Smith's complaint that he cannot be alive now and also ten years ago and ten years hence at the same time as being no different from the lamentation of a child who wants to have his cake and eat it too.

"S. M." says Smith's "elegant expressions" might be translated thus:

- *All the few days we live are full of Vanity; and our choicest Pleasures sprinkled with bitterness:*
  All the few Cakes we have are puffed up with Yeast; and the nicest Gingerbread is spotted with Flyshits!
- *The time that's past is vanish'd like a dream; and that which is to come is not yet at all:*
  The Cakes that we have eaten are no more to be seen; and those which are to come are not yet baked.
- *The present we are in stays but for a moment, and then flies away, and returns no more:*
  The present Mouthful is chewed but a little while, and then is swallowed down, and comes up no more.

- *Already we are dead to the years we have liv'd; and shall never live them over again:*
  Already we have digested the Cakes we have eaten, and shall never eat them over again.
- *But the longer we live, the shorter is our life; and in the end we become a little lump of clay.*
  And the more we eat, the less is the Piece remaining; and in the end the whole will become Sir-reverence!
- *Oh vain, and miserable world! how sadly true is all this story!*
  Oh vain and miserable Cake-shop! Etc.

"S. M." then closes by saying that we should stand with Solomon, who advises us to eat with joy and drink wine with a "merry heart": "Let us rejoice and bless God that we are neither oysters, hogs, nor dray-horses; and not stand repining that he has not made us angels; lest we be found unworthy of that share of happiness He has thought fit to allow us."

So what is the world we actually live in? Not some perfectly made and smoothly ticking grand clock, not some best of all possible worlds or glorious great chain of being—but a cake shop with a good wine cellar attached. We die, it's true. But what we regret about death is leaving behind the cakes and the wine. Seen in this light, who is better off, the angels, who as such eat no cakes and drink no wine (and have no sex, we could add), or we human beings, who enjoy all of these things? If our heads were clear, should we really even *want* to be angels?

When we think of angels, do we not perhaps confuse two things: the continuation of life as we know and love it in the world and some strange incorporeal consciousness? Might we not, as remembering angels, be bored stiff and long eternally for past mortal delights? And if as angels we are spared this longing by remembering nothing of life, could we here on earth really yearn to be, much less know what it would mean to be, an angel? It is thus not clear in which direction the great chain of being might run: The oysters and hogs do not know what they are missing, but then neither might the angels. What is at the end of the great chain of being, at least for us? A turd. What a glorious thing. But even so, if we really think clearly about death, we will see that although life must disappoint us by turning the cakes and the wine and ourselves eventually into dirt, it is foolish to think that the cakes and the wine and ourselves, while we have them, are nothing but Sir-Reverences.

Here Franklin puts some serious thoughts in our heads, it seems to me. One might think that in this little spoof Franklin recommends that with cakes and wine—especially with wine, if we drink enough of it—we can simply put death out of mind. Or one might think that he means to say that we have to put death out of mind in order to enjoy the cakes and the wine. But another thought occurs as well and is, I think, suggested by the example of the angels: that we *have to keep death properly in mind* in order fully to enjoy the cakes and the wine. When we imagine ourselves as angels, perhaps we are just confused: We want life, but not the life we have; we fear death, but we think of it as escape from our woes. Perhaps there is something better beyond the life we have in hand. But we certainly cannot know this and have to admit that, because of death, the life we have may be the only one we will *ever* have.

Thus, the idea of death may, if we think about it clearly, shake us from the dissatisfactions that make us dream of being angels. Death ends life, and most of us cannot be happy about this fact. But it's not death that spoils life as we live it, it's how we think about life that does. We have no control over death, but we do have some control over what we think. So perhaps we can discern the following simple truth: Death is bad, but death is one thing and life is quite another. The life we have is a bird in the hand. Whatever cares it may bring, there is no good reason for us to make those cares worse than they are. And there is no good reason to ignore the delights that bird can offer. At the very least, Franklin's comedy puts these thoughts before us to consider for ourselves.

Much later, while in Passy, Franklin wrote another spoof of general providence in the form of a letter from the Abbé Franklin to his friend the Abbé Morellet on the subject of wine.[44] Franklin opens by thanking his friend for the drinking songs he sent and by saying that he will provide some edifying and Christian, moral, and philosophical reflections on the same topic. *In vino veritas* is proven by the fact that with the aid of this great drink, Noah "discovered numberless important truths" and by the fact that Joseph "took it upon himself to *divine* by means of a cup or glass of wine."[45] And furthermore, the flood was occasioned by mankind's previous lack of wine and preference for drinking only water, which led to mankind's wickedness. All this explains why the word "to divine" comes from *vin*, and "even the Deities themselves, have been called *Divine* or *Divinities*." Even the miraculous conversion of water into wine at the marriage in Cana was but the speeding up of what God does for us every day, as the rain falls to the vineyards and is changed into wine. And the miracle goes in the other direction as well, as wine is turned into water. What sort of water? "Eau-de-vie": Men perform the miracle by converting "common water into that excellent species of wine which we call *punch*." So eschew water, says the Abbé Franklin, and learn from the fact that while the apostle Paul advised Timothy to put wine into his water, "not one of the apostles or holy fathers ever recommended *putting water to wine*."

To this lighthearted blasphemy Franklin then adds a postscript to help the abbé confirm his "piety and gratitude to Divine Providence"— by reflecting on "the situation it has given to the *elbow.*" Then follows commentaries on several illustrations in his letter. In the animal world, those with long legs have been given long necks so that they may drink water without kneeling down (Figures 1 and 2). To man, divine providence has been equally kind. Destined as we are to drink wine, we must be able to get the glass to the mouth. For this the elbow must be placed just right. Were the elbow too far down or too far up the arm, the glass would miss the mouth (Figures 3 and 4). "But by the actual situation, (represented in Figure 5), we are enabled to drink at our ease, the glass going exactly to the mouth (Figure 5). Let us, then, with glass in hand, adore this benevolent wisdom;—let us adore and drink."

Little needs to be said by way of commentary on this sidesplitting account of how divine providence is manifest in the world. What the Deists saw as the fixed and wonderful moral order embedded in the great chain of being, Franklin presents here as the well-ordered means for our getting well crocked. The world a miserable cake shop? No indeed. With enough wine, easily supplied by art and delivered by the divinely designed elbow, what will it matter if the flies have deposited the shits of their repasts on the gingerbread we enjoy!

And Not Even Jesus

Franklin was usually careful, at least in public, not to offend the religion of his fellow citizens *too* egregiously. This is especially true for the person of Jesus, if not exactly so for Jesus understood as the miraculously resurrected Son of God. Indeed, in describing the "bold and arduous project of arriving at moral perfection," Franklin listed as the thirteenth virtue humility, and he

Fig. 3.

Fig. 4.

Fig. 5.

described its precept as the admoni-
tion to imitate Socrates and Jesus.
But in a 1745 letter to the lawyer
James Read, son of Deborah's cousin
Charles, Franklin went well beyond
the edge in the matter of imitating
Jesus.[46]

Franklin addresses a letter James
wrote, in the heat of anger, to ask
Franklin's advice, apparently about a
disagreement James had with Franklin's wife, Deborah. Franklin admires
James's having chosen to write when
angry, rather than speaking directly
and with temper; but Franklin, being cool in the affair, would speak as
well as write if he had the opportunity. Then, as regards seeking calm,
Franklin suggests that James's copy
of Thomas à Kempis's *Imitation of
Christ* must be corrupt if, as James
must have written, it said, "*in om-
nibus requiem quaesivi, sed non inveni, nisi in angulo cum libello*" ("repose is
sought in all things, but is not found, unless in a quiet corner with a
book").[47] Then, says Franklin, the "good father understood pleasure (requiem) better, and wrote, *in angulo cum puella*" (in a corner with a girl). But
then, rather than leaving the quip at this naughty suggestion, Franklin follows it with the obscene comment that there is yet another reading, which is
"more *to the point*" but which James should reject as an "expression too indelicate": "*in angulo puellae*" (in a girl's corner).

The obscene implication is pretty clear: If the young man, angry at Deborah, wants to calm down, it will be most to the point to follow the good father and author of *The Imitation of Christ* and find his repose in his wife's
cunnus. If he wants to ease his anger at Franklin's wife, the first thing he
should do is to bed his own. And that is the most modest reading: *Puella* can
mean young girl or maiden as well as young wife.

So, according to this, how does one imitate Jesus? Get laid. Franklin does
not say that the obscene reading is wrong—indeed, he says it is "more *to the
point*"—but only that James should reject it as being too indelicate. But of
course, if this is too indelicate, why would Franklin have mentioned it, since
poor young James had not? As far as Franklin is concerned, it could well be

the only rational lesson to be drawn from the otherworldly "good father."[48] The excellent old philosopher Socrates comes off much better in the rest of the letter. As Socrates teaches, in disputes between friends, the wisest is the one that makes the first concession. Franklin then hints to the young man that if he is "not very speedy in [his] acknowledgements," he is in danger of losing the honor of being the wisest.

Franklin was not so reckless as to publish his obscene joke at the expense of *The Imitation of Christ*. But he did make it in private correspondence. The joke applies, we might add, as much to Jesus considered as merely human as it does to Jesus considered as divine, and it is hard to miss the similarity between this letter and the *Old Mistress Apologue*.

Both concern sex and repose, and both consist of confidential advice from an older Franklin to a younger friend. With the joke at the expense of Jesus, we are reminded of the alternative "remedy" for the "violent natural inclinations" ruled out by the advice contained in the *Old Mistress Apologue*. In the *Apologue*, the argument is that the sexual urge should be diminished and managed by means of marriage, masturbation, or sex with old ladies. That advice proved limited, however, to those incapable of clearheaded affairs with beautiful women. The clear implication is that both sex and sex connected with beauty, though often the source of trouble when not understood clearly, are still good things for human beings. If Jesus were merely human, this implication would apply to him as well. His chastity would then, on the *Apologue*'s terms, be unnecessary and a needless and even foolish self-denial of a natural human good. Denying oneself sex is not an obvious moral sacrifice, since sex need not necessarily result in harm to others. Indeed, just the opposite is often the case: The old ladies are so grateful. And this is not to mention the good that sex provides the community: Young people to take care of the old ones.

So how could chastity make sense for a human being? At least as Franklin presents the matter, chastity could make sense only if one refrained from sex in order to rule out the possibility of the moral harms that sex *might* cause or if refraining from sex somehow produced a better good here or in some other world to come. In the first case, chastity has to appear as an extreme remedy used when simpler and more effective ones are available. What is more difficult, resisting the inclination altogether or following Franklin's advice? In the second case, chastity could be an effort to atone for a supposed human depravity—the sin that caused men to be ashamed of their nakedness, to feel desire and the pain of childbirth, and to toil and sweat for bread. We know that Franklin thought original sin an absurd bugbear.[49] His opinion by itself surely does not prove false the account of an original Fall, and it remains to be seen if he had good reasons to think the Fall absurd. Even so, we wonder, could there be some reason for chastity apart from the fear of divine punishments for harms committed or atonement for original sin? And what might that be, at least in the light of Franklin's wise advice about old ladies?

Perhaps something like the following: One could find in the objects of one's erotic desires such an overwhelming and profound promise of perfect happiness that the thought of actual carnal knowledge (making the grunting beast with two backs) disgusts and spoils the yearning for the beautiful object. From Franklin's point of view, such "romanticism" would surely be comical: The chaste romantic would understand the delights and the troubles associated with sex (why else feel the desire and also think that satisfying it would besmirch the beloved and the promise of happiness?) and would then yearn erotically for the beloved as if she (or he) had no body—as if she were an angel, with whom sex is impossible. Here we're back to the cake shop of mere human life: Is it not a confusion—is it not wanting to have one's cake and eat it too—to wish to be an angel or to wish such a condition on one's beloved? Here, chastity is giving up the bird in hand not for two possibilities in the bush but for no bird at all.

A Shameless Politician?

In order to frame the context for considering Franklin's philosophical humor, we must remember that Franklin was for most of his life a political man. We keep this fact in mind because it poses a problem: Politics has more to do with anger and indignation than it does with laughter. Anger and indignation do not jibe with philosophical humor that finds nothing sacred and knows no shame. As soon as Franklin became rich he retired from business, and as soon as he retired from business (indeed, slightly before) he embarked on a long and varied political career. My own view is that Franklin was above all else a political elitist and fixer and something of a cool opportunist—more akin to a big city boss than to an ideological partisan. But even taking Franklin as an opportunistic political boss does not make our fundamental problem disappear.

No matter how hard-boiled and personally opportunistic a politically ambitious man or boss might be, such types are almost always, contrary to appearances, moved by some moral imperative. Such men at the very least think that they deserve to rule more than do others and that power and glory and fame and, for the big city boss, public improvements attest to that fact. Whatever passions moved Franklin—the charity of his party of virtue, desire for fame and recognition, love of power, resentment at having been born poor, love of the British Empire, hatred of the Penns—they would seem to reveal a morally serious man. To take politics seriously—even for the grittiest fixer-opportunist—requires one to think that the public's business really matters and that one deserves rewards for managing such important affairs.[50] Political ambition almost always betrays the love of justice, and the love of justice is never far removed from anger and indignation.

But for such men there is a limit to permissible raillery, and there are some things that cannot be treated lightly or mocked. And herein lies the problem. Franklin's humor goes all the way up, so to speak. Nothing is spared: religion, divine providence, the life of Jesus, the great chain of being, philanthropy, the family, sex and love, moral virtue, human and divine justice, our political attachments and obligations, Newton's laws, Baconian science, or the Masons, a secret and universal party of and for virtue.

It seems clear that Franklin disagreed with Philoclerus that "true wit and humor cannot be employed in ridiculing things serious and sacred." Indeed, when we penetrate Franklin's humor, we are left with questions in our minds and with work to do on our own, but always in directions that leave us wondering about confusions that may afflict our commonly held opinions about the things we admire, hold dear, or consider "serious and sacred." Religious fanatics take a drubbing, no doubt about that, and so too do miracles and the Bible. Here, Franklin (not so tolerantly) ridicules religion. But we cannot say with great confidence that he does so for the sake of "Deism," since, when he does an about-face and shores up the believers, he upends the metaphysical grounds of Deism's rejection of miracles and revelation. At this point Franklin leaves us unable to settle the dispute between the seeming lunatics and the seeming rationalists—at least if settling it depends on resolving the metaphysical dispute between materialism and spiritualism.

But Franklin does not simply abandon us before an insoluble metaphysical dilemma. By this I mean not that he solves the dilemma but, rather, that what the comedy leads us to consider has nothing to do with metaphysics at all. The focus is rather on ourselves—on our hopes and longings and on our common and apparently sensible opinions about the serious and sacred matters that are spoofed. Poor Prouse and Mitchel were believers. But Prouse was torn between hope for divine mercy and fear of divine punishment. Mitchel, the doubting believer, was fully converted by the stunning discovery that God cared for *him* and intervened on behalf of the justice *he* deserved. But then we meet Polly, whose argument in her defense makes us wonder about divine justice. Were God to punish Prouse and Polly, could the punishment ever fit the crime? Is there any sin or misdeed that deserves the eternal fire, or if not the fire, even the loss of eternal life, or any punishment worse than death? Even if we do not find the eternal fire an appalling indictment of God, then at least we have to wonder about such a God.

One could reply, of course, that the ways of divine justice are beyond our powers to comprehend. Perhaps. But then Polly and Father Abraham make us wonder not just about divine justice but about justice as such, whether human or divine. We cannot make sense of justice or the evil against which it strives without assuming that the wicked choose their wickedness. Polly and Father Abraham suggest that this assumption may be hopelessly confused. Thus, when we blame the wicked for their evil, we might as well shake our fingers at skunks or snakes while yelling at them: "Shame on you!"

Then again, Father Abraham makes us think some perplexing things about virtue as well as about vice. When he tells us that virtue provides for inner satisfaction, we are reminded that we think of virtue as noble and that, as such, virtue at its peak requires sacrifice or devotion of our good to that of others. Yet it is hard to think of the noble deed rewarded by the wrinkling of all noses, and harder still to think the noble deed should be the choice of being esteemed by all, including God, as stinking to high heaven. Again, it is hard not to think of inner satisfaction at the nobility of our sacrifice as itself a good of *our own*. It is hard not to think of the reason for that satisfaction, our virtue, as itself a good, perhaps the greatest good, of our own. It seems that as regards virtue, and especially as regards the noble, we want to have our cake (the noble sacrifice) and eat it too (be worthy of our just rewards, even if we never get them).

The same confusion seems to rule in our more mundane affairs as well: We want the objects of our erotic desires, but not as they really are—and hence, we expect happiness from beauty or fall in love with angels. We complain about death but spoil the life we have in wanting to *be* angels. But what we want from being angels, no angels as we conceive them can provide. In trying to be good, we wind up being bad—whether we take white scalps or starve the red Indians. And having starved the Indians or scalped the whites, we think that for our troubles (either by taking the scalps or donating them) men or God or the whole cosmos, or all three together, owe us respect. Thus, Mitchel discovers that God provides justice to *him, right now,* by altering the course of events in this world. And the more rational Deists think the world, just as God made it once and for all time, was made for *us*— the farthest star is connected through all time and space to the elbow that gets the wine through our grinning lips. Is this piety (rational or otherwise) and the love of a loving God, or is it rather plain old human vanity?

Franklin begins the *Autobiography* by commenting that "in many cases it would not be quite absurd if a man were to thank God for his vanity among the other comforts of life."[51] "Not quite absurd" says Franklin, which means almost absurd. How could it be *simply* absurd for God to give us vanity as one of the comforts of life? If that vanity were the grounds for our believing in a God or a universe that cares for us and gives us comforting vanity. Franklin does not say that by writing the *Autobiography* he *will* indulge his vanity, only that *perhaps* he will. It is thus possible that vanity can be understood and overcome—and so perhaps by understanding "God's gift" of vanity we lose our reasons for believing in the donor.

Moreover, Franklin does not just assert that we humans are vain: He suggests ways for us to see for ourselves that we are vain. Perhaps vanity is exposed for what it is when we see ourselves clinging with all our might to opinions—such as that we merit divine reward—that do not make any sense when we think about them clearly. But why is God's gift of vanity not simply absurd but just *almost* absurd? Because we can never be absolutely certain, no matter how well we understand ourselves, that the divine reward does not exist. As usual, Franklin proceeds with care, never makes assertions about what cannot be certain, and instead directs us to think about the serious and sacred matters on our own.

But if Franklin's humor is philosophical and not simply the product of an irrepressible jokester, then in going all the way up it goes all the way down to the grounds of political seriousness. Franklin's humor leads us to doubtful thinking about those issues the political man cannot take lightly or mock, and cannot really doubt, either.

So then what are we to make of Franklin's lifelong involvement in political life? This fact, more than anything Franklin relates in *Autobiography,* seems to tell against a skeptical Franklin and for the founder of the party of virtue and the man for whom public service was the most important service of God. If we are to discover the single, clear-sighted, philosophical Ben Franklin, then we will have to account for his political life. And the philosophical and political lives—so apparently at odds—must be shown in his case to have been compatible. Only then can we understand the ultimate unity of Franklin's several personae: new man and scientific inventor, self-improving moralist, civic-minded philanthropist, tireless politician, jokester and prankster, lover and musician, monarchist and British imperialist, republican revolutionary patriot, proponent of rational religion, and the radical and skeptical philosopher.

But if our task is to find the one and only Ben, we cannot do so without getting to the very bottom of his thought. Franklin's humor is revealing, but it does not by itself take us to the core, which remains to be uncovered. As I noted earlier, Franklin wrote the *Autobiography* at least in part to provide the frame for evaluating his most important theoretical and moral writings. To get to the bottom of his humor—and thus to his deepest thought and the unity of his personae—we return, in chapters 5 and 6, to the *Autobiography* and the other texts to which it points.

5 · The Metaphysical Follies

Although the *Autobiography* is written with great care and by itself presents enough puzzles to put our minds to work, it is not wholly self-contained. In presenting the saga of fall and redemption, Franklin tells us not only about what he read but also about some of the things he wrote. Two of them begin a trail that leads to still another three—a letter and two additional relevant pieces. Together these pieces are important because they concern the issue of particular providence, and they figure prominently in the conventional and scholarly assessment of Franklin's intellectual and spiritual journey.

Let's briefly recapitulate that journey as we know it from the *Autobiography*. Franklin's corruption began with reading his father's books of polemical divinity, which led to his doubts about revelation and then ultimately to a thorough Deism and doubts about the tenets of Franklin's religion. These doubts were buttressed along the way by his reading of such Enlightenment thinkers as Shaftesbury, Collins, the authors· of the *Port Royal Logic,* and Locke. As regards his resulting behavior, he began with a habit of obnoxious disputation but then, after discovering Xenophon and the Socratic method of disputation, turned to aggressive refutations covered by the guise of the humble doubter, which he practiced for some few years before gradually giving up the aggressiveness and retaining the guise of modest diffidence alone. That behavior also led to his flight from the good people of Boston, the moral errata Franklin committed as the result of his moral corruption and lack of religion, and the harms he suffered at the hands of those corrupted by his arguments.

While in London, Franklin wrote the *Dissertation on Liberty and Necessity, Pleasure and Pain,* which led to his introduction to London intellectual society. But in the light of his reflections on the bad effects of his freethinking doctrine on his own and others' behavior, he came to suspect that the *Dissertation* might have suffered from an insinuating error, common in metaphysical reasoning. Following on his reflections and his suspicion about metaphysics, he came to his moral reformation, which at first lacked religion. Then, after getting religion, he wrote in 1728 his *Articles of Belief and Acts of Religion*—his own private liturgy. He returned to that liturgy about the time he conceived of the "bold and arduous project of arriving at moral perfection." After next conceiving the great and extensive project for the united party of virtue, he used his newspaper, along with *Poor Richard's Almanack*, as means for public instruction. To this end, he published (in addition to *Poor Richard*) the Socratic dialogue proving that a vicious man cannot be considered a man of sense and a discourse on self-denial proving that virtue is not secure until it is free of opposing inclinations. These two pieces, Franklin said, "may be found in the Papers at the beginning of 1735."

So in the course of relating and then undermining the moral and religious saga, Franklin identifies four of his own writings that are directly relevant to the crucial matters at hand: The *Dissertation* was the product of his "fallen" period, and his changed view of it was the product of his moral "reformation." The other two writings on virtue (the Socratic dialogue and the discourse on self-denial) were apparently the products of that moral reformation. And the *Articles of Belief* was the product of the moral reformation and the religious beliefs he had "never doubted" (including particular providence). Franklin had good reasons to think that his readers—especially the puzzled ones—would have access to these relevant pieces. He tells us where to find the Socratic dialogue and the essay on self-denial: in the "Papers [the *Gazette*] about the beginning of 1735." At the time he wrote Part One of the *Autobiography*, he surely knew that the *Dissertation* was still available (the *Dissertation* had been pirated and reprinted in Dublin in 1733), and, far more important, he left a copy of it to his grandson and literary executor William Temple Franklin.[1] He also left the manuscript of the *Articles of Belief* with William.

Moreover, by the time he wrote Part Two of the *Autobiography*, Franklin clearly knew that his writings would be published after his death. His London publisher, Benjamin Vaughn—the same Vaughn whose 1783 letter comes before Part Two of the *Autobiography*—had been working on an edition of Franklin's political and miscellaneous writings since 1776 and had published them as *Franklin's Political, Miscellaneous, and Philosophical Pieces* in 1779. These were the first of Franklin's nonscientific and as-yet-unpublished writings to be set in print. The *Autobiography* was not published in Franklin's lifetime (and it was first arranged that Vaughn would publish it after Franklin's death, a plan that did not pan out), and the manuscript of it was bequeathed to William, who published the work in England after Franklin's death.[2]

Thus, at the time he wrote the *Autobiography*, Franklin had as much reason to expect these four writings to be available to the public as he did for the *Autobiography* itself. If the contradictions and clues in the saga prompt careful readers to wonder about Franklin's moral and religious views, that same saga prompts these readers to find and consider these four writings, identified so clearly by Franklin, that might shed light on the questions raised in our minds.

Franklin had equally good reason to think his readers would have access to an additional piece of the puzzle. In 1779 Franklin, then in Passy, wrote a now-famous letter to Vaughn concerning the soon-to-appear *Political, Miscellaneous, and Philosophical Pieces*. Franklin took great care to preserve this letter. In addition to the copy sent to Vaughn, Franklin put one (written in the hand of his secretary) in his letterbook of the time, and he gave another copy to his grandson William.[3] So Franklin took all the steps he could—short of publishing the letter himself, something he never did with any of his correspondence—to see that the 1779 letter would survive and be in the hands of those who would eventually publish the *Autobiography*.

Franklin thus had, again, as much reason to expect the 1779 letter to be published as he did for the *Autobiography*. Moreover, he would not have been surprised that when William took over the task of publishing the *Autobiography* from Vaughn, William included the Vaughn letter along with the *Autobiography* (and along with the later 1783 letter from Vaughn set between Parts One and Two) when it eventually was published. William included the 1779 letter because it concerned the *Dissertation* and Franklin's view of it and writings like it. In the letter, Franklin tells Vaughn that he wrote the *Dissertation*, and after describing it (and its conclusion that "all is right"), he briefly says:

There were only an hundred copies printed, of which I gave a few to friends, and afterwards disliking the piece, as conceiving it might have an ill tendency, I burnt the rest, except one copy, the margin of which was filled with manuscript notes by Lyons, author of the Infallibility of Human Judgment, who was at that time another of my acquaintance in London. I was not nineteen years of age when it was written. In 1730, I wrote a piece on the other side of the question, which began with laying for its foundation this fact: "That almost all men in all ages and countries, have at times made use of prayer." Thence I reasoned, that if all things are ordained, prayer must among the rest be ordained. But as prayer can produce no change in things that are ordained, praying must then be useless and an absurdity. God would therefore not ordain praying if everything else was ordained. But praying exists, therefore all things are not ordained, etc. This pamphlet was never printed, and the

manuscript has been long lost. The great uncertainty I found in metaphysical reasonings disgusted me, and I quitted that kind of reading and
study for others more satisfactory.[4]

Now, this story is different from the one told in the *Autobiography* in two
very important respects. First, in the *Autobiography*, Franklin tell us nothing
about having burned the piece because it might have had an "ill tendency."
This fact is astounding, since reporting the burning would have counted as
rectifying the moral erratum of printing the *Dissertation*, and Franklin takes
pains in the *Autobiography* to report his rectifications of the errata. It strains
credulity to think Franklin could have forgotten about the burning in 1771
and then remembered it again in the 1779 letter to Vaughn. Franklin could
be lying to Vaughn, but even then the effect is the same as regards what we
are to make of the *Dissertation* in light of the letter. And second, Franklin
tells Vaughn that he became disgusted with metaphysics because of its "great
uncertainty." This is in tone and content a somewhat different description
of the problem identified in the *Autobiography*, which complained not of
great uncertainty but, rather, of a possible error that had "insinuated itself
unperceived, . . . so as to infect all that followed, as is common in metaphysical reasonings."

We'll come back to these important matters in a moment. But first we
need to make our way down the trail before us. In the letter to Vaughn,
Franklin tells him—and us—that in 1730 he wrote the metaphysical piece
"on the other side of the question," that is, in favor of particular providence,
that argued from the existence of prayer. Franklin was still at "metaphysics,"
though to an opposite end, at least five years after he wrote the *Dissertation*.
The prayer pamphlet was never printed, and the manuscript was lost (odd, is
it not, that Franklin would remember—or at least claim to remember—the
exact year in which he wrote this long-lost piece). Franklin then explains
why it never appeared: "The great uncertainty I found in metaphysical reasonings disgusted me, and I quitted that kind of reading and study for others
more satisfactory."[5]

So according to the story Franklin tells Vaughn, it was metaphysics in service of particular providence that finally disgusted Franklin with metaphysics. When we turn to the *Articles of Belief*, one thing becomes clear. It
too belongs to the category of metaphysical writings. In the course of the argument of the *Articles*, at a point where Franklin asserts that by virtue and
holiness we merit from God a suitable share of temporal blessings, he refers
readers by an asterisk to "the Junto paper of Good and Evil, etc." The piece
referred to by the asterisk is apparently lost, but it must certainly have assumed or argued for the existence of good and evil and particular provi-

dence, as is clear from the context of the asterisk in the *Articles*.[6] There is a Junto paper on just this topic, probably written in 1732, never published but nevertheless carefully preserved by Franklin. The Junto essay is entitled "On the Providence of God in the Government of the World."[7] This piece is indeed on the "other side of the question" from the *Dissertation* and is clearly one of Franklin's metaphysical pieces.

At the end of the trail, we have the following scene before us: Between 1725 and probably as late as 1732, Franklin wrote four metaphysical pieces on particular providence: the *Dissertation* against it and then, after his moral and religious "reformations," the *Articles*, the missing piece on prayer, and the essay "On the Providence of God," all in favor of particular providence. After becoming disgusted by the great uncertainty of metaphysical reasoning, he abandoned metaphysics and published, in 1735, for public edification, the pieces in defense of virtue—the Socratic dialogue and the essay on self-denial. As we will see, these last two pieces are not metaphysical and are rather dialectical in form. And both before 1725 and after 1735, Franklin was using his two forms of the Socratic method—the first with its aggressive religious refutations that persisted for some few years and then were gradually abandoned, and the second in which he retained (until and beyond the writing of the *Autobiography*) the guise of modest diffidence in matters of dispute (and as we know concerned especially religion).

The now-standard view of Franklin's intellectual and spiritual journey began with the important scholarship of Aldridge. It pretty much follows the story as told in the *Autobiography* and as supplemented by the famous letter to Vaughn.

According to the standard view, Franklin followed a path (to use the spectrum described in the preface, note 4) from dry Deism (no free will or particular providence) to very wet Deism (no miracles but free will and particular providence). The first position, based on metaphysics, was early, radical, and even nihilistic and is expressed in the *Dissertation* and described in the *Autobiography*. After his reflections on the harmfulness of his dry Deism, Franklin then moved to a very wet Deism, at first based also on metaphysics. This position is expressed in the *Articles of Belief*, the essay "On the Providence of God," and in the missing piece on prayer described in the letter to Vaughn.

Franklin then became disgusted with metaphysics and grounded his very wet Deism on humanistic and practical considerations. This final position is described in the *Autobiography*, where Franklin tells us that he rejected the conclusions of the *Dissertation* because they were not useful even if they might have been true; that metaphysics commonly contains some insinuating error; that truth, sincerity, and integrity in relations among men are of the utmost importance for happiness; that things are commanded or forbidden because they are good or bad for us and not vice versa; and that the religious principles he never doubted (including particular providence) are the essentials of every religion and serve "to inspire, promote or confirm morality."[8] His final position is also revealed in the letter to Vaughn, where Franklin says that he abandoned metaphysics in disgust because of its great uncertainty.[9]

There is, however, some scholarly confusion about the precise content of the first and radical position as expressed in the *Dissertation*. Aldridge sees it as atheism rather than a form of Deism and argues that in describing the *Dissertation* in the *Autobiography*,

> Franklin made the same confusion between deism and atheism which was then common to many orthodox Christians. He lumped them together as forms of freethinking which lead to the obliteration of the distinction between virtue and vice. Actually, deism insists on high standards of moral conduct, and Franklin himself remarked elsewhere that it is as different from atheism as chalk is from charcoal. Franklin's pamphlet is atheistic rather than deistic in its metaphysics as well as in its ethical overtones. When Franklin says in his *Autobiography* that he later renounced the metaphysical conclusions of his pamphlet because of practical reasons . . . he was giving up his own form of atheism, not deism.[10]

Now it is simply incredible that Franklin could have succumbed to a popular, orthodox confusion on the issue of atheism and Deism. Thus, another scholar says more recently, and with greater respect for Franklin's brain, that when Franklin described the *Dissertation* "the position under discussion was not Deism at all, but his earlier freethinking."[11] In this case, however, the argument simply ignores Franklin's clear indication in the *Autobiography* that the *Dissertation* reflected "this doctrine," which is in the context just as clearly identified by Franklin as Deism.[12] At least according to Franklin, Deism could and did grant the existence of God and deny the existence of virtue and vice and particular providence. The problem here springs in part from the vague and slippery historical term "Deism." But aside from this issue of historical terms, the real problem is that the scholarship is insufficiently attentive to the complicated but carefully written evidence Franklin actually presents to our view. Hence the scholarship jumps to hasty conclusions and ignores significant problems.

To say that Franklin renounced the conclusions of the *Dissertation* "because of practical reasons" is very hard to square with Franklin's claim about that very practice—that he came to believe that "*truth, sincerity* and *integrity*

in dealings between man and man, were of the utmost importance to the felicity of life." If the "doctrine" of the *Dissertation* might be true and yet was
not useful, then Franklin would have to renounce what might well be *really*
true theoretically, in order to serve truth, sincerity, and integrity in dealings
between man and man.

But could he, then, *tell* the theoretical truth about the *Dissertation* to
other men: that its denial of virtue and vice might well be really true? How
could he tell the truth about the *Dissertation* and at the same time say that
truth, sincerity, and integrity are of utmost importance? Here we need to apply some simple common sense. Suppose someone said to you: "It's really important for practical purposes to tell the truth, but I also believe that it's very
likely true that there is no such thing as the virtue of telling the truth, or
any kind of virtue, for that matter. But hey, I've got some property in Florida
I'd like to sell you." I wouldn't buy; would you? Moreover, I would think the
salesman a fool as well as not to be trusted: "If he wants to bilk me, why give
himself away? Perhaps he's really telling the truth here, but I'm not about to
risk my dough to find out."

Now, if we generalize to Franklin addressing all mankind, why, after saying that truth, sincerity, and integrity are of utmost importance, does
Franklin then add that it may well be true that there are no virtues, including those virtues? That might incline others to think: "What you're saying is
that truth is very important in practical matters but it very likely is not a
moral virtue—because there really are *no* moral virtues. Well, you know as
well as I do that telling the truth is certainly useful in practice; no one
likes—much less deals with—a habitual liar. But when the stakes are high
enough, what you're saying is that what men also know to be true in practice—that a lie is sometimes very useful, very practical indeed—may well be
supported by theory, since virtue isn't and can't be the issue; usefulness is."

Can this thought—so clearly put in our minds by Franklin's equivoca-
tion—be good for spreading the practical view that "*truth, sincerity and integrity* are of the utmost importance in relations among men"? It does not
seem likely. Rather, the practically useful thing to do would be to lie to people about the probable truth of the *Dissertation*'s doctrine about virtue and
vice. But then, how can telling the truth be of the *utmost* importance in relations among men? It cannot. The amazing thing about Franklin's artful
rhetoric here is that he *does not* lie about the *Dissertation*, and the effect
upon careful reading is to make us think that for practical purposes he
should have lied.

To put the matter bluntly: From the evidence Franklin supplies, the most
plausible and indeed consistent conclusion is that Franklin learned from
experience, and for the sake of relations among men, to say falsely that truth,

sincerity, and integrity are of the utmost importance in relations among men. And it follows as well that he learned from experience to say falsely that he believed in particular providence.[13] But aside from this enormous interpretive wrinkle, the most serious problem with the scholarship is that it jumps well beyond the evidence in speaking of Franklin's radical and atheistic point of view. Franklin never, anywhere, says openly that he was an atheist. Even at the time of the obnoxious disputations and the Socratic refutations, we learn only that he came to be considered an atheist or infidel by good people. (It is hard not to miss the clear reference to Socrates, of whom it was concluded by those who listened to his first accusers—who reported what Socrates had investigated and argued—that he did not believe in the gods.)[14]

For all of his daring, Franklin was not so foolish as to rule out completely plausible deniability. Moreover, Franklin is open and quite precise about his "want of religion": When he says he lacked religion, we have a clear standard from the six principles of all religions by which to judge this lack—and the crucial issue was the denial of particular providence, not atheism as such. And finally, Franklin does point to a difference between his skepticism and that of the Deists, which the scholarship ignores: the strange and dangerous dialectical aggressiveness that got him run out of Boston and put him at risk until he gave up the Socratic refutations for the practice of modest diffidence.[15]

This last point indicates the deepest flaw in the now-standard scholarly story: The scholarship simply assumes, without a shred of evidence, that the radical and skeptical view is expressed in the metaphysical *Dissertation* and that the Socratic refutations and the skepticism of the *Dissertation* were the same. On its face this assumption is unwarranted: There is a world of difference between deductive arguments that are based on abstract metaphysical assumptions and Socratic, dialectical refutations that draw out the consequences of an interlocutor's commonsensical and practical opinions and beliefs. And again, we have no grounds for simply assuming, as the scholarship does, that the "doctrines" of the Socratic refutations and the metaphysical writings were the same. On the contrary, in having learned the Socratic method from Xenophon's *Memorabilia*, Franklin would have known that Socrates' conversational activities as reported there concerned everyday moral, practical, and religious matters and also that Socrates thought it foolish to think about the cosmos and the necessary causes of the heavenly things (which is not to judge of the general question as to whether Socrates ever studied natural philosophy, for which there is conflicting evidence, or what importance his dialectical investigations might have had for that philosophy).[16]

At this point we have to recall again Franklin's intellectual situation. According to the letter to Vaughn, Franklin gave up metaphysics sometime after 1730, and we know that the last such piece Franklin wrote (in favor of particular providence) was probably written for the Junto in 1732. It is certain that Franklin was still at the Socratic refutations at the time of writing the *Dissertation*. We know this because he tells us that he continued the aggressive refutations by the humble doubter for "some few years, but gradually left it, retaining only" the method of modest diffidence when advancing anything that might be disputed. He began the aggressive refutations at age sixteen and was almost nineteen when he wrote the *Dissertation*—not quite three years later, which surely qualifies as "some few years." We know that it does qualify because the *Dissertation*, although not dialectical, is surely aggressive in religious matters that might be disputed. Moreover, as he tells us in the *Autobiography*, Franklin did not simply drop the Socratic refutations. Rather, after the "some few years" he *gradually* left them and then retained only the method of modest diffidence. The period of the gradual abandonment of the aggressive Socratic refutations could easily have stretched from just after the writing of the *Dissertation* in 1725 until the writing of the *Articles* in 1728 (more about this later), and it is indeed likely that they were still going on, though more rarely, at the time he wrote the last metaphysical piece, in favor of particular providence, sometime between 1730 and 1732.

But even if we cannot be sure of the far end of this temporal stretch, it does not really matter, because in describing his methods of conversation, Franklin never tells us anywhere that in leaving the aggressive Socratic refutations, he changed his mind about anything that transpired in them. On the contrary, in describing the retained diffidence of the Socratic method, Franklin tells us, by way of a poetic reference to Pope, that he learned "to speak tho' sure, with seeming diffidence."[17] Franklin here tells us that by the time he turned away from the aggressive refutations, he had become sure of something important regarding religion, no longer needed to take the risk of humble but aggressive refutations, and could then simply keep his mouth shut about the matter.

It could very well be (and is, as I will argue) that Franklin answered the question of particular providence in the course of the Socratic refutations, that the answer was the same as the one in the *Dissertation*, but that it was derived from an argument having nothing in common with any of his metaphysical writings. If we consider just the most obvious difference between metaphysics and conversational dialectics (that the former is theoretical, the latter practical), then for Franklin the practical consideration of religion both followed *and preceded* his metaphysical writings (so there can be no simple turn from metaphysics to a newly discovered "humanism"). The important questions thus become: What were the substantive differences between the Socratic refutations and the metaphysical pieces on both sides of the particular providence divide? And how are they related? To pursue them, we have to remember what we learn from the *Autobiography* and the 1779 letter to Vaughn: The problem with metaphysics is not just its great uncertainty but great uncertainty that springs from an insinuating and hard-to-see error.

Let's again consider Franklin's intellectual and spiritual journey, this time exactly as he describes it in the several stages of the *Autobiography* (as I detailed in chapter 1). From reading his father's books of dispute about religion, Franklin picked up his habit of disputatiousness that produced "disgusts and perhaps enmities" (Stage Two). We can presume, but we don't know for sure, that these disgusts and possible enmities concerned religion. We get powerful confirmation that they did from the later account of his moral reformation (Stage Six), where Franklin tells us that when he was barely fifteen years old he began to doubt revelation from the points disputed in the different books he read, which seem clearly to be his father's. After that (again according to Stage Six), Franklin read the books (apparently new ones) against Deism, from the lectures endowed by Boyle, that had the opposite effect of turning Franklin into a "thorough Deist."

Ben's own deistic arguments then led him to pervert and harm others and to be harmed by those he had perverted. We don't know the exact time frame of these arguments, but we do know that the harms produced by them occurred as late as the affair of Mrs. T. (recounted in Stage Five, Erratum Five). In the course of this intellectual progression (as we learn from Stage Three), at "about sixteen" years old Franklin read Locke and the *Port Royal Logic* and then read Xenophon and discovered the aggressive, Socratic method number one, which he practiced for some few years. He found this method "safest" for himself (and embarrassing to others) because he had by then from reading Shaftesbury and Collins become "a real doubter in many points of our religious doctrine."

A year later he fled Boston as an accused atheist or infidel (Stage Five, Erratum One) and a year and a half later, in London, he wrote the *Dissertation* (Stage Five, Erratum Number Four). Some time after that he gradually abandoned the aggressive Socratic refutations, and after becoming sure of something regarding religion, he retained the diffidence of Socratic method number two (Stage Four). And between the *Dissertation* and after the (supposed) moral and religious reformations (Stages Six and Ten), Franklin wrote three other metaphysical pieces in favor of particular providence, somewhere between 1730 and 1732. And then, after abandoning metaphysics in "disgust" (as we learn from the letter to Vaughn) and after conceiving the great and extensive project for a "united party for virtue" (Stage

Eleven), Franklin, "about the beginning of 1735," published the Socratic dialogue and the essay on self-denial, for the sake of public instruction (Stage Twelve).

Franklin makes the precisely defined steps of the journey hard to assemble and see, and the effect is that we lose sight of the details, especially the place of the Socratic refutations and the crucial fact that he never abandoned what he became sure of by their means. It's thus no wonder that the scholarship lumps everything together and then divides between an early radical, freethinking metaphysical position and a subsequent humanistic and practical Deism that followed the moral and religious reformations.

But nothing in the precise progression allows us quickly to identify its various steps—the early doubt, the influence of the Boyle lectures, the impact of Locke and the *Port Royal Logic*, the influence of Shaftesbury and Collins, and the experience of the Socratic refutations. Moreover, it is easy to conclude that because Franklin had, from reading Shaftesbury and Collins, become a doubter in many points of "our religious doctrine," the Socratic refutations were used to promote that doubt on the deistic and metaphysical grounds supplied by Shaftesbury and Collins. But this too would be a jump to an unwarranted conclusion: At the very least, to repeat an essential point, metaphysical and dialectical arguments are simply not the same. And if Franklin never abandoned what he learned in the dialectical refutations, then we'll surely want to know what's going on in the two essays written for public instruction, which, as I noted above, are dialectical.

Franklin, as usual, leaves us to think on our own, albeit with the important clues about the insinuating error in the metaphysical treatises on both sides of the particular providence divide and the aggressiveness and risk of the Socratic refutations. At this point, the really curious reader wants very much to check out the writings identified by Franklin as relevant to the saga of fall and redemption.

IN THE CASE OF THE *DISSERTATION*, Franklin *really* makes us eager to check it out. How so? We know that if Franklin never doubted particular providence, as indeed he says, then the saga of fall and redemption never happened. This is one of those fundamental contradictions that we cannot ignore or explain away. But it also then leads to another. If it's true, as Franklin says, that he never doubted particular providence, then when he wrote the *Dissertation* he *did not believe the doctrine he was presenting*. Stated otherwise, when he wrote that piece *he did not take it seriously*.

Perhaps Franklin never doubted particular providence and wrote the *Dissertation* to test that lack of doubt. In this case, all the stuff about his having once thought it clever and then coming to think of it as infected with some insinuating error would be part of the pious fraud of his fall and redemption. As we saw earlier, however, this plausible explanation simply does not jibe with the extraordinary suspicions to which Franklin's contradictions draw our attention: that a skeptical Franklin did not believe in particular providence and lied both in saying that he always did and in saying that he did, then did not, and then did again.

Moreover, we're still left not only with these utterly corrosive suspicions but also with the thought in our heads that, for whatever reason, Franklin may not have taken the *Dissertation* seriously at the very time that he wrote it. What are we to make, we then wonder, of the error he came to think may have insinuated itself into the *Dissertation*? In particular, the following possibility comes to mind: Perhaps Franklin came to doubt—and never stopped doubting—particular providence but did so before he wrote the *Dissertation* and on grounds other than those supplied by that treatise. But if he did not take the piece seriously when he wrote it, why did he write it? Again, the question becomes this: What was the error that had insinuated itself, unperceived, into the *Dissertation's* argument? So we turn, now, to the infamous and subsequently burned metaphysical treatise.

The pamphlet has as its motto the following lines from Dryden:

Whatever is, is in its Causes just
Since all things are by Fate; but purblind Man
Sees but a part o' th' Chain, the nearest Link,
His Eyes not carrying to the equal Beam
That poises all above.[18]

Then follows the dedication to Ralph, in which Franklin says he will give his "*present* thoughts of the *general state of things* in the universe," and the dedication is followed by the body of the pamphlet, which consists of two sections. The first purports to demonstrate that since God is all-wise, all-good, and all-powerful, there is no free will and no such things as vice and virtue.[19]

The argument consists of nine steps. The first two stipulate that (1) "*there is said*" to be a God who made the universe, and (2) he "*is said to be all-wise, all-good, all-powerful.*" Franklin says that he "supposes" these two propositions to be granted because they are "allowed and asserted by people of almost every sect and opinion." The argument that follows thus "will stand or fall as they are true or false." The principle of contradiction establishes the next two propositions: (3) If God is all-good, whatever he does must be good. (4) If God is all-wise, all that he does must be wise.

From these follows a fifth proposition: (5) If God is all-powerful, there can be nothing existing or acting in the universe without his consent, and that to which God consents must be good, because God is good, and therefore evil does not exist. Franklin does not deny that there are things that we *call* evil (pain, sickness, want, theft, and murder), but he does mean to say that "these and the like are not in reality *evils, ills,* or *defects* in the order of the universe." To suppose anything done contrary to the will of God is to suppose him not almighty or to suppose as the cause of evil something mightier than God. To deny that anything consented to by God is good is "entirely to destroy his two attributes of *wisdom* and *goodness.*"

We cannot repair to the philosophers' distinction between what God does and what God permits, as if God does only the good things but permits those things that are bad or not for the best. This is because if God permits an action to be done, it is because he lacks either the power or the inclination to stop it. If he lacks the power, then he is not almighty; if he lacks the inclination (in the case of an action we call evil), then either he is not good or the action is not evil. Thus, if God is good, there can be no such thing as evil. And we cannot say that God permits evil actions to be done for wise ends and purposes. This argument "destroys itself," says Franklin, "for whatever an infinitely good God hath wise ends in suffering to *be,* must be good, is thereby made good, and cannot be otherwise."

The sixth proposition stipulates (echoing Baruch Spinoza) (6) that if a creature is made by God, it must depend on God and get all of its power from God and can do nothing contrary to divine will, because God is almighty. And since what is not contrary to divine will must be agreeable to it, it must be good since God is good. Hence, a creature can only do what is good. It follows from this, says Franklin, that although creatures do things their fellow creatures call evil, and for which they suffer pains called punishments, the creature "cannot act what will be in itself really ill, or displeasing to God." That the painful consequences of the so-called evil actions "are not, as indeed they ought not to be, *punishments* or unhappinesses, will be shown hereafter."

Before turning to the seventh step, Franklin addresses the argument, made by Wollaston in *The Religion of Nature Delineated,* that what is good is what is done according to truth and what is evil is what is done contrary to truth. Thus, for example, if A steals a horse, he treats that horse as his own property when in truth it is not, so A thus commits an evil act. This argument makes no sense to Franklin. For it is also true that A is covetous and as such is moved by nature to an inclination to steal that is stronger than the fear of any punishment. And besides this, adds Franklin, "if it is proved to be a *truth,* that A has not power over his own actions, it will be indisputable that he acts according to truth, and impossible he should do otherwise."

Franklin then comments that he means not to encourage theft but only to make an argument, which will, at any rate, have no ill effect: "The order and course of things will not be affected by reasoning of this kind; and 'tis as just and necessary, and as much according to truth, for *B* to dislike and punish the theft of his horse, as it is for *A* to steal him."

The seventh proposition asserts: (7) If a creature is able only to do those things that God would have him do and cannot refuse to do what God wills, then the creature can have *"no such thing as liberty, free will or power to do or refrain an action."* (The implication here is that no creature has power simply of its own, that every creature has only that power that God gives it and directs through it.) Franklin grants (echoing Hobbes) that there is liberty in the sense of absence of opposition, but this is just like the liberty that a heavy object has to fall to the ground if it meets with nothing to hinder its fall; the fall itself is entirely necessary.

To bolster his case, however, Franklin looks at the matter from a different view. Let us grant, he says, that men are free agents in the commonsensical understanding of the term. If man is part of the great machine of the universe, then his regular acting is essential for the regular moving of the whole. (So in this respect, "good" means the good of the whole. Later Franklin shows that "good" also means "good for us.") And if he is free to choose his actions, then there is at any moment that which is best to be done and which is good, in comparison to which every other possibility is at that time evil. But in order to make the choice, however, this free agent would have to know "at one view all the intricate consequences of every action with respect to the general order and scheme of the universe, both present and future; but they are innumerable and incomprehensible by anything but omniscience." Since we cannot know these consequences, we would, as free agents, be "blundering about in the dark, and putting the scheme in disorder; for every wrong action of a part, is a defect or blemish in the order of the whole." Is it not thus necessary, concludes Franklin, that our actions should be "overruled and governed by an all-wise Providence?"

Then Franklin says, clearly borrowing from Shaftesbury:

How exact and regular is every thing in the *natural* world! How wisely in every part contrived! We cannot here find the least defect! Those who have studied the mere animal and vegetable creation, demonstrate that nothing can be more harmonious and beautiful! All the heavenly bodies, the stars and planets, are regulated with the utmost wisdom! And can we suppose less care to be taken in the order of the *moral* than in the *natural* system? It is as if an ingenious artificer, having framed a curious machine or clock, and put its many intricate wheels and powers in such a dependence on one another, that the whole might move in the most exact order and regularity, had nevertheless placed in it several other wheels endowed with an independent *self-motion*, but ignorant of the general interest of the clock; and these would every now and then be moving wrong, disordering the true movement, and making continual work for the mender; which might better be prevented, by depriving them of that power of self-motion, and placing them in a dependence on the regular part of the clock.[20]

From all this, the eighth and ninth propositions follow: (8) If there is no free will, then there is no merit and demerit in creatures. (9) Therefore, *"every creature must be equally esteemed by the creator."* There is no good reason why the Creator should prefer any of his works to another, since all are the product of his wisdom and goodness and since any defect would be contrary to his nature and his power. It is impossible for the Creator, given his will and his power, to have wanted the world to be other than it is now, so it has to be concluded that all things "exist now in a manner agreeable to his will." Thus, all things are equally good and equally esteemed by God.

Franklin closes the first section by returning to his earlier point (in the sixth proposition) that painful consequences of so-called evil actions are not punishments or unhappiness, which he there says they "indeed . . . ought not to be." He will now proceed to show, he says, "that as all the works of the creator are equally esteemed by him, so they are, as in justice they ought to be, equally used" (that is, treated by God).[21]

The second section of the pamphlet establishes this fact of equal divine use, which at this point is not clear as regards the role of justice—it is not clear if God's equal use accords with justice or follows from justice.[22] The argument consists of five propositions. First, *"when a creature is formed and endowed with life, 'tis supposed to receive a capacity of the sensation of* uneasiness *or pain."* By "'tis supposed," Franklin means (echoing Locke) that the capacity to sense unease or pain is what distinguishes "life and consciousness" from unconscious matter. Consciousness does not begin until the soul is acted upon from without and there is a subsequent feeling of pain, which is the source of actions to dispel the uneasiness. We are first moved by pain, "and the whole succeeding course of our lives is but one continued series of actions with a view to be freed from it." As soon as the spur of pain ceases, we are dead and think and act no more.

The second proposition is that pain produces a desire to be free from it, and the desire is proportional to the unease or pain. Pain or unease, therefore, is actually a necessary and beautiful part of the universe, for without it all animal creation would cease to move—would be "reduced to the condition of statues, dull and unactive." Even God agrees about the necessity and beauty of pain, Franklin argues: "And how unlikely [it is] that the inhabitants of the world ever were [without pain], or that the Creator ever designed they should be, exempt from it!" This proposition, Franklin notes, establishes on other grounds the eighth proposition of the first section: that there is no merit and demerit. "For since *freedom from uneasiness* is the end of all our actions, how is it possible for us to do any thing disinterested?" And "how can any action be meritorious of praise or dispraise, reward or punishment, when the natural principle of *self-love* is the only and the irresistible motive to it?"[23]

The third proposition is that the desire to escape pain is always fulfilled or satisfied "in the *design* or *end* of it, though not in the *manner*." For example, if I think my house is going to fall on me, I feel unease and the desire to relieve the unease, which I can do by getting out of the house. But this same end can be had if I become convinced that the house is not going to fall. Even if the infinitely varying means for expelling unease—such as fame, wealth, or power—are not attained, if the unease is "removed by some other means, the *desire* is satisfied." During our life, "we are ourselves continually removing successive uneasinesses as they arise, and the *last*, we suffer is removed by the *sweet sleep* of death." (If I remain convinced the house will fall and do not get out before it does, not to worry: Death will relieve the unease!)

The fourth proposition is that pleasure springs from the satisfaction of the desire to remove uneasiness, and the pleasure is "*great or small in exact proportion to the* desire." Since pleasure is the mind's satisfaction at the accomplishment of desire and since desires are caused by pains or uneasiness, "it follows that *pleasure* is wholly caused by *pain*, and by no other thing at all." (What about the things that satisfy our desires, we wonder?)

From this follows (says Franklin) the fifth proposition: that the "*sensation of* pleasure" is equal to or in exact proportion to the "*sensation of* pain." One of the arguments to prove that the soul outlives the body is the "generally supposed" inequality of pain and pleasure in the present, which leads us to assume the need for a "future adjustment." But in fact, since pleasure and pain are always equal, there is no need for such an adjustment, and "thus are all the works of the Creator *equally* used by him; and no condition of life or being is in itself better or preferable to another"; the king is not "more happy" than the slave and the beggar is not "more miserable" than Croesus. To illustrate: Assume A and B, both animate, and C, an inanimate piece of matter. If A gets ten degrees of pain, followed by ten of pleasure, and B gets fifteen degrees of pain followed by fifteen of pleasure, A has no reason to complain that he gets five degrees less pleasure than B, because B got five degrees more pain than A. And both A and B are on the same footing as C, because, like C, they are neither gainers nor losers.

Now against the obvious objection of common sense that we see some people "hearty, brisk, and cheerful perpetually" and others "constantly burdened with a heavy load of maladies and misfortunes, remaining for years perhaps in poverty, disgrace, or pain, and [dying] at last without any appearance of recompense," Franklin says first that we cannot trust our judgment in such matters because we are often deceived, and what appears to us to be the case turns out in fact to be the opposite. Those who appear unhappy may enjoy being thought unhappy. These are reasons, along with others that might be given, why "we cannot make a true estimate of the *equality* of the happiness and unhappiness of others" and so cannot establish this fact against the hypothesis of the argument presented so far. We cannot even be sure of judgments about our own happiness or lack thereof, since we take no mind of our pleasures and have a more vivid memory of our uneasinesses. But even if in fact we live in pain and sorrow and die by torments, the torment does not last until the last moments of life, and so we have the pleasure to behold the approach of relief, which is in exact proportion to the sum of the pain endured—a single moment of pleasure thus compensates for a lifetime of pain.

Franklin continues that it was from ignorance of the nature of pleasure and pain that the ancients conceived of Elysium. Elysium's pure pleasure is impossible in nature: Is not the pleasure of spring "made such" by the disagreeableness of the winter? In perpetual spring, would not the pleasure "pall and die upon our hands?" Franklin then turns, abruptly, to the question of the soul's condition after death.[24] Even if we allow that the soul is immaterial and thus not subject to dissolution, it is still the case that it can cease to think and hence cease to act—for instance, when we are in a sound sleep or swoon. The soul can exist, then, while it does not act. With the death of the body—and in particular, with the dissolution of the brain—the ideas contained in the brain are destroyed. With no ideas upon which to think or act, the soul, though itself not subject to destruction, ceases to think or act. "And to cease to *think* is but little different from *ceasing to be*." It is not impossible that our souls will be united to a new body and get a new set of ideas. But this latter fact will not concern us, since our identity will be lost and we will no longer be the same self but will have become "a new being."

Franklin ends the pamphlet by repeating its argument in short form: The nine propositions of the first section are summed up in five quick steps, and the five propositions of the second section are repeated in nine quick steps.[25] In the fifth step of the first summary, Franklin concludes that "*evil is hereby excluded, with all merit and demerit; and likewise all preference in the esteem of God, of one part of the creation to another.*" Before presenting the summary of the second section, Franklin makes a final remark about divine justice:

> Now our common notions of justice will tell us, that if all created things are equally esteemed by the Creator, they ought to be equally used by Him; and that they are therefore equally used, we might embrace for truth upon the credit, and as the true consequence of the foregoing argument. Nevertheless we proceed to confirm it, by showing *how* they are equally used, and that in the following manner.

So to confirm that God treats all creatures alike, the second section ensues.

Franklin concludes the summary of that second section by noting that if he were to publish this doctrine, it "would meet with but an indifferent reception."[26] Why? Because "mankind naturally and generally love to be flattered." Whatever "soothes our pride, and tends to exalt our species above the rest of the creation, we are pleased with and easily believe, when ungrateful truths shall be with the utmost indignation rejected." Franklin puts this indignation into the mouth of a supposed angry reader: "What! Bring ourselves down to an equality with the beasts of the field! With the *meanest* part of the creation! 'Tis insufferable!" To this, Franklin says that our geese are geese even though we may think them to be swans—and truth is truth even when "it sometimes prove mortifying and distasteful."

Now, THE FIRST THING TO NOTE is that although the *Dissertation* draws its conclusions from the attributes of God, the argument is in fact entirely hypothetical. The first two propositions—that there is a God and that he is all-wise, all-good, and all-powerful—are merely supposed as granted and laid down, on the grounds that they are "allowed and asserted by people of almost every sect and opinion." Franklin clearly means that they are "allowed and asserted" by almost every religious persuasion. In other words, the first two propositions are supposed because that is what most believers already believe. Not a very persuasive beginning, to say the least. Moreover, Franklin makes it clear that the entire chain of consequences, "truly drawn" from the first two propositions, "will stand or fall as they [the first two propositions] are true or false." Franklin says nothing of where he stands on these first two propositions. It is thus entirely possible that he did not believe them and thought, in fact, that all that follows "will . . . fall."

But regardless of what Franklin believed about the propositions, the argument of the *Dissertation* is noteworthy in these respects: The argument of the second section is so stupid and lame as to make that part of the *Dissertation* sheer metaphysical slapstick. Is there a living soul who could be convinced that for a person who is utterly wretched for an entire life and who then dies in torment, the beholding of relief in "the *last* moments of life" will afford an "*exquisite pleasure*" that counterbalances all that came before? Would not the wretch rather opine, "So is *this* what I get for all of my misery?" And what if the wretch dies in his sleep? Or what if he is tortured and, while the rack is still being turned, shot through the head from behind? Although some pleasures spring from the relief of pain (scratching an itch), others clearly do not (smelling a flower). Do we really think that justice consists in the equality of pleasure and pain? It is very hard not to read this part of the *Dissertation* as pure parody.

Furthermore, the second section also looks stupid in contrast to the first, which is for the most part well argued and rigorous and contains some shocking implications. If we grant the two propositions that most people accept, we soon face a powerful and disturbing conundrum: If there is in truth a God, then virtue and vice as we know them in common sense do not exist. And conversely, if virtue and vice as we know them in common sense do exist, then God cannot, at least as we think of God in the terms presupposed. It seems that we can have morality or God, but not both. Moreover, in his refutation of Wollaston's argument from truth, Franklin says by way of excuse that he argues "for the sake of argument" and not to encourage theft. Yet he follows this up with a further defense: That his argument will not change the necessary order of things and "'tis as just and necessary, and as much according to truth, for B to dislike and punish the theft of his horse, as it is for A to steal him." If I had a good horse, I would not want Ben Franklin to move in next door.

Finally, Franklin suggests two quite different arguments about God's equal esteem for and treatment of all creatures. We note the following four statements about the matter. First, in proposition six of the first section, Franklin says that what we think of as painful "punishments" of "so-called" evil actions are really not, "as indeed they ought not to be, *punishments* or unhappinesses," as "will be shown hereafter," in the second section.[27] At this point, it is not clear where the force of the "ought" comes from—just why all are equally well-off in this life. Then, in proposition nine of the first section, we get an answer in Franklin's second statement about the matter.[28] Franklin explains that God esteems all creatures equally because "no reason can be given, why the Creator should prefer in his esteem one part of His works to another, if with equal wisdom and goodness he designed and created them all, since all ill or defect, as contrary to his nature, is excluded by his power." God esteems all creatures equally because it is *reasonable* for him to do so. As regards esteem, God would seem not to have justice on his mind.

Then, in the very next paragraph, which is the brief transition to the second section, Franklin says in his third statement about the matter that he will next proceed to show "that as all the works of the Creator are equally esteemed by Him, so they are, *as in justice they ought to be*, equally used" (my emphasis).

And then, in the interval between the two summaries at the end, Franklin repeats this last point much more forcefully in his fourth statement about the matter. He says that "our common notions of justice" tell us that if all things are equally esteemed by God, "they ought to be equally used by Him; and that they are *therefore* equally used, we might embrace for truth upon the credit, and as the true consequence of the foregoing argument. Nevertheless we proceed to confirm it, by showing *how* they are equally used, and that in the following manner" (my emphasis).[29] In this last statement, Franklin says nothing about God acting as he does because he has no reason to do otherwise.

In the first three statements, we could say that God uses all creatures equally because there is no good reason for him not to, and this equal use then accords or coincides with what we human beings think (erroneously) ought in justice to be done. But one could also with some plausibility take the third statement to mean that God treats all alike *because* it is just to do so. In the fourth and last statement, however, it is possible to conclude more strongly, from Franklin's use of "therefore" and his silence about divine reason, that God uses all creatures equally simply *because* he ought to and because he is moved by "our common notions of justice." Moreover, this fact "might be" embraced for true even on the argument of the first section and without the confirmation of the second section.

Why, we wonder, does Franklin suggest two different things—that God acts from wisdom that *accords* with our erroneous notion of justice, and that God acts *because* of our common notions of justice? And if, because of divine wisdom and goodness and power, there is no merit and demerit, why refer to justice at all? Why, indeed, say that the punishment of the horse thief is as *just* as the theft of the horse? And why the ridiculous confirmation of God's equal use, in the second section, so as then to confirm that God either acts according to or because of our common (but erroneous) notions of justice?

If we look carefully, we see that the two different explanations of God's equal treatment of his creatures are consistent with the declining coherence of the argument: God esteems and also treats all creatures equally because there is no good reason not to, and this fact *accords* with our notion of justice, a notion that is erroneous because there is no merit and demerit, as is shown in the first section. The much stronger suggestion—that God treats us all equally *because* of justice as we commonly understand it—is patently inconsistent with the argument of the *Dissertation* as a whole: How can there be divine justice if there is no merit and demerit? But this just-discredited suggestion occurs in and fits with the equally discreditable and ludicrous second section, where we are told that the wretch is just as happy as the king.

This progression accords perfectly, I suggest, with the *comedy* at work in the *Dissertation* as a whole. What in the first section deserves to be parodied in the second? Not what most believers believe: that there is a first mover and that he is all-wise, all-good, and all-powerful. That's not stupid on its face. Not that all he does is both good and wise. That's not stupid either. Not that, as a consequence of his power and goodness, evil does not exist, and not that there is no such thing as free will, virtue and vice, or merit and demerit. We (believers and unbelievers) might not want to hear these things, and we might even become indignant upon hearing them, but they are not stupid or patently ludicrous. And God's equal esteem for all his creatures is neither shocking nor ludicrous, since the believer can easily believe that God loves all his creatures, even sinners and the lowliest sparrow.

But things look shaky for the conclusion that "*a creature can do nothing but what is good.*" We can think of reasons, having nothing to do with God, that evil might not exist—for instance, if people do only what they think is right and therefore act from ignorance and not from free will and hence not from evil. Again, a believer might get mad upon hearing this, but he would not necessarily laugh, since he is not asked to conclude that the horrible things these ignorant people do are "good." But that "a creature can do nothing but what is good" is a stronger statement, a statement that what is done is good. Rape, torture, and murder are *good?*

And things look really shaky for the argument for the clockwork-perfect moral order: If rape, torture, and murder are "good," then to suffer rape, torture, or murder is good as well. Tell this to our poor wretch stretched out on the rack—which is just what Franklin then does, but with arguments of such lunacy that they make us laugh. That wretch will not die not happy but, rather, furious, or with a prayer on his lips for divine justice in a world to come.

So what, or who, deserves to be and is parodied in the second section? Deism and the Deists—those who argued from the divine origin of nature and from the perfect order of nature to the fact of a *morally perfect* "system" in no need of revelation or particular providence. By the end of the first section, we are sorely tempted to ask: "Maybe the whole of creation is a morally perfect 'system,' but what about *me?*" Once we ask this simple question, the second section follows with its ludicrous answers: "Hey you on the rack, you're just fine, and God's wisdom and justice have made you as happy as the king of Siam. You might not be able to understand (since metaphysics is the last thing on one's mind while being lengthened on the rack), but in God's creation, everything is just fine with you right now because the extent of your suffering is determining the compensatory 'exquisite pleasure' that awaits you at the moment before death."

In the *Dissertation*, Franklin comically makes a very serious point: There will be no persuasive defense of God's wisdom, goodness, and power without an equally persuasive account of particular providence. Such an account of particular providence might be difficult to come by if we think strictly and deductively from divine wisdom, goodness, and power, but we will not make up for the lack of such an account by deistic and metaphysical claptrap about the morally perfect whole or "system." If these Deists are not themselves jokesters—covert atheists making fun—then they must be extremely naïve. Or, as is more likely, they deceive themselves: While rejecting particular providence metaphysically and for the sake of theoretical consistency, they unwittingly sneak it in the back door.

To see this last point, we have to return to the one real contradiction in the first section (proposition 7). Franklin says we cannot have free will because we do not have the omniscience required to grasp "all the intricate consequences of every action with respect to the general order and scheme of the universe." Yet in almost the next breath he says: "How exact and regular is every thing in the *natural* world! How wisely in every part contrived! We cannot here find the least defect. . . . All the heavenly bodies, the stars and planets, are regulated with the utmost wisdom!" We cannot know the whole. We do know the whole. The contradiction is obscured by Franklin's poetic (and Shaftesburian) presentation of its second term. But once we notice it, we see that it is too big to ascribe to Franklin's youth. It is preposterous to think he did not see it. Moreover, once we see it, we are forced to think twice about the issue of the "whole" that is either known or not known. When we do, we discover a subtle and telling shift in the argument of the first section, and this shift discloses what is wrong with deistic talk of a morally perfect system.

In proposition 5 of the first section, Franklin says, "that there are both things and actions to which we give the name of *evil*, is not here denied, as *pain, sickness, want, theft, murder*, etc., but that these and the like are not in reality *evils, ills*, or *defects* in the order of the universe, is demonstrated in the next section, as well as by this and the following proposition." Here, Franklin seems clearly to refer, as he said to Ralph, to "the *general state of things* in the universe." And thus he seems clearly to mean that the general whole may be perfect at the expense of its parts—just as the beehive is maintained through the suicidal stings of the bees.

But in proposition 7 of the first section (and as is "demonstrated" in the ludicrous second section), he speaks of "*every action* with respect to the general order and scheme of the universe" and says that we can see that the natural world is "in *every part*" wisely contrived (my emphasis), and we can reason from this fact about the "natural system" to the "moral system." Here, he implies that every single thing and motion in the universe is good, even the bee's suicide for that bee—and it's this claim that prompts the ludicrous "explanation" of the second section showing that the wretch on the wheel is as happy as a king.

It would be one thing simply to say that God made this beautiful beehive called the universe and we bees suffer and die as part of its internal motion. But, at least as Franklin presents it, the Deists do not just leave their account of creation at that. And so the *Dissertation* slides from the good of the whole, considered by itself and in indifference to the parts, to the exact and regular goodness of "every part" of the moral "system."

With the subtle slide or shift, Franklin shows, without broad comedy, that when the Deists speak of the "goodness" of the whole order of nature, they are of course thinking in moral terms. And if they think in moral terms, they cannot really think of individuals as suicidal and expendable bees with nothing, especially justice, coming to them. Again, somehow the bee's sacrifice for the good of the whole must also be good for the bee. So the Deists say, along with Dryden, that "whatever is, is in its Causes *just*" (my emphasis). If the Deists explain this claim without particular providence, as indeed they do, they could do no better than the ridiculous pain-and-pleasure argument of the second section. So again, as Franklin implies in the *Dissertation*, the Deists, unless they are unbelieving jokesters, must be powerfully inclined to deceive themselves and unknowingly sneak particular providence in (even if ridiculously) by the back door. However they might deny the fact in theory, they too cannot really abide a world in which divine justice does not obtain for each and every individual as an aspect of divine goodness. In the *Dissertation*, Deism is the butt of comedy because it presumes that divine justice is at work in the world but cannot explain the fact on its own grounds without lapsing into absurdities—not the least of which is the patent contradiction between the nonexistence of merit and demerit and the claim that "whatever is, is in its Causes just."[30]

In the *Autobiography*, Franklin tells us that publishing the *Dissertation* was "another erratum." It is not immediately clear, however, just how the *Dissertation* was an error and who was harmed by it. It could have been among the arguments that corrupted Ralph, to whom the piece was dedicated. This could be true whether or not Ralph missed the obvious comedy of the piece. And if it did corrupt Ralph, it might have only partly contributed to the fact, since Ralph could well have been a happy victim of Franklin's Socratic refutations prior to leaving with Franklin for London. Indeed, Ralph was at the time of the departure abandoning his wife and thus already something of a scoundrel. Franklin intimates that Ralph would agree with the *Dissertation*, since in the dedication he tells Ralph that he knows his "scheme will be liable to many objections from a less discerning reader than your self; but it is not designed for those who can't understand it."[31]

On the other hand, we might reasonably suppose that the piece would have corrupted not so much Ralph but the general public had it become widely available—it cannot be good for them to hear that stealing horses is just, especially if in hearing this they do not understand the whole treatise. But corrupting the public turns out not to be much of a danger, at least according to what Franklin tells us in the *Dissertation* itself.

There, Franklin says that since the *Dissertation* concludes that we are no better than the beasts of the field, the treatise will, since it ruffles human pride, meet with an "indifferent reception." By this Franklin means not that it will be ignored but, rather, that it will be "with the utmost indignation rejected." Now it is perhaps possible that parts of the pamphlet might have been believed by some, and all of it by a very few who could understand it, and they might have thus been corrupted. But this cannot be the most serious danger posed by the piece, since most who read it would be moved not to corruption but to indignation on behalf of common sense.

Franklin here comically understates the issue: The conclusion is that God esteems all of his creatures equally—that he loves them all equally—and this is hardly a revolting or shocking idea. But what about the claim that horse theft (not to mention rape, torture, and murder) is just? That would seem guaranteed to outrage our common sense and to move those who hear it to indignation against Franklin. Who was most likely to be harmed (the "ill tendency" reported to Vaughn) by the *Dissertation?* None other than Ben Franklin himself—but the danger loomed from the good people, not from those few he might have corrupted.

So here is the situation: We know from the *Autobiography* as well as from the *Dissertation* that Franklin argued explicitly in the latter that virtue and vice are empty distinctions, "no such things existing." We know from the *Dissertation* that the danger in making this argument was primarily moral indignation directed at Franklin. And yet the *Autobiography* tells us nothing of the step Franklin took to protect himself from the "ill tendency" remarked of to Vaughn: burning all of the pamphlets but the one Franklin evidently secured from Lyons.

We now can conclude with confidence that Franklin was, at the time he wrote the *Dissertation*, still practicing his aggressive Socratic refutations, since he would not have turned to Socratic method number two and *then* have written and published the *Dissertation* with its shocking and infuriating claims about virtue and vice and just horse theft. But he also had not completely given up the "pre-Socratic" and less guarded refutations—in the case of the metaphysical *Dissertation*, we see direct, positive, and shocking confutation, not the conversational dialectics of the sham humble doubter.

But Franklin's nonchalance in the *Autobiography* makes it seem that this last, positive confutation posed no serious danger to himself. Indeed, it paved the way for his introduction to London's intellectual circles. If we consider the *Autobiography* and the *Dissertation* and the letter to Vaughn together, we are surprised by the *Dissertation*'s positive and shocking tone, by the *Autobiography*'s nonchalant indifference to the danger to Franklin posed by this tone, by the *Autobiography*'s astounding silence about what would have been the exculpatory burning remarked to Vaughn, and by the fact, revealed in the *Autobiography*, that as far as Franklin sees, the *Dissertation*'s only problem is not that it is a danger to himself or an erratum whose amends are worth mentioning but, rather, that it might possibly have contained an insinuating error that crept in unperceived.[32] These facts are not easy to discern and assemble. But once we do, they are suddenly obvious.

We can thus with some confidence conclude the following: While in London, Franklin was still at his aggressive Socratic refutations, having learned the lesson of too much positive disputatiousness. But then, again while in London, he took one more stab at the more risky disputatiousness and published the shocking but also slapstick parody of Deism, borrowing from Spinoza, Hobbes, Locke, and Shaftesbury. This got him introduced to the likes of Mandeville, and he then burned (or at least claims to have burned) the copies, thus protecting his briefly exposed flank. But he wants the careful readers of this parody to focus not just on its obvious burlesque of Deism or on the brief danger to himself but also, more seriously, on the insinuating error that creeps in unperceived. The latter is the sore thumb that sticks out the most. These writings are commonly subject to great uncertainty. But that uncertainty is not obvious and in our faces—it sneaks in by way of an error that is hard to see.

We have to look at the *Dissertation* with an eye to error, but we have to look for an error that is sneaky and hard to perceive. Now in this light, we first have to admit the obvious: The deistic argument of the first section of the *Dissertation* is clever and (with the exception of the contradiction regarding knowledge of the whole) valid and consistent. But even so, it is not in general convincing, and it is not at all hard to see why. Franklin himself points out this very fact. In the dedication to Ralph, he says, "I need not give you any caution to distinguish the hypothetical parts of the argument

from the conclusive: you will easily perceive what I design for demonstration, and what for probability only."[33]

In fact, the whole argument is merely probable, since the first two crucial
propositions are "supposed" granted and laid down as the foundation of the
argument, and all else that follows "will stand or fall as they are true or
false." And in proposition 7 of the first section—the one that concludes
against free will—Franklin follows the Hobbesian argument, that liberty is
the absence of opposition to a necessary event, with an "argument in another view." This other argument is the Shaftesburian and favorite deistic
argument that "as man is a part of this great machine, the universe, his regular acting is requisite to the regular moving of the whole," and that "those
who have studied the mere animal and vegetable creation, demonstrate that
nothing can be more harmonious and beautiful" and that the universe is
completely ordered and that we cannot suppose less order in "the *moral* than
in the *natural* system." We cannot but remember that Philoclerus appealed
to those who contemplate the nature of animals to defend the possibility of
ongoing and miraculous divine revelation. And apart from that fact, it is
clear even here that the supposed great machine is no real challenge to orthodox believers in the miracles of revelation, particular providence, and divine rewards and punishments.

First, that reason discloses an order to nature does not by itself rule out
the possibility of miracles. On the contrary, miracles are, by definition,
events outside the regular courses of nature and hence presume the very regularity that is here presented as evidence against them. Second, even if the
world appears to be regular to those who have studied the mere animal and
vegetable creation and the heavenly bodies, stars, and planets, this fact cut
no ice with John Calvin, with whose doctrines the Presbyterian Franklin
was undoubtedly familiar.[34] For Calvin, faith in the active and miracle-
working God allows the manifest irregularity of the world (if you look
closely, you can see that the regular change of the season proceeds irregularly) to bear witness to miraculous, divine power.[35] And thus, we cannot
with any confidence reason from a supposed absence of divine intervention
into nature to a similar absence of divine intervention into human affairs
and thence to a supposedly self-subsisting and divine moral order.

And most important for the *Dissertation*, the mysteries that attend orthodoxy (that there is free will and evil in a world governed by an all-good, all-
wise, and all-powerful God) are hardly foreign to our common experience
(the ways of God are not fully known to us), but the "mysteries" of Deism as
Franklin presents it (the world is ruled by divine justice but there is no such
thing as merit; the world includes things merely given the name of evil and
rape, torture, and murder are good) are simply ridiculous and incompatible

with our common moral experience. And this is not to mention the comically absurd argument of the second section, where it is confirmed that God treats all creatures alike and the wretch on the rack is as well-off as the king, apart from divine rewards in a world to come.

In the *Dissertation* Franklin's ironic rhetoric works backward: The broad comedy on the surface prompts us to think our way through to the butt of that comedy, and the much more subtle shifts and slides then corroborate our conclusion about that butt, the Deists. The comic second section parodies the deistic moralism of the first section—the fact that when the Deists speak of the whole of creation as a "moral system," they cannot really give up on divine justice for each and every cosmic bee. That this is the problem Franklin wants us to see is then borne out by the subtle change, from the first section to the second, in the meaning of divine justice—first that God's equal treatment of his creatures *accords* with our common but erroneous notions of justice, and then that God's equal treatment of his creatures is *caused* by our common notions of justice.

We thus see the perfect contradiction between the essay's theme—that our common notions of justice are erroneous—and the motto from Dryden that "whatever is, is in its Causes just." How could our common notions of justice be erroneous if God obeys them, and how can there be justice if there is no merit and demerit? And thus we see why the Deists in the same breath say that we cannot and then that we can apprehend the whole of God's creation. When they say we cannot, it is to deny free will and to speak as if God's whole is good at the expense of its parts. But when they say we can, it is because they cannot think that we—or they, for that matter—are seen by God as expendable bees. The problem with the Deists is that their "moralism" contradicts our common moral experience, and even they cannot rest easy with this result and so resort to absurdities to square the result with our common moral opinions.

If God's power merely accords with justice, then it is not absolutely necessary that it always be just. On the one hand, we think of God as all-powerful and limited by nothing. But on the other hand, we think of God as all-good and therefore perfectly just. It is not clear theoretically that he can really be both, and so, theoretically, we cannot be absolutely sure that God is fully just—we cannot be absolutely sure whether we should worship God out of love of justice, whose foremost *servant* is God, or out of fear of the power of God, whose will we cannot ultimately know and whose good side (whether just or unjust) we want to be on.

The comedy suggests, and the shift from accordance to necessity confirms, that though we might think of God's power as unlimited and that he may not always be absolutely good and just, in our hearts we really cannot *believe* this to be true. And if we think in more cosmological terms, as the Deists surely do, in our hearts we want the whole to be good not just as a whole but as a collection of parts, one of which each one of us is. We'll take God's absolute goodness over his power. But if we want both, as the Deists do, we'll jump through absurd theoretical hoops to explain how God's goodness still works for each of us in the world.[36] So when we're angry with God, it's not because we think of him as simply harmful—as if he were a very powerful and capricious spider. We don't get angry at wild beasts; we just try to tame them or placate them as best we can. So perhaps we're angry precisely because we think God is and must be just, but for some reason he has not fully heard our case (forget about infinite wisdom). In the *Dissertation*, the subtle theoretical errors and contradictions are driven by what the comedy discloses—a longing of the human heart.

In the *Dissertation* the contradictions and shifts and slides corroborate what the broad comedy suggests, and the broad comedy makes sense of the obvious impotence of the argument in the face of orthodox faith. If we think of the subtle contradictions, shifts, and slides as errors, then they are not wholly insinuating if they corroborate what is evident from the surface of the text— the slapstick parody that, rather, smacks us between the eyes. We cannot yet say, therefore, that we have uncovered the insinuating error that Franklin tells us is common to metaphysical reasoning. Is there something more, some error deeper and even harder to see than just the metaphysical propensity to fall prey to the longing of the human heart? If so, then there is really but one candidate for consideration. Granting that if God *must* be just, then he cannot be all-powerful, how can it be an error to believe that God must be just?

IT COMES AS NO SURPRISE that the next metaphysical piece identified by the *Autobiography*, the *Articles of Belief and Acts of Religion*, presumes a just but less-than-all-powerful God.[37]

A moment's glance at this bizarre piece shows that it belongs in the category of metaphysical reasoning. Despite its title and its role in Franklin's purported worship, it has the form of a deduction from first principles.

The first principles are stipulations of Franklin's belief (just as the *Dissertation* began with a stipulation of what almost all believers believe) and some acts of his imagination as to the infinite space of the universe. Franklin believes that there is one supreme and most perfect being that is father of the gods, for he believes that there are many degrees of beings inferior and superior to man. When he imagines the infinite universe, with all of its other worlds, this one of ours seems almost nothing. When he thinks this, he imagines it a great vanity to think that the supremely perfect being would care about man, and since he (Franklin) cannot have a positive or clear idea about something infinite and incomprehensible, he cannot "conceive other-wise" than that the infinite father expects or requires no worship from us and that he is infinitely above any such worship. However, there is in man a natural inclination to worship some unseen power, and since men being en-dowed with reason are superior to the animals of the world we know, there-fore "I think it seems required of me, and my duty, as a man, to pay divine regards to SOMETHING."

Franklin conceives that "the infinite" has created many gods vastly supe-rior to man, and he further thinks that these gods can better conceive "the infinite's" perfections and render "more rational and glorious praise" than can we. The created gods may be immortal or mortal, but each is "exceeding wise and good, and very powerful," and each has made a sun and system of planets. The wise and good god that made our system, "our" God, is the one Franklin proposes for the object of his praise and adoration. For Franklin "conceives" that God has some human passions and that since he has given men reason with which we can observe "his wisdom in the creation, he is not above car-ing for us, being pleased with our praise, and offended when we slight him, or neglect his glory." Franklin then says that for many reasons he conceives that God is "a *good being*" and that, since he, Franklin, should be happy to have such a wise, good, and powerful being as his friend, he then allows himself to "consider in what manner I shall make myself most acceptable to him."

Next to the praise that is due to his wisdom, Franklin believes that God delights in the happiness of his creatures, and since virtue is essential for happiness, God delights when he sees Franklin virtuous because he is pleased with his happiness. And since God has created many things de-signed solely for man's delight, God is not offended to see his children "so-lace themselves in any manner of pleasant exercises and innocent delights, and I think no pleasure innocent that is to man hurtful." Thus, Franklin loves God for his goodness, adores him for his wisdom, and hopes that he will not fail to praise God continually, as is his due and as return for favors and goodness. He resolves to be virtuous in order to be happy and so he will please God, "who is delighted to see [him] happy."

Then follows a section that Franklin calls the "Adoration," praising God for all of the attributes derived from the first principles—including that God hates treachery and deceit, malice and revenge, intemperance, and every other "hurtful vice" in his creatures and that he loves justice, sincerity, friendship, benevolence, and every virtue.[38] This is followed by a suggestion that Franklin read some work, such as John Ray's "Wisdom of God in the Creation" or the "Demonstration of the Being of a God" by the archbishop of Cambray (Fénelon), or else spend some time in silent contemplation and then sing John Milton's *Hymn to the Creator*, which is printed as the sequel.

The "Adoration" is followed by a "petition" in which Franklin asks for his God to help him have the virtues and avoid the vices—including atheism and infidelity.[39] The "Petition" is introduced by a brief "Prelude": Franklin has reason to hope and believe that God's goodness will not "withhold from me a suitable share of temporal blessings, if by a VIRTUOUS and HOLY life I merit his favor and kindness." He thus asks for help in pursuing virtue and eschewing vice, rather than anything more specific, since we cannot be certain that the specific things we might pray for will turn out to be real goods were we to possess them.[40]

The Articles of Belief concludes with a brief section called "Thanks" in which Franklin thanks his God for peace, liberty, food, clothes, corn, wine, milk, every healthy nourishment, air, light, fire, water, knowledge, literature, every useful art, his friends and their prosperity, the fewness of his enemies, all God's innumerable benefits, life, reason, speech, health, joy, and every pleasant hour.[41]

Now, unless we think Franklin had completely lost his marbles, this piece is at least as deliberately funny and tongue-in-cheek as the second section of the Dissertation. The argument is silly to the point of being moronic: The most supreme and perfect God would not care for us (shades of Aristotle and Lucretius). But in all men there is a natural inclination to worship some unseen power, and since human beings are reasonable, Franklin therefore thinks it is his duty to pay divine regards to something. Since Franklin is reasonable, his reason compels him to this perfect non sequitur.[42]

From this duty he conceives that there are many lesser creator gods who are wise and good and who care for us and answer our prayers for virtue as the means to our happiness. We make a powerful friend of "our" God, and receive from him a suitable share of temporal blessings, if we merit these blessings by leading a virtuous and holy life. How do we get that virtue? By leading a holy life—that is, by asking for God's help in securing virtue. We thus pray for the means to get what we pray for—the real goods that only God decides we should get, since we cannot know if the rewards we pray for will or will not be real goods. God is not offended to see us solace ourselves in pleasant exercise and innocent delight, but only he knows what they really are!

God hates treachery, deceit, malice, revenge, intemperance, and every hurtful vice (are there nonhurtful vices?) in his creatures. And he loves justice, sincerity, friendship, benevolence and every virtue (presumably also in his creatures, since God needs none of these things, or perhaps this lesser God needs justice too, and so loves it). But why does God hate these vices and love these virtues in his creatures? Because the virtues cause happiness, and presumably the vices cause misery, in his creatures. God sees the virtues as means to happiness, not as goods in themselves. We have yet to consider the substance of Franklinian virtue, but suffice it to say that the argument here depends on the unproved assumption that virtue is a necessary means for happiness. Says Franklin, "without virtue* man can have no happiness in this world." (The asterisk asks us to "see Junto Paper of Good and Evil, etc.")[43]

But this unproved assumption aside, the whole kit and caboodle of the *Articles* depends on our knowing God and his nature on the basis of our natural urge to worship something. The central argument of the *Articles* has thus exactly the same non sequitur form as the unpublished and lost 1730 metaphysical piece that argued the case for the existence of good and evil and particular providence simply from the existence of prayer. (Since people pray, what they pray to and for must exist. Since men have the natural urge to worship, what they worship must exist.) With the idiotic *Articles*, however, the non sequitur amounts also to a wonderful joke.

Franklin starts out by declaring his belief in a supremely perfect being who is "author and father" of all the gods. But that belief is then explained in the following three moves: (1) The supreme being is incomprehensible, utterly indifferent to men, and above worship (well, not so incomprehensible after all, since we know of his indifference and superiority to worship). (2) There is in men "something like a natural principle" that inclines them to devotion or the worship of "some unseen power." And therefore he (Franklin) thinks it required of him and a duty to worship something. (3) And so he "conceives then" that the "infinite," the supremely perfect being, created lesser gods that can worship him, and these gods are the ones who create systems of planets, including our own. And the god who created our own is the one Franklin describes (exceedingly wise and good and very powerful) and the one he worships and is really happy to have as his friend (like the strongest kid on the playground).

Now if we stop laughing and actually think carefully about this argument, we recognize it as exactly the same argument Hobbes makes *against* the existence of active "powers invisible" whom we worship and who intervene in our lives.[44] Says Hobbes: Reason can conceive an incomprehensible first cause. But beyond that, all religion springs from a natural seed: the desire to worship the powers invisible to which we attribute our fates in this world. That is, the intervention by active gods is a figment of the human imagination—a figment of the natural urge to worship things we cannot see but take to be causes in the world.

Anyone familiar with Hobbes—and Franklin certainly was—knows that the argument about the natural origins of divine intervention is an attack on miracles. Divine intervention (including revelation) is not an inexplicable miracle; rather, it can be explained naturally, as a figment arising from the natural constitution of the human mind. Hobbes learned this from Bacon, and Shaftesbury saw it in Bacon and called him an atheist for saying it out loud.[45] In the *Articles*, the very heart of the argument for particular providence is the central rationalist argument against revelation and particular providence. More metaphysical follies, I am afraid. And Franklin was still up to them two years later when he put the Deist-busting argument in favor of orthodoxy and against Hobbes in the mouth of Philoclerus.

Franklin says that after writing the *Dissertation* and the patently stupid opposing piece on prayer, he rejected metaphysics out of disgust for its great uncertainties. He had just as much reason to reject the *Articles*, and out of the same disgust. But in all three cases, he would have been *genuinely* disgusted only if he had at one time really taken them seriously. That, I submit, is very hard to believe. With his contradicting sleight of hand, Franklin makes us consider that, for some reason, he did *not* take the *Dissertation* seriously when he wrote it. The consideration is borne out by the comic character of the piece. And the metaphysical *Articles* in support of particular providence is every bit as screwy and laughably absurd as is the *Dissertation* that opposed particular providence. And the *Dissertation* is not even in full opposition to particular providence (some kind of divine justice operating in the world for each and every individual).

The Deists are subject to burlesque because they cannot help sneaking divine justice for each and every individual, particular providence, in the back door. We cannot establish from any of the metaphysical pieces that Franklin ever believed in that providence at all. Nor can we conclude that he ever took any of the metaphysical writings seriously. On the contrary, all the evidence points to his comic mockery of the pretenses of reason, whether on the side of radical Deism or on the side of the more orthodox view, to decide the issue metaphysically or physically.[46]

Aldridge is correct to say that Franklin rejected metaphysics. But he did so by the time he wrote the *Dissertation*. And the alternative was not practical and humanistic morality and religion, but whatever he learned or was learning from the Socratic refutations.

In the Articles there is broad and obvious comedy, a subtle and central joke, and great uncertainty. But there is not, so far as I can tell, an insinuating error. If such errors are "*common* in metaphysical reasonings," it follows that they are not simply ubiquitous. However, there is another comical metaphysical piece, also in favor of particular providence, in which (as we are told would be the case with the *Dissertation*) we find what looks at first like such insinuating error: the Junto essay, probably written in 1732, "On the Providence of God in the Government of the World."[47]

Franklin begins the essay with an amusing double entendre. After some ironic opening remarks about the weakness of his intellect by comparison to that of his audience, Franklin says that he will appeal to no

> books or men how sacred soever; because I know that no authority is more convincing to men of reason than the authority of reason itself. It might be judged an affront to your understandings should I go about to prove this first principle, the existence of a deity and that he is the creator of the universe, for that would suppose you ignorant of what all mankind in all ages have agreed in.

In the blink of an eye Franklin says he will respect only the authority of reason, and then says we should grant as reasonable "what all mankind in all ages have agreed in." "All mankind" obviously does not mean all men, since in the sequel Franklin refers to the existence of men who "blaspheme him their Creator in the most horrible manner," and since it is reasonable to think that some who blaspheme horribly do not just hate or disrespect God but, rather, do not believe in God.

Franklin begins by appealing to the authority of reason alone and then interprets that reason to consist in what most men have always agreed to. Shades of the *Dissertation*, where he supposes that there is a God because that is what all believers believe. We are thus forced to wonder what the affront to the authority of reason might be: to assume his audience ignorant of what most men believe, to attempt a proof of what most men believe, or to think that the fact of their belief establishes the reasonableness of that belief? The essay thus begins with more of Franklin's comic sleight of hand.

At any rate, the essay thus begins with the supposition that God exists, based on the fact that mankind in all ages has agreed that God exists. Even though he does not make the point explicitly, as he did in the *Dissertation*, the conclusion of the essay is entirely dependent on this prior agreement. Franklin does not say where he stands on this agreement, but it soon becomes clear, again, that the agreement of all mankind is not simply universal.

Franklin then "observes" three things about God: "1. That he must be a being of great wisdom; 2. That he must be a being of great goodness and 3. That he must be a being of great power."[48] He then proceeds to defend these three observations. Turning to God's wisdom, he says not that it is *great* but that it is *infinite*, as is demonstrated by God's "admirable order and disposition of things"—the heavenly bodies, the earth and its elements, the structure of animal bodies, and their adaptation to life on the earth, in the air, or in the water. The most "exquisite human wisdom" cannot find fault with this order or say that it might be better, and when we consider it attentively, we are "astonished and swallowed up with admiration."

Turning then to God's goodness, Franklin shows only that it is *great*, with no mention of its being infinite, on the grounds that God gives life to so many creatures, who show that this is a great benefit by "their unwillingness to leave it." Other proofs of this great goodness are God's provision of food and useful things such as water, air, light, and sunshine to almost all animals, and vegetables, iron, and useful animals to men, each of which, if we consider them, fill us with love and affection. Again we see Franklin's tongue well in his cheek: There is no mention here of the facts that we have to work hard for vegetables and even harder for iron and that for every useful animal there are many others that make our lives miserable, such as the bugs that eat our vegetables, the wolves that eat our useful animals, and the lions, tigers, and bears that eat us.

Then, turning finally to God's power, Franklin again argues not merely that it is great but that it is infinite, as is demonstrated by the fact that God has formed such vast masses of matter as the earth and the sun and the planets and governs their prodigious motions and speeds. It is easy to think of this power if we consider God's infinite knowledge and wisdom, for if we feeble minds can make acid and gunpowder, what power must God possess who knows the nature of everything in the universe and can make new natures as well?

After presenting these three arguments, Franklin says: "Agreeing then that the world was at first made by a Being of *infinite Wisdom, Goodness and Power*, which Being we call God; the state of things ever since and at this time must be in one of these four following manners, viz" (my emphasis).[49] And then follows the bulk of the argument about the nature of providence.

Now here I recommend to the reader that you keep one hand on your wallet. It was never argued that God is *infinitely* good, only *greatly* good. Moreover, the very evidence for God's great goodness—the reluctance of every living creature, including mankind, to leave the benefit of life—is also possible evidence against God's infinite goodness. We not only live, but we and every other living creature also die, and the discussion that follows concerns just whose fault that might be and what it means for God and man. Thus, the argument to follow depends on an argumentative shell game: the quick slide from the argument for God's great goodness to the undemonstrated "agreement" about God's infinite goodness.

On the basis of the sneaky "agreement" as to infinite divine wisdom, goodness, and power, Franklin lays out four positions on particular providence.[50] (1) God ordained everything and allows for no creature's free agency. (2) God ordained nothing and left everything to general nature and the events of his creature's free agency, which he never alters or interrupts. (3) God decreed some things unchangeably and left other things to general nature and free agency, which also he never alters or interrupts. (4) God sometimes interferes by his particular providence and sets aside things that otherwise would have followed from the course of general nature or free agency.

If the first position is asserted, says Franklin, two unacceptable consequences follow.[51] First, God undermines his own power to act and so turns himself into a nongod, no better than a wooden or stone idol, with no reason to be worshipped. Second, God must have decreed all manner of evils and injuries committed by men, including the most horrible blasphemies, and must have decreed that the "greatest part of mankind" should pray in public and in private but to no avail. "Surely," says Franklin, "it is not more difficult to believe the world was made by a God of wood or stone, than that the God who made the world should be such a God as this."

If the second position is asserted, the result is again twofold and unacceptable.[52] First, God must utterly hide himself from his creation and take no notice of natural and moral proceedings. Or second, he must indeed take notice, in which case he looks on as an indifferent spectator while virtuous men ("heroes in virtue") labor and suffer hardships and miseries while endeavoring to serve the good of others and in order to please God and earn his favors, for which they pray. But the spectator-God will think that those heroes will have to take such favors as chance provides, since he does not intervene in their affairs. And thus he watches other men commit all kinds of evil and harm to others, to which he can say that if chance should reward these evildoers he will not punish them. He sees the just and the innocent and the beneficent in the clutches of wicked oppressors, and when the good pray for deliverance, he only says that there is nothing he can do, it is none of his business, and he does not regard such things. As with the first position, Franklin asks how we can imagine a wise and infinitely good (not to mention even very good) being to be like this, and how we can imagine his power, wisdom, and goodness to have become idle in this way.

If the third position is granted, the result is still similar to the results of the first two.[53] God "ungods" himself and has nothing to do; he is "no more to be regarded than a lifeless image, than Dagon, or Baal, or Bell and the Dragon." The being who is most able to act (is powerful), knows best how to act (is wise), and would always act best (is good) becomes idle—an absurdity that we cannot swallow "without doing the greatest violence to common reason, and all the faculties of the understanding."

We are thus "necessarily driven" to the fourth position, says Franklin.[54] God does sometimes interfere in human affairs by his particular providence, changing the way things would have transpired by the unimpeded course of nature or by human free agency. Since some may doubt the existence of human free agency, Franklin provides just one "short argument" in favor of free will: Since God is acknowledged to be infinitely powerful, wise, and good and also himself a free agent, we will not deny that he has given us some part of his wisdom, power, and goodness, and if he has, then is it impossible for him to have given us some part of his free agency? It is enough for Franklin to show that it is not impossible for men to have free will and that no one can demonstrate that it is improbable. Although much more could be said to demonstrate that men are in some way free agents, Franklin says that he will reserve the topic "for another separate discourse hereafter if I find occasion."

Continuing with the main argument at hand, Franklin says that if God does not use his particular providence, it is either because he cannot or will not. Take the example of a nation in the grip of a terrible tyrant, whose people pray for divine deliverance. If God cannot deliver them, then we deny his infinite power, which we "at first acknowledged." If he will not, then we deny his infinite goodness. It is thus "highly reasonable," Franklin abruptly concludes, to believe in particular providence because it is absurd to deny it. Franklin concludes that since it is unreasonable to deny particular providence, that providence is "the foundation of all true religion," and we should love and revere God for his goodness, thank him for his benefits, adore his wisdom, fear his power, and pray for his favor and protection. This religion "will be a powerful regulator of our actions, give us peace and tranquility within our own minds, and render us benevolent, useful and beneficial to others."

Now here Franklin's tongue is clearly and broadly in his cheek. The crux of the argument is that reason requires us to exclude the possibilities that God cannot or will not intervene to save the nation in the tyrant's claws. The inevitable conclusion is thus that if good men pray for relief from the tyrant, an infinitely powerful, wise, and good God *always* answers their prayer. But this, even more than a divine refusal to intervene in this or that case, is absurd on its face. Tyrants may suffer in some world to come, but to say that God always answers prayers for deliverance from them on this earth is enough to make any sensible person laugh. And this is not to mention the problem of why an infinitely powerful, wise, and good God would allow tyrants to torture his creatures in the first place.

Close inspection shows this essay to be the mirror image of the *Dissertation*. Like the conclusion of the *Dissertation*'s second section (the wretch dies as happy as the king of Siam), the central conclusion of this essay (God always rescues nations from the tyrant) is comically absurd and an affront to reason and common experience. Again, we would have to take Franklin for a dunce to think he ever took this argument seriously. And like the *Disserta-*

tion, with its corroborating slides from the good of the whole to the good of the parts and from God's accordance with justice to God's necessary justice, this essay also contains a corroborating argumentative slide, also having to do with the character of divine justice: the slippery shell-game move from the argument for God's great goodness to the "agreement" on God's infinite goodness. I have brought this slide to the reader's attention, but it took me more than a few readings of the essay before I noticed it. It is hard to see, but once one does, it is equally hard to think that Franklin just goofed and did not know what he was doing in the course of three carefully written paragraphs. The move is too artful and its implications too important for us to think of it as a mindless slip.

If God is greatly but not infinitely good, then we can, I think, make better sense of our common moral intuitions as regards divine justice. A greatly good God could give men free will, which would make him the ultimate but not the proximate cause of the evils men commit, and that greatly good God could then punish the wicked (perhaps with eternal fire, perhaps with something less) and reward the virtuous (perhaps with eternal happiness, perhaps with something less). We can then at least make consistent sense of our common view that God with his providence rewards virtue and punishes vice, if not in this world (as when he refuses to intervene against the tyrant), then in the world to come.

But with the slide to the agreement that God is infinitely good, we wind up with exactly the three postulates of the *Dissertation* that led to no free will and no virtue and vice. In the essay "On the Providence of God," Franklin simply ignores the conclusions drawn consistently from these postulates by the *Dissertation*. Moreover, once Franklin makes the slide, the same silly and absurd things are asserted: God somehow makes everything just fine right here and now—just as the wretch is as happy as the king of Siam, so God always answers the prayers of those who beseech him to free them from the tyrant's claws.

We have now to ask: If the assumption that God is but greatly good in fact makes the best sense of our ordinary experience, and if it does not involve us in the absurd final move (God always redeems us from the tyrant), why the slide to God's infinite goodness, which is precisely to the *Dissertation*'s proposition that God, the first mover and maker of the universe, is "allowed and asserted by people of almost every sect and opinion" to be all-wise, all-good, and all-powerful?[55] If "*almost* every sect and opinion" believes that God is all-good, then some do not, and it cannot be impossible for them to conceive of God as merely greatly good. But with the slide, Franklin indicates again, it seems to me, that most men simply *want* God to be all-good and thus think it absurd to say that he is not.

Why? If God is all-good, then it is certain that my good is in his sights, right now, whatever else might be the theological consequences for God's infinite power. According to Franklin, this goes not just for ordinary believers but also even for the Deists, who, according to the *Dissertation's* burlesque, want God to have "answered" the poor wretch with a compensating end-of-life pleasure, so that "whatever is" is in fact "in its Causes just." The only interpretation that makes sense is that people—ordinary folks and metaphysical Deists alike—want divine justice so much for themselves that they want God's infinite goodness over all other divine attributes. Whatever people might say, they are not in their hearts fully satisfied if God's power merely accords with justice, because we cannot then be sure that such accordance is strictly necessary. Rather, they want God to be infinitely good and thus necessarily just—they want God's power to be bound by the demands of justice.[56]

Now, that we think of God as all-good and all-just is obvious and hardly an insinuating and hard-to-see fact. In the *Dissertation* and in "On the Providence of God," it marches in with a flourish. And so the slide from great to infinite goodness looks insinuating, but (again) it is not really so because it corroborates what is evident from the broad comical conclusion about the nation in the tyrant's claws. This is just what we saw with the subtle contradictions, shifts, and slides in the *Dissertation*.

But at this point we can see something new about the contradictions, shifts, and slides as they work in the two essays. This new fact is not obvious, easy to see, or announced boldly on the surface of the text: It is the general fact that our hope for justice *determines* how we think about God. That fact *is* insinuated by way of the corroborating slides. But again, how is this insinuated fact about belief, the connection between our longing for justice and our understanding of God, an error? Why should it matter if our faith in God is preceded and determined by our longing for justice? Would a just God really care if this were so? Could we not say that according to God's providence, he planted the love of justice in our hearts both for the sake of that justice and so that we would then hearken to him? But then how could this be an error first on God's part and then on ours?

WE CANNOT SAY—so I do not claim—that Franklin wrote the metaphysical pieces with a prospective eye on the *Autobiography*. We can say—and I do claim—that the *Autobiography* is retrospective, and so too is the trail to these texts that Franklin blazed in the *Autobiography* and the letter to Vaughn. And thus, so too is the emphasis that, once it emerges, sticks out like a sore thumb: that the problem with the *Dissertation* was not its danger to Franklin or to others and not a moral erratum whose amends were worth mentioning in the *Autobiography* but, rather, its probable infection by an insinuating error that is common to metaphysical thinking.

Franklin was quite young when he wrote his metaphysical pieces. But they are far from immature. They consist of his multilayered comedy, ironic form, and telling contradictions, clues, and sleights of hand. They all make fun of Deism, and especially of Shaftesbury as he was conventionally understood.[57] In none of its forms (from very dry to very wet) could Deism, in Franklin's mind, resist the human longing for justice. When Franklin wrote these pieces, he was engaged in or just finished with the dialectical Socratic refutations, from which he became sure about some matter of religion. At the very least, when he wrote the metaphysical pieces he thought it was a problem to think of God as perfectly just, as all Deists and most people are sorely tempted to do.

Franklin suggests that when we shrug our shoulders and aver that God's providence on earth is mysterious, we really don't mean it in our hearts. If we really believed that God were a cruel spider, who tortures or rewards us capriciously and just for fun (as do little boys who catch some flies and let others go, and pull the wings off those not so lucky), we would fear him, but we could not possibly love or revere him. Rather, when we love God despite being unsure of his ways on this earth, we really believe that when all is said and done divine justice will be coming to each and every one of God's unfortunate bees and that all of our sufferings are in fact "good" as parts of God's ultimate plan. (It may take a providential while to work it out, but in fact the wretch on the rack really is as happy as the king of Siam.)

By the time he wrote the retrospective *Autobiography* and the illuminating letter to Vaughn, Franklin had come to see that the hope for divine justice is an irresistible longing, not just for ordinary people but even for free-thinking metaphysicians. That longing is an insinuating error in metaphysics because of the causal link between our moral intuitions and our thinking about God. But strictly speaking, we can at this point say only that the causal link is insinuating, not that it's an error. We still have to see how our longing for justice and its insinuating effect on our thinking about God together make an error.

6 • Dialectics and the Critique of Morality

By the time a fully "reformed" Franklin published his essays intended "as another means of communicating instruction," he had written the metaphysical burlesques identified along the trail marked out by the *Autobiography* and had abandoned metaphysical writings, on both sides of the particular providence divide, in "disgust." We can say with confidence, however, that, at least as regards the metaphysical burlesques, he never really abandoned them in disgust because he had never taken them seriously in the first place. At the time of writing them, he practiced his aggressive Socratic refutations—at least through the time of the *Dissertation* and very possibly through the writing of the *Articles*, and perhaps beyond even that time. But although he gradually "left" these aggressive dialectical refutations, Franklin says nothing of having done so in disgust.

On the contrary, the turn from the aggressive to the diffident Socratic methods left him "sure" about matters pertaining to the refutations—and his arguments about these matters in Boston led the good people to call him an atheist or infidel. We thus *cannot* simply equate the Socratic refutations with the radical point of view presented in the *Dissertation* and then later "abandoned." We're thus led to wonder about these refutations and about the conclusions of which Franklin became sure. Franklin presents the refutations in much the same way that Aristophanes presents Socrates' conquest of Pheidippides in *The Clouds:* We know it happened and see the result (conversion to "philosophy") but don't see actually how it transpired.[1] So too with Franklin's refutations: We're told they occurred and were dialectical, we're told of the result (embarrassment and anger), but we get no depiction of what actually went on. But at this point, we have to remember the immediate effect of the refutations on Franklin, and then we'll get an important clue, and both the effect and the clue lead us to think matters out on our own.

When Franklin says that his aggressive Socratic argumentation was "safest for myself and very embarrassing to those against whom I used it," it is not immediately clear if he means that the method was "safest" because it effected success despite his relative lack of knowledge, and thus gave him sometimes undeserved victories, or that it protected him from some dangerous consequences of his refutations, consequences arising from the embarrassment of its victims.[2] As regards the first possibility, we cannot conclude that the method simply made for undeserved victories, because Franklin tells us only that with his method he obtained victories that he and his cause did not *always* deserve. The clear implication is that he mostly deserved his victories and only sometimes did not.[3] And even if he sometimes did not deserve his victories, it is not impossible for a dialectical refutation to reveal something to the refuter even though the victory is undeserved.[4]

As regards protection from dangerous consequences, the Socratic method provided Franklin with better deniability and cover, but it did not, at least in Boston, as we recall, prevent his being identified as an atheist or infidel.[5] This danger posed by the "good people," which made Franklin decide to flee Boston, was a lesson he never forgot. As he said later on several occasions, to speak against religion is to spit into the wind or, even worse, to unleash a tiger that can and will bite.[6] That tiger is the good people who bite out of indignation. And, as we learned from the *Autobiography*'s nonchalance about the *Dissertation*, they are more likely to bite if they have been victimized by a Socratic refutation than if they have read an obscure and comical metaphysical treatise (however shocking to the good it might in fact be, and especially if most copies are burned).

What, we wonder, did Franklin learn in the course of the aggressive Socratic refutations? He must have considered them important, since he continued them "continually" even after his bad reputation in Boston forced him to go on the lam. Indeed, all the evidence suggests that he kept at them while in London (where he wrote the metaphysical *Dissertation*) and could well have been still at them, although not continually, when he wrote the metaphysical *Articles* in favor of particular providence. He may even have been still at them, though only rarely, when he wrote the metaphysical spoof in favor of divine providence.

Does Franklin provide any clue as to what actually transpired in these dangerous private conversations? Indeed he does—and he reveals his hand with a wonderfully subtle and clever move. When describing his turn from the aggressive to the diffident Socratic method, Franklin tells us that his method of modest diffidence has been of great help to him on those occasions when he has had to inculcate his opinions into others and persuade them of things he wanted to promote.[7] He says that a "positive dogmatical manner in advancing" one's sentiments only provokes contradiction and prevents attention and the exchange of information and the correction by others of one's own errors.

With this remark, Franklin lulls us into forgetting that the method replaced by modest diffidence was not the positive and "dogmatical" one of his first disputations but, rather, the Socratic refutations that confounded the religious opinions of his interlocutors on the basis of their own opinions. When we wake up and see clearly what we're tempted to forget, we see that the more important comparison is between the method of the humble inquirer and doubter that confounded and embarrassed (Socratic method one) and the more diffident method that pleases and persuades (Socratic method two). Then, to characterize this second method, Franklin quotes Pope from *An Essay on Criticism*. As Pope "says judiciously":

Men should be taught as if you taught them not,
And things unknown propos'd as things forgot,—[8]

"farther recommending it to us," says Franklin,

To speak tho' sure, with seeming diffidence.[9]

Franklin changes Pope's "must be taught" to his own "should be taught" to make the verse less positive and dogmatic and thus to accord with the end of gentle persuasion. He who wants simply to persuade should do as Pope suggests and use what Franklin "retained"—the mantle of diffidence. He who wants to refute should do as Franklin did in the Socratic refutations, which is to combine the mantle of diffidence with the aggressive inquirer and doubter.

Again, by the time of this important switch, Franklin had become *sure* of something important, although, as befits a sensible person, he remained open to being convinced otherwise. The switch from the dangerous Socratic method number one to the safe Socratic method number two thus makes sense: The risk of method number one could be avoided once Franklin had become sure of what he was seeking in the refutations. One could say that in the present context, Franklin simply argues in general terms about Socratic method number two—that one should speak diffidently even when sure of something, whatever that something might be. But the immediate sequel belies such generality. It points, rather, to something as specific as it is important and surprising.

Franklin next performs some referential and editorial prestidigitation. He says first that "he," meaning Pope, "might have coupled" the line about speaking diffidently with "that which he has coupled with another, I think less properly":

For Want of Modesty is want of Sense

If we put this all together then Franklin would have Pope saying:

Men should be taught as if you taught them not,
And things unknown propos'd as things forgot, —
To speak tho' sure, with seeming Diffidence
For want of Modesty is want of Sense.

Now, as much as all this rhymes, the line about modesty and the want of sense is not in Pope's *Essay on Criticism*. The following kindred ones, however, are in his *Essay*:

No pardon vile obscenity should find
Though wit and art conspire to move your mind
But dullness with obscenity must prove
As shameful sure as impotence in love.[10]

In Franklin's composite, immodesty is failing to practice wise diffidence, and it is lack of sense or imprudence or stupidity. In the relevant lines in Pope, clever obscenity (immodesty) is never pardoned, while dull or stupid obscenity is as shameful as impotence in love. Needless to say, impotence in love is a misfortune, not a vice. Pope thus treats immodesty as a moral vice, which in one circumstance (when motivated by wit and art) can be blamed and in another (when moved by dullness) can be excused. But in Franklin's composite we get only the argument that immodesty is simply an unfortunate lack of sense.

Franklin then speaks as if Pope had not treated immodesty as a sometimes blameworthy moral vice. In an almost accurate rendition of the lines as they really occur in Wentworth Dillon (and to whom Pope was clearly referring), Franklin explains why the following couplet is "less properly used":

Immodest Words admit of no Defense
For want of Modesty is want of Sense.[11]

Why is this coupling of lines "improper"? Because, says Franklin, "Now is not *Want of Sense,* (where a man is so unfortunate as to want it) some Apology for his *Want of Modesty?* and would not the Lines stand more justly thus?"

Immodest Words admit *but this* Defense
That Want of Modesty is Want of Sense.

So Franklin first speaks as if Pope had not treated immodesty as a moral vice
and then introduces the Dillon lines to make the point that it's improper to
say, as the lines clearly do, that immodesty isn't a moral matter ("no defense") because immodesty simply *is* in *all* cases just pitiable lack of prudence. And then we get the lines changed so that (supposedly, as we'll see)
the only *moral defense* of immodesty is the unfortunate lack of prudence.

Franklin thus does two sneaky things: He changes Pope's position that (1)
smart immodesty is indefensible (moral) and (2) stupid immodesty is defensible (moral), to Franklin's position that (1) all immodesty is stupid (and so
never a matter of morality at all), which is rejected as improper, whereas (2)
some immodesty (caused by an unfortunate want of sense) is morally defensible, and by implication, some immodesty (caused by wit?) is not.

Franklin—who starts out by referring to Pope—turns to Dillon so as to in-
troduce a matter that Pope had not taken up. And what is that matter? It's
the possibility that what looks like a moral vice (immodesty) might in *every*
case be a matter of mere imprudence (want of sense).

But this supposedly improper conclusion is, we have to remember, exactly
the one described in the four composite lines, intended to explain why one
should speak with seeming diffidence (modesty): that immodesty as such—
no qualification as to wit or dullness—is lack of sense.

So let's now consider the two final couplets simply by themselves—as if
we had not made our way through the missing lines from Pope. The lines as
Dillon presents them and Pope does not ("Immodest Words admit of *no* Defense / *For* want of Modesty is want of Sense") make perfect sense for
Franklin's context just as they are: Simple prudence teaches that there is no
"defending" immodesty since the immodest speakers simply harm themselves (in the context, they don't convince anybody), and that goes for the
smart ones as well as the dumb ones. There is no defending immodesty because there is no issue of blame and hence no issue of excuse—it's simply
stupid to be immodest, and those who are inevitably suffer from it. When we
come across an immodest person, rather than feeling the urge to blame or
excuse, we should feel pity for one so stupidly and unfortunately imprudent.

In changing the wording as he does to the second couplet ("Immodest
Words admit *but this* Defense / That Want of Modesty is Want of Sense"),
Franklin changes the merely prudential consideration to a moral one. In
taking the prudential matter as a moral one, Franklin says subtly that the
very thing (want of sense) that *makes* immodesty inherently nonmoral is the
only defense for it taken in a moral sense.[12] But then he fails to make the

emendation in the second line that would be needed to make sense of any understanding of immodesty as a moral vice: "That want of modesty is *sometimes* want of sense." Without that, we're left with the "improper" conclusion that when we take immodesty as a moral vice (to be blamed or excused), we err, because it's not a moral matter at all, just a matter of a pitiable misfortune. We then can at least wonder if the same error is involved when we consider (to blame or excuse) any moral vice.

All this opens a moral can of worms. We find ourselves projected back to the issues raised in the "Speech of Miss Polly Baker," and two lines of thinking emerge that are especially interesting and important.

In the first line of thinking, we are led to wonder if the distinction between prudence and moral virtue is as clear as our common sense leads us to think. Are there grounds for considering prudential and moral matters as the same? When we think of moral virtue and vice, we think of praise and blame and rewards and punishments. But we also wonder about the rewards, if not the punishments. That is, we think that moral virtue at its noble peak consists of sacrifice or service to others; to think of virtue as simply a means to some gain or good, a reward such as money or reputation or even self-satisfaction, is to diminish the purity or splendor of the virtuous deed.

That is why, in defense of nobility and righteousness, we say (confusedly, as we will see) that virtue is its "own reward" or that virtue is "good in itself." Now, if virtue is good in itself and its own reward, then the same goes for vice: It is bad in itself (for the vicious person, not just for the victim), and hence it is its own punishment. But then we're left with a puzzle: The odd result of thinking about vice as bad in itself, or as its own punishment, is obviously to make vice the same as imprudence in the sense of being bad for the agent. And then if we think about virtue as good in itself or its own reward, the same result occurs: Virtue at its peak, noble sacrifice, is also good for the agent—a gain and not a sacrifice, and so a matter of prudence.

Noble sacrifice is a loss (perhaps of everything good that we have) for the sake of others, and it is noble *because* it is a loss for the sake of others; but we hardly say of one who has made such noble sacrifice: "Poor man, what a calamity and bad thing he has brought upon himself." We think that noble sacrifice makes us worthy or deserving of reward, but only if the sacrifice was not done for the sake of that reward.

But then what about the worthiness itself? Even if the noble deed is done righteously for the sake of no reward, and even if no reward in fact ensues, is it bad, or no gain at all, to be *worthy* of them? Would we say, again: "What a catastrophe has befallen this poor man, to become such a one who is worthy"? Speaking from the greatest moral high-mindedness, would we not rather say that such a one has gained the *greatest good*—moral worthiness?

But if so, is this nobility not then the highest form of prudence, and again, if so, can it really be a sacrifice? When with common sense we praise nobility and righteousness, do we really know what we're talking about? Is this not like wanting to have one's cake and to eat it too?

The second line of thinking follows from the first. If, no matter how hard we try, we cannot really separate noble moral virtue from prudence, then three other startling conclusions follow.

First, if virtue is its own reward, then, strictly speaking, it needs nothing by way of other rewards. And if vice is its own punishment, then, strictly speaking, it needs no other punishment to make amends for the harm done to others. In becoming vicious by doing the vicious deed, the vicious person harms himself while thinking erroneously that he secures what is good at the expense of others. If vice is indeed a sickness and deformation of the soul, committing a vicious deed would be akin to shooting oneself in the foot. In this case, punishing the vicious person would be like saying, "This man just shot himself in the foot, so let's shoot him in the other foot."

Just as we saw with Polly, the second shot would seem to be piling on. And why would we pile on, unless we had some suspicion that in fact the vice is not really its own punishment and, conversely, that virtue is not really its own reward? Or, to put the matter differently and as we came to suspect in the case of Polly, we think that when the virtuous sacrifice and the vicious gain, the vicious get something good (a roll in the hay, not a bullet in the foot) and that the virtuous should get the same thing by other means—and just to make sure the vicious do not get to keep or enjoy the memory of that good thing, the virtuous pile on. Again, it seems that we don't have a coherent understanding of just what virtue and vice really are.

To see the second startling conclusion, let's start again. If virtue is its own reward, then, strictly speaking, it needs nothing by way of other rewards. And if vice is its own punishment (like shooting oneself in the foot), then, strictly speaking, vice needs no other punishment to make amends for the harm done to others. In becoming vicious by doing the vicious deed, the vicious person harms himself while thinking that he secures what is good at the expense of others.

But in that case, is not the viciousness merely ignorance, "want of sense"? If the vicious person *knew* that, in fact, he was harming himself, would he—at least if he were in his right mind—do the vicious thing and so shoot himself in the foot? And if he suffers from ignorance, can we hold him responsible for the deed? We do not consider children or idiots or madmen responsible for what they do. For them, moral ignorance is a defense or excuse for the vicious things they might do. But should not the same be true for one who simply does not know what is really good and bad?

The first response of common sense is that they should have known better. The second response of common sense is that the wicked person does know better but simply chooses his own good at the expense of others out of wickedness.

As regards the first response of common sense (that he should have known better), it isn't clear that the common sense really does make sense. If someone fails to seek the knowledge they would certainly want to have if they could, is there not some plausible reason why that person fails while another does not? Let us say the person fails simply because he is lazy. Is he responsible for being lazy? Or better, is he responsible for being the kind of person who is lazy? Does anyone *want* to be the kind of person who becomes lazy, so as to harm himself by not coming to know what is really good for him? Does anyone willingly choose what he knows to be bad for himself? Does anyone willingly choose to be ignorant of what is good for himself?

And thus, as Franklin says, is not the "want of sense" a *misfortune?* A misfortune is a condition suffered, not chosen. And this leads us to the second objection of common sense (that he did know but acted out of wickedness). When we consider the issue of wickedness, we come to the third startling conclusion.

What can it mean to think that wickedness causes the wicked person to choose what he knows is wrong? Assume that person A makes wicked choice a, knowing that b was really the right thing to do. What kind of person makes such a wicked choice? A wicked person. How did A become wicked? By ignoring what he knew to be good and making the wicked choice, we say. But to make that wicked choice knowingly, A had already to be wicked.

So where is the *choice* for wickedness? If in blaming we appeal to wickedness as opposed to ignorance that should have been otherwise, then we're stuck with saying that a wicked person is one who is wicked, and *no more*. We might want to kill such a person as we do a rat or harmful snake, but it makes no more sense to say of the wicked person than it does of the rat or snake that they "deserve" to be killed or "punished," that they "had it coming" or "got their just deserts" for what they "willingly chose to do." Just as we surmised with Polly, wickedness or evil is, like the want of sense, a *condition* (like being in the grip of the "Devil"), not a choice.

However we look at it, we cannot really make sense of the commonsensical notion that one chooses to be ignorant or chooses to become wicked. It thus makes no sense to say that a person is "willingly" ignorant or "willingly" wicked. And if not, then free will, merit and demerit, moral virtue and moral vice, and wickedness make no sense. We say the peak of virtue, nobility, consists in freely chosen sacrifice or devotion and that vice consists in freely chosen wickedness. But the nobility and the free choice and the wickedness make no internal logical sense. And when we speak of noble and worthy sacrifice, the voice of our hearts makes us think of that sacrifice—at the same time—as two completely incompatible things. Franklin's move, in describing his turn from aggressive Socratic refutations to Socratic diffidence, is the feather-light nudge that sets us thinking. And when we do, it seems that the moral house of cards comes down.[13]

RATS, SNAKES, AND WICKED PERSONS . . . and why not skunks as well? We've of course seen all this before, with comical Polly's self-defense and comical Father Abraham's scatological advice to his beloved son. These two comic pieces clearly followed Franklin's turn from the aggressive Socratic refutations to Socratic diffidence. Given this similarity between the lines of thinking provoked by the comedies and by the nudge-like but powerful clue about the dialectical refutations, it is reasonable to conclude that the two comedies reflect precisely those issues of which Franklin became sure before turning to his Socratic diffidence.

This conclusion is powerfully supported by the fact that Franklin leads us to similar lines of thinking, and more, in the other two pieces explicitly mentioned in the *Autobiography:* the 1735 "Socratic dialogue" and the essay on self-denial. Both are dialectical, not metaphysical.

In the *Autobiography,* Franklin describes the essay on self-denial as having shown "that virtue was not secure, till its practice became a habitude, and was free from the opposition of contrary inclinations." Franklin here fudges the thrust of the second piece, which actually bears the title *"That SELF-DENIAL is not the ESSENCE of VIRTUE."* In that brief essay, Franklin does *not,* in fact, argue that virtue becomes secure only when it is habitual and free from contrary inclinations.[14] This is a clear implication of the piece, but it is not the basic point he wants to make, which is, rather, the one declared by the title.

Why does Franklin fudge this matter? To make us wonder, I think, about the relation between "perfect virtue," or moral virtue at its peak, and self-denial. The title does point to the deep contradiction in what we commonly think about moral virtue—that it *is,* at its peak, self-denial, but also the gain of the greatest good. Let's see how this plays out in the course of the essay.

Franklin begins by granting that it is "commonly asserted, that without *self-denial* there is no virtue, and that the greater the *self-denial* the greater the virtue." This makes sense, Franklin says, if we think of a man who cannot deny himself anything he is inclined toward, even though he knows it to be harmful. In this case, the man would lack resolution and would have to practice self-denial in order to practice that resolution. "But as it stands," he says, the common assertion "seems obscure or erroneous." To show just how it is obscure or erroneous, Franklin then considers "some of the virtues singly."

A man who is never inclined to wrong people, feels no temptation to do so, and never does must be considered a just man and thus one who has the virtue of justice. Ditto for the man who is never tempted by idle diversions: He is industrious and has the virtue of industry. Franklin could make the same argument for all of the virtues, but to make things short, he says, it is certain that the more we strive against the temptation to any vice and the more we practice the contrary virtue, the weaker becomes the temptation and the stronger the habit of virtue, until the temptation simply vanishes or has no force. Do we by this striving against vice thus become less virtuous until "at length we have no virtue at all?" If self-denial is the essence of virtue, then a person who has become fully temperate or just—that is, whose inclination is simply toward temperance and justice and has no temptation to the opposite—must be accounted not virtuous, and to become virtuous he would have to drink to excess or harm his neighbors.

Now what, we ask, is at the bottom of this obvious sophism? If we look carefully we can see the move involved: Franklin makes the same identification of virtue understood prudentially and virtue understood morally that we saw in his description of the turn from the aggressive Socratic method. If we think of virtue as prudence, then it makes perfect sense to deny that self-denial is its essence. On the contrary, virtue so understood is wise self-serving. For three of the virtues Franklin mentions—resolution (fortitude), industriousness, and temperance—being able to avoid what would be one's "hurt" and stick to what is one's good—for example, being able to work hard enough to make one's fortune or to stay sober enough to do so—is precisely what is in one's interest to do. These virtues are necessary for happiness by securing the specific goods at stake.

Matters are surely different in the case of justice. In that case, even the man who is naturally temperate and just—who has simply "no inclination to *wrong* people in his dealings"—would still have to practice self-denial in those instances when being just could be counted a moral as opposed to a prudential virtue. Usually, of course, being just is the prudent thing to do. It would be stupid to be habitually unjust, since being so would soon get one the reputation of being an obvious and untrustworthy scoundrel. But that's not what we mean when we think of justice as a moral virtue.

Consider an important case for the just man with no inclination to harm his neighbors: If he does not steal his neighbor's cow, his own child will die. The issue here is not a desire simply to harm the neighbor but, rather, to secure a crucial good at the neighbor's expense. It is really *not* good to be drunk all the time (unless, like Winston Churchill, you can really handle your liquor), to be unable to act for what is good, and so on. But it really *is* good to have one's child live rather than die. Or an even better case would be this: A man has struggled hard in life and finally has the opportunity to become very rich, but the only way to get the necessary capital is to steal his neighbor's cow, a one-time theft that will never happen again since he will be rich and since he has no inclination to wrong people. (And since he feels bad, he'll give the neighbor a cow once he's rich, if the neighbor has not starved by then.)

Again, the inclination at work here is not to wrong the neighbor just for the sake of the harm but, rather, to secure a good, great wealth. Even for the man who has no inclination to wrong his neighbors or who is naturally just, the just thing in this case would involve the sacrifice of an obvious good for himself: great but otherwise unattainable wealth. It is in these cases that we would admire the justice as an instance of self-sacrifice or devotion or putting another's interest ahead of one's own. It is in these cases that we would admire the just act as noble and moral.

Just as we see what common sense reveals to be *Franklin's* sophism, Franklin next traces that sophism straight to common sense. "But perhaps it may be said, that by the word *virtue* in the above assertion, is meant, *merit;* and so it should stand thus; without self-denial there is no merit; and the greater the self-denial the greater the merit." But then he says: "The self-denial here meant, must be when our inclinations are towards vice, or else it would still be nonsense." This makes somewhat better sense than did the previous argument, but just barely: If we deny our inclination to drink, perhaps we merit praise. In this prudential case, we could beam to hear "way to go!" and "good for you!" But it is hard to see why we would morally deserve or merit reward. If, by denying one's inclination to drink, one achieves the good of a clear head, why should one "deserve" *more* than the obvious good one has procured for oneself? The matter seems clearer if one refrains from injustice, as in the pinch cases just discussed. In those cases, a man denies himself an obvious good—the object of the injustice such as a live child or significant wealth. In this case, it seems more sensible to say, we may deserve both praise *and* reward.

Before addressing the matter, however, Franklin makes two brief remarks. First, we do not merit anything from God, because God "is above our services; and the benefits he confers on us, are the effects of his goodness and bounty." And second, "all our merit then is with regard to one another, and from one to another."

"Taking then the assertion as it last stands" (that is, without self-denial there is no merit; and the greater the self-denial, the greater the merit),

Franklin asks a series of questions: If a person does me a service out of natural benevolence, do I owe him less than I owe one who does it against his inclination? Should I pay a lazy worker more than an industrious one for the same job equally well done? We pay more for a naturally honest servant in affairs of trust than we do for a natural rogue who has recently acted honestly, but that is because the former has more merit in spite of his lack of self-denial. Is a patriot to be thought not praiseworthy if public spirit is natural to him? Is a pacing horse less valuable for being a natural pacer? Neither does a man have less merit "for having in general natural virtuous inclinations."

The truth, concludes Franklin, is that temperance, justice, charity, and the like are virtues whether they are practiced with or against our inclinations, and one who practices them "merits our love and esteem." "Self-denial is neither good nor bad, but as 'tis applied: he that denies a vicious inclination is virtuous in proportion to his resolution, but the most perfect virtue is above all temptation, such as the virtue of the Saints in Heaven."

According to Franklin's argument, we cannot merit anything from God, because we can render such an exalted being no service. There is merit, then, only among men who need things, or at least who can use unnecessary things that might be given them. Then follows not arguments but the series of questions. To the first, we can answer: No, the one who does me a service out of natural benevolence deserves *no less* than the one who serves me against his inclination and who deserves *no more*. But that does not mean that either one deserves *anything* at all for a gift freely given.

The implied answers to the next questions clarify the matter: If a workman or servant serves for wages, I owe no more to an industrious workman than to a lazy one for an equally good job, and I pay an honest servant more than I pay a servant who is just lately honest because I expect better work from the former than from the latter. A naturally virtuous man is like a horse that is a natural pacer—both have no less merit for not having to go against their inclinations.

This last comment at first glance seems to be a joke. A morally virtuous man can be likened to a naturally fast horse? What do we suppose that horse "merits"—hay? This is hardly an edifying description of moral virtue. But the joke really is that the description isn't a joke at all, at least if we consider the answers to Franklin's rhetorical questions. So what is the equivalent of our hay? What does a man have coming for a job done for free? Our *love and esteem*, says Franklin. This is as much as to say: "If you do me a service for wages, I owe you for what you do. We are both unlike gods and have needs—I for your work and you for your wages. But if you do your work or service for free, and for whatever reason (according to or against your inclination), then thanks a lot, I esteem you and love you for it. But money, or some other reward? Forget it—I didn't ask for the favor. I love and esteem that naturally fast horse for winning, and I feed it the hay it needs to go fast. But do I *owe* it anything more? Not a chance; horses run, that's what they like to do. You with your free gift are no different, except that since we agreed on no wage, we assumed you can feed yourself."

The movement of the piece is thus from a sophism that makes us discern between prudence and noble sacrifice, and then from noble sacrifice to merit or deserving of praise or reward, and then to wages for work performed for wages, and finally to esteem and love for work or services performed for nothing. This subtle movement catches perfectly our conflicting intuitions about moral virtue. On the one hand, virtue understood as the noble, as opposed to prudence, does consist in self-denial, self-sacrifice for the sake of others, or devotion to others. But on the other hand, we think that by noble sacrifice we become deserving of praise or reward. Praise, perhaps. But if reward (even its being its own reward), then it is not clear how virtue understood as noble sacrifice is not also understood as gain—as a high form of prudence.

So what about the praise? Do we not praise the noble deed for its *worthiness* of reward and because it was done with no concern for that reward and even if that reward does not come? We do. And do we not praise it because that worthiness, simply by itself, is good—and good for the worthy person? We do. Again, do we not count it much better to be morally worthy of reward than not to be worthy, even if the reward never comes?

Yes. But as regards reward, if the worthiness is such a great good, why should one then get still more? And then the conclusion: For services rendered for free—even sacrifices rendered for free—one "merits" love and esteem but nothing more, nothing along the lines of wages, reward, or even admiration. This is as much as to say: "I like you and regard you for doing me this sacrificial favor, but I owe you *no admiration, only praise*. In other words: Way to go! Good for you for getting such a good thing as worthiness for yourself by giving me what I did not ask for! I, however, owe you nothing. But this isn't just me talking. It's what you think as well: that your sacrifice is, by earning you your merit, by itself your greatest gain."

As regards the patriot, it is hard to believe he thinks our love and esteem is a sufficient reward should he wind up sacrificing his life, gratis, for others. He wants and believes he deserves our admiration—that we should feel incomplete, less good, if we cannot be like him. He thinks that noble deeds are services done for free. But he also thinks they are not for free because they pay their own wage, admirable worthiness. So when people admire and praise the noble, they think two contradictory things at the same time.

Since God (if there is such a thing) has no need for our services, we can merit nothing from him. There is nothing like a wage that he is obliged to provide us for services we render. But you and I, like any creature less exalted than a god, have needs—things that are good for us. There is good reason for you to get what is good for you (wages) by helping me get what is good for me (service). There is no good reason why—if you want—you should not help me get what is good for me (free service, or a gift) at your cheerful expense and with nothing expected in return. And the same is true even if that free service entails a real sacrifice, like a dead child or the loss of a major financial opportunity or even your life. But when you do me this favor, it is not clear that you really know the reason why: You want me to admire you for doing it for free. But how can I *admire* you for doing it for free if your unrewarded "worthiness" is the best wage, the best gain, you can get? And if you are noble and have the best wage one can get, why should I feel obliged to give you anything of mine for free?

If we read the essay with care, Franklin points us to the conclusion that our common moral intuitions are a tangle of confusions. No wonder Franklin ends his essay with a picture of moral derangement: "And he who does a foolish, indecent or wicked thing, merely because 'tis contrary to his inclination, (like some mad enthusiasts I have read of, who ran about naked, under the notion of taking up the cross) is not practicing the reasonable science of virtue, but is lunatick."

It is hard to see how such naked self-abasement could be wicked, since, however misguided and against the naked men's inclinations it might be, it is done at their expense and for the sake of "taking up the cross." And while it may seem indecent, its intention is not. It is, however, in Franklin's view, without question lunatic. But this bizarre case is also in his view no more lunatic than are our common intuitions and opinions about moral virtue: The pious streakers, apparently, want to serve Christ by sharing his suffering. But how can the divine Jesus, who needs nothing, benefit from their suffering? And if he is not divine but merely human, how does the streakers' suffering diminish his? And if in some way it could and were thus like a good he needed and could really use, why do the streakers provide it, if it's bad for them and good for him?

From all that we've seen so far, the best explanation we could expect from them would be something like the following gibberish: "We do it for his good and for no reward and it's noble for that reason; its excellence consists in its being pure sacrifice for another who is worthy. But because we do it for no reward, we merit that reward. And that merit is reward in itself—the highest one. So the fact that we have reward coming, even if it never comes, is really getting it! And because we have it coming and really get it, we're then worthy of being given something else for free. But no—if we have it and are worthy of something else too (but don't get that something else), then we're not noble, and so deserving, since we've gained such a wonderful thing, our worthiness, for ourselves. So we'll shed not just clothes but skin for him as well, and for no reward, so we'll merit that reward. And that merit is by itself the greatest gain a man can have, and so we'll shed our merit, so that we'll *really* merit . . . BLAAAGH!!!"

Again, the issue here is not that when the righteous sacrifice for another's good, they really just aim for some reward. Franklin makes no such cynical and dogmatic assumption. The issue is, rather, that when we think noble deeds make us deserving, we think that the deed is both *in essence* a sacrifice for another's good and hence a loss for us and, at the same time, *in essence* a good and highest gain for us. Righteousness makes no internal sense. Our moral common sense tells us that a square is round, and Franklin thinks that's "lunatick" and often makes us act like lunatics.

WE TURN NEXT TO THE LAST PIECE identified on the *Autobiography*'s trail, the delightful Socratic dialogue "A Man of Sense."[15] The dialogue opens with Socrates asking Crito about the identity of a well-dressed man who has just passed by. Crito says that "he is a gentleman of this city, esteemed a *man of sense,* but not very honest." Socrates then asks whether a man who is dishonest can deserve the appellation "a *man of sense.*" To this Crito answers: "Yes doubtless; there are many vicious men who are nevertheless men of very good sense."

In the next exchanges, Socrates and Crito agree that just to have knowledge is not to be a man of sense, since there are many who know things like cards and dice and music who are silly, and there are even masters of languages, rhetoric, and logic who are "senseless fellows." And there are some who understand logic and rhetoric but are no better at convincing and persuading than those who do not. Not even knowledge of the sublime sciences of mathematics, astronomy, or natural philosophy will earn a man the right to be characterized as "a *man of sense.*"

As regards the latter sciences, Crito says that he might have thought they did, but that he knows of masters of these sciences who, in the conduct of their lives, have acted weakly—he does not mean viciously, but foolishly. From all this, Socrates then concludes that the only knowledge whose possession permits us to say of the possessor that he is "a man of sense" is the knowledge of our "*true interest;* that is, of what is best to be done in all the circumstances of human life, in order to arrive at our main end in view, HAPPINESS."

Crito then asks Socrates whether he still doubts that a vicious man can deserve the character of a man of sense, "since 'tis certain that there are many men who *know* their true interest, etc. and are therefore *men of sense,* but are nevertheless vicious and dishonest men, as appears from the whole tenor of their conduct in life." Socrates responds by asking Crito if vice can "consist with any man's true interest, or contribute to his happiness." Crito replies: "No certainly, for in proportion as a man is vicious he loses the favor of God and Man, and brings upon himself many inconveniences, the least of which is capable of marring and demolishing his happiness."

So how, then, Socrates asks, can it appear "that those vicious men have the knowledge we have been speaking of, which constitutes a *man of sense*, since they act directly contrary?" By the fact that they talk well about virtue and vice and express their thoughts about the good effects of the former and bad effects of the latter, responds Crito. So, asks Socrates, is it knowing how to talk about shoemaking, or knowing how actually to make shoes, that makes a shoemaker? The latter, of course, says Crito. And so if one could only talk about shoemaking and then were to set to work, he would soon discover his ignorance of the art? Yes, says Crito. So if someone can talk "justly" about virtue and vice, and say that drunkenness and gluttony and lewdness destroy a man's constitution and wreck his happiness, and despite his talk "continues in those vices," can such a one deserve the character of a temperate and chaste man? Or does "not that man rather deserve it, who having a *thorough sense* that what the other has said is true, *knows* also *how* to resist the temptation to those vices, and embrace virtue with a hearty and steady affection?"

The latter, says Crito, who is now inclined to think that those mere talkers are men who "speak only by rote" and repeat what they pick out from the books or conversation of wise men, but that what they have learned by rote, "having never entered or made any impression on their hearts, has therefore no influence on the conduct of their lives." So, concludes Socrates, "vicious men, then, do not appear to have that knowledge which constitutes the *man of sense*."

Crito agrees, but then says that instead of defining the man of sense, he and Socrates have annihilated him, "for if the knowledge of his true interest in all parts of the conduct of life, and a constant course of practice agreeable to it, are essential to his character, I do not know where we shall find him." To this Socrates replies that it is not necessary that the man of sense never make "a slip in the path of virtue, or in point of morality," provided he sees his failing and tries hard to rectify what has been "done amiss" and to prevent it in the future. "The best arithmetician may err in casting up a long account; but having found that error, he *knows how* to mend it, and immediately does so; and is notwithstanding that error, an arithmetician; But he who *always* blunders, and cannot correct his faults in accounting, is no arithmetician; nor is the habitually-vicious man a *man of sense*."

To this Crito says that it will "look hard" that one could master all the other arts and sciences and not be called a man of sense unless he is also a man of virtue. Socrates replies: "We shall agree, perhaps, that the one who is a *man of sense*, will not spend his time in learning such sciences as, if not useless in themselves, will probably be useless to him?" Crito agrees. "And of those which may be useful to him, that is, may contribute to his happiness, he ought, if he is a man of sense to know how to make them so." Again, Crito agrees. "And of those which may be useful, he will not (if he is a man of sense) acquire all, except that one only which is the most useful of all, to wit, the science of virtue." Crito again agrees.

And so it "seems to follow then" that the vicious man who is master of many sciences is ignorant and foolish, because since he is vicious he is unhappy, and so he has acquired only useless sciences, "or having acquired such as might be useful, he knows not how to make them contribute to his happiness; and though he may have every other science, he is ignorant that the SCIENCE OF VIRTUE is of more worth, and of more consequence to his happiness than all the rest put together." And since he is ignorant of "what *principally* concerns him, though it has been told him a thousand times from parents, press, and pulpit, the vicious man however learned, cannot be a *man of sense*, but is a fool, a dunce, and a blockhead."

Now, this charming and clever little piece begins with a wonderfully subtle indication of what is to follow. At the very outset, when Socrates asks Crito about the identity of the well-dressed man who has just passed by, Crito does not give the obvious first response—"that's Joe Blow." He instead says that the passer-by is a man of the city, esteemed a man of sense, but not very honest. As Crito expresses the matter, it is not absolutely clear if we're to think the man is esteemed wise but is in truth and unbeknownst to most people dishonest, or is esteemed both wise and dishonest (the comma between "sense" and "but" points to the former meaning, but not perfectly). We might think the latter meaning silly but for the fact that Crito's response in fact speaks in that direction.

Crito remembers the man's reputation for sense and remembers his dishonesty better than he remembers the man's name. The man, then, must have a widespread reputation for dishonesty, for even the notoriously stupid Crito would have remembered the name had Crito, by having been himself a victim of the well-dressed man's dishonesty, learned what others did not know. So before another step is taken Crito makes a revealing mistake: It cannot be wise or prudent even for a dishonest man to have a widespread reputation for dishonesty. Indeed, it's absurd, because for such a one dishonesty cannot be effective or useful. ("Hi, I'm your local con man and I'd like to fix your driveway.") If one is to use dishonesty wisely, it should not be practiced often, or at least not obviously, and one cannot afford to be caught too many times, if at all. We can guess, then, that even though the gentleman walking down the street is currently well dressed, he should not count on being able to replace his fancy duds when they wear out or on still having a reputation for wisdom at the time.

The very first lesson we can draw from Crito's stupidity is not that dishonesty in itself is unwise but that having a reputation for dishonesty is unwise. And so for all we know, real wisdom may consist in knowing when and how to be dishonest so as not to earn a reputation for the "vice." In this way and properly understood, we can conclude with Crito that there are many vicious men who are nevertheless men of very good sense.

In the immediate sequel, Socrates establishes that the knowledge that makes a man a man of sense is not the likes of mathematics, astronomy, or natural philosophy, but "the knowledge of our *true interest*; that is, of what is best to be done in all the circumstances of human life, in order to arrive at our main end in view, HAPPINESS." So far so good. But then, as Crito points out, there are men who know their true interest and so are men of sense and are still vicious and dishonest "as appears from the whole tenor of their conduct in life."

Crito thus blatantly repeats his error, which is to think that it can be sensible for a vicious and dishonest man to have a widespread reputation for these vices—to make himself "appear" vicious and dishonest "from the whole tenor of [his] conduct in life." Then, when asked point-blank if vice and true interest and happiness can coexist, Crito corrects his error, but without knowing what he is doing: He says no, and that a person loses the favor of God and man and brings on many inconveniences in proportion to his viciousness. But, despite the fact of proportionality, he says at the same time that the *least* inconvenience is "capable of marring and demolishing" a man's happiness. It is thus certain that what is *apparent* in the whole tenor of the vicious man's conduct, a reputation for vice, is simply foolish. But a much lesser degree of vice and a smaller proportion of trouble and disruption of happiness may not be so foolish. Indeed, under some circumstances, it might not be foolish at all and might be a small disruption of happiness that produces a net gain in happiness. Crito doesn't see this possibility, however, because he thinks that the smallest inconvenience, resulting proportionally from the smallest vice, can wreck a man's happiness.

Still not seeing the correction he has just made, Crito responds to Socrates' question as to how it can appear that such a one, the obviously and reputedly vicious man, can have the knowledge of his true interest. Crito yet again misses the obvious point and makes an even stupider one: Rather than saying that such people are obviously just imprudent and ignorant fools, he says that they appear to have the knowledge of their true interest because they know how to talk well about virtue and vice, how to praise the former and condemn the latter.

Now, knowing how to talk well on this subject would make good sense for the prudently vicious man, the one who uses vice rarely and carefully and does not have or get a reputation for vice and dishonesty. But it makes no sense at all for one who has such a reputation: It could not be effective, since known liars are unlikely to be believed, and it would serve only to augment the reputation for viciousness with one for ridiculousness.

Kind Socrates, however, lets both the foolish Crito and the foolish vicious man off their respective hooks. He changes tack and describes the obviously vicious good talker not as a ridiculous fool but, rather, as one who knows about an art (shoemaking) but not how to put that art to work (how to make shoes). The real man of sense, then, is the one who "having a *thorough sense* that what the other has said is true, *knows* also *how* to resist the temptation to those vices, and embrace virtue with a hearty and steady affection." The necessary knowledge, then, is twofold: It consists of knowing what is in one's interest, in this case knowing that drunkenness, gluttony, and lewdness destroy the constitution, cause trouble, and mar happiness, and it also consists of knowing how to avoid the vices. By this point, we note, Socrates drops any mention of honesty and refers instead to drunkenness, gluttony, and lewdness—and honesty never returns.

So Crito next agrees that the vicious good talkers speak only by rote about the "true interest of all men," which is virtue, and that what they say by rote has never impressed their hearts and so does not influence their conduct. Thus, he agrees with Socrates' claim that they have not "embrac[ed] virtue with a hearty and steady affection," but he says nothing about the matter of how to put to work what one knows. The latter is a different matter, since one could well embrace virtue and not know how to become virtuous—one could want it very much but not know how to get it. Here the slow-witted Crito has made another slip. With Socrates, he agreed that the knowledge of our true interest is knowledge of what is best to be done in all the circumstances of life in order to arrive at the chief end: happiness. There, our interest is to know the means to happiness. Now Crito says simply that "the true interest of all men" is virtue, with no explicit mention of happiness or the means to happiness, and as if happiness *consisted* in virtue as opposed to virtue being the means to happiness.

Crito isn't very bright, but he is, it turns out, a righteous man. No wonder, then, that he reacts with dismay and says that they have annihilated the man of sense. If happiness consists in virtue, as opposed to virtue being the means to happiness, then it is far more likely that rare acts of viciousness, "the least inconveniences," will mar our happiness than if virtue is just the means to that happiness.

This is exactly what Crito has said: that the least "inconvenience" can mar and annihilate our happiness. Socrates said that knowledge of our true interest is knowing what is best to be done "in all the circumstances of human life" in order to secure our happiness. Crito now says of the man of sense that if he is required to know "his true interest in all parts of the conduct of life, and a constant course of practice agreeable to it," then such a one will not be found. Socrates spoke of all the *circumstances* of life, while Crito here speaks of all the *parts* of the conduct of life: Crito speaks of all our acts, not all the contexts of our acts.

Crito thus speaks as if he and Socrates had agreed that to be a man of sense is to know that happiness consists in virtue and therefore that constant happiness consists in constant virtue. The latter is not such an extreme conclusion if we assume that happiness consists in virtue. On this assumption, think of a virtuous man who lives half his life well and then makes a one-time mistake and neglects a duty so important that others die because of that neglect. One could argue that even if such a man spent the rest of his life virtuously, his happiness (again, on Crito's righteous assumption) would be forever ruined. Crito is not so stupid as to miss the fact that by his measure of righteousness, the man of sense will not be a very often sighted bird.

Socrates then comes to the rescue again. Don't worry Crito, it's not necessary that the man of sense never make a slip in the path of virtue, so long as he sees his error and tries not to make it again. This might for a minute soothe Crito's worry that happiness might be impossible if we think it consists in virtue. But before Crito can see the still-remaining problem—what if the slip is really big?—Socrates makes an odd and telling comparison.

To whom does he compare the slipping man of sense? To an arithmetician, the very scientist earlier identified as among those who, despite their knowledge, have been known by Crito to be weak (meaning foolish, not vicious) in the management of their affairs and the conduct of their lives.

As Socrates presents the comparison, there are two figures opposite to the slipping arithmetician: one who always blunders in the matter of accounts, who is no arithmetician; and, by comparison, the "habitually-vicious man," who is no man of sense. The telling move is this: The opposition is between the occasionally slipping arithmetician, on the one hand, and the always blundering arithmetician and the habitually-vicious man, on the other hand. But the comparison is subtly but importantly wrong. Arithmetic is a science, not a habit, and even a constantly blundering nonarithmetician is so not out of habit but, rather, out of stupidity or incompetence.

Were the comparison to be strictly appropriate, the opposition should be between a slipping arithmetician and a man who always sizes up the situation wrongly and chooses in every case for vice—but as an error in judgment, not out of habit. Such a dunce probably does not exist, but then neither does one who knows about arithmetic but can never get an account right. Thus the real comparison would be between a slipping arithmetician and one who sometimes judges falsely that a given situation calls for vice rather than virtue. But this does not rule out—indeed, it rather suggests—that to correct the error is to discern correctly when a situation calls for virtue and *when it calls for vice*.

The issue at the beginning, we recall, was knowing what to do in every circumstance to secure our happiness, and Crito himself unknowingly disclosed the possibility that the favor of God and man, and inconvenience and dangers to our happiness, are proportional to a man's viciousness. It was never established, but only assumed by Crito in his proportionality remark, that virtue is in fact the sole means to our true interest in happiness. Nor was it later established, but only assumed by Crito, that happiness consists in virtue. The comparison to the slipping arithmetician is thus free to suggest, as it does, that in a given circumstance some vice might be an essential means to maximized happiness.

Moreover, Crito's remark that he has known of foolish but not vicious arithmeticians reveals the limits of his experience or the dullness of his wit or both. If an arithmetician is one who can find an error he has committed, he is also the one who knows best how to hide an error he has committed, which of course he would do if he had committed the error on purpose. (Who is better equipped to rip us off than our accountant?)

Everything in the dialogue points to the following: We are supposed to be able to recognize "a slip in the path of virtue." But the question is whether there is but one way to understand such a slip. One way is to see the slip as a falling away from what is otherwise a habit of acting virtuously. Another way is to see the slip as a failure to judge in a given set of circumstances what is in one's "true interest," happiness. This would be a failure of what Socrates calls, in his concluding remark, the "science of virtue." Thus, the only "science of virtue" can be knowing when not to slip in the pursuit of our true interest in happiness. And in this case, the slip to be avoided would be to *fail* to commit, when necessary, what is called a slip in the first sense.

The man of sense would not be one who is known to be habitually dishonest; rather, he would be one who always knows when, where, and how to be dishonest. This conclusion does not jibe well, we have to admit, with the doctrine of Franklin's moral reformation: that "*truth, sincerity and integrity* in dealings between man and man" are of the "utmost importance to the felicity of life."

OF THE THREE VIRTUES truth, sincerity, and integrity, only sincerity wound up on the list of thirteen virtues for the project of attaining moral perfection. Sincerity, for the reformed Franklin, is somehow the core of moral virtue. At the end of Franklin's trail, however, we cannot possibly take him seriously when he praises this most pragmatic and public-spirited of the moral virtues. And so the trail has an especially illuminating terminus.

Since we are directed to the "Papers about the beginning of 1735" and since Franklin knew that his readers could find all issues of the *Gazette* between 1728 and 1747 in the Library of Philadelphia, he could expect them to find his anonymous 1732 *Gazette* essay "On Simplicity."[16] In this piece, it turns out, Franklin hides so as to let another famous writer, Francis Bacon, speak in his place.

"On Simplicity" is especially of interest since it treats simplicity as "the homespun dress of honesty" and treats both the dress and what is underneath it, honesty, in contrast to cunning and dissembling. There is in human nature, says Franklin, a certain "charming quality, innate and original to it, which is called SIMPLICITY." Lately, he says, this virtue has been thought of as folly, and cunning and artifice have replaced it and are thought of as wisdom and understanding. He believes, on the contrary, that simplicity is "the homespun dress of honesty" and that chicanery and craft are in fact the adornments worn by vice and knavery. In the first ages of the world, before the advent of luxury and ambition and "a thousand fantastic forms of happiness," simplicity was the "dress and language of the world." But now the arts of cunning have "attained their utmost perfection" and are practiced among the "necessary arts and knowledges of life." If we look at history, we see that the original simplicity has worn off gradually in every age, as we see when we consider the great characters of the ancient Greeks and Romans and compare them to our own times.

If one wants to see the charm of simplicity, we need only retire from the great cities and consider the "simple and unaffected dialogues of uncorrupted peasants." But perhaps we do not have to repair to the rustics, says Franklin, for he believes that simplicity will be found sometimes in "the men of the truest genius and highest characters in the conduct of the world." Those who resort to cunning are in fact only pretenders to "policy and business."

Cunning, says my Lord *Bacon*, is a sinister or crooked wisdom, and dissimulation but a faint kind of policy; for it asks a strong wit and a strong heart, to know when to tell truth and to do it; therefore they are the weaker sort of politicians, that are the greatest dissemblers. And certainly there is a great difference between a cunning man and a wise one, not only in point of honesty but in point of ability; as there are those that can pack the cards, who cannot play the game well.

Cunning will not succeed in "free and mixed assemblies," and as a result, the cunning man is "obliged to hunt his game alone, and to live in the dark." And so "none but fools are knaves, for wise men cannot help being honest," and cunning is the wisdom of a fool.

To draw his remarks to a close, Franklin asks us to consider that if cunning is thought good, how are we to explain that the greatest and ablest men eschew it and the weak and the low perfect it? And then follows a soaring encomium to simplicity: Simplicity, "we are sure," is "natural and the highest beauty of nature," and all that is excellent in the arts is to demonstrate this natural beauty or to show us how to copy it "in every thing." Simplicity in speech and manners is the "highest happiness as well as the greatest ornament of life; whereas nothing is so tiresome to one's self, as well as so odious to others, as disguise and affectation." What is more, no one is so cunning as to be able to hide the fact of being so, and "those cunning men, though they are not declared enemies to the world," "are really spies upon it, and ought in the justice of things to be considered and treated as such, whenever they are caught." Moreover, cunning men have no friends, for the honest catch them out and rascals betray them, and Franklin hopes his reader by this time agrees that "wisdom and virtue are the same thing, as knavery and cunning are generally so too; and that for the future, we shall resolve to be what we would seem, which is the only sure way not to be afraid to seem what we really are."

Despite this ending flourish, Franklin is not, in fact, quite finished. "Perhaps it is not necessary to add," he continues, that by simplicity he does not mean the pretenses to it that are made by good people who honestly mistake it and who while striving for it "are guilty of very gross affectation." What Franklin means by simplicity is not "quaintness of habit or oddness of behavior" or taking great care not to appear unfashionable. And he states "on the other side" that the term "*cunning*" is related to the word "king" and that in its ancient sense, it implied knowledge. He has no quarrel with these facts; his quarrel is with what "cunning" now signifies, which is "the little subtlety of base minds." He is, after all, aware that this "crooked wisdom" has become so well established that it is not to be "immediately exploded," and although he hopes that his reader will be ashamed to live in the world by its means, he also warns him to beware of those who do and to arm himself against them with better weapons: "the integrity of a wise man, and the wisdom of an honest one."

Now, the first thing to note is Franklin's abrupt reversal at the end of the essay: He has no problem with the fact that the ancient term "cunning" meant knowledge and that the word is related to the word "king." His quarrel is not with that understanding of the term but only with what the term has now come to signify: the "little subtlety of base minds, who are incapable of great and honest actions." Well, what about the big subtlety of those who are capable of great and honest actions?

In his description of the project for achieving moral perfection, Franklin says that sincerity—as simplicity is known in the list of virtues—requires the use of no *hurtful* deceit.[17] If indeed wisdom and virtue are the same, and if great minds are allowed cunning, then it looks as if the essence of virtue is knowing when, how, and to what end to lie—that is, to use no hurtful deceit. To put this point in the terms used by Francis Bacon, whom Franklin quotes with accuracy, the essence of virtue—and strength of heart and mind—is not always telling the truth but knowing "*when* to tell truth and to do it." Franklin's reference to Bacon is obvious yet itself very subtle. It is in fact a hybrid, a combination of Bacon's opening remarks in two separate essays: "Of Cunning" and "Of Simulation and Dissimulation." In order to make sense of the virtue of simplicity, as Franklin presents it, we have to consider Bacon's discussion of cunning, simulation, and dissimulation.

According to Bacon in "Of Cunning," cunning is a kind of cheating or "packing" the cards.[18] It consists then in small tricks; the cunning are "haberdashers of small wares" used by men who lack the knowledge and ability for success in serious practical affairs. In the course of the essay, Bacon "set[s] forth their shop" with a list of stratagems used by the cunning, including such small ruses as varying the way one looks upon persons with whom one deals, bringing up unpleasant business, provoking curiosity in another, breaking bad news, presenting a main point as an afterthought, getting another to use to one's own advantage words one put in his mouth, and so forth.

Now, as Bacon presents the wares of the cunning, not a single one is unsuccessful. On the contrary, in each case the stratagem described works and in none is it strictly dishonest or unfair. The comparison to cheating at cards is, then, not exact, but the effect of the inexactness is to emphasize what cheating at cards and the stratagems do have in common—pettiness. As Bacon presents them, the problem with the stratagems is not that they are immoral or ineffectual. The problem is that, as regards serious business, they do not get to essential truths and are concerned only with small wares and are thus better for short-term and minor practice than they are for counsel about important and broad matters. For this reason, it is important in matters of state to be able to tell a cunning man from a wise one. The cunning look competent in practical affairs—and to a degree they are. But their competence is superficial and concerns only the beginnings of enterprises. Those who are merely cunning lack the ability to "examine or debate matters."

The problem with cunning, as Bacon reveals it, is that it is not deep enough: It does not get to the heart of practical matters of state and hence to those matters for which simulation and dissimulation are relevant. About those matters, as we learn in Bacon's essay "Of Simulation and Dissimula-tion," it is important then to know "when to tell truth, and to do it."[19] Knowing when to tell the truth and doing it require a strong wit and a strong heart. That is why "the weaker sort of politics . . . are the great dis-semblers." It is the *habit* of dissembling that marks off the weak from the strong. As Bacon says: "For if a man have that penetration of judgment as he can discern what things are to be laid open, and what to be secreted, and what to be showed at half lights, and to whom and when (which indeed are arts of state and arts of life, as Tacitus well calleth them), to him a habit of dissimulation is a hindrance and a poorness."

Here, we learn that simulation and dissimulation are relevant not only for practical matters of state but also for one's private affairs as well (the "arts of life"). While the habit of dissimulation is the fallback of the weak, of those without sufficient judgment of particulars, the appearance of the habit of "openness and frankness" is an element of well-used dissimulation: "Cer-tainly the ablest men that ever were have had all an openness and frankness of dealing; and a name of certainty and veracity." But these men are like well-trained horses, says Bacon, and hence "could tell passing well when to stop or turn; and at such times when they thought the case indeed required dissimulation, if then they used it, it came to pass that the former opinion spread abroad of their good faith and clearness of dealing made them almost invisible."

According to Bacon, there are three forms or degrees of the "hiding and veiling of a man's self." The first is "closeness, reservation, and secrecy," when a man simply hides himself from observation. The second is dissimula-tion "in the negative," when a man "lets fall signs and arguments, that he is not that he is." And the third is simulation "in the affirmative," when a man expressly "feigns and pretends to be that he is not." Secrecy is useful because no one will open himself to a "blab or a babbler," and thus the secret man comes to the knowledge of men's hearts. And nakedness is "uncomely" both in mind as well as body. Thus, says Bacon, "an habit of secrecy is both politic and moral." Moreover, if one is to be secret, it follows that one must also be a dissembler to some degree. Men will try to pick the truth from a secret man, and lest an absurd silence be the response, "no man can be secret, ex-cept he give himself a little scope of dissimulation; which is, as it were, but the skirts or train of secrecy."

As regards the third degree—"simulation and false profession"—Bacon says that it is "more culpable, and less politic; except it be in great and rare matters." Thus, a general custom of simulation is a vice that springs either from natural falseness or fearfulness or from great faults of mind that must be disguised. Simulation and dissimulation have three advantages: First, they "lay asleep opposition, and [then] surprise." The second advantage is that they allow for a "fair retreat." And the third is that they enable one to discover the minds of others. But then there are three disadvantages as well: They convey a show of fearfulness, they puzzle and perplex the conceits of those who might cooperate, and they deprive a person of one of the best instruments for action—trust and belief. The best mix of these qualities, Bacon concludes, is to have the reputation for openness, the habit of secrecy, "dissimulation in seasonable use; and a power to feign, if there be no remedy."

The import of Bacon's argument in the two essays could not be clearer: As regards honesty, the only habit that is good is the habit of secrecy mixed with well-used simulation and dissimulation. And although the third degree of lying—simulation—is to be used only in great and rare matters, these matters are not confined to matters of state but are, as Tacitus says, also important for the general "arts of life." Habitual liars are, of course, no good for themselves or for others. The best mix for both politics and life in general is the appearance of habitual honesty, the reputation for it, and the capacity for well-chosen dishonesty.

Franklin knew Bacon's argument perfectly well, and we cannot miss the impact of his explicit reference to "my Lord Bacon"—not just "Lord Bacon." For all of his moralizing praise of simplicity, there is no doubt that for Franklin, virtue properly understood is wisdom, and that wisdom includes knowing well when and how to lie, not just in matters of state and so for a public or common good but also in matters of life in general—that is, in the successful pursuits of one's political and personal self-interest. It is by that measure that we judge the "hurtfulness" of any deceit.

WE CAN NOW HAZARD some conclusions about Franklin's path of thinking. After considering the evidence—and after following up the subtle clues, contradictions, and sleights of hand that set us on our own paths of thinking—it is very hard to believe the moral and religious saga told in the *Autobiography*. The religious conversion, depicted as a return to belief in particular providence, is made less convincing by Franklin's claim never to have doubted particular providence. So we could not at first be sure if the story told is a pious comedy and fraud, or a comic fraud to cover a story that might cause the pious tiger—the good people—to bite Franklin (or the likes of Franklin) again.

The evidence Franklin reveals with his rhetorical art, however, points overwhelmingly to the latter, but not because Franklin came to a settled theoretical or metaphysical view of God's wisdom, power, and goodness.

Rather, he came to think that the background notions essential to any belief in divine, particular providence—justice and injustice, virtue and vice, merit and demerit, rewards and punishments, nobility and evil—are fundamentally and hopelessly confused. There is no particular providence that metes out divine justice, because the very idea of justice is in fact a chimera.

Recall the nudge-like but powerful implications of Franklin's account of his turn to retained Socratic diffidence. When, in presenting the flawed final couplet modeled on Wentworth Dillon, Franklin asks whether the lines would not stand "more justly thus," he makes a joke with enormous implications.[20] If free will, and merit and demerit, and moral virtue and wickedness make no sense, then justice as we understand it can make no sense. And thus, it can make no sense to speak of rewards and punishments that are deserved.

Again, Franklin did not come to this conclusion from his metaphysical speculations. On the contrary, as he presents metaphysics and Deism in the comic burlesques, despite all their theoretical huffing and puffing, both the hard-nosed and the soft-nosed freethinkers blithely accept our moral common sense, essential as that common sense is to the contention that "whatever is, is in its Causes just."[21] Franklin ended the essay on self-denial with a description of moral lunacy. He certainly does not mean that we are all crazy, but he does mean to say that the grounds of the bizarre and the extreme in human behavior can be traced to confusions at the heart of our normal, moral orientation in the world. Moreover, the insinuating error in metaphysics is not confined to "that kind of reading and study" but applies also to the thinking of orthodox believers: Our moral intuitions powerfully influence what we think about God. This fact is an "error" because the intuitions make no sense. And if so, then one would expect that if people's intuitions about justice are shaken and revealed to be incoherent, so too might their faith in God (if they do not, as is much more likely, become furious and chase the likes of Franklin out of town).

Franklin's rhetorical bag of tricks discloses the following course of his spiritual and intellectual journey: As a boy, his voracious reading of his father's theological books led him to be a contentious smart aleck about religion who disgusted and angered people with what must surely have been heterodox views. He soon came to doubt revelation and, at barely fifteen years old, became a thorough Deist by reading attacks on Deism. This Deism was sufficiently dry—denying particular providence and the existence of vice and virtue, merit and demerit—that when he argued for it with his friends, they became less than trustworthy, as if they had perhaps come to think that horse theft was "just."

In the course of the year after adopting thorough Deism, up to the time he was about sixteen, Franklin read Shaftesbury and Collins, who were suffi-

ciently influential to have led him to become a "real doubter" about orthodoxy, and had read Locke, the *Port Royal Logic*, and, lastly, Xenophon. We
know Xenophon came last and that the "real doubt" about orthodoxy was
crucial because the Socratic method of the humble but aggressive doubter,
learned from Xenophon, was safest for Franklin as one who had already become the real doubter and because he practiced the method full blast at least
through the 1725 writing of the *Dissertation* in London and then gradually
abandoned it, most likely through and perhaps even well beyond the 1728
writing of the *Articles of Belief*. But while the doubts about orthodoxy may
have remained the same, we cannot assume that the grounds of the doubts
discovered from Shaftesbury—the metaphysical doctrine of the perfect natural and moral order—were the same as the grounds discovered in the
course of the Socratic refutations.

Along the way, and certainly by the writing of the 1730 "Letter of the
Drum," he had read Hobbes and Spinoza and had come to think the likes of
these "impious free-thinkers" ultimately to be dogmatic atheists who, beginning with materialistic metaphysical premises, came to materialistic metaphysical conclusions. This view of Hobbes and Spinoza accords with
Franklin's "disgust" with metaphysical reasoning, which led him, as he reports later to Vaughn, to quit "that kind of reading and study."

Although Franklin abandoned metaphysical reasoning in disgust, he left
off the aggressive Socratic refutations only after having become sure
(though open to changing his mind) about the important matters discovered in the course of those refutations. The disgust with metaphysics, we recall, was from the "great uncertainty" that "insinuated itself unperceived"
into such reasoning. By the time he left off the aggressive Socratic refutations, Franklin had no disgust at any uncertainty—he had, within reason,
become sure. He could then retain only the habit of modest diffidence in
matters of religion, and he retained this diffidence for the rest of his life. But
it pertained to conversation, not to writing. For the latter and when he
wanted to, Franklin used his rhetorical bag of tricks to set his careful readers
to thinking for themselves, to soothe and elevate those in a hurry or those
with no desire to see their most cherished opinions put to the test, and, especially, to protect himself from the angry tiger's bite.

From Franklin's brief description of the Socratic refutations, from the
blockbuster clue about the substance of those Socratic refutations, and from
the later evidence from the comedies and the dialectical essays he wrote after he had become sure and turned to Socratic diffidence, we can think
about how the refutations might have differed from Franklin's metaphysical
reasonings and arguments.

Unlike metaphysics, which proceeds deductively and from groundless and dogmatic assertions about the beginnings and the order and the essence of the world or God, the Socratic refutations concerned simply our homely, everyday moral opinions. They revealed the internal incoherence and the contradictory double-sidedness of those opinions. They drew out the contradictory consequences of those opinions, which is why the refutations proved to be embarrassing to those who suffered them.

An orthodox believer might be enraged by metaphysical arguments or conclusions, such as the *Dissertation*'s conclusion that horse theft is just or that we are no better than the beasts of the fields. But he need not be embarrassed, because these conclusions need not be traced to his doorstep. Not so with the Socratic refutation, which shows that contradictions follow from the interlocutor's own opinions. And these contradictions must have threatened, to one degree or another, the one thing men most want in their hearts from God when they cannot get it from men: the justice they believe in and think coming to them for their virtue, for their merit, and for their worthiness.

Moreover, the metaphysical arguments were, well, metaphysical and also dogmatic, and so, in addition to containing the insinuating error, they were obviously uncertain as well. The Socratic refutations concerned our common moral opinions. If they blow up in our faces because they do not, in fact, make sense, there is nothing uncertain about that.

Franklin had two radical positions that denied particular providence: One was dogmatic and metaphysical, and the other sprang from the dialectical critique of morality. Metaphysics—and metaphysical Deism—is dogmatic not only because it presumes things about beginnings and essences that cannot be surely known but also because, at least in Franklin's view, it had not freed itself from a moral horizon that is, if truth be told, incoherent.

Franklin gave up metaphysics. But he did so in favor of a dialectical critique of morality, of whose methods and conclusions he remained sure. In the course of working his way to this critique, Franklin wrote the metaphysical spoofs on both sides of the particular providence divide. (According to what Franklin told Vaughn, we have no grounds to think that Franklin ever wrote any sincere metaphysical pieces. He says only that he gave up "that kind of reading and study.")[22] All were great fun. All pointed to the insinuating error—common to orthodoxy and metaphysical freethinking alike—discovered ultimately in the dialectical critique of morality. The comical pieces in favor of particular providence had the added benefit of providing Franklin with theological cover. Even the comic *Dissertation* was profitable, since it got him introduced to London's intellectual society. It was dangerous, to be sure (with its crack about horse theft), but it was not in effect all that dangerous because he quickly burned it, because the piece was circulated in cosmopolitan London, not in Boston or Philadelphia, and because he later covered himself again by professing regret about the "horrible errors" he was led to, as a young man, by metaphysics.[23]

As it turns out, the "pre-Socratic" disputatiousness and the Socratic refutations were, separately or together, *in effect* far more dangerous than the publication of the *Dissertation*. The *Dissertation* did not get Franklin run out of town. No doubt the guise of the humble doubter was safer than the provocations of the heterodox loudmouth. And the humble doubter was not accused of atheism between Franklin's flight from Boston and his turn to retained Socratic diffidence. But the fact is that these refutations had to have involved some risk, aggressive and embarrassing as they were, and the question then must then be why, after suffering the tiger's bite in Boston, Franklin continued these refutations as he did.

Again, we have to think the matter out on our own. But I think the most plausible explanation is as follows: Franklin did not have to engage in the Socratic refutations to *discover* the critique of morality. This he surely could have done in the privacy of his study and through private consideration of his own opinions and those of others. We can discover that critique by following up the subtle clues and twists and turns in his writings. We do not have to witness the refutations, or even read a detailed description of them as they transpired and confounded and embarrassed the victims. And anyway, Franklin does not present one to us. It is even possible that the refutations never happened and that Franklin has simply made them up. They might not have actually happened, and Franklin would still have set us on our way to thinking about the critique of morality. But what matters is that we are told that the refutations took place, and told in such a way as to make us wonder why he tells this story and why it contains his persistence in the dangerous refutations.

What *more* could he have learned from the refutations than he could already know from his own private reflections? From these private reflections, Franklin concluded that our commonsensical concepts of morality—justice, free will, deserving (merit and demerit), devotion, virtue and vice, the noble, evil, and reward and punishment—make no internal logical sense, despite the fact that they seem so obvious. He came thus to understand the contradictions in common moral behavior: the angry jealousy implied in punishment, as in the piling on suffered by Polly, the smashing of the good china, and the roasting of the poor wife's tongue; the unnoticed tension between sacrifice and gain, as displayed most vividly in the bizarre antics of the pious streakers and the self-castrator who wants a ticket to heaven's gate. He came to see that when we speak of free will and evil, we presume causes that make no logical sense, and so we blame poor smelly boys for trying to do their best and blame people for being bewitched by the Devil.

From the critique of morality, Franklin came to a profound doubt of particular providence, free of the dogmatism and uncertainty of metaphysics. It makes no sense to hope for divine justice, not because God is not just or for any other reason having to do with God but because justice makes no sense. If we want divine rewards and punishments, we would have to think that God had lost his senses. If he rewards the virtuous as we hope, then he gives first prize to the one who won first prize. And if he punishes the wicked as we hope, then he punishes a poor skunk, who never asked to be a skunk, just for being a skunk.

With this conclusion alone and by Franklin's own measure of the essentials of all religion, we can say that Franklin first came to lack religion on dogmatic metaphysical grounds but then came to lack it on the quite different grounds of the dialectical critique of morality. The latter would dispose of "religion," at least in Franklin's mind, and would have disclosed, as regards his own experience, the connection between religious faith and our moral hopes. But it would not necessarily dispose of those who claim that God (or the Devil) miraculously speaks to them, such as the drunken preacher giving the funeral service and the Reverend Gentleman in the "Letter of the Drum," or even such as those who might claim to have seen a witch cause sheep to dance and pigs to sing Psalms. (Nor would it dispose of the argument that God is a big, mean, and dangerous spider.)

As we saw with Philoclerus, we may scoff at such persons, but it is not so easy to prove them wrong. According to the *Autobiography* and its trail to the texts, by the time Franklin wrote the metaphysical comedies he had come to understand the insinuating error: that what we think about morality determines what we think about God. That certainly was so with his own stance on particular providence. The refutations concerned religion, but what Franklin became sure of in the course of them, the critique of morality, he did not need the refutations to discover. He discovered the critique of morality in *the course* of the refutations, but not *through* those refutations.

What then, could he have discovered only through the refutations? Why did he take the risk at all, and why did he persist in taking it after suffering the tiger's bite? I think only the following makes good sense: What Franklin discovered in the refutations was some external evidence for the insinuating error—that the refutations' effect on him (making him not able to reasonably believe in divine justice or particular providence) could be shown to be similar to their effects on others too. If the Reverend Gentleman were to be pushed on matters of morality, he too might undergo some change in matters of faith. And more important, there might be a change not just concerning particular providence but also in his conviction that the drum had really been banging. If the drunken preacher were to be pushed on matters of morality, he too might undergo some change not just in matters of faith but in his conviction that God had spoken to him while he was drinking in the pub.

Franklin could be sure that no God could speak to him intelligibly about justice. From this, he became sure that if there is a God, he provides no rewards or punishments in this world or in the next. Or if he does, one had better be scared because that God is powerful and completely out of his senses. *Franklin* could not take such a God seriously. But he could not be sure that if the drunken preacher or the Reverend Gentleman or poor Mitchel heard God's voice or felt his spirit within, that that voice and that spirit would become mute if their common notions of morality were refuted on their own grounds and in their own heads.

Perhaps they only think God speaks to them because they believe they deserve to be spoken to by God. And perhaps their ears would be stuffed up if they came to see that it makes no sense for them to think they could deserve anything, not to mention the attention of God. Franklin could have learned that only by poking at the Reverend Gentleman, or others like him, in the course of conversation and then interpreting the results. Mostly he made his victims mad; and Franklin would doubtless have wanted to see just how and when and what exactly made them angry, so as to see what that anger might reveal.

Franklin was much too careful to have revealed, in a brief and clear picture, what went on in his Socratic refutations. We have at best the clues that set us to thinking as best we can and that point us to the most plausible explanations of his clues. Moreover, we have only Franklin's clues, since he says he learned his method, and thus what it concerned, from Xenophon but says nothing more about what he might have learned from Xenophon, or from Plato, for that matter. We cannot then infer from Franklin's conclusions to those of his dialectical predecessors. From just what we know from Franklin alone, it is possible that he disagreed with them.

The best explanation for Franklin's humble aggression, it seems to me, is that the dialectical refutations were his first scientific experiments, not unlike the literary one he performed on poor Prouse and Mitchel. When he finally turned from the aggressive refutations to the retained Socratic diffidence, the only thing of which Franklin was *sure* was the critique of morality and his own resulting take on God. About the Reverend Gentleman, we can surmise that he had the best experimental evidence that he or any rational man could get. But in the end, though he could prove that lightning was in fact electricity, Franklin knew that no one, not even the most intransigent atheist, could prove demonstrably that electricity is not a divine fire.[24]

7 · The Political Principles of the Good Life

We can now consider Franklin's view of the good things in life, including and especially the importance of politics. We had to wait so long because only now can we see that Franklin's delight in politics cannot have been grounded on a view that it is the most important thing in life—and certainly not if that importance is understood as the highest service to God or somehow a moral and ennobling obligation that trumps natural science, philosophy, and other goods. Rather, he delighted in politics because it was one, but surely not the only or the highest, of the good things in life. We thus turn now to Franklin's understanding of the good life and to the political and other practical principles to which he adhered.

With the critique of morality, Franklin came to conclusions, on entirely different grounds, identical to those of the *Dissertation:* that free will and merit and demerit make no sense and "that vice and virtue were empty distinctions, no such things existing." It was from these conclusions that he further concluded against particular providence and, we can surmise, probably against belief in any God. But he did not then come to the *Dissertation's* absurd conclusions that "nothing could possibly be wrong in the world," that "all is right," or that we are brought "down to an equality with the beasts of the field! with the *meanest* part of the creation!"[1]

To be more precise, Franklin did not accept the *Dissertation's* clear and absurd argument that all things in the world—horse theft, murder, human beings, horses, and oysters—are equally good; or, if we prefer not to say "good," with its moral connotations, he did not accept its argument that there is no way we can find some things more attractive than others. It's one thing to say that moral virtue consists of empty distinctions. It's quite another thing to say, against reason, that all things in the world and in life are or wind up as equally good: that eating oysters is the same as being stretched on the rack; that it's no better to be me eating the oyster than to be the oyster; or that theft, rape, torture, and murder are as good as peace and prosperity. For Franklin, only an Enlightenment metaphysician could come up with such nonsense.

Franklin actually came down quite sensibly in between the Enlightenment view that we live in the best of all possible worlds and the contrary Enlightenment refusal ever to be satisfied with life as it is, or at least as it is handed to us. This latter position is most vivid in Hobbes and Locke. According to them, human needs are unlimited and human life is moved by pain or unease. We saw this principle at work in the metaphysical *Dissertation*, which Franklin did not really believe in precisely because it was metaphysical and ultimately dogmatic. For both Hobbes and Locke, the idea that there exists for human beings some condition of genuine satisfaction or fulfillment or happiness—a *summum bonum* (highest good)—is mere superstition or the product of vain philosophy.

Listen, for instance, to Hobbes, whose theoretical account of human life amounts to the claim that to be human is to be condemned to shop until we drop:

> The felicity of this life, consisteth not in the repose of a mind satisfied. For there is no such *finis ultimus*, (utmost aim,) nor *summum bonum* (greatest good,) as is spoken of in the books of the old moral philosophers. Nor can a man any more live, whose desires are at an end, than he, whose senses and imaginations are at a stand. Felicity is a continual progress of the desire, from one object to another; the attaining of the former, being still but the way to the latter. The cause whereof is, that the object of mans desire, is not to enjoy once only and for one instant of time; but to assure for ever, the way of his future desire . . . so that in the first place, I put for a general inclination of all mankind, a perpetual and restless desire of power after power, that ceaseth only in death.[2]

Or consider Locke, who argues in the *Essay Concerning Human Understanding* that "the philosophers of old did in vain inquire, whether *summum bonum* consisted in riches, or bodily delights, or virtue, or contemplation" and who said to the contrary that

> our desires look beyond our present enjoyments, and carry the mind out to *absent good*, according to the necessity which we think there is of it, to the making or increase of our happiness . . . [and] because the indolency and enjoyment we have, sufficing for our present happiness, we desire not to venture the change; since we judge that we are happy already, being content, and that is enough. For who is content is happy.

But as soon as any new uneasiness comes in, this happiness is disturbed, and we are set afresh on work in the pursuit of happiness.[3]

In a 1753 letter to his scientific friend Peter Collinson, on the topic of support of the poor, Franklin made it clear that he disagreed with Hobbes and Locke on this score. Far from being by nature continually spurred on by unease and acquisitiveness, human beings are by nature prone to desire "a life of ease, of freedom from care and labor."[4] This proneness can work in two opposite directions: toward industry to provide for such an easy life, as is the case among civilized peoples (such as Hobbes and Locke); or toward an extreme simplicity and a wandering, careless life, as is the case with the Tartars in Europe and Asia, the Negroes in Africa, and the Indians in America.

Of the Indians, Franklin commented that the natural proneness to ease is demonstrated by their reluctance to become civilized. They are not "deficient in natural understanding," he said, and see the advantages of the arts and sciences among the whites, yet they refuse to give up their indolent ways. And that this fact springs not from their being Indians but simply from their being human beings is demonstrated by the fact that when young whites of either sex are taken prisoner and then raised by the Indians and are then subsequently ransomed, they soon "become disgusted with our manner of life, and the care and pains that are necessary to support it, and take the first good opportunity of escaping again into the woods, from whence there is no reclaiming them." The Indians have few wants, and those wants are easily satisfied. "With us" there are infinite artificial wants that are no less pressing than the natural ones but are much more difficult to satisfy.

Franklin thus supposes that "close societies subsisting by labor and arts, arose first not from choice, but from necessity: when numbers being driven by war from their hunting grounds and prevented by seas or by other nations were crowded together into some narrow territories, which without labor would not afford them food." As things stand now among the civilized, "care and industry seem absolutely necessary to our well being." But human beings are by nature indolent, and only by convention and artificial needs (though no less powerful than natural ones) are they driven to hard work, restless and endless desire, and acquisitiveness.

Thus, it is on these grounds at least possible for the human individual, even in civilization, to step outside the general proliferation of new needs and even to act toward the existing and powerful artificial needs as if they can be satisfied. In the letter to Collinson, Franklin points out that the civilized poor are, like the Indians, prone to laziness. But because they are civilized, these poor are not lucky enough to be able in the end to afford their laziness. Too bad for them; but for a lucky and talented person it is possible, and not contrary to human nature, to work hard and then to retire (which is exactly what Franklin did, at the age of forty-two) to pursue the leisured activities of philosophy and politics.[5]

As early as 1732, Franklin made clear his view that we can speak intelligibly about the good things in life and even about the good life in the sense of a complete happiness. In the "Proposals and Queries to be asked in the Junto," Franklin asked whether a man can arrive at perfection in life.[6] His humorous answer is that, indeed, it is possible. The perfection of a thing is "the greatest the nature of that thing is capable of." Different things have different degrees of perfection, as do single things at different times. "Thus a horse is more perfect than an oyster yet the oyster may be a perfect oyster as well as the horse a perfect horse. And an egg is not so perfect as a chicken, nor a chicken as a hen; for the hen has more strength than the chicken, and the chicken more life than the egg: yet it may be a perfect egg, chicken and hen."

Franklin goes on to say that it may well be true that we cannot be as perfect as an angel or as we ourselves might be in heaven. But that does not alter the fact that we can be as perfect here as we are capable of. To deny this fact makes no sense: "It is as if I should say, a chicken in the state of a chicken is not capable of being so perfect as a chicken is capable of being in that state. In the above sense if there may be a perfect oyster, a perfect horse, a perfect ship, why not a perfect man? That is as perfect as his present nature and circumstances admit?" This charming philosophical doodle is followed immediately by an argument that a rational creature can be happy if he knows three things: "such truths as relate to . . . happiness," that wisdom is knowing what is best for oneself, and that some people are wiser than others.[7]

Humorous doodle that it is, Franklin's reflection on perfection and happiness is really pregnant with important implications. Different things have greater degrees of perfection in ascending order: "A horse is more perfect than an oyster," and a man is more perfect than a horse. By this time, Franklin did not think this fact means that, as humans, we deserve and the world owes us our existence; nor does it mean that we somehow deserve to rule those creatures endowed with lesser perfection; nor does it mean that the less perfect owe obedience or service to the more perfect; nor does it mean that if the less perfect defer to or devote or sacrifice themselves to the good of the more perfect that the less perfect cannot share, the less perfect come thereby to be "worthy" and thus to "merit" reward.

Franklin thus does not mean there is any "great chain of being" in a moral sense. He means, rather, that horses can do and experience more things than can oysters, that, likewise, men can do and experience more things than can a horse, and that some men can do, experience, and know more things than other men.

Socrates would never choose to be the stupid Crito. No one, knowing what it is like to be a human, would wish or choose to be an oyster or a horse. And this really means that we prefer not to be dead, since if we really became a horse we could not be aware of what we had lost. No horse—could it know what it is to be a horse—would rather be an oyster. So far so good. Given these simple facts, it is possible and makes sense to do and experience the things we can as fully as we can: If we are capable of strength, then it is better to be strong than weak; if we are capable of knowing, then it is better to know than to be ignorant. Again, so far so good.

By the same logic, however, if we happen to be stupid, then it is best to know whatever we can within the limits of that stupidity. This is the clear implication of Franklin's conclusion that if there can be a perfect oyster and horse, there can also be a perfect man—"as perfect as his *present nature and circumstances*" admit. If we add this conclusion to the stipulation that specific things have different degrees of perfection at different times, the result is that for human beings there is a possible state of perfection for every nature and for every set of circumstances as they come and go and change. At the very least, for Franklin, it is better to be what one is than to be dead. Of course, life could be so wretched that happiness is crushed and death really is preferable to life—that's not impossible. Surely that's the situation of the wretch on the rack. In most such awful circumstances, life clearly affords the possibility of having what is at least preferable (death) to the miserable life we're stuck with. The poor fellow on the rack, it's true, can't choose his end, but even he can at least remind himself that the torment can't go on too long.

Franklin does not mean that for human beings everything is at any time as perfect as it can be. And he does not mean that the wretch on the rack is as happy as the king of Siam. These propositions are both absurd. Nor does he mean that we should not endeavor to change our circumstances for the better as much as we can. That always makes sense. He means, rather, something like this: Happiness consists in knowing what can and cannot be done in life and in knowing that what can be done is circumscribed by conditions and events over which we have absolutely no control.

If a person is born poor and doesn't like it, it makes sense to try to become rich. But if he is born poor and doesn't like it but lacks the temperament or brains or luck to do better, then wisdom would disclose that there is no one morally to blame for this, that there is nothing to be done, and that it makes sense for the person to take as much delight as possible in what goods life still presents—not the least of which is not being an oyster but, rather, eating them when possible. So Franklin might say: Just ask a poor, lazy, stupid, and unlucky man who can still smell and taste and hear music and get drunk and have sex if he would rather be a horse or a chicken than a man? It makes sense to want what the rich have and even to take it if that can be done safely; but it makes no sense to envy or resent the rich for having things or to feel that one deserves these things and the rich do not—since no one "deserves" anything. It makes no sense at all to be angry (sad and regretful, perhaps; angry, not at all) about the bad hand life may deal, any more than it makes sense to be angry with someone who does one harm (any more than it makes sense to be angry at a snake).

Likewise, it makes no sense to think that, beyond the reasonable best a man can do, he can ensure for the future the circumstances that obtain at any time. People may think that they can command life altogether and thus act as Hobbes says we do by nature, striving incessantly and restlessly "to assure for ever, the way of . . . future desire." But for Franklin, people act this way not because they are hardwired to do so but only because they lack wisdom (which most do and always will). Though Franklin does not say so explicitly, it is reasonable to conjecture as follows: Just as the murderous turmoil of this world can be traced not to "evil," which does not exist, but, rather, to our moral intuitions and righteous indignation, so too can the anxious turmoil in the soul be traced to these moral intuitions. We think that if we strive—for power after power—somehow the world will reward our deserving efforts. And just in case the world does not oblige, God will, provided that we have been good. It is not so much fear or unease that disturbs the soul as, rather, our deeply rooted sense that we are deserving and have something coming to us.

Franklin's understanding of wisdom and happiness is simply and beautifully expressed in a letter he wrote to his sister, Jane Mecom, from London in 1766. He begins by sending his condolences to Jane for the death of her husband, and he then turns to Jane's earlier report about the circulation, in Philadelphia, of harmful stories that Franklin was complicit in the passage of the Stamp Act. Says Franklin:

> As to the reports you mention that are spread to my disadvantage, I give myself as little concern about them as possible. I have often met with such treatment from people that I was all the while endeavoring to serve. At other times I have been extolled extravagantly when I have had little or no merit. These are the operations of nature. It sometimes is cloudy, it rains, it hails; again 'tis clear and pleasant, and the sun shines on us. Take one thing with another, and the world is a pretty good sort of a world; and 'tis our duty to make the best of it and be thankful. One's true happiness depends more upon one's own judgement of oneself, on a

consciousness of rectitude in action and intention, and in the approbation of those few who judge impartially, than upon the applause of the
unthinking undiscerning multitude, who are apt to cry hosanna today,
and tomorrow crucify him.[8]

The moral pieties are, of course, for the sake of his sister's sensibilities. But
the lesson here is clear enough. True happiness consists in knowing the limits of circumstances and making the best of them and of whatever happens.
Just as Franklin did what he could to oppose the Stamp Act (within the limits of his own ambitions, of course), he then, when it became law, made the
best of the situation by trying to get a friend to administer it and thought his
countrymen foolish to get so worked up about the matter. As he wrote about
the Stamp Act to his friend Charles Thomson, some months prior to the letter to Jane: "We might as well have hindered the sun's setting. That we
could not do. But since 'tis down, my friend, and it may be long before it
rises again, let us make as good a night of it as we can. . . . idleness and pride
tax with a heavier hand than kings and parliaments; if we can get rid of the
former we may more easily bear the latter."[9]

No doubt Franklin was covering his tracks and explaining the extent to
which he had "misjudged his countrymen," as Carl Van Doren describes
Franklin's surprise at the Americans' moral outrage at the tax. And no
doubt, as Van Doren rightly says, Franklin's temporizing with the Stamp Act
was a strategic judgment about how best to secure the long-range goal of imperial unity.[10] But these words also reflect Franklin's deepest understanding
of life and happiness: that happiness consists in accepting and living with
the inevitable and unalterable "operations of nature." Nothing could be further from the Hobbesian restless pursuit of power after power, or from
Locke's perpetual flight from unease, or from the mechanical and greedy Enlightenment idea of the "perfectibility of man" derided by D. H. Lawrence.
Assuming some good fortune, which must include the good fortune of possessing wisdom, and assuming the world does not put one on the rack, the
world, just as it is, is a pretty good one.[11]

In Franklin's view, there were lots of good things in the cake shop of life.
Knowing the world as it really is, and not as we wish it were or hope it will
be, was very high on his list of good things. As Poor Richard said in 1736,
"He that lives upon hope, dies farting."[12] Natural science was also right up
there, as was invention, and of course the challenges of politics and public
service, followed very closely by wine and food, women and song, good
jokes, and witty conversation.

So what was Franklin's positive "moral doctrine"? What were the rules to
be used for securing the cakes in the cake shop of life? He tells us in the *Au-*

tobiography's list of moral virtues that constitute moral perfection.[13] In presenting the list, Franklin says that from his reading he found the "catalogue" of the virtues "more or less numerous," since different writers used a term, such as temperance, more or less widely. Some spoke of temperance as referring to eating and drinking, whereas others used the term as referring to "every other pleasure, appetite, inclination or passion, bodily or mental, even to our avarice and ambition." Franklin chose to use more names with fewer ideas, rather than vice versa, for the sake of clarity.

There are, he says, thirteen virtues, and to each he appended "a short precept, which fully expressed the extent I gave to its meaning." The first is temperance: "Eat not to dullness, drink not to elevation." The second is silence: Say only what will benefit oneself and others and avoid trifling conversation. The third is order: Keep each thing in its place and each business in its time. The fourth is resolution: "Resolve to perform what you ought, perform without fail what you resolve." The fifth is frugality: Only spend for what is good for yourself and others; that is, waste nothing. The sixth is industry: Do not lose time and always be employed in useful actions and avoid all unnecessary actions. The seventh virtue is sincerity: "Use no hurtful deceit. Think innocently and justly; and, if you speak, speak accordingly." The eighth is justice: "Wrong none, by doing injuries or omitting the benefits that are your duty." The ninth is moderation: Avoid extremes and "forbear resenting injuries so much as you think they deserve." The tenth is cleanliness: Do not tolerate uncleanness in body, clothes, or house. The eleventh is tranquility: Do not be disturbed at trifles or at common or unavoidable accidents. The twelfth is chastity: "Rarely use venery but for health or offspring; never to dullness, weakness, or the injury of your own or another's peace or reputation." And the thirteenth and last is humility: "Imitate Jesus and Socrates."

In the sequel, Franklin makes it clear that his ordering of the list's elements is not random.[14] The order is hierarchical because it springs from Franklin's practical desire not just to know what is right and wrong but to become habituated to doing what is right and not doing what is wrong: "As the previous acquisition of some might facilitate the acquisition of certain others, I arranged them with that view as they stand above." Temperance comes first because one needs a clear head against old habits and temptations. This makes silence easier.

Why does silence come next? Because Franklin says he desired "to gain knowledge at the same time" that he improved in virtue and thus needs his ears more than his tongue, with its habits of prattling, joking, and punning. Order comes next because it provides the time for his project. Resolution, once it becomes habitual, will keep him firmly to the task of obtaining the remaining virtues. Frugality and industry come next, so as to free him from debt and produce "affluence and independence" and "make more easy the practice of *sincerity* and *justice*, etc. etc."

Franklin tells us that he did not succeed in mastering the practice of all the virtues—he was especially deficient in order and in general fell far short of the perfection at which he aimed—but he was a better and happier man for having tried.[15] It was "to this little artifice [aiming high so as to do the best he could], with the blessing of God," that he owed "the constant felicity of his life down to his 79th year." To temperance he owed his health and constitution; to industry and frugality he owed his wealth and success, which enabled him to acquire the knowledge that made him a good citizen and esteemed among the learned; and to sincerity and justice he owed "the confidence of his country, and the honorable employs it conferred upon him." And it was to the whole of the virtues, so far as he achieved them, that he owed his even temper and the cheerfulness in conversation that made his company so agreeable and so sought after.

Close attention to this charming presentation shows Franklin up to his usual tricks. There are two accounts here: one in which he details and explains the functional order of the list and another in which he comments on how those virtues he attained contributed to the felicity he achieved in life.[16]

In the first account, some of the virtues are presented as means to the other virtues: temperance, silence, order, resolution, frugality, and industry (by way of freedom from debt, affluence, and independence) are all, by making them easier, means to sincerity and justice and (the "etc. etc.") moderation, cleanliness, tranquility, chastity, and humility. It is hard to see how cleanliness, chastity (as Franklin describes it), and tranquility are moral virtues, since they concern simple matters of prudence and not the good of others. But we could, if we try, see them also as means to sincerity, justice, moderation, and humility. The latter would seem easier to achieve if we are sufficiently concerned with decorum not to be dirty, sufficiently in control of our sexual desires not to be maddened by them, and undisturbed by trifles and accidents.

It seems, then, that ten of the virtues are means to sincerity, justice, and humility—the three that on first glance seem like genuinely moral virtues since they involve deference to the good of others. Of sincerity Franklin says in the list that it requires us to "use no hurtful deceit." Lies are acceptable so long as no one is hurt and so long as these lies comport with thinking innocently and justly. Thinking so should then produce doing so—being just, which is doing no wrongs to others or omitting benefits that are one's duty. No mention here of seeking the just punishments of the wrongs others commit, but so far, so good.

And then comes the rug-pulling sleight of hand. Moderation is the avoidance of extremes and requires that one should "forbear resenting injuries so much as you think they deserve." By "injuries" Franklin clearly means moral wrongs, since we do not resent a mere injury, and resentment implies moral indignation.

Now one's first inclination is to suppose Franklin means simply that we should avoid thinking erroneously that a wrong is greater than in fact it is. Hence, we should not resent it as much as we might at first passion. But he does not speak in this straightforward and obvious way. As he expresses the matter, by asking us to forbear our resentment, he could just as easily, and in fact more probably, mean that if we suffer a wrong and address it correctly, we should be moderate and *want* less punishment than we *think* it deserves. On the first and less likely reading, we should not jump to false conclusions about the extent of wrongs. But on the second reading, we should not want the punishment we think is really coming to one who has wronged us.

Franklin provides no evidence to let us decide between these two readings. But if we read the sentence to mean we should want less punishment than a wrong really deserves, then why does he not just say that? Why "so much as you *think* they deserve" as opposed simply to "what they really deserve"? We cannot just jump back to the first reading and say that he must mean that in our passion we have measured the wrong incorrectly. If we make this jump, we're chasing our tails: We're still faced with the alternative and more likely possibility that he means that we *should not want what we think is really deserved for a wrong accurately assessed*—another matter altogether.

This second reading accords better with serious moderation, since the first reading has more to do with getting things right and not jumping passionately to false conclusions. The seriously moderate man is one who, knowing what is deserved, does not demand the full measure of retribution. To use Franklin's words, the moderate man would "avoid extremes" in the measure of the law. But in this most plausible reading, Franklin speaks as if "what X deserves" is the *same* as "what one *thinks* X deserves." Is this not the same as to say that a right is but what one *thinks* is a right? (As we will see, this is just what Franklin did indeed say.) Such a right, dependent as it is on our mere opinions, is no moral right at all. But then likewise for what an injury might deserve by way of resentment: If the deserved resentment is just what *I or anyone thinks*, then it is really everything and nothing at all. But then there are no wrongs, only injuries—and for injuries there is no place for resentment or justice.

The *Autobiography*'s account of moderation pulls the rug out from under justice, and then the whole rug unravels. If there are no wrongs, then there can be no such thing as justice and injustice, no benefit one is duty-bound to provide to others. If there is no such thing as injustice, then it makes no more sense to say we should think innocently and justly than it does to say one should act justly and according to one's duty, and thinking innocently and justly can have nothing to do with defining the hurt one should avoid in telling deceits. In that case, the hurtful deceits one should avoid are not those that harm others and so cause a "wrong" but those deceits that hurt oneself. The only moral virtue left unscathed and still standing is humility, which tells us to imitate Jesus and Socrates. But when Franklin concludes Part Two of the *Autobiography* with the story of how he came to add the virtue of humility—at the urging of the Quaker Friend—even humility takes a final hit.[17]

In his account of how the virtues led to the felicity he has had in life, Franklin makes no mention at all of humility. And when he later tells us of how he came to add that virtue to his list, he describes the diffidence that looks like, but really isn't, Socratic method number two. He then says nothing of how to imitate Jesus, but instead concludes with a brief paragraph about how hard it is to subdue pride. The reason for this conclusion would seem to be obvious: By his own admission, he had achieved merely the appearance of humility, and that cannot be a successful imitation of Jesus. Nor can implying, as we see in the letters introducing Part Two of the *Autobiography*, that Franklin was a moral model as good as the Bible, with no imitation suggested.

So Franklin says that pride is the hardest of all the natural passions to subdue. We may "disguise it, struggle with it, beat it down, stifle it, mortify it as much as one pleases, it is still alive, and will every now and then peep out and show itself. You will see it perhaps often in this history." Franklin's remarks here make it sound as if he—like any other sinful mortal—were simply in the grip of a natural passion and hence could not measure up to the divine Jesus. But that is not quite what Franklin says next: "For even if I could conceive that I had completely overcome it, I should probably be proud of my humility."

"Probably"? In other words, it is not certain that he would be proud were he to have overcome pride altogether. Now suffice it to say, if the critique of morality makes sense, then it can never make sense to feel the swelling chest of pride. If there is no moral free will, then how can one be proud of one's accomplishments? Glad and happy, perhaps, not to be an oyster or Crito— but proud for simply being what one is? So it looks as if Franklin had, in fact, overcome pride, but not on grounds he could readily reveal.

But if we assume, for the sake of argument, that we could sensibly if sinfully be proud of our accomplishments, and especially of our moral virtue and worthiness, it is possible to see how, if we were perfectly humble, we could not be humble.

In its starkest, Calvinist form, humility is the awareness and feeling of our lack of worthiness for anything before God, of our utter powerlessness and lack of virtue, of our being nothing and having humility alone as our refuge.[18] Were we to achieve perfect humility, we would have to deny our worthiness to receive it as a gift from God: We did and could do nothing to deserve or to receive the gift of perfect humility. If we were to *become* by God's gift and through no doing or merit of our own *perfectly* humble—if we get through no effort or merit of our own the only refuge available to us—we could not then be proud for having received it.

But would we not then, having become perfectly humble, have also *then become* righteous and justified as well? So it would seem, and Calvin agrees.[19] And if we become righteous and justified, even if we did nothing to deserve to become righteous, are we not *then* also worthy? Would we say that we are, *as then justified*, worthless in the eyes of God? No. Are we not *then*, for whatever reason God may have, worthy in God's eyes while others (the unjustified) are not? Yes. And if we are *then* worthy—even if that worthiness is an unearned gift from God for which we were previously unworthy—can we *then* be *perfectly* humble? Not if perfect humility is recognizing our utter lack of worthiness. Are we not here in the dilemma of the pious streakers and the tension between loss and gain?

Franklin's point is not that we, being mere mortals, are incapable of becoming perfectly humble. For Calvin, God sees to it that we can, even if it is by his justifying grace alone. Franklin's point is, rather, that if we think about the justifying gift of humility, it turns out to be a round square. It may be possible for us to imitate Socrates. But if we try to imitate Jesus, we cannot really know what we're doing.

There is one more sleight of hand at work in the list and description of the virtues. In the first account, Franklin tells us that since silence prevented him from prattling, punning, and joking, activities that only made him acceptable to trifling company, he gave silence second place in the order of progress because his desire was "to gain knowledge at the same time that I improved in virtue." According to this statement, knowledge is an end of the virtue of silence, but knowledge is not the same thing as virtue or understood as a means to other virtues, or to anything else, for that matter.

Then, in the account of how virtue produced his felicity in life, Franklin praises industry and frugality as virtues that led to the wealth and success that enabled his acquiring "all that knowledge which enabled him to be an useful citizen and obtained for him some degree of reputation among the learned."

There seems at first glance a contradiction between knowledge first understood as an end in itself and knowledge understood as a means to service or reputation among the learned. But Franklin expresses himself with a precision that clarifies the issue. In speaking of knowledge as a means, Franklin clearly refers to it in the restrictive—"that knowledge which"—and so marks it off from knowledge otherwise understood. Thus we see two kinds of knowledge that result from two different means: knowledge understood as choice-worthy in itself, and facilitated by silence; and knowledge understood as a means to service (useful citizenship) and esteem, and facilitated by industry and frugality.

According to the critique of morality, useful citizenship cannot be good because of the sacrifice and nobility involved. And so it is good ultimately for oneself; but, at least according to the letter to his sister Jane, that good does not consist in the esteem of the "unthinking [and] undiscerning multitude." We can assume with some confidence that the esteem of the learned, won by knowledge, is more valuable. But that knowledge is not the same as the knowledge facilitated by silence, the knowledge that is not presented as a means but is presented as choice-worthy in itself.

As usual, Franklin gives us the clues to work the matter out for ourselves. An experience or activity or thing can be understood as good or choice-worthy in three senses: as simply a means (money or the drilling that fixes my tooth); as choice-worthy simply in itself (a good smell or taste, seeing a beautiful sunset, or happiness); or both as a means and as choice-worthy in itself (health, and perhaps knowledge).

From all we have seen so far, the following seems to be the most plausible account of Franklin's understanding of knowledge: Industry and frugality both produce and facilitate the knowledge of how to get along in public affairs and the knowledge of those things, like natural science, that gain the esteem of the learned. The esteem both causes pleasure for oneself and also facilitates one's getting along in public affairs (as indeed it did for Franklin). This does not rule out the fact that the knowledge that gains the esteem of the learned, and is useful therefore for public affairs (including providing public goods like protection from lightning), is also choice-worthy in itself, just as is health—good all by itself and good for those things it allows us to do. Were there no payoff in the form of protection from lightning, popular reputation, and the esteem of the learned, or even pleasure for oneself, it would still be better, for Franklin, to know what lightning is than not to know this fact—or any other truth about nature, for that matter.

What then, we wonder, is the knowledge facilitated by silence? The most plausible contender is the knowledge required of a man of sense—the knowledge of our true interest, happiness. Such knowledge consists, most importantly, in the knowledge of virtue and vice and divine rewards and punishments. Franklin came to this knowledge not just by giving up prattling, punning, and joking in order to associate with more than trifling company, but also by giving up his loud and obnoxious disputations, by disguising—a form of silence—his aggressive refutations, by keeping his mouth shut about what he came to understand about true happiness, and by writing ironically in such a way as to speak at one and the same time to all and just to some (another form of silence).

That knowledge was both choice-worthy in itself and a means for happiness. Regardless of the outcome, it is better to know the truth about happiness than not to know. But happiness does not consist simply in knowing the truth about happiness, first because the cake shop of life has more things in it than knowledge, and second because part of the truth about happiness is that there are no guarantees in this life—there is nothing we can do to assure that life will not break us with its misfortunes, and there is nothing we can do to make us "deserve" the happiness we want.

So what was Franklin's positive "moral" doctrine? What were the rules to be used for securing the cakes in the cake shop of life? In the light of all we know, and in the light of Franklin's list of virtues, we can see that the rules are as follows: It is unwise to eat and drink or fornicate to the point of dullness, derangement, or ill health (temperance and chastity). It is unwise to prattle and blab everything one knows (silence). It is useful to have some tidiness in one's life (order), or at least to marry someone who can provide it. It is very smart actually to do what is good for oneself (resolution) and, if one is poor, to be able to save and work hard enough to become rich and independent (frugality and industry). It is smart to avoid extremes and not only sensible but also completely rational to "forbear resenting injuries so much as you think they deserve" (moderation), since nothing is ever "deserved." Of course, it is better to be clean than to be filthy (cleanliness). It is wise to be calm and unperturbed by small things and accidents (tranquility). One should think and speak innocently and justly because habitual knavery is foolish and a reputation for justice is useful (sincerity), and also because there is no good reason for more than necessary harms to others.

And one should not lie so as to cause hurt, which means that one should lie only when necessary and as much for one's own as others' good, and one can lie well only if one has the reputation for being honest (sincerity, again). And by extension from sincerity, it makes perfect sense *whenever possible* to be just (justice)—to avoid stealing and murder and cheating and such things.[20] But necessity ultimately rules in life, and so one should not feel remorse for those "injustices" one cannot avoid, nor should one think one deserves anything on account of having avoided "injustices" whenever possible. Above all, it is wise to know that the most fundamental truths about life are cards to hold very close to one's vest, and that although it is impossible to imitate Jesus because even Jesus could not, it is very smart to have a reputation for humility (the thirteenth virtue).

OF THE GOOD THINGS in life's cake shop, politics was high on Franklin's list. If we think about the broad trajectory of Franklin's political career, we see that from the beginning to the end he was, to put it bluntly, a political fixer and more like a big city political boss than a crusading ideologue or a righteous partisan. For Franklin, politics was a form of mechanics. (Boss Tweed admired Franklin and got his start in politics in much the same way Franklin had: by helping organize a fire engine company almost named for Franklin.)[21]

Franklin's earliest political foray was as a pamphleteer in the controversies involving evangelical challenges to the Presbyterian establishment in 1734 and 1739, when Franklin skirmished with an eye to fracturing that establishment. His more concrete organizing of the militia for defense against Spanish and French privateers in 1747 coincided with his experiments in electricity and brought him to the untoward attention of the proprietor, Thomas Penn, who took him for an ambitious and democratic rabble rouser. In this first political fix, Franklin successfully united the wrangling parties (Quaker moderates, wealthy commercial gentlemen, and middling artisans), who for different reasons had been unwilling to pay for the defense of the city during King George's War. With his retirement as a rich man from business in 1748 and the takeoff of his career in elected office—to the City Council in 1748 and to the Pennsylvania Assembly in 1751—Franklin's policy interests focused first on schemes for basic public infrastructure (fire protection and a hospital) and higher education (the Philadelphia Academy).

The premier issue for Franklin was, however, defense. It dominated his political activities throughout the 1750s. This was without doubt the issue that set Franklin against the Proprietary Party and the person of Thomas Penn and gave birth to his ill-fated Albany Plan for colonial union in 1754 and his long and equally ill-fated project to secure Crown rule over Pennsylvania.

By the time Franklin published the famous Canada Pamphlet ("The Interest of Great Britain Considered") in 1760—in which he argued that in the aftermath of the Seven Years' War, Britain should retain all of Canada and not worry about retaining Guadeloupe—the glue that combined Franklin's policy interests had become well set: America would be the place where the British Empire would achieve unheard-of expansion and grandeur. Until as late as the beginning of 1774, Franklin remained a staunch imperialist and worked at fixing the ever-worsening breach between the colonies and the Crown. It cannot be said that Franklin was, at least until the Revolution, particularly good at his political mechanics. Although he certainly did well in his early years in Pennsylvania and performed well before Parliament in the Stamp Act crisis, he just as certainly misjudged popular and partisan opinion in the colonies in general and in Pennsylvania in particular—in the election of 1764, which he lost, and in the Stamp Act crisis—and overestimated the British government's support for Crown government of the colonies, which of course never succeeded. And one could well argue that his faith in political mechanics and deafness to American opinion led him in the end to the almost-harebrained scheme of the Hutchinson letters affair, a catastrophe that finally dashed his hopes for cabinet office and served only to exacerbate the imperial crisis.

With the final collapse of Franklin's imperial hopes, he turned to the revolutionary and republican cause. Luckily for Franklin, he had just signed on to the American cause when he got the job that suited him best, head of the diplomatic mission to France. This job required strategic skill in the rarified circles of finance and international diplomacy, great charm and wit, and the respect of French intellectual circles. But it did not require a keen sense for the ebb and flow of popular public opinion in America. It thus afforded Franklin the opportunity to pull off the single most important feat of the Revolution: the depletion of French royal coffers for the republican cause. For his troubles, the French foreign minister, Charles Gravier de Vergennes, got a polite letter of apology from Franklin for having come to terms with England behind Vergennes' back.[22] And for France's troubles, it later got the Revolution and the Terror.

Franklin returned to America in limited triumph, since he still had powerful enemies and detractors, but even that fact did not prevent him from his final and successful attempt at a fix, his efforts for the Connecticut Plan that solved the deadlock over representation in the Constitutional Convention. (In this instance, Franklin, a longtime unicameralist, did another switch of "principle" and saw the wisdom of an upper house.) Also at the convention, Franklin's speech against limiting the suffrage to freeholders put an end to the dangerous matter. The speech was a beauty and made the hardheaded point that the Americans had just won a war with the steadfast courage and loyalty of the common people, whose behavior in captivity had been just the opposite of that of English sailors, who, when captured, eagerly switched sides. The message could not have been clearer: If the common people were disenfranchised, their help couldn't be counted on again. For a poor public speaker, his word did well enough on that important score.[23] Note again Franklin's flexibility: a nod toward aristocracy on the issue of representation, a nod toward democracy on the issue of suffrage. In his waning days,

Franklin did what he could for the abolition of slavery, but this problem was well beyond the efforts of a few smart and farsighted people.

In assessing and explaining Franklin's checkered political career, the most recent and best scholarship has painted Franklin as an odd combination of moralist and selfish hothead. In explaining Franklin's bungled scheme for royal governance of Pennsylvania, Robert Middlekauff argues that Franklin was simply blinded by personal hatred of the proprietor Thomas Penn. Gordon Wood doubts this interpretation and argues in favor of Franklin's typical rationalism: Franklin was an ardent royalist and imperialist, and this commitment explains his behavior in the early 1760s. Franklin's elitist rationalism, not his anger, led him to misjudge colonial public opinion, both with respect to the scheme for royal government and in the Stamp Act crisis.[24]

But as regards Franklin's turn to the revolutionary cause, Wood says that Franklin became "more passionate in fact than nearly all the patriot leaders." Wood grants that Franklin, who was suspected as a dubious "patriot" and even thought by some, including James Madison, to be a possible British spy, had good opportunistic reason to fake his patriotic zeal. But in end, says Wood, Franklin was motivated by his intense and personal anger at what he took to be betrayal by his beloved British Empire. For Franklin, says Wood, the Revolution was "an unusually private affair."[25] Thus Wood opts ultimately for Middlekauff's view of a more irrational Franklin.

Wood says, however, that despite these irrational foibles, Franklin was motivated to political ambition by the moral imperative of public service. Franklin became convinced, says Wood (joining all the recent biographers and the Aldridge tradition), "that science and philosophy could never take the place of service in government. Being a public official—that was what counted, that was how the community was best served, that was where true greatness and lasting fame could be best achieved." "Franklin took his project to achieve moral perfection quite seriously," says Wood, and his successful efforts in diplomacy can be seen as the real embodiment of his related project for establishing a united party for virtue.[26]

The evidence for an angry Franklin is, in my view, very thin and wholly speculative.[27] (For an account of the evidence, interested readers should see note 27 here.) Wood is right to say that Franklin's scheme to bring royal rule to Pennsylvania was in itself perfectly reasonable, given his views about the empire and America and his hopes for the Grand Ohio Company (a scheme, involving Franklin and Thomas and Richard Walpole, to sell land in the American West). That Franklin misjudged public opinion in America and ministerial opinion in England is best laid at the door of Franklin's rationalism: Men like Franklin, no matter how skeptical they are, often in practice assume that others like themselves see the world just as clearly as they do, and men like Franklin often cannot take seriously those fools whom they know cannot see the world clearly at all.

The question of Franklin's anger is not trivial and, indeed, matters to my argument. If the philosophical Franklin is the real one, then we should not see palpable evidence that he was in character an angry man. How could he be if, as a philosopher, he understood why anger is always foolish?[28] I do not mean to imply that Franklin was the completely cool cucumber he presents in the *Autobiography*. He was, after all, a human being and could get mad (and sad) and be uncaring and even mean (especially when it came to his family). But he cannot, I think, be counted as an "angry man" for whom some deep resentment or sense of injustice framed his politics. Rather, he was always able to reflect philosophically on the perfect irrationality of anger as the wellspring of moral and political commitments.

He thus left us with a wonderful and charming picture of how reason tells us we should look on those occasions when our passions get the best of us. It occurs in the account of his treatment at the hands of Sir William Keith.[29]

The freethinking Keith, governor of Pennsylvania, was impressed by the young Franklin and supported his endeavors as a printer. Keith provided the lad with a letter of recommendation to Franklin's father, encouraging him to finance a new printing firm for his son. And when Franklin's father refused, Keith himself promised to finance the boy and suggested that Franklin go to London, armed with letters of credit and recommendation from Keith, in order to purchase the necessary printing equipment. When Franklin sailed for London, he was under the impression that the letters were among the governor's dispatches, held in a bag that would be opened before they landed in England. Franklin discovered that there were no letters, and he was left high and dry in London, with no credit and no introduction. When Franklin immediately related the business to his friend Denham, the latter informed him that Keith was notorious for his empty promises and that it was comical to think of a letter of credit from one who had no credit.[30]

After relating the story, Franklin then poses a question to his readers: "But what shall we think of a Governor's playing such pitiful tricks, and imposing so grossly on a poor ignorant boy!" Now for all we know, Franklin could well have been furious at Keith at the time, and we should well expect some condemnation of his character and his dirty trick. But Franklin's reply to the question is as dispassionate as can be: "It was a habit he had acquired. He wished to please every body; and having little to give, he gave expectations.—He was otherwise an ingenious sensible man, a pretty good writer, and a good Governor for the people, though not for his constituents the proprietaries, whose instructions he sometimes disregarded.—Several of our best laws were of his planning, and passed during his administration."

"It was a habit he had acquired." Such is Franklin's response to one who really had mistreated him. (It is not really clear that his brother James ever really did.) But Franklin's reaction—at least in the hindsight of the *Autobiography*—is perfectly in accord with his critique of morality. To be indignant would have required Franklin to believe that Keith's conduct merited blame and punishment. But there is no such thing, in Franklin's view, as blameworthy ill conduct. Had the mistreatment not been the result of Keith's habit, it could have been the result of Keith's opinion that the boy had some mistreatment coming. That opinion would, likewise, make no sense—not because it could not have been true on its own ground but because the ground, that someone could have something coming, is unintelligible. But as Franklin explained to his parents in the Masonic initiation affair: "It is no more in a man's power *to think* than *to look* like another . . . and if after all I continue in the same errors, I believe your usual charity will induce you rather to pity and excuse than blame me."

It would not have been Keith's fault that at the time of the affair he was less wise than Franklin was when he recounted the story. Or Keith could have had some other end in view, unknown to Franklin, which required his mistreatment of the young boy. Were it really necessary, there is no blame. And were it not really necessary, there is still no blame. Keith would simply have misjudged the matter; he would have failed in the science of virtue, for which he suffered because of his tarnished reputation. However we look at the matter, Franklin wants us to see that there was no good *reason* for Franklin to have been angry, even if in fact he was.[31]

Anger, for Franklin, is for fools. But he did not for a moment think it possible or wise to convince the good people—those angry tigers capable of righteously standing up for justice—of this fact. Franklin's take on anger did not make him soft. But it did make him profoundly humane. For Franklin, there is never a good reason to harm people more than clearheaded prudence requires. The harms others do are just what they think is really best even for those they harm. And when those harms are not really for what is best or exceed what is really necessary, the cause can almost always be traced to judgment distorted by the manifold forms of moral indignation. For Franklin, it only makes sense to be kind (or at least indifferent)—although only as far as one's own happiness allows and as far as possible in an unpredictable and hard world filled with human folly.

As regards the imperative of public service, there is likewise no persuasive evidence for the view, held by many, that Franklin saw and made a fundamental choice between the duty of public service and the delights of philosophy (both natural and moral) and invention, not to mention of wine, women, jokes, and song.[32] The mere fact of Franklin's political career does not by itself reveal his motive for pursuing it. All we have is what Franklin, especially in the *Autobiography*, makes us think about the noble, just, and good things. And from all the evidence uncovered so far, it is impossible to conclude that Franklin was moved to his political career by the usual motives of political ambition: the moral imperative of public service, a love of justice, righteous indignation, the longing for glory, or angry payback for personal injustices endured.

None of these motives are consistent with the critique of morality at the core of Franklin's deepest reflections about life. Rather, Franklin engaged in politics because it was for him a challenging and delightful aspect of invention and production. It was a part of the grand game of modernity, which promised, above all, new and hitherto unimagined possibilities for human life.

Franklin was, in short, a political Baconian, applying to the realm of social life what he applied to nature (electricity, smoke and wind, water, and vision, to name a few) and to music. "Life is," as Franklin said in his classic bagatelle *The Morals of Chess*, "a kind of chess, in which we often have points to gain, and competitors or adversaries to contend with; and in which there is a vast variety of good and ill events, that are in some degree the effects of prudence or the want of it."[33] Franklin played the games of chess and politics alike (and often played the former better than the latter), and he never simply gave up philosophy or invention. Franklin's Craven Street lodgings in London were as much a laboratory as they were the colonial agent's residence, and Franklin began the philosophical *Autobiography* in 1771. Franklin engaged in politics only because it was among the things he most liked, and what Franklin liked, Franklin did.[34]

For Franklin, politics was a delightful and high-stakes game. But I do not mean to suggest that he had no principles or project in mind. He most certainly did. In a nutshell, Franklin was first and foremost a political modern—again, a Baconian who thought that the technological conquest of nature could be coupled with a reasonable (and limited) reduction of politics to a form of wise administration.

He was an egalitarian, though of a very moderate stripe. Despite his profound skepticism, he thought that religion was crucial to social life. He liked the British Empire, especially as long as America was a part of it, and he then liked America by itself, because it constituted the widest horizon for new possibilities; the New World was where the action would be for a new world. He liked liberty, and he eventually disliked slavery. And yet for all his Baconianism, he never forgot that the rational animal is the only creature in nature's garden that lives most of its life in deluded folly. For this reason, we cannot say that Franklin was a full-blown man of the Enlightenment. To get a fuller picture of Franklin's political principles, we first have to understand how deeply he rejected the doctrine of natural rights and of rights in general, then grasp his political Hobbesianism, and then take the measure of his lifelong egalitarianism.

IN 1732 FRANKLIN COMPOSED a set of "proposals and queries to be asked the Junto," the club for discussion that he established in 1727.[35] In the manuscript as we have it, the remark in question comes among such questions as the origins of the dew, the value of importing servants, why converts to a sect are more zealous than those brought up in it, whether men can achieve perfection in this life, the nature of happiness for a rational creature, and the relation between knowledge and prudence. The important question is whether "it is justifiable to put private men to death for the sake of public safety or tranquility, who have committed no crime? As in the case of the plague to stop infection, or as in the case of the Welshmen here executed." As the questions have become deeper and more ominous, we then get the following absolute blockbuster: "If the sovereign power attempts to deprive a subject of his right, (or *which is the same thing*, of *what he thinks* his right) is it justifiable in him to resist if he is able?" (my emphasis).[36]

The blockbuster is not the question but the parenthetical explanation of the term. In civil society, a subject's right is "*what he thinks* his right," and that this goes for the natural condition as well is clear from the context: The issue is not whether the government can take a person's property but whether a man can resist when the government resolves to kill him though he has committed no crime—that is, when that person has, in relation to the governing power, returned to the state of nature. In the condition of nature and in civil society, a man's right is whatever he thinks is his right. If I think that my "right" is to take from you what I need *and also what I want*, then that is my "right." That is exactly what Franklin thought the right of the British Empire was with regard to Canada.[37] From the moral point of view—from the understanding of rights that takes them to be grounded in an inviolable moral dignity and accompanied by binding duties—such a right is no right at all. (Franklin thus said, but did not publish, in 1732 what we've seen he points to with subtle rhetoric in the *Autobiography* some fifty-two years later.)[38]

In his biography of Franklin, Esmond Wright says of the Declaration of Independence that "the war that was declared was not the war prepared for: the enemy now was monarchy, the goal no longer merely independence but republicanism, the rights claimed no longer 'the rights of Englishmen' but 'natural rights.'" As to Franklin's role in drafting the Declaration, says Wright, he left the matter to Jefferson because "Franklin was never an addict of grandiloquence in style, and the language of 'natural rights' was unusual to him."[39] Signing the Declaration was a big shift for Franklin. But the principles of rights espoused in the document involved for him no shift at all because, however robustly he embraced the Revolution, to say that the language of natural rights was "unusual" to him is a considerable understatement.

As we should expect from Franklin's critique of morality, he did not believe in natural rights any more in 1776 than he had in 1732. Moreover, he could not have believed that the "rights of Englishmen" had real moral gravity, as opposed to being quite useful arrangements that made for sensible politics and liberty. If I can merit no sacrifice or deference from others (whether human beings as such or just Englishmen)—if I have nothing coming to me simply because of what we all are or what I do—then it is hard to see how I bear a right that, according to justice, must be deferred to by others.

If I have a natural right to x (say, my life, or an apple) but you have no duty to recognize and defer to that right, then at the very least my "right" means only this: You can't give me a moral reason why I shouldn't take the apple, and I can't give you a moral reason not to kill me and take it away. In either case, I cannot say that I "deserve" my life or the apple, on the basis of the right; and neither can you "deserve" your life or the apple, on the basis of the right. From a moral point of view, a natural right with no corresponding natural duty is really no right at all. Animals kill only for what they need. But if we humans have natural rights but with no deserts, that is, rights with no corresponding natural duties, then there is no moral reason for us not to take whatever we want, and what we get we do not deserve, and so we cannot expect anyone else to respect our possession of what we have. Franklin did not like the language of natural rights because he did not believe in natural duties; and he did not much like, so it seems, to trade on the (chimerical) moral connotations of the language of rights.[40]

Now, to the extent that the Revolution was fueled by the theoretical doctrine of natural rights (along with fuzzier notions of classical republicanism), that doctrine sprang, as is well known, primarily from Locke's *Second Treatise of Government*. The two key principles of that treatise were the origins of government in a contract of free and equal individuals in the prepolitical state of nature, and a consequent natural right of revolution by the governed against the governors. The former doctrine, the origin of government in a contract of free individuals in a state of nature, was worked out in Hobbes's earlier *Leviathan*. But Hobbes, unlike Locke, was by no means held in high repute, for reasons that will become obvious below.[41] Franklin, of course, knew Locke's *Second Treatise*. And he knew Hobbes's *Leviathan* very well, as is clear from the argument of Philoclerus and from a comment to Joseph Priestly, in a letter of 1780, that Franklin wished "that men would cease to be wolves to one another."[42] As it turns out, Franklin was very much, but not completely, a political Hobbesian.

That Franklin knew Hobbes's political argument is clear from a letter, written probably in 1737, from Franklin to James Logan.[43] Logan's practice was to send chapters of his writings to a friend for criticism, and he sent Franklin a chapter, entitled "On Moral Good or Virtue," of his work to be called "The Duties of Man Deduced from Nature." Poor Logan must have been dismayed to read Franklin's response, which is openly dismissive: The first bad sign is that Franklin says he gave the chapter the most attention possible given how busy he is. And then the best thing Franklin can say is that the design of the chapter is excellent and the management good, although summaries at the beginning and alongside each paragraph should be added to prevent "any disgust that the author's dilate manner of writing may give to some readers; and the whole is so curious and entertaining, that I know not where any thing can be spared."

Then comes the crucial remark: "It seems to me that the author is a little too severe upon Hobbes, whose notion, I imagine, is somewhat nearer the truth than that which makes the state of nature a state of love: but the truth perhaps lies between both extremes." Two brief paragraphs follow: As regards music, Logan could have done better by explaining what makes a tune agreeable, and as regards the virtues, it would have been good for Logan to have enumerated, distinguished, and defined them. And as regards temperance, Franklin thinks Logan may be incorrect, but he, Franklin, has no time to explain it in writing.[44]

Franklin obviously thought Logan's chapter—which argued, against Hobbes, that men in a state of nature recognize and act on the natural duty to love one another—worth quite a bit less than the paper on which it was written. Franklin obviously did not believe in such a natural duty. To Franklin's way of thinking, Hobbes's argument about the state of nature—that in it, life is "solitary, poor, nasty, brutish, and short"—is closer to the truth than is Logan's view that our natural condition is one of mutual love.[45] But the Hobbesian view is only *closer* to the truth, not the truth as such. That truth lies somewhere between the extremes, not midway but, instead, closer to Hobbes. Franklin thus tells Logan—and hence tells us—that he was not a full-blown Hobbesian. I will come back to Franklin's differences with Hobbes in chapter 8. But as regards natural duties that men might have to others, Franklin was even more skeptical than the widely despised Hobbes.

According to Hobbes, in the condition of mere nature prior to any government, all men are equal in their ability to kill one another and in their being endowed with the natural right to self-preservation—the natural right to do whatever is necessary to remain alive. For Hobbes, nature dissociates men: Because of competition, diffidence, and glory, there is in the natural condition a war of "every man, against every man," and there is no such thing as justice and injustice.[46] Hobbes argues that although this natural condition has never been general "over all the world . . . there are many places, where they live so now. For the savage people in many places of *America*, except the government of small families, the concord whereof dependeth on natural lust, have no government at all; and live at this day in that brutish manner."[47]

Franklin touched on the natural condition of mankind in his marginal comments on Allan Ramsay's pamphlet "Thoughts on the Origin and Nature of Government, Occasioned by the Late Disputes between Great Britain and Her American Colonies: Written in the Year 1766."[48] The pamphlet, which was published in 1769, addressed the representation crisis sparked by the Stamp Act. In it, Ramsay denied the principle, "frequently advanced," that men are free and equal in a natural condition, and he argued that an equal right to liberty and property had never been acknowledged by anyone but the lowest orders of society, who assert it for the sake of cutting the throats and taking the property of their betters. Franklin underlined the following remark by Ramsay: "*No history of the past, no observation of the present time, can be brought to countenance such a natural state.*" In the margin, Franklin responded to the remark as follows:

This writer is ignorant that all the Indians of North America not under the dominion of the Spaniards, are in that *natural state*, being restrained by no laws, having no courts or ministers of justice, no suits, no prisons, no governors vested with any legal authority. The persuasion of men distinguish[ed] by reputation of wisdom is the only means by which others are governed or rather led. And the state of these Indians was probably the first state of all nations.

Franklin ignores completely Ramsay's denial of a natural and equal right to liberty and property and comments only on his claim that there is no state of nature. There is, says Franklin, and the Indians are in it. As regards natural right, the most we hear from Franklin is in a marginal remark on another pamphlet on the same theme, this one anonymous, entitled "Good Humor." In it, the author comments that the colonies have a natural right to be treated fairly and that this right "derives from the natural right of all men to equity and justice, and it is indefeasible." To this, Franklin comments in the margin: "Here appears some sense."[49]

"Some sense," says Franklin, not the truth about our natural condition and our natural rights. Ramsay, later on in his pamphlet, denies that govern-

ment begins with a contract and claims that "society is composed of the ruling and the ruled, 'all equality and independence being by the law of nature
strictly forbidden: and it is farther declared by the same authority, that whoso-
ever is not able to command, nor willing to obey, shall forfeit his living or his
life'" (the emphasis is Franklin's).[50]

To this Franklin simply responds: "I do not find this strange law among
those of nature. I doubt it is forged, and not in the book." Ramsay next says
that the union between master and servant is both naturally and divinely
sanctioned. He says, moreover, "that the sole determination of [the master's]
right rests with the superior," because if that fact is not granted the determination does not rest anywhere and the union "so necessary in society . . . must
of course be dissolved."

To this Franklin responds: "That is, he that is strongest may do what he
pleases with those that are weaker. A most equitable law of nature indeed. . . . No man would unite in society on such terms."

In these marginalia, there is no clear indication or declaration that men
have natural rights of any kind, even though Franklin agrees with Hobbes
that the Indians of America are in a state of nature and even though he denies that there is any natural law that sanctions inequality. According to
Franklin, human beings are equal in the sense that the only terms on which
reasonable men would enter civil society are those where their livings and
their lives are in their own hands. But it does not follow that even human
beings such as these can claim a natural right to life and liberty in the sense
that there is a natural and binding moral duty of others to afford them these
goods of life and liberty, or in the sense that, because of some inherent or
natural worth or dignity, they have these goods coming to them, regardless
of the expense to be paid by others in providing them.

Ramsay argues, in the course of denying natural right, that if there were
such a natural right to equal liberty, it would be "inseparable from an equal
right to property."[51] Ramsay is clearly right on this score. If Franklin believed in a natural right to equal liberty, then he would necessarily have believed in a natural and equal right to property. But he did not. In a letter to
Robert Morris, written from Passy in 1783, Franklin complained of expenses
that had not yet been provided for by Congress, and he blames the "remiss-
ness" and the unwillingness of the Americans to pay taxes. He then says:

All property, indeed, except the savage's temporary cabin, his bow, his
matchcoat, and other little acquisitions, absolutely necessary for his subsistence, seems to me to be the creature of public convention. Hence the
public has the right of regulating descents, and all other conveyances of
property, and even of limiting the quantity and the uses of it. All the

property that is necessary to a man, for the conservation of the individual and the propagation of the species, is his natural right, which none
can justly deprive him of: But all property superfluous to such purposes is
the property of the public, who, by their laws, have created it, and who
may therefore by other laws dispose of it, whenever the welfare of the
public shall demand such disposition. He that does not like civil society
on these terms, let him retire and live among savages.[52]

Now, in this comment Franklin does acknowledge a natural right to such
property as is necessary for self-preservation, first of the individual and then
of the species, and this is property "which none can justly deprive [another]
of." This apparent right is the one that obtains in the state of nature, since
Franklin clearly refers to the natural property as belonging to the savages—
those identified earlier as just those who do live in the state of nature.
But then two facts confound the issue of the natural right even to natural
property of which men cannot "justly" be "deprived." First, in any state of
nature—and among the Indians, as Franklin says in the marginalia on Ramsay—there are no courts or ministers of justice. So how can we ever know if
a deprivation is or is not just? Hobbes, of course, makes this very point. Second, and far more important, Franklin makes an extraordinary comment on
Ramsay's argument concerning how governments come to be dissolved.
Ramsay says: "If you ask who has the right to judge which acts of power are
or are not contrary to nature, 'I answer, *no body*. The immediate impulse of
every man's feelings *stands in the stead of all judgment* in such cases.' For men
rise together against the government, and it falls."[53]
To this Franklin says: "Nobody; but every body." Whereas Ramsay claims
that no one has the right to be the judge of when power is ill used and that
governments fall, rather, by spontaneous and organically united *feeling,*
Franklin says coolly that each and every man can make this judgment—an
act of the head, not the heart. But if this is true of men who are governed, it
must also be true of men in the state of nature as regards the actions and persons of others. In the state of nature, every free and equal individual is the
sole judge of what deference he might owe or give to another, precisely as regards "the conservation of the individual."
Thus, if, in a state of nature, one judges one's preservation to be in danger,
then one is free to deprive another even of the temporary cabin, bow, and
matchcoat absolutely necessary for his subsistence—without moral blame
and without injustice. And just when such circumstances obtain is entirely
up to the judgment of every individual. In other words, the scope of an individual's "natural right" to self-preservation is *whatever* that individual thinks
it is. And if that scope is "whatever" an individual thinks it is, then there is

no criterion for judging what is and what is not a "mitigating" circumstance of necessity. There is, then, always a reason and a liberty for anything that anyone wants to do.

This is just what Franklin said in 1732, and it is exactly Hobbes's much more explicit position in the *Leviathan*. Says Hobbes:

> The right of nature, which writers commonly call *Jus Natural*, is the liberty each man hath, to use his own power, as he will himself, for the preservation of his own nature; that is to say, of his own life; and consequently, of doing any thing, which in his own judgement, and reason, he shall conceive to be the aptest means thereunto. . . . and because the condition of man, (as hath been declared in the precedent chapter) is a condition of war of every one against every one; in which case every one is governed by his own reason; and there is nothing he can make use of, that may not be a help unto him, in preserving his life against his enemies; it followeth, that in such a condition, every man has a right to every thing; even to one another's body.[54]

Here the argument is that if, in a state of nature, I judge it necessary to deprive another of his (necessary) temporary cabin, bow, and matchcoat, I commit no injustice. It's no wonder that Hobbes was not such a popular fellow. One could say, however, that Hobbes doesn't take the argument all the way down, since he speaks as if, should that necessity actually be objectively determined, it would justify the predations of the state of nature. And so, absent such objective necessity, my fellow natural man would deserve his cabin, bow, and matchcoat. Perhaps that's why Hobbes said, referring to Scripture, "the fool hath said in his heart, there is no such thing as justice."[55]

But according to Franklin's critique of morality, the very idea of justifying any taking in the state of nature, or any deserving there when necessity does not obtain, simply does not make any sense. On this score Franklin was more hardheaded than the hardheaded Hobbes—most probably, Franklin would say, because Hobbes had not examined the question of justice as fully as he had. For Franklin, there simply is no property, necessary or otherwise (including one's own body) that one "justly deserves" or of which one might be "justly deprived," under any circumstances, period. So when Franklin said simply, in 1732, that a right is what anyone thinks it is (that is, no moral right at all), he meant just that, period—with no reference to any circumstances or conditions, necessary or otherwise.

No wonder Jefferson reputedly did not want Franklin to put his pen to the Declaration of Independence for fear that pen might be tempted to a joke. It should come as no surprise that when Franklin was engaged in polemical defense of the Americans in the period from the Stamp Act crisis until the end of the Revolution, he almost never used the language of natural rights or the laws of nature and nature's God, and that on the rare occasions when he did, he always fudged.

In the 1765 letter to the *Gazetteer* directed at the anti-American polemic by "Vindex Patriae," Franklin said in conclusion that the Americans "have not the least desire of independence; they submit, in general, to all the laws we make for them; they desire only a continuance of what they think a *right,* the privilege of manifesting their loyalty by granting their own money, when the occasions of their prince shall call for it."[56]

In 1768 Franklin published in the *London Chronicle* an explanation of the American reaction to the Townshend Acts. The piece was reprinted again in the *Chronicle* in 1774, with some additions but with no reference to events subsequent to 1768.[57] In this famous essay, Franklin traces the then-current ill humor of the Americans to the indifference of the English government to American opinions as to representation and taxation and consent, and to the Americans' deeply held opinion that the actions of the House of Commons had the effect of rendering the American assemblies useless, which, in the Americans' opinion, would deprive them of "their most essential rights."

But Franklin speaks only from the vantage point of what the Americans "say as to Governors," and as "an impartial historian of American facts and opinions."[58] He speaks, thus, of what the Americans think or say their rights are, and he counsels the English from the standpoint of the prudential need to consider what the governed actually think. All this is again in perfect accord with the view expressed in the query for the Junto: a right is no more than what a person *thinks* it is.

So too is what Franklin says, in the *Chronicle* piece, as to the restraints on American trade and manufacture. "There cannot be a stronger natural right," says Franklin, "than that of a man's making the best profit he can of the natural produce of his lands." Expressing the case in the negative and the comparative is appropriately coy. That there is no stronger natural right does not mean that the natural right to profit from one's land is strong at all, or even that it is real, for that matter. And Franklin did not think it real—at least not real in the sense that it imposed a binding moral duty on others, including the English king.[59]

Thus, in the marginalia on the Ramsay pamphlet, Franklin makes the following comment on Ramsay's claim that there is no law of nature that requires consent to taxation. Franklin replies with Ramsay's own nonsense: "Does not *every man's feelings,* as he [Ramsay] says, Declare that his property is not to be taken from him without his consent?" (the emphasis is

Franklin's).[60] Our feelings tell us that there is such a binding natural right to profit from one's lands; but of course our feelings are no indicators of truth.

In defending the Americans, Franklin never really appealed to the principle of natural rights or to a natural right to be taxed only by way of consent and representation; he appealed only to such rights as had developed from practice, expectations, and opinions. And in a 1754 letter to William Shirley about the Albany Plan (reprinted in the *London Chronicle* at the time of the Stamp Act crisis in 1766), Franklin even defended the principle of consent to taxation as a useful method of getting people to bear difficult burdens—by inducing them to "have, or think they have some share in the direction."[61]

In 1775, as hostilities were under way, Franklin's old friend and fellow member of the Honest Whigs, Bishop Jonathan Shipley, wrote to Franklin in America, bemoaning the impending storm and blaming it on the administration and not on the English people.[62] In the course of Shipley's fond and kindly letter, the bishop comments on the objectionable argument of one John Lind in a book entitled *Remarks on the Principal Acts of the Thirteenth Parliament*. Lind approves of the most objectionable acts of the Parliament, but Shipley is most offended by Lind's argument about the origins of property. "The same author asserts that all property is derived from the liberality of government. . . . This doctrine is rare news for Ld. Sandwich and Rigby; but indeed it has not the merit of novelty; for it was taught by Hobbes long ago. I am not of an intolerant spirit and yet I should think it no great crime to hang the teachers of such principles."[63]

Franklin was, of course, grateful for Shipley's support, and he would not have thought it prudent for the English government—or for the American assemblies, for that matter—to confiscate and then redistribute all property. But he agreed in principle and more with Hobbes on this score, if not with the anti-American Lord Sandwich and Richard Rigby. As Franklin said in his remarks about the Constitution of Pennsylvania: "Private property therefore is a creature of society, and is subject to the calls of that society, whenever its necessities shall require it, even to its last farthing."[64] It's a good thing for Franklin that kindly Bishop Shipley was across the ocean and did not really mean his suggestion of using the rope on those schooled by Hobbes.

FRANKLIN'S PROFOUND SKEPTICISM about right, natural or otherwise, is of course in accord with his fundamental critique of morality. His skepticism about right is at the heart of his egalitarianism and what I have called his political Baconianism: the view that politics is an artful game aimed at getting things to work right and not a matter of setting things "right" in the sense of justice. The most powerful version of political Baconianism was outlined not by Bacon but, rather, by his student and protégé, Hobbes. And Franklin's most telling comment in this regard is almost a paraphrase of Hobbes's view of the matter.

It is commonly thought that Hobbes was absolutely in favor of absolute monarchy. This is not quite true, and there is an important and often over-looked subtlety in Hobbes's thought on the matter. According to Hobbes, monarchy is the best—the most convenient—form of the absolute power of government, the sovereign power, created when men agree to leave the state of nature. The sovereign power is absolute in the sense that—being willed by every individual as necessary for self-preservation—its actions (whatever they may be) cannot be described as unjust. If that power threatens the sub-ject's life (for any reason), the subject is not obliged to stick around (we take criminals to the gallows in chains because they have the natural right, by which Hobbes means the natural liberty, to self-preservation), but in no case can the actions of the sovereign be declared "unjust."

For Hobbes, this absoluteness characterizes sovereign power as such, in any of its forms, and not just the monarchical form. The three forms of common-wealths—monarchy, aristocracy, or democracy—are determined by where the absolute sovereign power created is placed: in the hands of one, or few, or all. In each of these different forms, sovereignty is the same and is absolute in terms of its powers and in the sense that we cannot decry its actions as un-just.[65] It follows from this that the differences in the forms of government are merely technical—like the difference between a flat-headed and a torque-headed screwdriver. They have no special dignity, nor do they warrant some claim of moral superiority or special capacity for justice. Says Hobbes:

> There be other names of government, in the histories, and books of pol-icy; as *tyranny*, and *oligarchy:* But they are not the names of other forms of government, but of the same forms misliked. For they that are dis-contented under *monarchy*, call it *tyranny;* and they that are displeased with *aristocracy*, call it *oligarchy:* So also, they which find themselves grieved under a *democracy*, call it *anarchy*, (which signifies want of Government;) and yet I think no man believes, that want of govern-ment, is any new kind of government: nor by the same reason ought they to believe, that the government is of one kind, when they like it, and another, when they mislike it, or are oppressed by the governors.[66]

Franklin agreed with Hobbes that government is a mere tool—no differ-ent really from a screwdriver—and that the forms it might take are deter-mined by prudence and practicality: In principle, any one will do. Although

Hobbes thought in practice that monarchy was the only sure bet, he held that opinion for reasons of feasibility and practice, and surely not because monarchy is sacred or glorious, much less because it is inherently more "just" than other forms. So too with Franklin, who eventually disagreed with Hobbes only on the technical matter of whether monarchy was the most convenient form. Until just before the Revolution, Franklin thought monarchy in the British form was the most convenient form. When it finally became clear that it was not, he concluded that for the Americans a republic was in order. But in principle, any form of government would do.[67]

Franklin's comment in his brilliant and effective concluding speech at the Constitutional Convention was thus not just soothing rhetoric; it also reflected his most deeply held theoretical view about the forms of government and is simply redolent of Hobbes:

> In these sentiments, Sir, I agree to this Constitution, with all its faults, if they are such: because I think a general government necessary for us, and there is no *form* of government but what may be a blessing to the people if well administered; and I believe farther that this is likely to be well administered for a course of years, and can only end in despotism as other forms have done before it, when the people shall become so corrupted as to need despotic government, being incapable of any other.[68]

The "best form" of government is the one best suited to a given set of circumstances. In that spirit, Franklin abandoned his long-held dislike of bicameral legislative branches, because the circumstances at the time required a solution to the problem of representation, and so those circumstances trumped any scruples that Franklin might have had from "principle." Even despotic government is not morally bad: It is what corrupted people most need and is good for them, however much this fact is their misfortune. And so Franklin's cool endorsement of the new, republican constitution was perfectly consistent with his earlier comments in a 1754 public letter to Shirley, speaking of the Grand Council proposed in the Albany Plan:

> It is very possible, that this general government might be as well and faithfully administered without the people, as with them; but where heavy burthens are to be laid on them, it has been found useful to make it, as much as possible, their own act; for they bear better when they have, or think they have some share in the direction; and when any public measures are generally grievous or even distasteful to the people, the wheels of government must move more heavily.[69]

For Franklin, government is the art of administration—and there are many ways to skin the political cat. One could better say that for Franklin, government and politics are matters of technology and not at all really about "sacred honor." Politics could be dangerous, he knew well. As he reportedly said to the Congress on making the vote on the Declaration unanimous, "Yes, we must indeed all hang together, or most assuredly we shall all hang separately." But so too was electrical experimentation, which almost killed him. The difference between political technology and material technology had to do with the greater recalcitrance and bad construction of the objects of political technology.[70]

Franklin's political Baconianism (and thus his Hobbesianism) explains his political opportunism. It's true that Franklin did what Franklin wanted and what he thought was good for him. But his abrupt shift from monarchist to republican involved no abandonment of moral principle. He was not and could not be a conscientious monarchist or republican or democrat, although in different times and circumstances he claimed rhetorically to be all three.

While Franklin agreed with Hobbes about the forms of government, and while he would have agreed with Hobbes that tyranny is but one form of government "misliked," at least in the sense that people mistakenly think one form of government more morally deserving than another, he did not hesitate to refer to the dangers of tyranny and despotism, when it served his polemical and rhetorical purposes and because he really believed in these dangers. For Franklin, the purpose of government is simply and only to provide the conditions for individual liberty and happiness, however we might see that happiness, and for such prosperity as is possible.

But human ambition and folly being what they are, bad and even dangerous government is always possible. Franklin thought that all administrative arrangements are subject to decay, abuse, and corruption and that it was up to the governed to prevent the decline of government as long as possible, to fix it if they can, or to take off for greener pastures if they cannot. Thus, although it would not be accurate to say that Franklin believed men get the good or bad government they *deserve*, he did think they get whatever government, from good to bad, of which they are capable. From the beginning to the end of his political life, he worried about the dangers of corruption in government that led to oppression, and he worried as well about corruption that would make the governed unwilling or unable to watch out for their interests.

Still, government is a matter of managing interests and necessities, not of justice and injustice. The latter make no sense, but people in general cannot see this fact, and their thinking too fervently that they do make sense is the biggest impediment to political clearheadedness.

If the government needs money, then it is in the interest of the governed to supply it, even if it is within the power of government simply to take what it needs regardless of what the governed wish to supply or might actually consent to supply. If the government takes too much, it is prudent to object and to point out to those who govern that it isn't good for anyone—the governed or the governors—to impoverish the many and prevent the freedom of trade that increases wealth. If the government takes too much and does so in a way that threatens the liberty of the governed, there is no moral obligation for the governed to stick around, and it is entirely up to the governed to judge when their own vital interests require either self-defense or flight. Of course, the government can try to prevent that flight—it is as much at liberty to do what it thinks is in its own and its citizens' interest as the citizen at liberty to do what is in his own interest. It is best if both genuinely listen to reason, since most serious conflicts do more harm than good. It is perfectly reasonable for the governed to denounce a dangerous government as tyrannical or despotic, if such denunciation will help bring the governors to their senses. But since governments as well as individuals do merely what they believe (even if stupidly) to be the right thing, in conflicts between the governed and those who govern, there is only a contest of liberties, not an issue of binding moral obligations and duties.

Franklin makes this last point clear in the marginalia to the essay by Ramsay. To Ramsay's claim that men have no right to desert their country, Franklin says:

> Have not all mankind in all ages had the right of deserting their native country when made uneasy in it? Did not the Saxons desert their native country when they came to Britain? Is it not tyranny in any government to make prisoners of its subjects, and is it not contrary to their rights? Will a Scotchman tell us this, whose compatriots are to be found in every country upon earth? Could there possibly be more than one legal government in the world at this time if this doctrine is true? Must not all nations but the first be deserters?[71]

And Franklin makes a similar argument in a 1773 pamphlet, "On a Proposed Act to Prevent Emigration," opposing a proposed ban on emigration. "God has given to the beasts of the forest and to the birds of the air a right when their subsistence fails in one country, to migrate into another, where they can get a more comfortable living; and shall man be denied a privilege enjoyed by brutes, merely to gratify a few avaricious landlords?"[72]

In both instances, as always, Franklin writes with wonderful subtlety. The analogy to the beasts and the birds is at first inappropriate and then on second glance perfect. Why inappropriate? The beasts have no rights, since after all we eat them. But they do have the freedom to wander where they will. Why perfect? Men have no moral natural rights either. But they do have the liberty to do whatever is necessary for them to secure their vital interests. And whereas the birds and the beasts know no "countries" of origin, all human emigrants do—and they go from one to another.

Is the other country obliged to take them? It is, if indeed the immigrant exercises a universal, morally binding natural right that establishes a claim on the other country. Franklin clearly did not think such an obligation exists—he certainly felt no obligation to the "Palatine Boors" (more about them later). And what goes for a potential host (that it is free to shut the door to keep out would-be immigrants) goes as well for the original home country (that it is free to bar it to keep in would-be emigrants). So while the governed have a liberty to leave, the governors have the liberty to prevent them if they think it is in the public interest; hence, all nations but the first can be *called*, if not actually be, deserters.

When Franklin was on his way back to America as the Revolution loomed, he wrote an account of his final attempts at reconciliation in the form of a letter to his son William. What irked him most about Parliament's rejection of the plan for reconciliation offered by William Pitt (Lord Chatham) was not the justice or injustice of the matter but the manifest stupidity of those in power in response to attempts to prevent the coming catastrophe. To the one (Chatham) who had brought England from its "lowest despondency, and conducted it to victory and glory through a war with two of the mightiest kingdoms in Europe," the "hereditary legislators" responded with such misunderstanding, ignorance, prejudice, and passion as to show them "in breach of all decency and prudent regard to the character and dignity of their body as a third part of the national legislature." This led Franklin to have

an exceeding mean opinion of their abilities, and made their claim of sovereignty over three millions of virtuous sensible people in America, seem the greatest of absurdities, since they appeared to have scarce discretion enough to govern a herd of swine. Hereditary legislators! Thought I. There would be more propriety, because less hazard of mischief, in having ([as] in some University of Germany,) hereditary professors of mathematics! But this was a hasty reflection: For the *elected* House of Commons is no better, nor ever will be while the electors receive money for their votes, and pay money where with ministers may bribe their representatives when chosen.[73]

As usual, Franklin could not resist a joke even in describing the calamity that had occurred. His tone here is unmistakable—not righteous indignation, or uncontrollable anger, but reasonable and bemused disgust at the political idiocy and incompetence he has witnessed.

Franklin did not believe in natural rights of any kind, nor did he believe in natural duties of any kind. And so he could not have and did not believe one human being could possibly be morally superior to another or that any form of natural inequality could be used to "justify" political or social inequality. He was, in short, an egalitarian—but a Franklinian egalitarian—and was so from the beginning of his literary career until the very end of his life.

When Franklin was still apprenticed to his brother and before his nighttime flight from Boston to Philadelphia, he published the satirical and pseudonymous Silence Dogood essays in the *New England Courant*—having slipped them under his brother's office door because he doubted his brother would have published pieces by one so young as he. The fourth essay is especially interesting for our purposes, because it reveals Franklin's almost-visceral egalitarianism.[74]

The piece is a satire directed at Harvard College and the clergy educated there. In a dream, Silence sees herself walking through small country towns and villages, all of which resound with the fame of "the temple of learning." She says, "every peasant, who had wherewithal, was preparing to send one of his children at least to this famous place; and in this case most of them consulted their own purses instead of their children's capacities: so that I observed, a great many, yea, the most part of those who were travelling thither, were little better than dunces and blockheads. Alas! Alas!"

She comes to the temple, at whose door she finds two porters, "*Riches*" and "*Poverty*," who guard the door and admit those with the former and turn those afflicted with the latter away. Then Silence tells, with heavy-handed mockery, of the stupid goings-on inside the great temple—a great tribe of numbskulls climbing up the great throne on which sits "LEARNING"; most, finding the climb difficult, content themselves with sitting at the foot of the throne with "Madam *Idleness*" and her "Maid *Ignorance*" and depend on others, paid off by a pint of milk or piece of plum cake, eventually to help them up. When the ascent was finally accomplished, at graduation "every Beetle-Scull seemed well satisfied with his own portion of learning, though perhaps he was *even just* as ignorant as ever." The class of dunces then leaves the temple, replaced by another just like it, with some making their way to business or travel or just nothing or even—for those with no patrimony—to poverty, but with the "most part of the crowd" making its way to "*the temple of theology,"* moved to it, despite its containing nothing worthwhile, by the lure of *"Pecunia."*

Much later, in the *Autobiography,* Franklin tells us that his first erratum, his abandoning of his apprenticeship, was at least in part to escape his brother's beatings. Even though the beatings (assuming they really happened) may well have been occasioned by Ben's saucy provocations, the boy took them amiss, we are told, and was on the lookout for a way to shorten his suffering. In the course of relating these facts, Franklin adds the following footnote: "I fancy his harsh and tyrannical treatment of me, might be a means of impressing me with that aversion to arbitrary power that has stuck to me through my whole life."[75]

Franklin felt in his very bones that such things as good education and health care should be available to all who could make real use of them, and he detested the unreasonable exercise of power in whatever sphere of life, whether public or private, it might occur.

He was thus at bottom, in his heart and in his head, and for all his life an egalitarian in the following sense: Outstanding human talents can turn up anywhere—say, in a soapmaker's son—and there is not a single good reason why the world in general or any society or government should prevent their flowering and prospering. The rich, by virtue simply of being rich, have no special claim on the basic goods of civil society. Franklin was always a proponent of equality of opportunity. It was with this end in mind that he devoted so much time to the building of public hospitals and institutions of higher education.

Despite his obvious political pragmatism and support for the English monarchy until quite late in his life, after the Revolution Franklin was, as we already know, a unicameralist, both at the Constitutional Convention (at first, that is!) and as regards the Constitution of Pennsylvania, because he believed that a second and upper house would lead to the predominance of the rich and to the renewal of aristocracy. Of the Pennsylvania Constitution, Franklin said: "The important ends of civil society, and the personal securities of life and liberty, these remain the same in every member of the society; and the poorest continues to have an equal claim to them with the most opulent, whatever difference time, chance, or industry may occasion in their circumstances." And "on these considerations," he was sorry to see "a disposition among some of our people to commence an aristocracy, by giving the rich a predominancy in government, a choice peculiar to themselves in one half the legislature to be proudly called the UPPER house, and the other branch, chosen by the majority of the people, degraded by the denomination of the LOWER."[76]

It is tempting to conclude that Franklin was driven to this egalitarianism

and to contempt for privilege and arbitrary power by his own difficult experiences. Indeed, it is easy to sympathize and understand how he must have
felt. Franklin was a powerful genius, perhaps the smartest American of his
generation, yet his family could afford but two years of formal education for
the boy,[77] after which he had to work with his hands and (perhaps) suffer
beatings at the hands of his intellectually inferior brother. He made his way
in life by his wits, the seat of his pants, some good luck and patronage, and
prodigiously hard work and aggressiveness in business. Small wonder that
such a man would despise assertions that from inherited wealth springs
virtue and a claim to rule, and small wonder that he would oppose political
arrangements that would establish such claims.

It would be a mistake, however, to think that Franklin's egalitarianism
sprang simply from his own experience in life. That experience was doubtless
important. But Franklin's egalitarianism was most importantly determined by
his understanding of morality and the roots of human folly. According to
Franklin, human beings are equal, but not because they share an equal natural dignity or glory in being created in the image of God or because they are
endowed with natural rights that entail natural duties. They are equal, rather,
because they can make no real claim to dignity or natural right at all. Indeed,
if man as a species is not more special, more deserving, or more worthy than
are the oysters—because being special or deserving or worthy is meaningless—then there certainly can be no reason why one human being is more
special, more deserving, or more worthy than another.

Franklin did not understand his egalitarianism as a moral principle, one
for which those who espouse and apply it deserve praise or for whose sake
anyone should be moved to righteous indignation. Thus, it comes as no surprise that he was in general good-natured about the matter. Not for Franklin
the extremism of Tom Paine or the revolting defense of the Jacobins and the
Terror that we hear from the humorless moral fanatic Thomas Jefferson,
who, though he had lost friends to the cause, would, rather than have that
cause fail, "have seen half the earth desolated."

Not for Franklin the Jeffersonian view that "were there but an Adam and
an Eve left in every country, and left free, it would be better than as it now
is."[78] Franklin was, of course, no pacifist and understood well the need for
security and the link between war and diplomacy. But to Jefferson, Franklin
would surely have responded as he did to Sir Joseph Banks in 1783, in a letter from Passy on the occasion of the peace with England: "*There never was a
good war, or a bad peace.* What vast additions to the conveniences and comforts of living might mankind have acquired, if the money spent in wars had
been employed in works of public utility!" In true Baconian spirit, Franklin
went on to say:

What an extension of agriculture, even to the tops of our mountains: what rivers rendered navigable, or joined by canals: what bridges, aqueducts, new roads, and other public works, edifices, and improvements, rendering England a complete paradise, might have been obtained by spending those millions in doing good, which in the last war have been spent in doing mischief; in bringing misery into thousands of families, and destroying the lives of so many thousands of working people, who might have performed the useful labor![79]

Franklin concluded this sentiment—meant obviously for America as much as for England—by informing Banks how pleased he was with the latest discoveries made by the Royal Society of London and by admitting that he is almost sorry to have been born so soon, since he "cannot have the happiness of knowing what will be known 100 years hence."

To Franklin, defending the blood that dripped from the guillotine, on the grounds that it justly watered the fields of equality, could be no more rational than defending the ancien régime as divinely ordained. Both positions would surely have impressed him as evidence of how far human beings are from being "reasonable creatures." It is telling that Franklin, the constitutional unicameralist on egalitarian grounds, arranged for the translation and publication in France of the constitutions of the American states, most of which were bicameral. Jefferson, on the contrary, apparently tried to suppress the French translation of John Adams's conservative defense of these models of balance, compromise, and moderation.[80]

So Franklin's egalitarianism was, indeed, good-natured, and he took it with a grain of salt. As a brash young smart aleck, even while he chafed as an apprentice under his inferior brother's harsh supervision and after having just recently mocked Harvard College, he published a spoof of William Penn's attack on titles and honors, *No Cross, No Crown; or, Several Sober Reasons against Hat-Honour, Titular-Respects* . . .[81] In his spoof, "On Titles of Honour," Franklin, speaking on behalf of his "club," begins by noting how stupid human beings are in the diversity of their opinions and in their opinion that their opinions are superior to all others' opinions. Even the most absurd and ridiculous of opinions give their proponents a feeling of superiority, from which they with great confidence pass a "sentence of condemnation upon the reason of all mankind, who dissent from the peculiar whims of their troubled brains." The club was led to this view by a reading of Penn's work, and Franklin presents a parody of some "excerpts" from Penn's work: There is in the Bible no "Noah *Esquire*" or "Lot *Knight* and *Baronet*," or "*The Right Honorable* Abraham, *Viscount Mesopotamia, Baron of Carran*," and the like, and even respectful doffing of the hat in our day makes no sense to the "zealous author."

To this, Franklin responds that "if common civility, and a generous deportment among mankind, be not put out of countenance by the profound reasoning of this author, we hope they will continue to treat one another handsomely to the end of the world." One of the club members thus intends to prove that though Abraham was not called *"Right Honorable"* he was called *"Lord"* by his wife Sarah, which Abraham then thought entitled Sarah to be called *"My Lady,"* and likewise for Rachel.

Franklin thought all men are equal because there is no moral meaning to the notions of dignity and honor. But all men are likewise equal in their propensity to vanity, foolish opinions, and condemnations of all mankind, and the latter included the stern and moralistic egalitarianism of the likes of William Penn—and surely Jefferson as well. Although Franklin thought that honor makes no sense, he was quite at ease with and approved of those honors and flatteries that made for common civility among men.

And this is not to mention the ease with which he lived among aristocrats and delighted in their company and tastes: He surely could have made London home once he was rich and famous. But this did not blind him to the subtle illusions that make aristocrats tick. When Franklin was in Passy, many years after the youthful spoof of Penn, he wrote in a letter to Robert R. Livingston that the French court was still well-disposed to America, even though it had been pressed at times with bad arguments and "indiscrete and improper language" (from the likes of John Adams): "Trade is not the admiration of their noblesse, who always govern here. Telling them, their *commerce* will be advantaged by our success, and that it is their *interest* to help us, seems as much as to say, 'help us, and we shall not be obliged to you.'"[82] This argument from commerce and interest is exactly what Franklin believed, but he understood too much about the French love of honor to say it to their faces.

The good-natured character of Franklin's egalitarianism is perhaps no better expressed than in two brief pieces, both written in Passy. The first is a piece Franklin published in February 1784 entitled "Information to Those Who Would Remove to America."[83] It is addressed to those (obviously aristocrats) who have asked advice of him, as one well acquainted with America, about moving to America but who do so under "mistaken ideas and expectations of what is to be obtained there."

These mistaken folk think of America as rich and capable of rewarding ingenuity, but also as ignorant in the arts and science. For this reason, so these Europeans think, they who have talents in the arts and letters will be well paid and will easily become rich if they move to America. The Europeans think likewise that there are many lucrative offices available in America, offices that the rude Americans are unable to fill and that will thus be available to persons of "birth" and "family," who will obviously be respected as suitable for the jobs, which will make them rich. They imagine that the governments of America will pay for their transportation and provide them with free land, Negroes, tools, and livestock.

All this is but wild imagination. The truth is, Franklin says, that there are few really poor people in America but also few really rich ones, at least in European terms. Most men work for themselves, and since there is little money available for luxuries such as art, the "natural geniuses" in such things all leave America for Europe. Letters and mathematical knowledge are "in esteem" in America, but they are better provided for in America than the Europeans think. And there are few civil offices and no superfluous offices, as there are in Europe. On the contrary, profitable offices are even forbidden by law, as can be seen in Article 36 of the Pennsylvania Constitution.

For all these reasons, he cautions, the Europeans will be better off staying home. Indeed, if all one has is one's high birth, then America is a very poor market for this commodity, "where people do not inquire concerning a stranger, *What IS he?* but *What can he DO?*" The person who can do something will be respected; one who cannot will be despised. Indeed, he says, one who has nothing but birth and can be nothing but a gentleman is considered to be no better than a hog. As regards the encouragement to immigration from the governments, these consist only in what comes "from good laws and liberty." There is room for strangers, and so the old inhabitants are not jealous of them, and laws protect them sufficiently and they have no need for the patronage of the great. America is the land of work, and not some land of milk and honey.

Franklin assures the would-be emigrants that in America land is plentiful and cheap, so that a poor man, after a few years of work for others, can have his own property, and many from Europe who would otherwise have remained poor have come and with work have become wealthy farmers. Good air and climate and food have made for rapid increase in the population, and this increase makes for greater demand for artisans of all kinds, which the poor can become, and so those with moderate means but many children can also do well in industry in America, and without the disgrace they would suffer in Europe.

Franklin then advises those who wish to understand government in America to read the constitutions of the several states, which have been translated into French and published in Paris. He then goes on to comment that the Europeans should not expect great government projects to encourage large-scale manufacturing in America, largely because labor is expensive and land is so cheap that few are willing to work for others for long. The Americans generally think that when the time is ripe for great manufacturing ventures, private persons will carry them on profitably. But that time is a long way off, according to Franklin: "Great establishments of manufacture, require great numbers of poor to do the work for small wages; these poor are to be found in Europe, but will not be found in America, till the lands are all taken up and cultivated, and the excess of people who cannot get land, want employ- ment." But the land is "not likely to be occupied in an age to come."

Franklin next condemns the mercantilist attempts of governments to de- velop industries, already well established in other states, by imposing prohi- bitions and duties on foreign goods. Such schemes just wind up taxing local consumers, and the workers' higher pay makes them neither richer nor hap- pier, since it winds up as liquor in their stomachs and induces them to work less, not more. The governments in America, therefore, do not encourage such schemes and prefer free trade and competition.

For this reason, artisans live better in America and make good provision for their children and for their old age. In Europe, all the arts, trades, and professions are full, so that the young are for the most part brought up igno- rant and are destined to be soldiers, servants, or thieves. In America, with its rapidly expanding population, artisans do not fear competition and gladly accept apprentices. Hence, it is generally easy for the poor to have their children educated, and they even find themselves paid by artisans to take on their children as apprentices; such pay has enabled many of the poor to buy land. Indentures are established according to law and require the appren- tices to receive education not only in a particular art but also in reading, writing, and the keeping of accounts, and in general the experience prepares them for lives as useful citizens.

In America, Franklin concludes, "an almost general mediocrity of for- tune" obliges most people to pursue some business, and as a consequence the vices that arise from idleness are rare. Bad examples for the young are rare, which is a relief to parents. And in addition, "serious religion under its vari- ous denominations" is tolerated and respected and practiced, and "atheism is unknown there, infidelity rare and secret, so that persons may live to a great age in that country without having their piety shocked by meeting with ei- ther an atheist or an infidel." The "Divine Being" seems to have approved of the mutual respect among the differing sects, as is evidenced by the remark- able prosperity of the whole country.

The second important piece is a letter written by Franklin to his daughter Sarah Bache concerning the hereditary Order of the Cincinnati, founded by Revolutionary War officers in 1783.[84] Franklin tells Sarah that his opinion is hardly of great importance in the matter. But he is surprised to see such an institution formed in obvious "opposition to the solemnly declared sense" of the country against established ranks of nobility, and he thinks the projectors of the society have been bedazzled by the ribbons and crosses worn by foreign officers. And those who oppose it have been silent out of almost maternal tolerance. Franklin says that he would have gone along with their badges and ribbons for such reasons of tolerance, but he does not agree with "the entailing it as an honor on their posterity."

Honor is a personal thing, says Franklin, and is not transferable to others who had no part in obtaining it. Ascending honor—as was practiced among the Chinese—makes good sense and is useful to the state. In ascending honor, if, for instance, a man earns the rank of Mandarin because of his virtues, his parents are afforded the same honors on the ground that they must have had much to do with his education and character. Descending honor, in which honor goes to posterity who had no part in earning it, is absurd and often harmful to the posterity because it makes them proud and lazy and likely to fall into poverty. Such is the case with the European nobility. And if, to keep family holdings intact, estates are entailed on the oldest male heir, the result is that "another pest to industry and improvement of the country is introduced, which will be followed by all the odious mixture of pride and beggary, and idleness, that have half depopulated and *deculti-vated* Spain."

It follows, then, that Franklin would wish the members of the Order of the Cincinnati to give their badges to their parents rather than to their children. He then argues that descending honor is not just a philosophical absurdity but can be shown to be a mathematical absurdity as well. Then follows a hilarious demonstration that in nine generations, "our present Chevalier of the Order of Cincinnatus's share in the then existing Knight, will be but a 512th part; which, allowing the present certain fidelity of American wives to be insured down through all those nine generations, is so small a consideration, that methinks no reasonable man would hazard for the sake of it the disagreeable consequences of the jealousy, envy, and ill will of his countrymen."

Reversing the path from the future knight, who is only 1/512th of the present one, it turns out that, taking into account that each knight has a mother and a father, "one thousand and twenty-two men and women, [are] contributors to the formation of one Knight." And if there are to be a thousand future knights, then 1,022,000 fathers and mothers will be needed to produce them. Deducting 22,000 to account for parents who give birth to more than one knight, and after a "reasonable estimation of the number of rogues, and fools, and royalists and scoundrels and prostitutes" that are mixed into the remaining million, "posterity will have much reason to boast of the noble blood of the then existing set of Chevaliers de Cincinnatus." As time goes on, it is clear that the right to the honor of an ancestor will diminish to the point of "an absolute nullity." So let the new order wear their badges, but they should let the distinction die with them.

And while he is on the subject of ribbons and badges, Franklin notes that some members have complained that the bald eagle on their badge looks too much like a turkey. In response, Franklin notes that he wishes the bald eagle had never been chosen as the "representative of our county," since the eagle is nothing but a lazy thief, and like all thieves, it is a poor, lousy coward; it flees from an attacking sparrow. So Franklin is glad that the figure on the badge looks more like a turkey, a bird that is at once native to our shores and "a much more respectable bird." Franklin closes with some jokes at the expense of the Latin mottoes selected for the society and with a story about a man whose newly built house—and the Latin motto over the door—is a monument to his vanity.

No brief pieces by Franklin better portray his sober and good-humored egalitarianism. Despite his having enjoyed the aristocratic life in Passy, Franklin's fondness for America is unmistakable in his advice to the Europeans and in his jokes at the expense of the Order of the Cincinnati. America is, simply, a more rational place than is Europe because in America a man is valued for what he does and not for illusory qualities such as high social rank or noble birth. In America the poor can prosper, just as Franklin himself had risen from obscurity to riches and fame. Although the concept of honor really makes no moral sense at all, it is useful to society when it works as it does in America, where it belongs only to the one who accomplishes those things men praise, where it acts as a spur to industry and prosperity, and where it does not have the perverse effect of spawning vice, crime, and poverty as it does in the Old World.

But Franklin did not think equality to be a burning *moral* imperative. And his egalitarianism was good-humored for another reason as well: Although he thought equality of opportunity the only social arrangement that makes good sense, if only because more-rigid or aristocratic societies were based on such stupid illusions, he was far from utopian in his beliefs about how far and how fast equality of opportunity could obtain on this earth, and he had no illusions about the reasonableness of the society that does make the best sense. He knew perfectly well, for instance, who those "Negroes" were who were falsely expected for free by the European and aristocratic would-be Americans. And so he knew perfectly well that the America of his fond account was idealized.

For all his zeal for science and invention, Franklin had a powerful sense of the weight of necessity and the limits of human endeavor—limits that spring from human nature and from the harsh circumstances of political economy. Americans owe their prosperity and their equality to liberty and good government and to the consequent security and promise of private property, but there is no doubt that they also owe them as much to raw good fortune: to the immense tracts of empty and cheap land, from whence Franklin thought all wealth ultimately derived.[85] Franklin believed that how one fares in life is considerably determined by luck and harsh necessity—even when conditions are as good as they can be, as they were in America, and especially where conditions are very bad, as they were in Europe.

As Franklin argued in the 1768 essay "On the Labouring Poor" (written and published in England), the poor in England are caught between a rock and a hard place.[86] On the one hand, in no other country are the poor so well cared for by the rich, who tax themselves to support the poor; everywhere else, "necessity reduces [the poor] to beggary." But at the same time, this support does nothing but corrupt them, for "giving mankind a dependence on any thing for support in age or sickness, besides industry and frugality during youth and health, tends to flatter our natural indolence, to encourage idleness and prodigality, and thereby to promote and increase poverty, the very evil it was intended to cure; thus multiplying beggars, instead of diminishing them."

Perhaps, says Franklin, the wages of the working poor could be raised. But that will not work, because the resulting higher prices of British exports would result in less work to be had, unless the English engaged in the mad attempt to conquer the world in order to compel it to buy British goods. And should the poor get higher wages, they might work fewer days, in which case they would spend their free time in the alehouse. But if conditions are right, and the poor do work hard, they will not become rich but, rather, will just avoid beggary. Tough luck to be born poor in England, where industry and frugality can at best keep one's nose just above the water. The only way out would be to come to America.

But that would be tough luck for the Indians. As Franklin argued in his 1751 essay "Observations Concerning the Increase of Mankind, Peopling of Countries, etc.," the Europeans "found *America* as fully settled as it well could be by hunters; yet these having large tracks, were easily prevailed on to part with portions of territory to the new comers, who did not much interfere with the natives in hunting, and furnished them with many things they wanted."[87] Franklin could see the potential result, but the unfortunate Indians could not, and so they did not see the obvious zero-sum game implied in Franklin's remarks—at least not until it was too late for their way of life and even, for many of them, for their lives.[88]

We cannot conclude that Franklin felt contempt for the Indians any more than he did for the poor. He did not. Indeed, he would have preferred the condition of the poor to be other than it was, as is clear from his touching comments on manufacturing and the poor of Ireland and Scotland.[89] In these wretched countries, he says, a tiny and opulent minority are landlords, while the tenants, the bulk of the population, are wretchedly poor. When he saw them, he thought of the happiness of New England, "where every man is a freeholder, has a vote in public affairs," and so on, and where manufacturing is for the most part done in the home.

Should these lucky New Englanders envy the manufacturing trade of Ireland and Scotland, they should think of the trade-off: a diet of potatoes and buttermilk and no shirts to wear, for the export of beef, butter, and linen; no shoes to wear, for the export of shoes and stockings; clothes of rags, for the export of cloths and stuffs for the rest of the world. Great manufactories require a large number of poor people willing to work for next to nothing, which is a misfortune for the poor. Says Franklin:

Had I never been in the American Colonies, but was to form my judgment of civil society by what I have lately seen [in Ireland and Scotland], I should never advise a nation of savages to admit of civilization: for I assure you, that in the possession and enjoyment of the various comforts of life, compared to these people every Indian is a gentleman: and the effect of this kind of civil society seems only to be, the depressing multitudes below the savage state that a few may be raised above it.

As we will see, the Baconian Franklin thought technology would in the long run make the world a much richer place. But that long run did the poor Irish and Scots of his own day no good, and so he could not say with Locke that the poorest laborer in England was better off than the chiefs of the Indians.[90]

But all this empathy notwithstanding, Franklin was not moved to indignation on behalf of the poor or the Indians. Indeed, he harbored no illusions about their superior virtues or merit. As things stand now among the civilized, he says, "care and industry seem absolutely necessary to our well being."[91] And thus, care and industry should get all the encouragement that can be devised and the poor should not be coddled by the dole, which maintains them in idleness (which they can come to see as just fine for them). They should, rather, be employed in workhouses. At least if they learn to work voluntarily, they will be able to provide for a rainy day and their old age and will not have to work for bare subsistence wages. Indeed, the poor are more industrious in Protestant than in Catholic countries (England excepted), because of all the provisions for the poor supplied in Catholic countries.

According to Franklin, the Indians reflect natural human indolence, civilization springs from artificial but inalterable necessity, and the civilized poor are caught in between—inclined to natural laziness but stuck in a world where that inclination is ultimately trouble for them and for society. But for Franklin, the Indians, civilization, and the poor are what they are. None is more worthy than the others—although civilization and wealth are surely good for Franklin, who loves its arts and sciences and many of its artificial wants. In Europe, it is possible for things to be better for the poor, but only marginally and within severe limits; but in America—with its vast expanse of land to be taken from the Indians—opportunities abound for the poor. Revolutionary redistribution of property would be required to turn Ireland and Scotland into New England. But such a remedy would never do, for Franklin, since the security of property is essential to an increasing population, and where that security is absent, people just depart for other countries.[92]

Of course, Franklin sees equality of opportunity as the only principle of society that makes any sense. But even so, for most people living where cheap land is not available, life is tough, unless they take off for the New World, where it will be cheap for a long, long time. For those poor who cannot or will not remove to America, life will be tough for a long, long time, and little can be done politically to change this fact.

Franklin's egalitarianism is so easygoing because it springs from the negative, not the positive. Human beings are equal not because they share an equal dignity but because they have no real claim whatsoever to *deserve* deference or any other good from someone else and because all are the products of the particular and necessary circumstances that determine who and what they are. It is senseless to be indignant about these circumstances, because they cannot be laid to anyone's moral fault. The fact of the circumstances is inalterable, and each social arrangement that sustains these circumstances is characterized by its own particular delusions. This does not mean that things simply cannot be made better with the exercise of good sense, especially in the world's bright spot, America, and even in Europe (as we'll see in chapter 8) with the eventual progress of the arts and sciences. If the Indians will not join in the American good fortune, however, they are doomed, and there is nothing that can prevent that fact.

Human beings are equal in another negative respect as well: They are equally prone to stupidity and folly and viciousness. As we have seen, Franklin made this view clear in his humor. And he made it equally clear in comments to his good friend and fellow natural philosopher Joseph Priestley. In a letter to Priestly written from Passy in 1780, Franklin noted that although he takes great delight in the progress of the sciences, he wishes that equal progress could be seen in "moral science." He wishes "that men would cease to be wolves to one another, and that human beings would at length learn what they now improperly call humanity!"[93]

Two years later, writing again to Priestley from Passy, Franklin continued his remarks on this theme—this time in a jocular tone of mock disgust. Franklin thanks Priestley for his reports on his natural philosophy and comments that he wishes he had the leisure to engage in such philosophy. But he longs for inquiry into the inanimate parts of nature, not the animate or "moral" works of nature. The more he learns of the former, the more he admires them; the more he knows of the latter, the more he is disgusted by them. He says:

> Men I find to be a sort of beings very badly constructed, as they are generally more easily provoked than reconciled, more disposed to do mischief to each other than to make reparation, much more easily deceived than undeceived, and having more pride and even pleasure in killing than in begetting one another; for without a blush they assemble in great armies at noonday to destroy, and when they have killed as many as they can, they exaggerate the number to augment the fancied glory; but they creep into corners, or cover themselves with the darkness of night, when they mean to beget, as being ashamed of a virtuous action. A virtuous action it would be, and a vicious one the killing of them, if the species were really worth producing or preserving; but of this I begin to doubt.[94]

Franklin says that he knows Priestley has no such doubts, since he (a preacher) spends so much time trying to save men's souls.[95] But "perhaps as you grow older, you may look upon this as a hopeless project, or an idle amusement, repent of having murdered in mephitic air so many honest, harmless mice, and wish that to prevent mischief, you had used boys and girls instead of them."

To show what superior beings think of us, Franklin tells his friend of some interesting news. An angel came to earth on business and was escorted by "an old courier-spirit" assigned as a guide. The guide flew over the "Seas of Martinico, in the middle of the long day of obstinate fight between the fleets of Rodney and De Grasse."[96] Upon viewing the carnage and suffering and the eagerness with which the survivors kept at their assaults, the angel turned to the guide and, calling him a blockhead, complained that instead of taking him to earth, his guide has taken him to hell. No, says the guide, "I have made no mistake; this is really the earth, and these are men. Devils never treat one another in this cruel manner; they have more sense, and more of what men (vainly) call *Humanity*." But then, continues Franklin, "to be serious, my dear old friend, I love you as much as ever, and I love all the honest souls that meet at the London Coffee-House. I only wonder how it happened, that they and my other friends in England came to be such good creatures in the midst of so perverse a generation."

For all of his enterprising spirit, his sense of American promise, his brash presentation of himself as the model of a new man for a new world, and his egalitarianism, Franklin knew that men are badly constructed—so much so that they outdo devils and are wolves to each other—and that at best we have to live with the cards that fortune deals, and in the best social arrangements we always live in a dream of one kind or another. Believing these things, Franklin could not be and was not an egalitarian fanatic. He could not even be a morally fervent partisan of equality. That would have been irrational and surely would have spoiled the good life he was lucky and smart enough to live.

8 • The Political Project
of the Good Life

Now that we have situated Franklin's more general political principles—his understanding of rights and obligation, the forms of government, and equality—in his broader and philosophical take on the good life, we turn next to the particular projects that occupied his political career. These projects reflect his political principles and his philosophical understanding of life in general. Therefore, they reflect at once the forward-looking projecting of Franklin's Baconianism and the deep skepticism with which he viewed the project of the Enlightenment. Within the general context of Franklin's Baconianism, he was preoccupied with three specific political issues: the modern political empire, toward the end of his life the question of slavery, and through the course of his life the practical circumstances of modern religion.

By early 1735, the year he published the two dialectical essays intended for "communicating instruction," Franklin had completed his critique of morality and religion and had come to his understanding of the good things in life. He had also become well versed in the thought of Francis Bacon, as is clear from the essay "On Simplicity." Franklin was, in fact, a *nearly* full-blown Baconian, just as he was a *nearly* full-blown Hobbesian. In the *Autobiography*, Franklin presents his work in natural philosophy as a brief interlude in his political career, and even then he presents it in terms of his personal reputation and not as part of a broad human project to understand and control nature. The *Autobiography* simply takes for granted the array of new possibilities afforded to those in America and more generally in the present age and then provides the lessons necessary for the ambitious and hard-working to seize these opportunities for themselves, as well as lessons to help such people combine for the improvement of themselves and their posterity. The new man is suited to a new world in which opportunities are freed from the confines of ossified societies and rigid inequalities.

Thus, in the *Autobiography*, Franklin's Baconianism appears as almost purely political—as pragmatic political fixing. But Franklin was keenly aware of the much broader horizon of modernity within which he depicted his American experience. In particular, he was aware of that horizon as defined by its architect, Bacon: the scientific and technological conquest of nature.

In his usual fashion, Franklin wrote little in direct, theoretical conversation with Bacon. But Bacon was very important to Franklin nevertheless. The crucial essay "On Simplicity" was rooted in Bacon's *Essays*. And Bacon was among the philosophical greats whose deaths were marked in *Poor Richard's Almanack*. In the 1749 *Almanack*, Franklin noted that "On the 7th of this month, 1626, died that *great little* man, Sir Francis Bacon; *great* in his prodigious genius, parts, and learning; and *little*, in his servile compliances with a *little* court, and submissive flattery of a *little* prince. *Pope* characterizes him thus, in one strong line; *'If Parts allure thee, think how Bacon shin'd, | The wisest, brightest, meanest of mankind.'"*[1]

Franklin begins this memorial by reminding us of Bacon's ugly moral reputation. (This reputation was well-earned by Bacon, by the way, who was one of the nastiest characters in the history of philosophy.) Lest we dwell on this reputation, however, Franklin immediately praises Bacon as the "justly esteemed" father of modern experimental philosophy. To Franklin, who in 1749 was newly retired from business and immersed in his experimental study of electricity, Bacon, as the father of experimental science, was one of the most important thinkers of the modern age.

It is no surprise, then, that he follows this praise with lines of another poet who excuses Bacon by "ascribing his blemishes to a wrong unfortunate choice of his way of life." In the mediocre poetry that follows, Bacon is described as having chosen a life of politics when nature had destined him for the life of the mind. Despite this choice, Bacon (who, according to Franklin, combined in "one rich soul" Plato, Aristotle, and Cicero) delivered philosophy from the cloistered monks and "jargon-teaching schools" and their "magic chain of words and forms, and definitions void." Bacon thus led philosophy to its slow ascent and investigation of the sure "chain of things" and thus let philosophy "with radiant finger point to Heaven again."

There is no moral blemish in Bacon's character if there is nothing but "a wrong unfortunate choice." Moreover, at least as regards the vices of servility and flattery, Franklin agreed completely with Bacon's teaching about them: It is important to have a reputation for honesty and to know when, how, and for what purposes (and those purposes include one's own interests) to lie. Franklin agreed with the Baconian moral teaching, and he surely agreed with the Baconian view that experimentation, rather than metaphysical contemplation, is the way to uncover the secrets of nature.

He was also a Baconian in his understanding of experimentation, in his belief that practice and utility are the means to the discovery of nature. We understand the courses of nature, at least sufficiently, when we demonstrate the things that can be done, first in experiment and then in practical applications, with the courses of nature. Said Franklin in his *Opinions and Conjectures*, published in 1750 and reporting on his electrical experiments of the previous year:

> Nor is it of much importance to us to know the manner in which nature executes her laws; 'tis enough, if we know the laws themselves. 'Tis of real use to know, that china left in the air unsupported, will fall and break; but how it comes to fall, and why it breaks, are matters of speculation. 'Tis a pleasure indeed to know them, but we can preserve our china without it. Thus in the present case, to know this power of points [that electricity is more readily attracted by a pointed rod than by a blunt one] may possibly be of some use to mankind, though we should never be able to explain it.[2]

Knowing why an object falls (why and by what ultimate means there is gravity) would be pleasant, but knowing the law telling us that and how an object must fall is all we need. It is by experiment that we uncover that and how the courses of nature move, which then makes it possible to control and bend the courses of nature to our uses. That we know at first but one use for a phenomenon—the electrocution of turkeys, in the case of electricity—does not mean that we cannot find others. And speculation can with experimentation be turned to further knowledge. Today, at the beginning of the twenty-first century, we know why a piece of china breaks: because of its particular molecular structure. Speculation, for Franklin, is not metaphysical contemplation. What we cannot know (by metaphysical reasoning or by natural science) is why the world is such as to have china break for the reasons that we can and do fathom.

Franklin was thus a Baconian as regards practical morality and as regards the ways and means of true natural philosophy. But he was also a Baconian as regards the practical ends of natural science: the "relief of man's estate."[3] Moreover, he understood, along with Bacon and with perfect clarity, how far that relief might go and what it might portend for religious faith.

A year after publishing the *Opinions and Conjectures*, Franklin published his "Appeal for the Hospital" in the *Pennsylvania Gazette*. The hospital project is featured in the *Autobiography*, not so much simply because it was inherently worthy but because it was, of all of Franklin's political maneuvers, the one that gave him the greatest pleasure and the one that "in after-thinking of it, I more easily excused my-self for having made some use of cunning."[4]

Franklin had, by his account, petitioned the Pennsylvania Assembly for a conditional grant, that is, one that would match the sum raised by the incorporated private contributors. That the public grant was to be conditional "carried the bill through; for the members who had opposed the grant, and now conceived they might have the credit of being charitable without the expense, agreed to its passage; and then in soliciting subscriptions among the people we urged the conditional promise of the law as an additional motive to give, since every man's donation would be doubled. Thus the clause worked both ways."[5]

In the *Autobiography* the hospital scheme is presented as an example of Franklin's charitable cunning—a cunning excused because it is charitable. But the "Appeal for the Hospital" is, beyond and beneath the rhetoric of an appeal, also a brief but subtle commentary on the relationship between charity and disease.[6]

According to the appeal, the remarkable thing about all living things is that despite the myriad differences of kinds and even of individuals within kinds, all are alike in that "none within our observation . . . *are by nature incapable of* DISEASES." The ancient poets made it clear that Achilles was vulnerable in his heel, and though all animals are subject to death, man is unique in having the greatest number of diseases, "whether they are the effects of our intemperance and vice, or are given us, that we may have a greater opportunity of exercising towards each other that virtue, which most of all recommends us to the Deity, I mean CHARITY."

Then follow three references to the Gospel according to Luke: the story of the Good Samaritan (Luke 10:30–37), the story of the rich man and Lazarus (Luke 16:19–23), and the story of Jesus and the ten lepers (Luke 17:11–19). The lesson Franklin draws from Luke is that care for the sick, regardless of who they are, "seems essential to the true spirit of Christianity." In particular and most important, the story of the rich man and Lazarus demonstrates that "*I was sick, and ye visited me* is one of the terms of admission into bliss, and the contrary, a cause of exclusion."

Franklin is here quite delicate, since the exclusion of which he speaks is, as regards the rich man, in fact condemnation to the anguishing flames of Hades. We should remember, Franklin continues, that our circumstances are subject to change, according to providence, and so we should be "mutual hosts to each other" and not harden our hearts against the lowly who are sick, lest we find ourselves in their position. But what we might suffer for this hard-heartedness in this world pales before what we will suffer for it in the next. And if we wish to be charitable to the sick, it is far better to do so by building the hospital, since so many more of the sick can be cared for, with much better skill and expertise.

In the second part of the "Appeal," Franklin contrasts pagan and Christian attitudes toward the charitable care of the sick.[7] Even the pagans thought that nothing made men more like gods than doing good to one's fellow men by *administering comfort and relief to the sick.*" If the pagans "without any other assistance than the dictates of natural reason, had so high an opinion of it, what may be expected from Christians, to whom it has been so warmly recommended by the best example of human conduct." The Christian doctrine has had an effect on human conduct, since the "sanctions revelation affords" produced conduct never produced by the heathens, who had but the "mere knowledge of duty."

Thus, in all states where Christians have sufficient influence, public and private money is spent on hospitals for the poor who are further burdened with disease. Then follow some historical examples, an account of the matching grant from the assembly, and a hardheaded account of the practical benefits—as regards both economies of scale and better medical care for rich and poor—that can be had from a hospital: "A beggar in a well regulated hospital, stands an equal chance with a prince in his palace, for a comfortable subsistence, and an expeditious and effectual cure of his diseases."

In the "Appeal," Franklin refers to the principle of wise self-interest: We never know when misfortune and a change of circumstances might befall us, so it makes good sense to have charitable provision made for the time that we might find ourselves both poor and sick. And hospitals lead both to cheaper and better care for all, since physicians and surgeons become more proficient when they practice in hospitals. It is not just that the beggar and the prince wind up on equal terms but, rather, that the prince also does better for himself if hospitals abound.

But by far the most stirring admonition in the "Appeal" is to the idea that disease is an occasion for charity, for the practice of which we are rewarded with heaven and for the neglect of which we are punished by the fires of hell. From this point of view, the object of charity is not primarily the cure of the disease but the exercise of mercy. From the biblical point of view, disease and death are the products of original sin and the Fall, and charity toward the sick and dying is one means of achieving salvation and eternal life.

Although there is no necessary tension between these two ends—the curing of disease and relief of suffering, and the exercise of charity and the winning of heaven—there could well be such a tension on the Baconian understanding of disease that Franklin actually held.

In the 1770 letter to Priestly, in which Franklin complained of the disparity between scientific and moral progress and wished that men would cease being wolves to each other, Franklin said of scientific progress that it

> occasions my regretting sometimes that I was born so soon. It is impossible to imagine the height to which may be carried, in a thousand years, the power of man over matter. We may perhaps learn to deprive large masses of their gravity, and give them absolute levity, for the sake of easy transport. Agriculture may diminish its labor and double its produce; all diseases may by sure means be prevented or cured, not excepting even that of old age, and our lives lengthened at pleasure even beyond the antediluvian standard.[8]

In letters to Joseph Banks and the Reverend John Lathrop, in 1783 and 1788, respectively, Franklin shortened his timeline considerably. To Banks, Franklin said that with Europe furnished with scientific academies and instruments and the "spirit of experiment," the progress of human knowledge will be swift, "and discoveries made, of which we have at present no conception. I begin to be almost sorry I was born so soon, since I cannot have the happiness of knowing what will be known 100 years hence."[9] To the Reverend Lathrop, Franklin concurs with the reverend's sentiment that human happiness is growing because of progress in philosophy, morals, politics, and the conveniences of common living. Indeed, so much is this the case, says Franklin,

> that I have sometimes almost wished it had been my destiny to be born two or three centuries hence. For invention and improvement are prolific, and beget more of their kind. The present progress is rapid. Many of great importance, now unthought of, will before that period be produced; and then I might not only enjoy their advantages, but have my curiosity gratified in knowing what they are to be. I see a little absurdity in what I have just written, but it is to a friend, who will wink and let it pass, while I mention one reason more for such a wish, which is, that, if the art of physic shall be improved in proportion with other arts, we may then be able to avoid diseases, and live as long as the patriarchs in Genesis; to which I suppose we should make little objection.[10]

It is not altogether clear how Franklin's wish to have been born two or three centuries later so he could gratify his curiosity is absurd. He probably means that it's silly to wish for what is now impossible. But even so, his embarrassment at such a wish does not prevent him from compounding it: He wishes to have been born two or three centuries later so that he could have lived, disease free, for more than 969 years (Gen. 5:27). The absurdity is to wish for satisfied curiosity before wishing for life "beyond the antediluvian standard." And if it is absurd to wish for both now, it is not absurd to regret that such distant but real possibilities are beyond one's time. A thousand years in the wonderful cake shop of life!! To this Franklin would "make little objection."

Two points are critical. First, everything Franklin says in these letters indicates that even the antediluvian standard is not insuperable. As Franklin says, it is impossible to imagine the height to which the scientific power over matter will ascend. This means, of course, that there is no limit to what we might imagine will some day be possible. In principle, then, all power over matter is possible.

Second, when Franklin says to Priestly that all diseases will be prevented or cured, he says "not excepting even that of old age." From the point of view of the experimental natural science, aging is a curable disease. If so, then it is not the inescapable path to the wages of sin. And if old age is a curable disease, so too is death.

In his oft-stated religious "creed," Franklin surely took death for granted as the condition of the rewards of heaven and the punishments of hell, for those sins for which men are responsible. In this sense, then, aging and death are the conditions for receiving the wages of sin. He cannot have really believed in such a creed if aging and death are diseases that will one day be cured on this earth. At the very least, then, Franklin had to understand the clear tension between the creed that answers to our moral hopes (and keeps us in line), on the one hand, and the promise of modern natural science, on the other. Even so, had Franklin died just today, we could imagine him lined up next to Ted Williams, in a cryogenic tube, "waiting" for the cure.

Franklin's view of the scientific project for the "relief of man's estate" was every bit as expansive as was Bacon's. If the vast uninhabited expanses of America could afford, in but a century, an enormous increase in the population and prosperity of the British Empire, as Franklin argued in the essay on population, then we can scarcely imagine what those same tracts (and all others and even in Europe, for that matter) will afford when transformed by one or two more centuries of progress in natural science.[11] Even if political technology can do little for the European poor, scientific technology can do a lot, albeit only in the distant future. If our power over matter has no real upper limit, then the earth, as the source of life and wealth, is, for all practical purposes, of infinite expanse.[12]

Franklin's lifelong political project—the Anglo-American empire and then America by itself—was a part of the larger project of modernity in which human reason, armed with science and technology, would relieve and expand the human estate.

Franklin's motive, however, was not the moral imperative of charity toward his fellow men and the ages to come. At least by 1735, when Franklin had come to his mature understanding of morality and religion, that would have been impossible. Rather, Franklin loved the projects to which he devoted much of his good life because, in his philosophically grounded view, they were where the action was to be found; they were the fields on which some of the most enjoyable and creative games of life could be played.

This fascination with the American project as a project—as a challenge of artful fabrication—is revealed powerfully in Franklin's remarks in and about the Canada Pamphlet. Franklin took the view that wise political economy spoke for Canada over Guadeloupe, but the real punch of the argument was that America enlarged by Canada was the true and almost limitless future of the British Empire.

America, says Franklin in the pamphlet, will for centuries increase in population, since people will be attracted by fertile land, "till they amount to perhaps a hundred million souls," and during those centuries, this population will consume the manufactured goods produced in England. Then Franklin says:

> The human body and the political differ in this, that the first is limited by nature to a certain stature, which, when attained, it cannot, ordinarily, exceed; the other by better government and more prudent police, as well as by change of manners and other circumstances, often takes fresh starts of growth, after being long at a stand; and may add tenfold to the dimensions it had for ages been confined to.[13]

With prudent craft, the imperial body politic can be husbanded to gargantuan proportions.

Franklin certainly knew that America was a good thing because it afforded more liberty and opportunity, definitely good things, than any place on the globe. But he *served* it because it harbored such amazing possibilities. And so to his philosophical friend Henry Home, Lord Kames, Franklin wrote the following just prior to publishing the Canada Pamphlet:

> I have long been of opinion, that the foundations of the future grandeur and stability of the British Empire, lie in America; and though, like other foundations, they are low and little seen, they are nevertheless, broad and strong enough to support the greatest political structure human wisdom ever yet erected. I am therefore by no means for restoring

Canada. If we keep it, all the country from the St. Laurence to Missis-
sippi, will in another century be filled with British people; Britain itself
will become vastly more populous by the immense increase of its commerce; the Atlantic sea will be covered with your trading ships; and
your naval power thence continually increasing, will extend your influence round the whole globe, and awe the world![14]

Franklin expressed himself in very similar terms about the events of the
Revolution. Arthur Lee reported in his diary entry for October 25, 1777, a
conversation that transpired between him and Franklin. Of the Revolution,
Lee reported: "He told me the manner in which the whole of this business
had been conducted, was such a miracle in human affairs, that if he had not
been in the midst of it, and seen all the movements, he could not have comprehended how it was effected."[15]

In other words, it looked like a miracle, but it was not. It was, rather, an
amazing human contrivance and accomplishment. After detailing all the
obstacles faced—laws and governments to be established and an army and
navy to be built from nothing, "in the face of a most formidable invasion,"
internal opposition and lukewarm friends of all kinds—Franklin said to Lee:
"It was, however, formed and established in despite of all these obstacles,
with an expedition, energy, wisdom, and success of which most certainly the
whole history of human affairs has not, hitherto, given an example."

To account for it, said Franklin, one had to

remember that the revolution was not directed by the leaders of fac-
tion, but by the opinion and voice of the majority of the people; that
the grounds and principles upon which it was formed were known,
weighed and approved by every individual of that majority. It was not a
tumultuous resolution, but a deliberate system. Consequently, the fee-
bleness, irresolution, and inaction which generally, nay, almost invari-
ably attends and frustrates hasty popular proceedings, did not influence
this.

As a consequence, all worked to do what they had "soberly determined"
and "the effects of anarchy were prevented by the influence of public
shame." The result was that within a few months, "the governments were established; codes of law were formed, which, for wisdom and justice, are the
admiration of all the wise and thinking men in Europe." And so,

the greatest revolution the world ever saw, is likely to be effected in a
few years; and the power that has for centuries made all Europe tremble,

assisted by 20,000 German mercenaries, and favoured by the universal concurrence of Europe to prohibit the sale of warlike stores, the sale of prizes, or the admission of the armed vessels of America, will be effectually humbled by those whom she insulted and injured, because she conceived they had neither spirit nor power to resist or revenge it.

Nothing could be clearer in these remarks. The Revolution was no miracle, nor was it a tumult; rather, it was "a deliberate system" that produced the greatest political event of human history. For Franklin, America was where the action was, and Franklin just loved being in on the action, especially if it concerned the greatest and most awesome political structure ever constructed by human wisdom. And the action was even better if it also included curing death and discovering the secrets of nature.

IT WOULD BE A GREAT MISTAKE to think that liberty and equality of opportunity did not really matter to Franklin. As we have seen, they most certainly did, although he did not think serving them his moral obligation and proper service to God. But in Franklin's view, they are ultimately the only political principles that make any sense, and a world in which liberty and opportunity flourish is simply better for all, and especially for Franklin and those like him. All the better, then, that the greatest political structure ever devised by human reason would grow in America, where liberty and opportunity really did abound.

But since Franklin did not believe in natural rights and thought human beings equal only in the negative sense that all equally lack moral dignity and owe no deference to anyone, it is reasonable to inquire into his views of race and slavery. One thing is clear: He could not have thought that any human being deserves to be a slave. But he could well have thought that because of tough luck, another's exercise of his own self-interest, and coercion, one might wind up a slave to someone else, and he could well have thought that the best advice to the slave, if he cannot get away, would be to make the best of a bad situation.

It is well known that, in fact, Franklin in his later years became an abolitionist. It is equally well known that Franklin came very late to abolition, owned slaves himself, profited from and temporized politically with the institution, blamed it on the British at the time of the Declaration and before, and objected to it on economic rather than moral grounds in his 1751 "Observations Concerning the Increase of Mankind, Peopling of Countries, etc." At the end of that same essay, Franklin made some notorious and nasty cracks about Palatine Boors and dark-skinned peoples.[16] The Palatine Boors comment haunted Franklin and cost him politically, and (along with other snotty comments at the expense of just about everyone—Quakers, Jesuits, Catholics in general, Presbyterians, and Calvinists, to name a few) earned him a reputation among some for bigotry. In the view of the editors of the Franklin *Papers*, the Boors remark demonstrated that in 1751 Franklin was "xenophobic" (by which they clearly mean "racist"), although he had changed his mind on these matters by at least as early as 1763.[17]

I doubt that Franklin was ever a bigot or a xenophobe, which is not to say that he was delicate in his polemics and afraid to appeal to the nasty sentiments of those he wanted to persuade. If my argument so far is correct, it is very likely that, at least by the early 1730s, Franklin had come to his mature understanding of moral life, religion, natural rights, and the roots of human folly and vanity.

That he could on occasion malign the various sects of Christianity is thus no big surprise—and it can hardly be described as bigotry, since it was based on his rigorous (and dangerous) dialectical critique of the dogmas not only of the believers but of the enlightened scoffers as well. It is likewise hard to imagine that he had real prejudices against various nationalities and races. To be sure, he thought many cultures were given to various kinds of weakness and stupidity and vices. But given Franklin's theoretical views, he cannot have thought one culture or civilization morally superior to another. To Franklin, all cultures, especially insofar as they are based on religion and believe in the moral superiority of their manners and ways, are just well-organized forms of moral delusion.

This fact seems clear even in the offending paragraphs of the essay on population. After insulting the Germans—though it is by far most likely that by "Boors" he meant peasants, not "pigs," especially since they *were* peasants—he makes it clear that what he dislikes about them is their disinclination to assimilation.[18] He thinks that they are as likely to adopt the English language and English customs as they are to acquire the English complexion. In a letter to James Parker in 1750, regarding the Albany Plan, Franklin makes it clear that he worried about the Germans' resistance to assimilation and its effect on the unity of the colonies.[19] About the Germans he may have been wrong—but the worries were not unreasonable.

Regardless of his view of the Germans, however, the offending final paragraph of the population essay is simply very hard to take seriously, and it betrays Franklin's typical subtlety. Here it is in its entirety:

Which leads me to add one remark: that the number of purely white people in the world is proportionably very small. All *Africa* is black or tawney. *Asia* chiefly tawney. *America* (exclusive of the new comers) wholly so. And in *Europe*, the *Spaniards, Italians, French, Russians* and

Swedes, are generally of what we call a swarthy complexion; as are the *Germans* also, the *Saxons* only excepted, who with the *English,* make the principal body of white people on the face of the earth. I could wish their numbers were increased. And while we are, as I may call it, *scouring* our planet, by clearing *America* of woods, and so making this side of our globe reflect a brighter light to the eyes of inhabitants in *Mars* or *Venus,* why should we in the sight of superior Beings, darken its people? Why increase the sons of *Africa,* by planting them in *America,* where we have so fair an opportunity, by excluding all Blacks and Tawneys, of increasing the lovely White and Red? But perhaps I am partial to the complexion of my country, for such kind of partiality is natural to mankind.

To the inhabitants of Mars and Venus—obviously "superior Beings"—we should show a white face? To take this argument seriously we would have to think Franklin had lost his mind. Even the absurd *Articles of Belief* did not populate Mars and Venus. Franklin clearly means war and love—and that was precisely his worry: the Germans' willingness to think of the common interest of Pennsylvania as he saw it.[20] Bigots may say that birds of a feather should flock together, but they do not often speak of their own partiality as a flaw, much less as a flaw that is natural to all men as men.

Moreover, the piece ends with a massive example of Franklinian sleight of hand: Why, he asks, bring Blacks into the country when "excluding all Blacks and Tawneys" would allow for "increasing the lovely White and Red." Red? The "Red" are, of course, the Indians, who are, according to Franklin's earlier account of the human colors, tawny: The inhabitants of America, "exclusive of the new comers," are "wholly" tawny.[21] If we limit Blacks and Tawneys, we can increase Whites and Tawneys! At the very least, Franklin quite deliberately makes this paragraph into nonsense. And what kind of skin-color bigot would prefer the tawny Indians, pagan hunters, to swarthy and civilized Italians?[22]

The population essay was written both to express Franklin's economic theory and to influence British colonial economic policy. In Franklin's view, the policy granting protection for British manufacturing and preventing colonial manufacturing would limit colonial population growth. Moreover, he thought that the use of slave labor was bad economics, since "the labor of slaves can never be so cheap here as the labor of working men is in *Britain,*" and because whites who have slaves are enfeebled and thus become less productive. For Franklin, both protection and slavery had bad economic effects in general, and they were especially bad in the light of the ongoing conflict between France and England for Canada. Franklin was an avid proponent of colonial and English expansion into Canada, and so the rhetoric of the essay makes sense in this regard.[23]

Moreover, Franklin's point in the essay is that customs and manners (such as tendency to see frugality and industry as religious duties, proneness to luxury, willingness to assimilate, and so on) have economic and political consequences. This aspect of the piece was immediately seized upon by Franklin's friend Richard Jackson, who wrote on just these points in his response to Franklin in 1755.[24] National mores matter in economics, thought Franklin. But this means that what people believe about life matters. He really did not like many things about the Germans. But his dislike had nothing to do with the color of their skin.[25]

Franklin was indebted to a "swarthy" (the Greek Xenophon) for the most important lesson he learned about Socrates (another "swarthy"). In 1769 he wrote to his friend John Bartram that the latter should take time to digest the information he gathered on his European travels and to compile and publish his "many observations."[26] True, says Franklin, many people enjoy accounts of old buildings and monuments. But there are also many who would be happier "with such accounts as you could afford them: And for one I confess that if I could find in any Italian travels a receipt for making Parmesan Cheese, it would give me more satisfaction than a transcript of any inscription from any old stone whatever." Philosophy and Parmesan cheese: Some of the very best things in life come from the "swarthies."

All this notwithstanding, the Palatine Boors remark raises an important matter: Franklin's views on slavery, especially in the light of his disbelief in natural rights. Whatever Franklin may have thought about slavery and blacks in his early life, he was, as early as 1757, solicited by the Anglican minister John Waring, secretary of the Bray Associates in London, a missionary and philanthropic association, to advise them in their efforts at educating and converting black slaves.[27] The letter arrived in Philadelphia after Franklin had sailed to England, and Deborah showed it to William Sturgeon, assistant minister of Christ Church in Philadelphia and an educator of blacks. Sturgeon then wrote to Franklin about the matter, and in 1758 Franklin answered Waring, in a letter written from Craven Street, in which he sent an extract of Sturgeon's letter. In the letter to Waring, Franklin recommended Sturgeon to Waring and the Bray Associates as a good person to direct the proposed Negro School in Philadelphia.

In that letter, Franklin commented to Waring that "at present few or none give their Negro children any schooling, partly from a prejudice that reading and knowledge in a slave are both useless and dangerous" and also lest white parents be disgusted and take their children out of the schools that blacks might attend. It thus makes sense, says Franklin, to establish a "separate school" for blacks to see if it can be useful and not attended with the "ill consequences commonly apprehended" and, if so, if it can then be used as an example to other colonies and to the "inhabitants in general."

Already by that time, Franklin thought the idea that reading and knowledge were useless to blacks was a prejudice, and he recommended separate education as a matter of practicality, not because of any known inferiority of the blacks. Moreover, he recommended the project as an experiment to find out the truth of the matter.

In 1760 Franklin was elected to membership in the Bray Associates.[28] Then, in 1763, he wrote to Waring from Philadelphia after having visited the Negro School in Philadelphia along with Sturgeon and others. Franklin reports that he was impressed with the children and their progress in reading and in the catechism. Then Franklin says:

> I was on the whole much pleased, and from what I then saw, have conceived a higher opinion of the natural capacities of the black race, than I had ever before entertained. Their apprehension seems as quick, their memory as strong, and their docility in every respect equal to that of white children. You will wonder perhaps that I should ever doubt it, and I will not undertake to justify all my prejudices, nor to account for them.[29]

As the editors of the Franklin *Papers* comment, this was perhaps the very first comment by a prominent American that blacks and whites were equal in intellectual abilities.[30] It also powerfully reveals Franklin's skeptical open-mindedness. He admits to having doubted the intellectual equality of blacks and whites; most people did at the time. But although Franklin admits that his former doubt was a prejudice, it is clear from the letter to Waring that, before any evidence was in, he considered it as a prejudgment that could and should be put to the test.

Franklin was a rationalist and a scientist, and even if his doubts were provoked by general experience or prevailing opinion, he knew them as doubts—not certainties—and thus, he could and did view them with skepticism. Do you doubt that blacks and whites are equally intelligent? Want to know if this doubt is correct or well-founded? Says Franklin: Try an experiment.[31] Provide the blacks with education and find out. He did, and he found out. And from this point on, he knew that slavery inflicted a deformation of the minds, the hearts, and the souls of all involved.

When Franklin reprinted the essay on population in his 1769 *Experiments and Observations on Electricity*, he followed Cadwallader Colden's advice and omitted the penultimate paragraph on the Palatine Boors and the final, satirical paragraph on the human colors. But he also made a small but extremely telling change for which there was absolutely no polemical or rhetorical call. In the first version, Franklin said in the course of describing the economic disadvantages of slave labor that it was inefficient in part because "almost every slave [is] *by nature* a thief." In the later version, he changed that to "almost every slave [is] from the nature of slavery a thief."[32]

Slavery, not the slave, is responsible for the slave's degraded condition. But even so, Franklin was hardheadedly matter of fact about the matter as he saw it: In the 1770 "Conversation on Slavery," Franklin described American slaves as no worse off than the English working poor and the blackened slaves in Scottish mines, and as being "of a plotting disposition, dark, sullen, malicious, revengeful and cruel in the highest degree."[33] Just two years later he wrote to Anthony Benezet expressing his approval of the growing "disposition" against slavery in America.[34] Franklin by this time clearly thought slavery bad for America and bad for the slaves, who are equal to their masters in intellectual capacities. But he thought other men who are free suffer just as much, and he had no illusions about how ugly slavery makes the slaves.

In the address at the Cooper Institute, in which Abraham Lincoln refuted Senator Stephen Douglas on the constitutional framers' view of congressional control of slavery in the federal territories, Lincoln counted "Dr. Franklin," along with Alexander Hamilton and Gouverneur Morris, as "among . . . the most noted anti-slavery men of those times."[35]

There is no doubt that Lincoln's judgment of Franklin was correct. In 1787 Franklin was appointed president of the Pennsylvania Society for Promoting the Abolition of Slavery and the Relief of Free Negroes Unlawfully Held in Bondage, and in 1789 he wrote, signed, and submitted a remonstrance against slavery to the first Congress. Franklin by then thought (and had thought before then) that slavery was "an atrocious debasement of human nature" and that the elimination of slavery was in tune with the progress of "the luminous and benign spirit of liberty." [36]

He also thought it such a deformation of the slave's character that even "its very extirpation, if not performed with solicitous care, may sometimes open a source of serious evils." For a slave, degraded in heart and mind and, indeed, brutalized, freedom "may often prove a misfortune to himself, and prejudicial to society." Thus, along with emancipation, attention to the emancipated must become a national policy. It is hard to think that Lincoln would have disagreed with this advice.

But how did Franklin, who denied natural rights (God-given or otherwise) come to his agreement with Lincoln, who placed the Declaration of Independence at the center of the argument against slavery? According to the Declaration, the self-evident truths are that "all men are created equal, that they are endowed by their Creator with certain unalienable rights, that among these are life, liberty and the pursuit of happiness." With the first proposition, that all men are created (probably by sex alone) equal, Franklin agreed. But not so with the second, "that they are endowed by their Creator with certain unalienable rights." Indeed, Franklin proposed the change from Jefferson's original "We hold these truths to be *sacred and undeniable*" to "We hold these truths to be *self-evident*" (my emphasis).[37]

If all men are equal because none has a duty to defer to another's interest—and not from some inherent moral dignity or natural or God-given right—then under conditions of necessity, there is no duty not to enslave others. Of course there is no duty for the slaves to submit, which is why slavery is coercive. So on what grounds did Franklin oppose slavery?

Franklin's opposition to slavery was not just a whim or mere preference on his part. It is possible to deduce, from his thoughts about equality and human nature, how Franklin would have concluded that slavery is a very bad practice. The first deduction, it must be said, is disconcerting: If circumstances did really require one man to be a slave of another, Franklin would surely have said: "Better you than me." But he would have followed this up with the thought that the slave owner had better sleep with one eye open, because the slave is under no obligation to stick around or, for that matter, not to reverse the situation if he can. And Franklin probably knew that slavery—or institutions not unlike it—had indeed probably been necessary (or had at least been thought to be so) in times long past. He knew of course that the glories and beauties of Greece and Rome—not to mention the civilizations described in the Bible—all depended on the enslavement of those peoples who lose in wars or who are thought of as barbarians.[38]

Except under conditions of real necessity, however, Franklin did come to think of slavery as a very bad practice. It does not make society any richer than it could be with free labor because slaves are the worst possible laborers and are ultimately not worth their costs. It is of course bad for the slave, and especially so since the slave is just as capable of developing the human powers and excellences as is the master. It is also bad for the master, who by the practice of mastery is driven to pride and laziness.[39]

But I think that, for Franklin, the worst aspect of slavery by far is the link it must perforce forge between cruelty and moral indignation. As I have argued, Franklin thought that most human misery and folly spring not from "evil" but, rather, from wrong or stupid opinions and especially from moral indignation and claims about justice. Even the principle "Might makes right" demonstrates that the strong wish to rule not just because they are strong but, rather, because they are "right"—because somehow their strength is an indication that they have the service of others coming to them by some moral desert. There are surely some people who have a screw loose and just like to make others suffer, as do children who burn ants with a mirror or pull the wings off of flies. But in fact such people are rare.

Almost all those who deliberately inflict suffering on other human beings think the victims somehow deserve it. In the case of black slavery, there is no doubt that whites believed that they deserved to be the masters and that the slaves deserved to be the slaves (ditto for slaves who are losers in war or barbarians). With slavery, which requires such brutalizing of the slave, the pain inflicted had to be accompanied by a sense that the masters were fulfilling a moral obligation and by indignation on their part at the thought that some—at the very least the slaves—might wish to prevent their giving the slaves what they had coming, what they deserved. And if the obligation to enslave is commanded by God, then those who fulfill it bask in the knowledge that they, deserving as they are, have been noticed by God and have earned his favor. All this would surely make the Franklin we know shudder.

Do these deductions appear in any Franklin piece on slavery? They do. It was the last published writing of his life, written and then published in the *Federal Gazette* just three weeks before he died.[40] As usual, the piece, "Sidi Mehemet Ibrahim on the Slave Trade," is written as a hoax.

One Historicus, having read a speech by a Georgia representative in Congress (James Jackson) arguing against congressional interference with slavery, has been put in mind of a similar speech, made about a hundred years earlier, by Sidi Mehemet Ibrahim, who was a member of the Divan of Algiers. This speech argued against granting the petition of an Islamic sect called the Purists, who sought the abolition of piracy and slavery on the grounds that they were unjust. This speech of Ibrahim's is so close to Jackson's that it shows that "men's interests and intellects operate and are operated on with surprising similarity in all countries and climates, when under similar circumstances." Then, in a transition meant to make Jackson choke, Franklin continues: "The *African's* speech, as translated, is as follows" (my emphasis).

What follows is an African-Muslim version of all the arguments proffered by Jackson: Without piracy and (white) slavery, how will we get the commodities they produce, and who will do our hard work in our hot climate? We will have to become our own slaves. Do we Muslims not deserve more compassion than Christian dogs? Without a steady supply of these dogs, our lands and rents will decline in value and our governments will go bankrupt. All this to satisfy some extreme sect, who not only want to stop procuring slaves but also want us to free the ones we have? If we freed the slaves, who would compensate owners for their losses, and what would we do with the slaves, who, knowing life would be even harder for them at home, would not leave our shores? They will not convert to Islam or accept our manners and will not intermarry with us (who will be disgusted by them), so they will become an army of beggars and thieves.

Are they not better off here than in their home countries? Are not Europeans the slaves of despots? Are not the English impressed into slavery at sea? They are better off as slaves here, where at least the "sun of Islamism" is available as the true doctrine that will save their souls. Were we to let them settle on our frontiers, they would fail and become prey to the "wild Arabs." We, on the contrary, take good care of them, and laborers in their own countries fare worse. And there they are

> impressed for soldiers, and forced to cut one another's Christian throats, as in the wars of their own countries. If some of the religious mad bigots, who now tease us with their silly petitions, have in a fit of blind zeal freed their slaves, it was not generosity, it was not humanity, that moved them to the action; it was from the conscious burthen of a load of sins, and hope, from the supposed merits of so good a work, to be excused damnation.

But, continues Ibrahim, they are wrong about the Koran, which clearly countenances slavery. Plundering the world as we do is not only not forbidden, it is, on the contrary, "well known from it [the Koran], that God has given the world, and all that it contains, to his faithful Musselmen, who are to enjoy it of right as fast as they conquer it."

So on all these grounds, says Ibrahim, the Divan should prefer the interests of the true believers to the whim of the few Purists. Historicus then reports that the Divan rejected the Purists' petition, "and since like motives are apt to produce in the minds of men like opinions and resolutions," we should expect similar petitions in Parliament "and other legislatures" to receive similar treatment.

As close to death as he was, Franklin was still up to his old tricks in this hilarious piece. The first argument of the African Ibrahim is that white slavery is simply necessary, regardless of any claims about right. But as Franklin presents this argument from raw necessity, he also presents it as a matter of contingent and arguable facts, and so we are at least invited to consider whether the facts really do imply the necessity Ibrahim claims. Once we take up this invitation, it's not hard to think of how, in the case of the Islamic pirates, the facts really don't lead to the conclusion that white slavery is really necessary.

Without enslaving piracy against the Christians, says Ibrahim, the Muslims will not be furnished with the "commodities their countries produce, and which are so necessary for us." But since the Muslims clearly do not get by stealing all or most—an impossibility—or even little of what the Christians produce, they must settle for *less* than the Europeans have and, more important, must depend on the changeable fortunes of war. (And who, we wonder, is likelier to develop better weapons: those who know how to produce things, or those who know only how to steal?) Would not the Muslims be richer, then, if they produced on their own and did not steal? This certainly seems more than plausible. And why do they steal? Because, dependent as they are on slaves, they cannot think of themselves as laborers in their hot land (like Georgia?). To work, they think, is to become a slave. But if this is how they think, then to own slaves is also to become lazy and dependent on others for the relatively little one has.

A few moments' thought makes it clear that although white slavery might in some cases be necessary, it's most likely not so in the circumstances Ibrahim describes. The most likely outcome is that the slavery is on balance bad for the Muslim masters. And even if it's bad for the Muslim masters, it is surely worse for the Christian slaves. And we Europeans and Englishmen know, as readers of the piece, that life in our part of the world is not as bad as the Muslims think it is. Thus, we would not rather be slaves in their land than free men in our own.

So far, so good. But the conclusion of Ibrahim's speech is its most subtle and powerful part. As Franklin puts the words in the Muslim's mouth, we are led to scoff at his claim that the Muslims enslave the Christian dogs by right according the divine will revealed in the Koran. But *we* scoff only on the certainty that such revelation is false, either because Christian revelation is true and the Koran false, or because all revelation is spurious. Franklin does not say which of these is the case. As presented here, the right to hold slaves springs from divine will, but we have no way to know what that will really is or whether it even exists at all.

Moreover, what goes for the zealous Muslim Purists must also go for the orthodox Muslim "true believers" in piracy and slavery. As the Purists make their mad and bigoted request against slavery "from the conscious burthen of a load of sins, and hope, from the supposed merits of so good a work, to be excused damnation," so too must the true believers who would defend the right to piracy and slavery (and the way of life and conquests) as the gift of God. For Ibrahim and the true believers not to defend the right to piracy and slavery would surely be a load of sin, and likewise to defend it would be cause for moral satisfaction.

With this conclusion, Franklin forces us to spit into the wind. When Ibrahim speaks of the Muslim *Purist* abolitionists, it is impossible for us not to think of the Christian dissenting counterpart—say, Puritan abolitionists or Quaker abolitionists. What goes for the Muslim Purists would go for them as well, just as it would for the orthodox Muslim believers and the orthodox (or otherwise Christian) slave-holding Georgians.

Thus, unraveling the hoax reveals the following: As regards slavery, the right as defined by divine law applies equally well to any side of the issue: slaves, masters, pro-slavery orthodoxy, or antislavery dissenters. As regards divine law, *all* sides argue on the same nonprovable ground, and what helps one helps all and what subverts one subverts all. But aside from divine law, all sides argue on moral and not merely prudential grounds. And it is easier to convince men that slavery is imprudent than it is to convince them that their own moral principles—their own conceptions of right and deserving— are wrong. And this goes for all sides of the issue.

One can easily see Franklin remarking on the opposing combatants in the Civil War in the same terms he used for the sailors of George Rodney and François-Joseph-Paul de Grasse, fighting in the West Indies. For Franklin, there really was no "right" on any side of the issue. The really tough problem was, however, that almost everyone on every side thought there was. And that is why indignation, even more than interest, was at work, and to greater mischief, on every side.

Franklin was an abolitionist, but for the reasons deduced above. It follows, then, that he would probably have been a moderate abolitionist, willing to trim when necessary and with long-range results in mind. But if circumstances had required, he would not have been squeamish about the costs to be paid to get to the long-range result. And (unlike John Brown) he would not think of slavery as "a load of sins" for which the punishment would be "damnation."

Had Franklin been able to hear Lincoln's second inaugural address, there is no doubt he would have approved its sentiments and stern and moving beauty. But I doubt he would have agreed with Lincoln that the grievous war underway was the "woe due" from God to those by whom an offense had come into the world.

FRANKLIN WAS ALMOST a full-blown Baconian and Hobbesian, and what kept him from going with them all the way was the issue of religion. It is clear that Franklin agreed with Bacon's argument about the goal of natural science expressed in the *Wisdom of the Ancients*, a text Franklin knew well.[41] In Bacon's interpretation of the fable of Orpheus, the tale illuminates the character of natural philosophy: "For natural philosophy proposes to itself, as its noblest work of all, nothing less than the restitution and renovation of things corruptible, and (what is indeed the same thing in a lower degree) the conservation of bodies in the state in which they are, and the retardation of dissolution and putrefaction."[42] The lower degree is mere conservation: the prevention or retarding of old age and decay. The higher degree is the achievement by natural science of what Orpheus tried to achieve by persuading the infernal powers: the return to life of the dead (in Orpheus's case, his beautiful wife).

When this higher degree fails, says Bacon, it does so from "no cause more than from curious and premature meddling and impatience." And when from these causes it does fail, philosophy turns from nature to moral and civil things, "for true it is that the clearer recognition of the inevitable necessity of death sets men upon seeking immortality by merit and renown."[43] Bacon's experimental method was meant to prevent "curious and premature meddling and impatience"—bad science not based on observation and disclosure of the latent courses of nature.

According to Bacon, that meddling and impatience springs from the idols of the human mind—those inherent and acquired flaws of mind that incline human beings to think of the world as they hope it must be and not as it actually is. The most pernicious effect of the idols, in Bacon's view, is the persistent inclination to think of the world as if it were held together as a collection of "formal causes" by some "final cause." This is to understand the world as a kind of god existing especially for us, as if we human beings somehow deserve to have a perfectly ordered home and road map to life handed to us on nature's plate.[44] Bacon had little faith in general enlightenment in the short run. And so he thought that for most human beings, the idols of the mind would be, for a very long time, to some degree at work. Thus, in the scientific society depicted in his New Atlantis, the scientific establishment operates largely in secret, and the populace is ruled by a political elite from above and by religion and faith in miracles.[45]

But in the long run, Bacon thought that with the technological conquest of nature, religion would fade away. According to Bacon's comment in the fable, men seek immortality in merit and renown when they are clearly aware of the necessity of death. Put slightly otherwise, this means that men seek immortality in moral experience because they fear death. That is, they seek redemption by God, on the basis of their merit, because they fear death. By this argument, if and when death is overcome, human beings will no longer sense their merit and hear the call of God.

Franklin, I think, sees the matter in precisely the opposite way: For Franklin, human beings fear death only because they have a prior sense of deserving either the life they have or things others have in life but they do not. We fear death because we are moral, not vice versa; and it is thus only because we are moral that we fear divine punishment and hope for divine reward.

Even if death were to be overcome by science, the fear of God would not be overcome, because morality cannot be overcome. So Franklin could well imagine that at the verge of the final scientific conquest, the believers will fall into paroxysms of condemnation of man's "playing god" and will tremble in fear that God will, with a final miracle, destroy the entire world and human race, including its modern Tower of Babel, science. And if God does not step in, believers might well take matters into their own hands. A poetic wag inspired by Franklin might say that, just as was the case with those drowned before the Flood, we would be better off with just good wine and October than we are with modern science.[46]

Like his teacher Bacon, Hobbes too envisioned the achievement of a fully rational and demystified society. Again, Franklin did not buy this dream, and the point of disagreement emerges most clearly if we consider Franklin's comment that Hobbes's account of human beings in the state of nature was only "closer" to the truth, and not the truth as such.

On close inspection, we see that although the state of nature for Hobbes is "solitary, poor, nasty, brutish, and short," this is not because men are depicted as evil. The *Leviathan* is, among other things, an attack on the concept of original sin, as those who decried Hobbes as an atheist knew perfectly well. According to Hobbes, all men are equal in the state of nature because they are equally able to kill one another and are equally served and satisfied by such wit or reason as they possess.[47] For Hobbes, all men are equal in being sufficiently rational. This fact does not afford them any special dignity; rather, it simply means that "the difference between man, and man, is not so considerable, as that one man can thereupon claim to himself any benefit, to which another may not pretend, as well as he."

As to this conclusion, Franklin and Hobbes agree. But Hobbes's focus on equality of wit points to a utopian rationalism that Franklin simply could not accept. For Hobbes, the violence of the state of nature springs not from human viciousness or ignorance or folly. It is, rather, the inevitable outcome of the rational calculation of all in a state of nature. It is true that some men are moved to aggression by glory and the desire for reputation. These are individuals who take "pleasure in contemplating their own power in the acts of conquest, which they pursue farther than their security requires." But it follows, then, that those who "otherwise would be glad to be at ease within modest bounds" are forced to the offensive with such glory-lovers in mind. And even though men by nature and in the state of nature fear invisible powers and in a state of nature could only agree to covenants on the basis of an oath invoking the punishment of those invisible powers (and not the punishment of any man), Hobbes mentions and then denies the possible restraining role of such oaths in the state of nature.[48]

This silence is remarkable, to say the least. After all, which is more fearsome and likely to command obedience to our promises: death at the hands

of a man, or death and sure punishment at the hands of God? This is a
patent no-brainer: God's punishment wins hands-down. Hobbes thus clearly
implies that oaths in the state of nature are in vain, but because we can only
know what a man tells us, he swears to God, and not what he really believes
and says to God in secret reservation.

But this clear implication is telling. Hobbes clearly presumes that in the
state of nature, whatever invisible powers men really believe in and fear and
regardless of the punishments those powers can inflict, those powers will not
punish us for what we do (make oaths with secret reservations) under conditions of uncertainty and according to our rational calculation and natural
right to self-preservation. In other words, Hobbes presumes that the invisible powers men fear opine exactly as Hobbes does about natural right and
duty: that when we lie and kill in our exercise of the right to all things, we
commit no injustice.[49] Although men in the state of nature believe in active
invisible powers, they apparently do not believe those powers intervene decisively in human affairs: They do nothing to put an end to the war of all
against all.

In Hobbes's state of nature, the war of all against all is not the result of
madness, evil, or even general viciousness. It is, rather, the collective result
of rational decisions made by free and equal individuals, who believe in rational, nonintervening gods that recognize the natural right to self-preservation and thus the right to all things—the right to attack and kill before
being attacked and killed.

For Hobbes, the argument moves from (sufficiently) rational individuals
endowed with the right to self-preservation who fear rational gods that recognize that right, to the state of the war of all against all, and thence to
those individuals' rational deduction, from the right to all things necessary
for self-preservation, of the "laws" of nature: the "Precept[s], or general
rule[s], found out by reason, by which a man is forbidden to do, that, which
is destructive of his life, or taketh away the means of preserving the same;
and to omit, that, by which he thinketh it may be best preserved."[50] From
this deduction comes, then, the rational agreement of all to submit to sovereign political power.

This power, being human and not divine, will have an interest in acting
in human affairs and will be sufficient to keep men in awe and to make it
possible for them to keep covenants. (Keeping covenants and obeying positive law is the only real meaning of the word "justice," for Hobbes.) Then,
and only then, will men be able to pursue "continual prospering," which has
nothing to do with that mere figment "tranquillity."[51]

In the general thrust of his political theory, Hobbes begins with rational
men and deistic "gods" and ends with individuals for whom the fear only of

violent death at the hands of men motivates them to obey the law and keep their agreements. As is clear from Hobbes's account of the origins and changes in religion, if the social and material circumstances are correct, the fear of invisible powers can simply disappear. Hobbes's cooked-up theology—in which there will be resurrection and heaven for the good, and resurrection and a second death for the bad, but no hell for anyone—was a first step in that direction.[52] Since, for Hobbes, religion has but a natural cause in the constitution of the human mind, and since that cause is fear and ignorance of causes, religion can be manipulated to any rational end and even, with the advent of secure long life and commodious living, be extirpated from human experience.

For Franklin, it was precisely this dogmatic hyper-rationalism that kept Hobbes from revealing the full truth about human nature and politics. As we know from the argument of Philoclerus, Hobbes merely assumes that religion has a natural as opposed to a supernatural cause, and he merely assumes that spirits or the spirit of God cannot intervene in the courses of nature and our affairs.

According to the dialectical Franklin, religion springs not so much from fear but also and more fundamentally from the powerful moral intuitions rooted deeply in the human soul—especially in our sense of merit and deserving. Human beings will always think that other men, society, even the universe, and especially God will answer their hopes about what they have coming to them, what they have earned by their moral worthiness. Since this, and not just fear, is the true source of religion, we have good reason to surmise that, for Franklin, Hobbes's rationalist project was ill founded and unlikely to work. And this is not to mention the fact that since Hobbes's lack of religion was merely dogmatic, he himself could in principle have been subject to the same conversion as the former Spinosist-Hobbist.[53]

The telling point as regards the natural human condition is Franklin's account of the American Indians. For Hobbes, the Indians are real examples of life in the state of nature, where the war of all against all ensues from the logic of rational actors' right to all things required for self-preservation. Franklin also considers the Indians to be in the state of nature.[54] But their lives are so far from being the war of all against all that Franklin can discuss the charms and attractions their way of life holds for civilized men and can contrast the simplicity, honesty, hospitality, and pleasant indolence of their lives to the laborious enslavement to artificial needs in civil society.

Moreover, the Indians are far from all being individually satisfied with their own wisdom, with its resulting dissociation. Rather, "the persuasion of men distinguish[ed] by reputation of wisdom is the only means by which others are governed or rather led."[55] The Indians are at once in the state of nature and subject to all manner of persuasion, not the least of which comes from those who communicated with the gods. Of course, Franklin knew that the Indians believed in all manner of spirits and hocus pocus no less than did civilized men, as is clear from his remarks in the 1783 essay "Remarks Concerning the Savages of North America."[56]

For Hobbes, human beings in the state of nature can be thought of as possessing nearly perfect clarity and reason; they are not blinded by any spurious claims to superior wisdom or status, by other claims to rule or exclusive benefit, or by any sense of binding moral duty; and they believe only in rationalistic Hobbesian "gods." This absolute clarity and reason has been lost in the course of history and civilization, especially at the hands of priests and self-interested philosophers. But the clarity and reason can be recalled, as Hobbes does in the *Leviathan*, and the cobwebs of false belief, superstition, and the fear of invisible powers can be completely dispelled.

For Franklin, human beings are equal for reasons partly akin to those of Hobbes: There is no credible reason for one person to claim or deserve a benefit not also available to others. But Franklin could and did argue, as the dogmatic Hobbes did not, that human beings are in truth equal because no one deserves anything, or has dignity, because deserving and dignity are internally incoherent ideas. Having thought this fact through dialectically, Franklin came to know that people in general do not and cannot know this truth. As simply human, and not just by historical or political accident, most people are equal in being equally credulous and misguided, and they are so because they are moral. They are thus "badly constructed" in the state of nature and remain so in the most advanced civilizations.[57]

Thus, for Franklin, it is pure folly for Hobbes to have thought that the "Kingdom of Darkness"—the realm of religion and fearsome invisible powers—could ever be dissolved by the light of perfect reason. Political technology will always have to worry about competition from those powers—from those who fear God's punishments more than those of men and from those who, like the deranged breaker of fine china, claim to dispense God's punishments.[58]

Franklin always (and unlike Hobbes) included divine punishments in his minimalist "doctrine to be preached."[59] He warned against debunking this doctrine not so much because the tiger needs to be kept frightened, lest it feel no restraint on its passions (although for sure it sometimes does), but, rather, because the vast majority of human beings are moral and think of themselves as acting for justice and for the good and are given to angry indignation (such as that in favor of or opposed to slavery).

Indignation, not fear, is the power to be managed, especially for the likes of Franklin, who had been nipped by the tiger and had to learn how to protect himself from well-meaning sharp teeth. But indignation is the power to be managed in general political life as well: The sailors going at it in the fleets of Rodney and de Grasse doubtless thought their respective causes were just and surely prayed to the same God to support them. Men in general are not and never will be "pragmatists."[60] For Franklin, this natural fact was an absolute limit to enlightenment, and not seeing this limit was another of mankind's dogmatic stupidities.

So for all of his cheerfulness, unbounded curiosity, and constructive Baconian inventiveness, Franklin had a profound understanding of the ineradicable roots of human folly and the limits of enlightenment. Enthusiasms of every sort will always be possible and will sometimes abound, and there is, therefore, a limit to the virtue of religious toleration. And thus, for all of his real efforts to foster his minimalist "creed" that would not "shock the professors of any religion," he always included divine punishment in that creed and was quite willing both to shock believers and to side with enthusiasts, whichever prudence required.[61] Franklin's concrete religious politics could be well described as inclined toward "managed enthusiasm."

Despite the whopper Franklin tells about his avoiding "all discourse that might tend to lessen the good opinion another might have of his own religion," Franklin weighed in heavily, publicly, and nastily in the religious politics of Philadelphia in the 1730s.[62] In the *Autobiography*, Franklin tells us that when the young Presbyterian preacher Hemphill arrived in Philadelphia, Franklin became his admirer because his sermons had little dogmatism and "inculcated strongly the practice of virtue, or what in the religious stile are called good works."[63] The orthodox Presbyterians and the older clergy objected to Hemphill's doctrines and brought him before the Synod on charges of heterodoxy. Franklin tells us that he "lent" Hemphill his pen and wrote three pamphlets and a piece in the *Gazette* in April 1735. The April piece was the "Dialogue between Two Presbyterians" and the pamphlets were *Observations on the Proceedings against Mr. Hemphill, Letter to a Friend in the Country*, and *Defense of Observations*, published in that order.[64]

As the last pamphlet was in press, Hemphill was exposed as having plagiarized his sermons (and from an Arminian, to boot); he was ruined, and Franklin's party on his behalf was defeated. Even so, says Franklin, he stood by Hemphill because he "rather approved his giving us good sermons composed by others, than bad ones of his own manufacture; though the latter was the practice of our common teachers." Franklin says that the pamphlets were soon out of vogue, as is the case with "controversial writings," and so he wonders if a single copy still exists.

Franklin was right about the theoretical or theological merits of these pieces—had they not survived it would have been no great loss. But they are valuable for revealing both the direction and the vehemence of Franklin's polemical stance toward the Presbyterian establishment in Pennsylvania. First, he was quite willing to say very nasty things about his fellow citizens' religious views, things obviously intended to make them have a lesser opinion of their own religion. The doctrine of original sin—so crucial to Calvinism—he described as an absurd "bugbear set up by Priests (whether *Popish* or *Presbyterian* I know not) to fright and scare an unthinking populace out of their senses, and inspire them with terror, to answer the little selfish ends of the inventors and propagators." It is monstrous, says Franklin, to think that one man can be subject to punishment for the guilt of another, and to believe this, as do the Presbyterians, is to make God arbitrary, unjust, and cruel.[65]

The doctrines of justification by faith alone and salvation by means of the merits and satisfactions of Christ, Franklin called antinomianism, "the most impious doctrine that ever was broached," which has "a natural tendency to make men act as if Christ came into the world to patronize vice, and allow men to live as they please."[66]

So much for the tender opinions of his fellow Presbyterians. The thrust of Franklin's position was very simple—and precisely in line with the creed he thought best for men in general. As the character S says in the *Dialogue*, "Faith is recommended as a means of producing morality: Our savior was a teacher of morality or virtue, and they that were deficient and desired to be taught, ought first to *believe* in him as an able and faithful teacher. Thus faith would be a means of producing morality, and morality of salvation."[67] According to Franklin—and he saw this in Hemphill's preaching—the doctrines absolutely necessary to be believed are given to us by our natural reason, and Jesus and the apostles serve to make that teaching more distinct to us. Anyone can achieve salvation by means of morality—by good works done to one's fellow man—and a moral heathen is more likely to get to heaven than will a rigid and dogmatic, but less than righteous, Presbyterian.

The important point to note is that Franklin was willing to defend his latitudinarian and tolerant public creed with nasty and even (apparently) intolerant attacks. Moreover, his aim, as Melvin H. Buxbaum has shown decisively, was less to advance his tolerant creed than to fracture the church's political power, which he feared.[68] In the *Letter to a Friend*, Franklin revealed this fear bluntly: "Nothing, in all probability, can prevent our being a very flourishing and happy people, but our suffering the clergy to get upon our backs, and ride us, as they do their horses, where they please."[69] It is hard not to think that Jefferson, in the last letter he wrote before he died, was thinking of Franklin when he penned his famous remark about the rights of man: "that the mass of mankind has not been born with saddles on their backs, nor a favored few booted and spurred, ready to ride them legitimately, by the grace of God."[70] So it is true that Franklin did not much like Presbyterians and Calvinists and was quite willing to attack them with an eye to diminishing their political and moral power.

But even so, he was also quite happy to hook up with Calvinistic *enthusiasts* when they further stirred and fractured the religious establishment. This he did in his later support of the Reverend Whitefield. In the *Autobiography*, Franklin soft-pedals his description of the reverend. There is no doubt that he was, in fact, a real Holy Roller. Ebenezer Kinnersly, a lay Baptist preacher and later a friend and scientific collaborator of Franklin's, in 1740 attacked Whitefield for his disruptive, "enthusiastic ravings."[71]

Franklin's intention in supporting Whitefield was another move in his attempt to break the Presbyterian establishment and to promote the multiplication of religious sects, which Franklin for the most part supported with his money and organizing efforts. On the one hand, he was perfectly happy to support Whitefield's ravings when they raised money for good works. But he was perfectly aware of Whitefield's beliefs, which included all of those Franklin derided in the polemics in favor of Hemphill—especially the "bugbear" of original sin and human depravity.

Franklin knew too much about human vanity to worry about Whitefield's "abuse" of his hearers in "assuring them that they were naturally *half beasts and half devils*."[72] Nor would he have worried later about the one-time Anglican's growing Calvinism and rantings about justification by faith alone.[73] Again, Franklin knew too much about human vanity to worry even about Calvinist enthusiasm: The good thing about enthusiasm, as regards predestination and justification by faith alone, is that, far from cowing those who experience it and preparing them for the saddle and the spur, it instead induces at least some of them to experience faith—that sure sign of God's grace and election—*actually* moving in *their* souls.

Knowing this, the saved can do perfectly well on their own. And those who, writhing on the ground in agony at the absence of that faith and grace and election, are in effect on their own because no one can help them but God. Whitefield's enthusiasm, regardless of its doctrinal hues, shook things up and freed his listeners from dependence on the religious establishment. That is what Franklin liked, and in supporting it, he practiced "managed enthusiasm." The fact is, Franklin knew, that faith and enthusiasm will always be with us and that the important task is to bend them whenever possible to liberty—to keep the clergy from riding us like horses.

Franklin never ceased to assert that well-managed religion—especially one whose doctrines include divine rewards and punishments—could be an important restraint on human viciousness.[74] But he knew well that the disease and the remedy spring from the same well of our common moral intuitions. If we think about the macabre and comic hoax of the scalps, the remarks about the Indians' manners, the comment to Priestly about the murderous sailors in the fleets of Rodney and de Grasse, and the spoof on slavery, and if we consider Franklin's view that the concepts of "evil," "moral virtue," and "justice" make no sense, it is clear that, for Franklin, the crimes and vicious horrors of life spring precisely from the manifold forms of indignation to which human beings are moved by their views of moral impropriety and justice abused.

And thus, claims of God's approval and encouragement of the crimes and horrors always follow. The fictitious Indian perpetrators of the scalping outrage are acting out of gratitude to their allies and against an enemy who has great and sharp claws and who has expelled the poor Indians from their land. What is this but moral tit for tat?[75] Franklin says of the Indians and their manners that we think them savages "because their manners differ from ours, which we think the perfection of civility," but they think the same of us.[76] And if the scalping Indians act out of their own moral convictions—their own sense of manners, civility, and justice—surely the same can be said of those who put them up to their vicious "crime": king, queen, Parliament, and bishops.[77]

Surely, as I've noted before, the sailors in the fleets of Rodney and de Grasse were all moved to their bloodletting by duty and by the conviction that justice and God were on their respective sides. And Franklin had earlier written to the marquis de Lafayette about Rodney's part in spreading English tyranny.[78] Sidi Mehemet Ibrahim does not find the Christians to be infidels because he thinks they are dogs. Rather, he thinks them dogs because they are infidels. They are better off as slaves to the true-believing Muslims because at home they suffer slavery to despots. And the Purists do not read the Koran incorrectly because they are "religious mad bigots"; they are mad bigots because they read the Koran incorrectly. And ditto, of course, for the Muslim slavers, the Christian slavers, and the Christian abolitionists.[79]

In Franklin's view, scratch a crook, and you'll find someone getting even. Scratch a bloodthirsty tyrant, and you'll find a moral fanatic. And examine what we think of as an outrage, and you'll find a moral explanation for it. For Franklin, there is no "evil" at work in such circumstances—if evil is understood as free, malevolent choice. In each case, the "evil" is simply the bad consequence of a given condition, and the condition is the moral conviction and understanding of the facts obtaining in each case.

For Franklin, the moral and the religious impulses are inseparable from each other, and thus, only a fool should expect the demise of religion or think that enthusiasm will not need to be managed. Indeed, those so fervent for enlightenment may well be moved by their own moral hopes and indignation—the very wellspring of the faith they so despise. The only recourse for a practical man of sense, then, is never to hope for the best from human beings and always to expect the worst. Human beings will always be more or less crazy—not because they want the worst for themselves and others but because they want the best.

Franklin's willingness to manage and manipulate religion appeared again at the very end of his life. This time it concerned not the Philadelphia Presbyterian establishment but the president of Yale College, Ezra Stiles. In January 1790, Franklin got a letter from his friend Stiles, who wrote:

> You know, sir, that I am a Christian, and would to Heaven all others were such as I am. . . . As much as I know of Dr. Franklin, I have not an idea of his religious sentiments. I wish to know the opinion of my venerable friend concerning Jesus of Nazareth. . . . I shall never cease to wish you that happy immortality, which I believe Jesus alone has purchased for the virtuous and truly good of every religious denomination in Christendom, and for those of every age, nation, and mythology, who reverence the Deity, and are filled with integrity, righteousness, and benevolence.[80]

Franklin, of course, knew that his educator friend posed this question to him as he, Franklin, had one foot in his grave. Heartfelt as were Stiles's wishes for Franklin's salvation, which he thought available through Jesus alone, Franklin cannot but have sensed the meaning of the question: Now that you are going to die, do you *still* believe you can be saved by your virtue alone, without intervention by the divine Jesus? And he cannot but have wondered if Stiles was asking him this question out of some more general doubts Stiles might have had not just about Jesus, but about God.

Franklin was still too prudent to puncture his friend's declared faith and dash his good wishes. But in typical fashion, he leaves some clues, if Stiles is willing to follow them up. So he answered exactly within the limits set out by Stiles.[81] He repeats and declares belief in his creed (which we have seen before) and then, as regards Jesus, says that he thinks "the system of morals and his religion, as he left them to us, the best the world ever saw or is likely to see." He has some doubts as to the divinity of Jesus, "though it is a question I do not dogmatize upon, having never studied it, and think it needless to busy myself with it now, when I expect soon an opportunity of knowing the truth with less trouble."

But he sees no harm in this being believed, if it reinforces respect for and observation of the moral doctrine. And then Franklin adds, as regards his doubts about and utilitarian calculation of the matter: "Especially as I do not perceive, that the Supreme takes it amiss, by distinguishing the unbelievers

in his government of the world with any particular marks of his displeasure."
As for himself, Franklin tells Stiles, since he has experienced "the goodness
of that Being in conducting" him prosperously through his life, he has "no
doubt of its continuance in the next, though not without the smallest conceit of meriting such goodness." To show his "sentiments on this head"
Franklin sends Stiles two letters, one Franklin had sent to a zealous believer
whose paralysis he had treated with electricity, and another that "will show
something of my disposition relating to religion."

Here is Franklin's penultimate sleight of hand. (The last was "Sidi
Mehemet Ibrahim on the Slave Trade," the spoof on slavery.) At first
glance, it seems as if God's lack of displeasure with unbelievers applies to
those who do not believe in the divinity of Jesus. Believing in Jesus's divinity
is fine if it makes us more moral; but it does not matter if one does not really
believe in that divinity, since God would not punish people for what they
believe to be true or false. This would seem to be the answer to Stiles, who
has asked Franklin about his belief in Jesus.

But it is by no means clear whether Franklin's phrase "his government of
the world" refers to God's use of Jesus in God's providence or to God's providence itself. The principle at stake—that God would not punish us for what
we truly believe—surely applies as much to belief in God's providence (and
especially to the particular providence of the Franklin creed) as it does to
belief in Jesus. It applies as well to those who believe their actions, whatever
they are, are really for the best. So Franklin leaves open the possibility that
he does not believe even in God and particular providence, while telling
Stiles that he—Stiles—even in that case has no reason to worry about
Franklin's soon-to-depart soul.

The letter to the "zealous religionist" is Franklin's 1753 letter to Joseph
Huey.[82] Huey had written to Franklin about Franklin's kindness in having
treated him with electrical therapy. Huey thanked Franklin by warning him
"impertinently" not to be proud.[83] Franklin says of his own "notion of good
works" that he no way believes that by them he actually merits heaven.
How, he asks, could we merit infinite and eternal happiness by all the good
works we do? Even one who would expect a plantation in exchange for giving a man a drink of water would be modest by comparison to our expectation of heaven for "the little good" one can do on earth. This wonderful
barb—that trying to cure Huey's paralysis was no better than offering a drink
of water—is then followed by Franklin's wish that the likes of Huey would
give more credit to good works as opposed to "holiday-keeping, sermon-
reading or hearing, performing church ceremonies, or making long prayers,
filled with flatteries and compliments, despised even by wise men, and much
less capable of pleasing the deity."

Now, in the letter to Stiles and in the accompanying letter to Huey, some telling hints of Franklin's view are presented for Stiles to consider if he wants. If God does not care about what men really think true about Christ, so long as they are virtuous, then doesn't the principle—that God won't punish for what we really believe true about Jesus—also apply to our genuine opinions about virtue and vice? Who wants to be wrong about such matters? Would anyone *choose* to be wrong about them, any more than one would choose to be wrong about Jesus? If the answer is no, then why would God blame us for our opinions about virtue and vice if he does not blame us for our opinions about Jesus? And while we're on the subject of punishment, wouldn't Stiles agree that, as virtue is its own reward, so too is vice its own punishment? It seems he would. But if that's true, then why does God pile his punishments on top of those piled on by men? And talk about piling on, can anyone deserve the eternal fire or eternal bliss, for *anything* he might do on this earth?

Which brings up another matter. According to Franklin's creed recited to Stiles, "the soul of man is immortal, and will be treated with justice in another life respecting its conduct in this."[84] By this Franklin clearly means that God's justice is a matter of proportion and that we reap in heaven or in hell what we sow on earth. But then, to Stiles and more strongly to Huey, he says we can't actually merit heaven, because the reward of eternal happiness can bear no proportion to the paltry good we do on earth. That sounds reasonable. But if so, is not the result just what he says to Huey: that "I can do *nothing* to deserve such reward" (my emphasis)?[85] Maybe if we're good we get a hundred years in heaven, but if God chooses, we get an additional eternity to boot.

But why would God so choose? Don't we have anything to do with the matter? It would seem we do. Still, it does seem reasonable that if we get the real first prize of heaven, there really is nothing we could have done on earth proportionate to *that* reward. So again, it would seem reasonable that we can do nothing to merit the first prize. But then, don't we then think that when we merit the first prize (we can't really believe we have nothing to do with the matter), we don't merit the first prize? Isn't there a problem here as regards salvation? And if we started to think, might we find a problem not just with salvation, but with the idea of merit itself? Is there a line of thinking we might follow up here?

Stiles can get the picture and set out on his own if he wishes. But none of this is shoved in the good reverend's face. The kind, benevolent, and fervent Christian is unlikely to follow up and put the pieces together unless he is really bothered by doubts of his own. And if so, and were he to come to Franklin's understanding of things, how sweet the liberation. If, as is likely, he does not, but still gets a whiff of Franklin's skepticism, he can rest easy that God will not forsake his dear friend because of what he has honestly believed.[86]

Franklin decided against particular providence dialectically and not by the dogmatic ways of metaphysics. And he decided against God as well and on the same grounds. But he could not be absolutely sure about every possible god—say, one like a big malicious spider. He went as far as reason can reasonably be expected to go and, having done so, had no deathbed conversion.[87] But still, since reason had not taken him to absolute certainty about every possible god, Franklin proposes an experiment: He will die and so find out for sure. Being proved wrong might conceivably be painful for quite some time. But discovering the truth always has some risk, as Franklin found out with his botched electrical execution of the turkey. What a charming way for Franklin to bow out. What a subtle and graceful note on his part, by which we take our leave, *nullum par elogium*.

Conclusion:
Will the Real Ben Franklin
Please Stand Up?

So who was the real Ben Franklin: First American and father of pragmatism? republican patriot and public servant? ambitious Tory imperialist? natural scientist? utilitarian hero of the plodding and middling folk? devotee of the moral sublime? selfish opportunist? Francophile Deist? debauched aristocratic wannabe? In one way or another, he at least looked like all of the above. And to some degree he was. That's why biographers and scholars, admirers and detractors alike, find the man behind the masks so elusive and such a puzzle. But Franklin is a puzzle only because the real Franklin—the philosophical Franklin that unifies all the masks—has for so long eluded us.

Moreover, the philosophical Franklin tells us why we find the mere existence of the masks such a problem: because we expect the human soul to be ordered according to our moral hopes. We think the several possibilities in the cake shop of life should be pursued as ends that have some binding moral order. We think the soul should be ordered by natural duties (callings) or, to use the language of more-modern moralizing, by authentic commitments. We think, for instance, that devotion to family trumps devotion to self, that devotion to country trumps devotion to family, and devotion to humanity (say, in some "united party for virtue") trumps devotion to country.

If a "committed monarchist" professes monarchy to be the best form of government but then, in different personal or political circumstances, suddenly becomes a republican, we suspect "mere opportunism." If we do not find a unity of soul anchored by these duties or callings or commitments, we see, at best, an enigma; if not that, then a ship unmoored in stormy seas; or at worst, a dangerous nihilist. There is much truth to this point of view, since a soul with no moorings at all can be useless to itself or dangerous to others. The real Franklin was neither an enigma nor an unmoored vessel, and he was certainly no nihilist (that would have required him to be too angry). The philosophical Franklin came to a clear understanding of the world

and life as they really are and, on that ground, had an equally clear understanding of the good things in life and the causes of the bad ones. And his
critique of morality exposed the reasons why we expect a tighter order and
unity in the soul than really stands to reason. The philosophical Franklin
was the real Franklin and explains why Franklin could and did do so many
things that seem to us exclusive of each other.

The deepest apparent contradiction is between Franklin the skeptical
philosopher and Franklin the political man. But this contradiction disappears when we understand Franklin's philosophy and his Baconianism. His
philosophy culminated in the critique of morality and religion. And although I doubt that he ever stopped thinking open-mindedly about that critique (even after he became "sure," he remained open to being persuaded
otherwise), neither the critique nor the ongoing reflection on it in any way
precluded his enjoyment of the other good things in life. The good things in
life for Franklin included natural science and invention, both of which were
extensions of philosophy in revealing the world as it actually is and not as
we hope it will be. Nor did they preclude his lifelong engagement in politics,
which was for Franklin an aspect of invention and one of the most enjoyable
games of life. They did preclude his being an angry political partisan, since
he knew that anger makes no sense. In all aspects of his Baconianism,
Franklin's efforts were (when they succeeded) good for others. But Franklin
engaged in them because they were good for Franklin, not because they were
good for others.

There is no real contradiction between his long and almost Tory-like efforts for the British Empire and his sudden "conversion" to the republican
cause. There is no contradiction because, as a political Baconian and
Hobbesian, he was no more a republican or democrat than a monarchist, if
by them we mean someone convinced that there is a best form of government as such or that either king or people—or anyone else, for that matter—deserves to rule. Franklin's abrupt change of allegiance was dictated by
circumstances and was entirely opportunistic and consistent with his broad
view of the course of modernity. And for Franklin, such opportunism was no
vice; it was the only political position that really makes sense.

Franklin was the First American, but not as a member of the moral community rooted in the experience and commitments of the Revolution. He
was, rather, the First American as the practical booster, example of the second chance and the clean slate, and enthusiast for modernity—liberty, invention, and opportunity for those born with nothing but their brains. But
Franklin was so cautious in his writing because his philosophical radicalism
far outstripped the homely American pragmatism he is so often credited
with founding.

Of this supposed pragmatism, Walter Isaacson, following James Campbell, tells us that for Franklin, "the truth of any proposition, whether it be a scientific or moral or theological or social one, is based on how well it correlates with experimental results and produces a practical outcome," and that Franklin's "moral and religious thinking . . . 'becomes a rich philosophical defense of service to advance the common good.'"[1] As we learned from Polly skating on her thin ice, pragmatists blithely overestimate the benevolence of a focus on practical outcomes: If we want to discourage adultery, we might well achieve the practical outcome as easily by taking the divine and eternal fire as our model and by forgetting about the simple principle of justice that punishments should fit crimes. And this is not to mention, as we have seen, that if the truth of a proposition depends on the practical outcome, then truth and lying go hand in hand, and it cannot really be true that "*truth, sincerity and integrity* in dealings between man and man" are "of the utmost importance" for happiness.

Franklin would point out, I think, that pragmatists always look on the bright side of things because they are not really pragmatists: They cannot really bear to revise the dictum that "nothing is useful that is not honest" and say that whenever it is useful one should not be honest, or better, if one is really in a pinch, all moral bets are off. The pragmatists are old-fashioned moralists in their way—and thus, their hearts too soar at the nobility and righteousness of service to the common good, and especially when that service is down to earth and practical. So too is their indignation stirred by absolutists who stand in the way of the common good. Thus, of Franklin's pragmatism, Isaacson says that Franklin's willingness to compromise was based on his "having the humility to be open to different opinions. For him that was not merely a practical virtue, but a moral one as well. It was based on the tenet, so fundamental to most moral systems, that every individual deserves respect."[2]

I doubt this assessment of Franklin. All the evidence suggests, rather, that Franklin appeared to be humble because he thought it was prudent and because there is simply no good reason for pride. And because there is not, it cannot really be true that any individual deserves respect, or anything else for that matter. Utilitarianism: The moral good is the greatest happiness for the greatest number. But if asked why the few should sacrifice for the many and be admired for that sacrifice, Franklin would say, I think, that neither he nor anyone else could ever come up with a really good answer. The good is one's own happiness, and a man of sense is the man who knows how to secure it as best and as clearheadedly as he can. Such thoughts as these, I think, might well make the coolest utilitarian or pragmatist very angry indeed.

Even if Franklin wasn't as American as apple pie, he was as American as the corndog. By this I mean that he was fully American in the sense of the exciting project—the ever-widening carnival of novelty and change—but not in the sense of American idealism, not in the sense of seeing America as the moral light unto the nations. No fan of aristocracy, he was nevertheless at home with aristocratic wit and good taste—and especially aristocratic feminine beauty and charm. He liked the French, as Adams said. But he was no Deist, however much he may have associated with them and was suspected of being one of them. He saw right through conscientious Deism. He was a utilitarian hero to those American boys (and now girls) of the middling classes who were warned by Mark Twain to expect torment in his name. But he was a "moral" hero—in the sense of practical but sublime devotion to public service and the public good—only in the fictitious light of the ironic *Autobiography*.

But most of all, Franklin could be all these things because he was *first* the careful, dialectical philosopher revealed in the *Autobiography*'s second ironic layer and in the writings, both comical and dialectical, to which that layer points. He was, in short, the radical and nondogmatic skeptic who peeps through all of his comic writings. This Franklin is no model, no paragon, no "first" anything. He is, rather, a helpful conversationalist who, having thought through as well as he could for himself the deepest and most pressing questions of life and never stopped doing so, helps us do the same—but for ourselves, and not as the recipients of a fixed and dogmatic system. In this sense, Franklin really does, if we read him with utmost seriousness and care, force us to the most important kind of bootstrap self-improvement.

Franklin speaks to his careful readers out of humanity and friendship, but not from duty. He speaks to them for the pleasing attachment to those he could imagine sharing in hours of conversation and a shared desire to see the world as it really is and not as we want it to be. He devotes to them much more effort than he did to poor Deborah, and ultimately he treats them with more consideration than he gave to his son, William.

I have argued that, as genuinely philosophical, Franklin was not an angry man (which is not to say that he did not feel anger and get mad). One fact that tells against this argument is Franklin's harsh treatment of his Tory son, William, after 1775. There is no doubt that Franklin's behavior was in large part opportunistic: He was suspected of being a spy and of being in secret cahoots with his son, the royalist governor of New Jersey. When William was arrested, Franklin "refused to lift a finger" on behalf of his release, which was eventually occasioned by Congress.[3] It was said that the two meetings between them in the summer of 1775 ended in shouting matches, and after the Revolution, Franklin replied coldly to William's request for reconciliation.

And in his will, Franklin left William almost nothing: "The part he acted against me in the late war, which is of public notoriety, will account for my leaving him no more of an estate he endeavored to deprive me of."[4]

Franklin had good reason to be angry. For the sake of some incoherent principle, some idea of duty, William was putting his own father seriously in harm's way. Had the Revolution failed, as Franklin reportedly said to his fellow cosigners of the Declaration of Independence, he would have joined them in having his neck stretched. Then William would have inherited everything, and for reasons that Franklin would not have liked at all.

Still, why would the philosophical Franklin stay mad at his son after the heat and danger of war had passed and he had asked for reconciliation? And why then disown him? Perhaps Franklin thought that since William was willing to have his inheritance by Franklin's unnatural death, why should he reward the rascal with the fruits of his own natural demise? But that consideration of justice would have made no sense to Franklin. As to the disownment, we could well surmise that Franklin thought William would be better off were he then to make his fortune on his own, and to better effect on his character. But we can as easily surmise that Franklin—a human being after all—just could not help being miffed, even knowing that the passion is irrational. That is perfectly compatible with a philosophical Franklin who was not, therefore, in general an angry man. We have wonderful evidence for just this fact. In the summer of 1784, while in Passy, Franklin wrote William a now-famous letter in which he responded to William's overture with equally famous "coolness."[5] To William, Franklin replied:

It [reconciliation] will be very agreeable to me; indeed nothing has ever hurt me so much and affected me with such keen sensations, as to find myself deserted in my old age by my only son; and not only deserted, but to find him taking up arms against me, in a cause, wherein my good fame, fortune and life were all at stake. You conceived, you say, that your duty to your king and regard for your country required this. I ought not to blame you for differing in sentiment with me in public affairs. We are men, all subject to errors. Our opinions are not in our own power; they are formed and governed much by circumstances, that are often as inexplicable as they are irresistible. Your situation was such that few would have censured your remaining neuter, *though there are natural duties which precede political ones, and cannot be extinguished by them.*[6]

Here, we're in the grip of the old conjurer again. There is no doubt that the letter is cool and that Franklin remained miffed. But Franklin is telling his son philosophically that he forgives and that he knows his own anger is irrational. *We* know that Franklin did not believe in natural duties. We know that what he means by them here is rather the attachments of the heart, not the requirements of morality. And he says as much to William, if William will read the letter carefully.

Franklin does not *say* that he means the attachments of the heart. He speaks only of natural duties as opposed to political ones. But as regards the latter, Franklin uses the very same argument he used in the letter to his parents excusing his involvement with the Masons (and the ghastly torment of the young lad at the faked initiation). He cannot blame William for his political opinions, and so for his notion of his political duties, because our opinions are not in our own power.

If we stop to think, however, the same must be true of our opinions about our natural duties. If our opinions about our natural duties (say, our obligation to Dad) are not in our own power, then we cannot be blamed for whatever we take them to be. But if we cannot be blamed, then neither can we be praised. But if we cannot be praised or blamed for whatever we take our natural duties to be, then does it not follow that our natural duties wind up being whatever we take them to be? And if that's true, can it make any sense to speak of natural *duties* at all? And of course the same line of thinking would apply to the attachments of the heart. Our opinions tell us how to comport toward those attachments—whether or not to prefer them to our political "duties." And over those opinions, we would have to conclude on Franklin's grounds, we have no power to choose.

Franklin the normal man could not help being hurt by and mad at his son. But even in this matter so close to his heart, the philosophical and humane Franklin could and did reflect on the groundless foolishness of the anger he just could not get over. That far, which is as far as is possible in real life, the philosophical Franklin is the one who stands up.[7]

Notes

Preface

1. Mark Twain, "The Late Benjamin Franklin," in *Collected Tales, Sketches, Speeches, and Essays, 1852–1890* (New York: Library of America, 1992), 425–427.

2. See Charles F. Angoff, *A Literary History of the American People* (New York: Knopf, 1931), 296–308; D. H. Lawrence, "Benjamin Franklin," in *Benjamin Franklin and the American Character*, ed. Charles L. Sanford (Boston: D. C. Heath, 1955), 57–64; Max Weber, *The Protestant Ethic and the Spirit of Capitalism*, trans. Talcott Parsons (New York: Charles Scribners, 1958), 48–56, 64–65, 71, 124, 180.

3. See John William Ward, "Franklin: His Masks and His Character," *American Scholar* 32 (1963): 541–553; and David Levin, "The Autobiography of Benjamin Franklin: The Puritan Experiment in Life and Art," *Yale Review* 53: 258–275.

4. Deism is a fuzzy creed, especially as it is understood as a historical movement. It can crudely be described as having had three forms: dry, wet, and very wet. Dry Deism claimed that we can know there is a God from the manifest order of the world. That order is fixed, however, and God does not intervene (no biblical miracles, and so on). There is no free will, and all is ordained by general providence; the world as it exists is the best of all possible worlds (there is no need for God to intervene). Wet Deism derived God in the same way and denied the existence of miracles, but it granted free will and morality by derivation from the laws of reason. Very wet Deism granted all that wet Deism claimed and also admitted rewards and punishments in the world to come.

5. Alfred Owen Aldridge, *Benjamin Franklin and Nature's God* (Durham, NC: Duke University Press, 1967), 81. See Donald H. Meyer, "Franklin's Religion," in *Critical Essays on Benjamin Franklin*, ed. Melvin Buxbaum (Boston: Hall, 1987), 147–167.

6. Walter Isaacson, *Benjamin Franklin: An American Life* (New York: Simon and Schuster, 2003), 84–85, 256.

7. H. W. Brands, *The First American* (New York: Doubleday, 2000), 94–95. I've borrowed the term "First American," used here and in the Conclusion, from Brands.

8. Edmund Morgan, *Benjamin Franklin* (New Haven, CT: Yale University Press, 2002), 17–25, 30.

9. Gordon Wood, *The Americanization of Benjamin Franklin* (New York: Penguin, 2004), 13–15, 29–30, 66–70.

10. John Updike, "Many Bens," *New Yorker*, February 22, 1988, 112. Quoted in Isaacson, *Benjamin Franklin*, 256.

Introduction: The Written Word Remains

1. Franklin did Machiavelli one better. In his final will, written in 1788, Franklin ordered that his tomb bear his name (and his wife, Deborah's) and nothing else. Contrary to the case with Machiavelli, no explanation, however terse, was needed for Franklin. This will, completely devoid of religious comments, differed in this respect from earlier ones and made sure that there was nothing like the early epitaph that foretold a new and corrected edition in another world. No last-minute conversion for Benjamin Franklin. See *The Papers of Benjamin Franklin*, ed. Leonard W. Larabee et al. (New Haven, CT: Yale University Press, 1959–),1: 111; Albert Henry Smyth, ed., *The Writings of Benjamin Franklin* (New York: Macmillan, 1907), 10: 493–510; and Alfred Owen Aldridge, *Benjamin Franklin and Nature's God* (Durham: Duke University Press, 1967), 250–267.

2. D. H. Lawrence, "Benjamin Franklin," in *Benjamin Franklin and the American Character*, ed. Charles L. Sanford (Boston: D. C. Heath, 1955), 64.

3. See Charles Francis Adams, ed., *The Works of John Adams* (Boston: Little Brown, 1856), 3: 220; Lawrence, "Benjamin Franklin," 22–26; Aldridge, *Benjamin Franklin and Nature's God*, 230. See also Benjamin Franklin, *Writings*, ed. J. A. Leo Lemay (New York: Library of America, 1987), 1079.

4. *Writings* 1008–1009.

5. *Papers* 23: 298–299.

6. *Writings* 1373.

7. *Writings* 1374–1379.

8. Gordon Wood, "Not So Poor Richard," *New York Review of Books*, June 6, 1996, 47.

9. For the doubters, see Melvin H. Buxbaum, *Benjamin Franklin and the Zealous Presbyterians* (University Park: Pennsylvania State University Press, 1975).

10. Adams, *Works*, 1: 661; see Aldridge, *Benjamin Franklin and Nature's God*, 8.

11. *Writings* 1409–1410.

12. There is nothing arbitrary or arcane involved in reading Franklin this way. The obscurities and problems may sometimes be hard to discern, but they have to be real and available for eyes to see. One then has to try to make sense of them by the lines of thinking they provoke. We have to take seriously what Franklin actually says in the texts and not jump first to speculations about what he must mean. We cannot ignore contradictions that no competent or sane person would commit. And one truly heterodox opinion trumps a sea of conventional pieties. (See chapter 2, note 39, and chapter 3, note 28, below.)

Franklin could easily have learned of these techniques first from Shaftesbury, who described it as "defensive raillery" to be allowed "in affairs of whatever kind—when the spirit of curiosity would force a discovery of more truth than can conveniently be told." Anthony Ashley Cooper, third Earl of Shaftesbury, *Characteristics*, ed. Lawrence E. Klein (Cambridge: Cambridge University Press, 1999), 30–31, 368. See David Berman, "Deism, Immortality, and the Art of Theological Lying," in *Deism, Masonry, and the Enlightenment: Essays Honoring Alfred Owen Aldridge*, ed. J. A. Leo Lemay (Newark: University of Delaware Press, 1987), 63–64. See also Lemay's comment in his introduction that covert atheism on the part of Deists was the reason they were abhorred by orthodox believers (12). Both Berman and Lemay are correct (and wonderfully unique in seeing) that Deists such as Anthony Collins could be atheists in disguise. But not all were, and it would be too simple a judgment of the ways of human thinking to paint with too broad a brush.

John Griffith comes very close to hitting the nail on the head when he says of Franklin: "To read Franklin at length and with real attention is to have one's imagination stirred by the sense of something unique and not wholly explicable going on between and behind the lines." Well, it is explicable, and so we can test to see if we are really just imagining things. See Griffith, "Franklin's Sanity and the Man behind the Masks," in *The Oldest Revolutionary*, ed. J. A. Leo Lemay (Philadelphia: University of Pennsylvania Press, 1976), 123–138.

13. The subtlest appreciation of Franklin's irony is, in my view, to be found in two essays by Ralph Lerner, "Franklin, Spectator," in *The Thinking Revolutionary* (Ithaca, NY: Cornell University Press, 1979), 41–59, and "Dr. Janus," in *Reappraising Benjamin Franklin*, ed. J. A. Leo Lemay (Newark: University of Delaware Press, 1993), 415–424.

14. *Writings* 1346, 1359.

15. *Writings* 435, 1016.

16. *Writings* 1382, 1396. See Aldridge, *Benjamin Franklin and Nature's God*, 81.

17. *Writings* 1359. A helpful critic asked if there is not a tension between this comment of Franklin's, that what is true might not be useful, and my claim that, for Franklin, the most important truths are to be had by thinking through our practical opinions and intuitions about morality and religion. There is no tension. One could think through one's opinions and discover that in fact what is true about life is not useful in this crucial sense: that a truth might harm others and might even harm oneself *if* one blabs it out loud.

18. *Writings* 1382.

19. In thinking about this I asked myself the following: If at some time in my life I concluded that God does not intervene in our lives and does not answer prayer and does not punish or reward in another life, and if for *really* believing such things I got yelled at for being an atheist, and if I wrote a treatise expounding such views and then burned it because I thought it was dangerous, could I, after an abrupt conversion to faith, forget all this and then believe that I had always *really* believed in particular providence? Impossible. To check, I did a simple empirical test: I asked several nonacademic friends at my gym whether, if they had once been virtual atheists and then got religion, they could possibly forget this fact about their lives. They all looked at me as if I were mad and answered: "Of course not; that would be impossible" (although one said maybe so if he were suffering from amnesia). It is simply absurd to suppose that Franklin could forget such a momentous fact about his life.

20. We might be tempted to explain the contradiction away by saying that Franklin means something like this: Although I once thought I believed particular providence does not exist, I came to see that in fact I had always, deep down and unbeknownst to myself, always really believed that it did. But Franklin *never* says this, and absent explicit corroboration in the text, this explanation is pure speculation, a flight of fancy. And as such, it will not make the contradiction go away. The question can surely be raised, however, as to why this massive and intentional contradiction has remained unnoticed in the scholarly literature. Two reasons come to mind. First, although the contradiction is a monster when one stares it in the face, noticing it in the first place is not at all easy. Each of Franklin's contradictory statements is explicit. But the connection between them is not so easy to see and only becomes explicit upon careful attention. Franklin does not just come out and say "A" and follow up immediately by saying "Not-A." Franklin separates the terms of the contradiction and states the second term in an offhanded way. The contradiction is hard to notice unless one is reading very carefully and assumes that Franklin might be writing very carefully and knew exactly what he was doing. Second, all but a very few scholars have been powerfully inclined to explanations beyond the texts and have not considered that Franklin might have written with great care and knew exactly what he was doing.

21. *Writings* 1397.
22. See Robert Middlekauff, *Benjamin Franklin and His Enemies* (Berkeley and Los Angeles: University of California Press, 1998), 73–76.
23. *Writings* 374.
24. *Writings* 830.
25. *Papers* 20: 277–286, 513–516.
26. See *Papers* 21: 37–70, 73–74, 78–83, 86–96, 99–101, 108–111, 112–115.
27. Quoted in *Papers* 21: 113n7.
28. See Wood, "Not So Poor Richard," 50.
29. The definitive account of Franklin's diplomacy and conflict with Adams is, in my view, Gerald Stourzh, *Benjamin Franklin and American Foreign Policy* (Chicago: University of Chicago Press, 1969). But the literature on this subject is large and rich. See especially Jonathan Dull, *Franklin the Diplomat* (Philadelphia: Transactions of the American Philosophical Society, 1982); Dull, *A Diplomatic History of the American Revolution* (New Haven, CT: Yale University Press, 1987); Ronald Hoffman and Peter Albert, eds., *Diplomacy and Revolution* (Charlottesville: University of Virginia Press, 1981).
30. Gordon Wood, *The Americanization of Benjamin Franklin* (New York: Penguin, 2004), 196.
31. Claude-Anne Lopez, *Mon Cher Papa: Franklin and the Ladies of Paris* (New Haven, CT: Yale University Press, 1990), 264–271.

Chapter One: The Autobiography: *A Comic Moral Saga?*

1. *Writings* 1307.
2. *Writings* 1359–1360.
3. *Writings* 1392.
4. *Writings* 1395–1397.
5. *Writings* 1313–1318.
6. *Writings* 1315.
7. *Writings* 1314.
8. *Writings* 1318–1320.
9. *Writings* 1320–1321.
10. *Writings* 1321–1323.
11. *Writings* 1323–1348. Here I identify these matters and the entire page span of the five moral errata.
12. *Writings* 1324.
13. *Writings* 1325–1326.
14. The last Dogood essay, which Franklin obliquely but clearly identifies as his own, was printed in the *Courant* on October 8, 1722, at which time Benjamin was three months shy of seventeen years old. The *Courant* listed Benjamin as publisher after January 25, 1723, when Franklin was seventeen. This much we know from clues internal to the *Autobiography*. He sneaked away on September 25 of that year.
15. *Writings* 1326–1335, 1335–1338.
16. *Writings* 1337.
17. *Writings* 1337–1340.
18. *Writings* 1340–1342.
19. *Writings* 1342–1345.

20. *Writings* 1345–1346.
21. *Writings* 1346.
22. *Writings* 1347–1348.
23. *Writings* 1348–1353.
24. *Writings* 1353.
25. *Writings* 1353–1358.
26. *Writings* 1358–1360.
27. *Writings* 1360–1366.
28. *Writings* 1366.
29. *Writings* 1366–1371.
30. *Writings* 1371.
31. *Writings* 1371–1372.
32. *Writings* 1373–1379.
33. *Writings* 1379–1382.
34. *Writings* 1382–1383.
35. *Writings* 1382.
36. *Writings* 1383.
37. *Writings* 1383–1394.
38. *Writings* 1391–1392.
39. *Writings* 1393.
40. *Writings* 1393–1394.
41. *Writings* 1395–1397.
42. *Writings* 1397.
43. *Writings* 1398.
44. *Writings* 1399–1400.
45. *Writings* 1400–1406.
46. *Writings* 1406–1410.
47. Douglas Anderson, *The Radical Enlightenments of Benjamin Franklin* (Baltimore: Johns Hopkins University Press, 1997), 15.
48. *Writings* 1417–1418.
49. *Writings* 1308.
50. *Writings* 1393–1394.
51. *Writings* 1390.
52. *Writings* 1339.
53. *Writings* 1424.
54. *Writings* 1399–1400.
55. *Writings* 1407.
56. *Writings* 1408.
57. Edmund Morgan, *Benjamin Franklin* (New Haven, CT: Yale University Press, 2002), 17–25, 30.

Chapter Two: The Autobiography: *Or Just a Pack of Lies?*

1. *Writings* 1406–1410, 1419, 1424.
2. *Writings* 1409–1410.
3. *Writings* 1409.
4. *Writings* 1410.

5. *Writings* 1409.
6. *Writings* 1396.
7. *Writings* 1382.
8. *Writings* 1307.
9. *Writings* 1348–1360.
10. *Writings* 1382–1394.
11. *Writings* 1395–1397.
12. *Writings* 1382.
13. *Writings* 1396.
14. *Writings* 1383.
15. Cf. *Writings* 1358–1360, 1382–1383.
16. See the bibliography in P. M. Zall, *Franklin's Autobiography: A Model Life* (Boston: Twayne, 1989), 119–120; see also J. A. Leo Lemay, "Franklin and the *Autobiography:* An Essay on Recent Scholarship," *Eighteenth-Century Studies* 1, no. 2 (Winter 1967): 185–211. A skeptical critic suggested that I implicitly accuse all of Franklin's readers of being "dunderheads." That I certainly do not do. But I do suggest that, at least to my knowledge, most who have *written* about Franklin have been powerfully inclined not to read him carefully and to rely first on evidence outside the texts. Again, the contradiction cannot be dismissed and really presents a fundamental problem. And again, it is simply impossible that anyone—not to mention Franklin—could forget such a crucial spiritual event of his life. I challenge any doubters to replicate the experiment noted above (see note 19 to the introduction, above).
17. *Writings* 1379.
18. See J. A. Leo Lemay and P. M. Zall, eds., *The Autobiography of Benjamin Franklin: A Genetic Text* (Knoxville: University of Tennessee Press, 1981), xii–xxiii. On the *Autobiography*'s "conscious symmetry in structural design" and the careful compositional interpolations Franklin used to achieve it, see Zall, "A Portrait of the Autobiographer as an Old Artificer," in *The Oldest Revolutionary*, ed. J. A. Leo Lemay (Philadelphia: University of Pennsylvania Press, 1976), 53–65. Zall does not mention the contradiction.
19. *Writings* 1358–1360.
20. *Writings* 1360.
21. See David Waldstreicher's wonderful *Runaway America: Benjamin Franklin, Slavery, and the American Revolution* (New York: Hill and Wang, 2004), 22–25.
22. *Writings* 1325.
23. Anthony Ashley Cooper, third Earl of Shaftesbury, *Characteristics*, ed. Lawrence E. Klein (Cambridge: Cambridge University Press, 1999), 46–47, 183–190, 268–271.
24. Cf. *Writings* 1392.
25. *Writings* 1382, 1396.
26. *Writings* 1318–1323.
27. *Writings* 1323–1326.
28. Melvin H. Buxbaum, *Benjamin Franklin and the Zealous Presbyterians* (University Park: Pennsylvania University Press, 1975), 73–74, claims that Franklin completely whitewashes his reasons for leaving Boston. As regards the supposedly bad treatment by his brother, it is entirely plausible that Franklin is lying through his teeth. But Buxbaum's claims that the Dogood essays, and not Franklin's "arguments on behalf of Deism," were the real reason for his departure and that Franklin's account of the departure is meant to hide his political radicalism are not persuasive. First, it does not matter what Franklin's real reason was at the time or that there is not a "shred of evidence available today" to

corroborate what actually happened: The *Autobiography* is a work of Franklin's art and thus what matters is its teaching. But as regards that teaching, Franklin covers his more serious radicalism but certainly, at this point in the text, does not simply hide it. Which is a more radical cause for flight: writing moralistic and politically controversial satire or earning a reputation among the good for being a horrid atheist and infidel? Buxbaum here also claims that Franklin describes his arguments on behalf of Deism as "rather formal disquisitions." Franklin says nothing of the sort, and Buxbaum here misses Franklin's very careful description of his methods of argument.

Douglas Anderson's claim in *The Radical Enlightenments of Benjamin Franklin* (Baltimore: Johns Hopkins University Press, 1997), 60–61, that Plato, not Xenophon, was really more important to Franklin is pure speculation with no evidence in the text: Franklin tells us it was Xenophon who moved him, and there is no reason here to second-guess him. Moreover, on Anderson's own view of Shaftesbury's importance for Franklin, it makes no sense to doubt Franklin's claim. Here is Shaftesbury on Xenophon's superiority to the poetic (Plato) and comic successors of Socrates: "He joined what was deepest and most solid in philosophy with what was easiest and most refined in breeding, and in the character and manner of a gentleman. Nothing could be remoter than his genius was from the scholastic, the rhetorical or mere poetic kind. He was as distant, on one hand, from the sonorous, high and pompous strain as, on the other hand, from the ludicrous, mimical or satiric" (Shaftesbury, *Characteristics*, 114).

29. *Writings* 1321–1322.

30. *Writings* 1392–1394.

31. *Writings* 1393.

32. *Writings* 1395.

33. *Writings* 1318, 1321.

34. *Writings* 1392.

35. For a different account, with which I disagree, see Arthur Burnon Tourtellot, *Benjamin Franklin: The Shaping of Genius. The Boston Years* (Garden City, NY: Doubleday, 1977), 226–228.

36. *Writings* 1321–1322.

37. *Writings* 1360.

38. *Writings* 1391–1392.

39. His doing so is akin to what Franklin's hero Shaftesbury said of another Franklin hero, Francis Bacon. Here is Shaftesbury on Bacon's *De augmentis scientiarium* 2.13: "It was a good fortune in my Lord Bacon's case that he should have escaped being called an atheist or skeptic when, speaking in a solemn manner of the religious passion, the grounds of superstition or enthusiasm (which he also terms a panic), he derives it from an imperfection in the creation, make or natural constitution of man" (Shaftesbury, *Characteristics*, 368). Shaftesbury's point is that despite Bacon's having said a hundred times that God created the world and all things in it, just the one isolated remark that human beings were by nature ill-formed was enough to reveal Bacon's true view—and that view was atheistic.

Chapter Three: The Philosophical Wag

1. See Daniel Royot, "Benjamin Franklin as Founding Father of American Humor," in *Reappraising Benjamin Franklin*, ed. J. A. Leo Lemay (Newark: University of Delaware Press, 1993), 388–395.

2. Albert Henry Smyth, ed., *The Writings of Benjamin Franklin* (New York: Macmillan, 1907), 1: 171.

3. I have excised a remark that Franklin was the inventor of the supermarket tabloid, since Norman S. Grabo beat me to the punch. Norman S. Grabo, "The Journalist as Man of Letters," in Lemay, *Reappraising Benjamin Franklin*, 37.

4. *Writings* 137.

5. *Writings* 155–157.

6. Cf. Thomas Hobbes, *Leviathan*, ed. Richard Tuck (Cambridge: Cambridge University Press, 1996), 300–306.

7. *Writings* 180.

8. *Papers* 2: 357. See *Writings* 1172–1173.

9. *Papers* 2: 364.

10. *Writings* 1382.

11. *Papers* 4: 97; *Writings* 149, 748–749.

12. *Papers* 2: 214.

13. This view of Franklin's Deism and toleration is most powerfully expressed in Alfred Owen Aldridge's *Benjamin Franklin and Nature's God* (Durham: Duke University Press, 1967), a book that continues to influence scholarship on Franklin's religious views. I will return to this scholarship in some depth below, but for now I will note that it in general accepts the view of Franklin's religious attitudes—and especially his toleration—as presented by Franklin in the *Autobiography*. There is quite a different point of view, however, most powerfully detailed in Melvin H. Buxbaum's *Benjamin Franklin and the Zealous Presbyterians* (University Park: Pennsylvania State University Press, 1975). According to Buxbaum, Franklin engaged in a sustained attack on Calvinism and on the Congregationalist and Presbyterian establishments in Boston and Philadelphia. He weighed in (often intemperately and intolerantly) on the Hemphill controversy and then first supported and then turned away from the revivalist Whitefield, in order to attack, weaken, and provoke schism in the Presbyterian church, which he thought of as a danger to liberty. By the time Franklin wrote the first part of the *Autobiography*, he was concerned to fend off attacks in the British press on the Americans for their religious extremism and bigotry. So Franklin, now coming to the defense of the Calvinists, glossed over the extent and vehemence of his earlier radicalism and bigoted hostility to Calvinism. Franklin said he became a Deist, but "in truth he acted in a manner quite different from the benevolent deistic persona of the *Autobiography*" (Buxbaum, *Benjamin Franklin and the Zealous Presbyterians*, 56, 111, 115, 151–152).

That Franklin lied about these matters in the *Autobiography* is entirely plausible, and Buxbaum makes a persuasive case. In one respect, however, I am not persuaded: Buxbaum, again, thinks of the *Autobiography* as a complete whitewash of Franklin's character and machinations in the religious politics of Boston and Philadelphia. That it is, to be sure. But the *Autobiography* also—however subtly and indirectly and by forcing us to think on our own—reveals how radical a thinker Franklin really was. Not seeing this fact, I suggest, leads Buxbaum to some unwarranted conclusions about the *Autobiography*. If Franklin softens the vehemence of his attacks on Calvinism, especially in the hard-hitting defenses of Hemphill, he also does not hesitate to inform us of his authorship of the pamphlets, presented anonymously when first written, and also to direct us to the date of the piece in the *Gazette* (the *Dialogue between Two Presbyterians*), which was also published anonymously. Although Franklin says that he doubts any copies of the pamphlets still exist, the fact is that they sold very well indeed (*Writings* 1399–1400). If we want to find out what Franklin actually thought and wrote at the time, it is the *Autobiography* that points us in the right direction.

14. *Writings* 145–148.
15. *Writings* 148–151.
16. Hobbes, *Leviathan*, 76–77.
17. *Writings* 145; see Hobbes, *Leviathan*, 304–306.
18. Aldridge, *Benjamin Franklin and Nature's God*, 81.
19. See, for instance, Franklin's letter to George Whatley, in which Franklin argues from the divine conservation of all in his creation to the eternity of the soul: If God does not waste even a drop of water, why would he every day waste the millions of souls that already exist and continually trouble himself to make new ones? (*Writings* 1106).
20. *Writings* 1339. See J. A. Leo Lemay's wonderful essay "The Theme of Vanity in Franklin's *Autobiography*," in Lemay, *Reappraising Benjamin Franklin*, 84–85.
21. *Writings* 1091. See the wonderful discussion of Franklin and Mesmer in Claude-Anne Lopez, *My Life with Benjamin Franklin* (New Haven, CT: Yale University Press, 2000), 114–126.
22. *Writings* 138–142.
23. Says *Poor Richard*, "He that lives upon hope, dies farting" (*Writings* 1200).
24. *Writings* 305–308.
25. Cited in *Papers* 3: 122; see also note 4 on that page.
26. This argument goes for rewards as well as punishments. See *Writings* 427, where Franklin says to Jane Mecom that it is impossible to merit heaven; see also *Writings* 475, where Franklin says the same thing to Joseph Huey. Compared with eternal bliss in heaven, all good deeds on earth are paltry.
27. See Franklin's letter to Hume, *Papers* 10: 81–83.
28. A skeptical critic objected to my reading of Franklin on the grounds that such careful irony as I ascribe to Franklin is psychologically impossible for any author. The critic asked: "Is any writer in complete control of his text?" The implication is that all human beings make mistakes and that there is a limit to how attentive any author can be to the whole of a text, not to mention to the whole of a corpus of texts. So we cannot assume that contradictions or inconsistencies or strange obscurity or confounding sleights of hand are intentional. They may just be mistakes and slips. This argument is not unreasonable. But it does, without further consideration, incline us to ignore the evidence of all those powerful thinkers who claimed that either they or others practiced such careful irony (Plato, Cicero, St. Augustine, Hobbes, Franklin's heroes Bacon and Shaftesbury, Edward Gibbon, Jean Le Rond d'Alembert, Jean-Jacques Rousseau, and the Baron de Montesquieu, to name some). See Leo Strauss, *Persecution and the Art of Writing* (Glencoe, IL: Free Press, 1952), 22–37. Perhaps most men make mistakes and cannot keep the whole of a text in mind. But what about geniuses who say or imply that they write with such care as to speak to some but not others? Is it not plausible that such powerful minds as these *could* keep a whole text in mind? It seems plausible to me. Perhaps our modern egalitarianism inclines us to see ourselves in the great minds of the past. However, the issue is not what we assume, but the evidence. Whether or not we believe an author is sufficiently well equipped to pull off what we might think is beyond anyone's capacities depends on whether we can find the evidence for it or not. We just have to look and see. But that means we have to look.

The same skeptical critic in the same breath quite rightly pointed to the problem of the reliability of printed texts and mentioned, as an example, that we "have no uncontroversial text for 'Polly Baker.'" The critic is correct: There are variations among the several printed versions of Franklin's hoax. That printed texts may sometimes differ is a fact. But this fact does not, a priori, tell against reading an author as I have done with Franklin. Rather, if a printing difference exists, it imposes an obligation to see if the difference *matters* and constitutes a problem or oddity in the text. (And the same goes for genuine but trivial errors.) If it does, then that is a real problem for the interpretation. In the case of Polly, the differences in the several printings do not cause an oddity or problem. All but two are trivial and involve no differences of meaning. The one substantive difference is that the text printed in the *Maryland Gazette* in 1747, by Franklin's former employee and friend Amos Green, who claimed to present a version based on a correct copy of the text in his possession, contains the passage in which Polly asks her judges to "reflect a little on the horrid consequences of this law" and in which Polly rattles off the ill effects, such as abortion and infanticide. Some think Green stuck this in as his own hoax, but, as Max Hall says, "when all is considered, however, one cannot feel certain that Franklin did not originate the passage." See Max Hall, *Benjamin Franklin and Polly Baker: The History of a Literary Deception* (Chapel Hill: University of North Carolina Press, 1960), 123; see 121–125, 157–167. I think it is pure Franklin, since it is so much like the high dudgeon of the *Narrative of the Late Massacres* and since it played such an important role in convincing so many that the piece was genuine. But that is beside the point because the passage poses no problem or obscurity and adds nothing to the ironic and revealing twists and turns of the rest of the piece. The controversy about the passage simply does not matter.

The same holds for the only other substantive difference. Against all the other versions, two (in the *New Haven Gazette* in 1786 and in *James Parton's Life and Times of Benjamin Franklin* in 1864) omit the sentence "You believe I have offended heaven, and must suffer eternal fire: Will not that be sufficient?" There is no good reason to think these two later versions should trump all the rest (two of nine). Consequently, there is no scholarly controversy about the matter. The phrase serves to highlight the problems of secular and divine punishments and piling on. But even if the sentence *should* be struck, we could still make our way to the problems without it. Just before the sentence, after raising the difference between secular and religious punishments for transgressions (Acts of Assembly versus precepts of religion), Polly has said: "You have already excluded me from all the Comforts of your Church Communion: Is that not sufficient." The remark about eternal fire puts the icing on the cake, but we can without it infer the consequences of Polly's excommunication: condemnation to the fires of hell. See also J. A. Leo Lemay, "The Text, Rhetorical Strategies, and Themes of 'The Speech of Miss Polly Baker,'" in *The Oldest Revolutionary*, ed. J. A. Leo Lemay (Philadelphia: University of Pennsylvania Press, 1976), 91–120. I think Lemay ultimately misses the boat, but the discussion is otherwise excellent and reminds us of Franklin's clear reference to Jonathan Swift's *Modest Proposal*.

29. *Writings* 511–518.
30. *Writings* 517–518.
31. *Writings* 1263.
32. *Writings* 511–513.
33. *Writings* 513–517. J. A. Leo Lemay is absolutely correct to fault the editors of the *Papers* (8: 124) for rejecting this section as having not been written by Franklin. Its arguments are absolutely at the core of Franklin's philosophical concerns in general and in this piece from beginning to end. Lemay, "Franklin and the *Autobiography*: An Essay on Recent Scholarship," *Eighteenth-Century Studies* 1, no. 2 (Winter 1967): 187.
34. *Writings* 511.

35. *Writings* 514–515.

36. *Writings* 513.

37. *Writings* 518.

38. This comic piece clearly undermines the claim Franklin made in his *Journal of a Voyage* in 1726 that it is impossible to live and die a villain with a reputation for being honest (*Papers* 1: 78–79).

39. *Writings* 1294–1303, 1200–1201; cf. 1296.

Chapter Four: Shameless Ben

1. *Writings* 148.

2. *Papers* 3: 27–29.

3. *Writings* 302–303.

4. See Daniel Royot, "Benjamin Franklin as Founding Father of American Humor," in *Reappraising Benjamin Franklin*, ed. J. A. Leo Lemay (Newark: University of Delaware Press, 1993), 392.

5. See my "Pious Princes and Red-Hot Lovers: The Politics of Shakespeare's *Romeo and Juliet*," *Journal of Politics* 65 (2003): 350–375.

6. *Writings* 1371.

7. There is thus an explanation of why, as Claude-Anne Lopez perceptively remarked, "Franklin somehow never committed himself wholly in love; a part of him was always holding back and watching the proceedings with irony." Lopez, *Mon Cher Papa: Franklin and the Ladies of Paris* (New Haven, CT: Yale University Press, 1990), 10–20.

8. *Writings* 827–828.

9. *Writings* 924–925.

10. As we know from the wonderful books by Claude-Anne Lopez, Franklin was as deficient as a husband and father as he was charming and delightful as a lover of other women and children. See Lopez, *The Private Franklin*, with Eugenia Herbert (New York: Norton, 1975).

11. Albert Henry Smyth, ed., *The Writings of Benjamin Franklin* (New York: Macmillan, 1907), 1: 166. I wish we knew whether this is true, and it certainly could be. But I have been unable to corroborate it, and it is not to be found in P. M. Zall's edition of *Ben Franklin Laughing: Anecdotes from Original Sources by and about Benjamin Franklin* (Berkeley and Los Angeles: University of California Press, 1980).

12. *Writings* 956–960.

13. *Writings* 960.

14. *Writings* 1046–1047.

15. *Writings* 969.

16. Gordon Wood, in his fine study of Franklin, sees in this hoax evidence of Franklin's personal indignation at the British for the Revolution and its horrors. Wood can see this as evidence, and infer Franklin's anger, only by ignoring the comic elements of the piece and, most importantly, the pathos of the Chief's plea. Wood, *The Americanization of Benjamin Franklin* (New York: Penguin, 2004), 160.

17. *Writings* 952–955.

18. Francis Bacon, *Essays* (Amherst, NY: Prometheus, 1995), 5, Epistle Dedicatory.

19. Francis Bacon, *Novum Organum*, trans. Peter Urbach and John Gibson (Chicago: Open Court, 1994), 1: 129.

20. *Papers* 2: 187.

21. *Papers* 2: 198–202.

22. *Papers* 2: 199.

23. *Papers* 2: 201.

24. *Papers* 2: 201–202.

25. Moreover, it is not at all unlikely that Franklin would have enjoyed both the first and second practical jokes. Even Aldridge has his suspicions that Franklin "probably witnessed the weird ceremonies of the Brothers of Saint Francis, known also as the Monks of Mendenham Abbey and the Hell Fire Club." Aldridge, *Benjamin Franklin and Nature's God* (Durham, NC: Duke University Press, 1967), 166–173. "Weird" is hardly the word to describe the drunken orgies at the house of Sir Francis Dashwood (Baron Le Despencer), in which whores were dressed as nuns and the club's members were dressed as monks. Franklin said that he was as much at home at Le Despencer's house as he was at his own (see *Papers* 20: 339–40, 343–352). We will never know what Franklin knew about the goings-on there—or for that matter what he did. Except for the horrible accident, the Masonic spoof was far less shocking than the obscene and blasphemous sport that transpired in Le Despencer's club. Francis Jennings thinks it "more than probable" that Franklin joined the "good, clean fun" that transpired when "boatloads of prostitutes" were brought in for the orgies. Jennings, *Benjamin Franklin, Politician* (New York: Norton, 1996), 183–184. See also Daniel P. Mannix, *The Hell-Fire Club* (New York: Ballantine Books, 1959), and Carl Van Doren, *Benjamin Franklin* (New York: Penguin, 1991), 437–440.

26. *Papers* 2: 202–204.

27. *Papers* 1: 219.

28. *Papers* 3: 364–365.

29. *Papers* 4: 112–113.

30. *Papers* 4: 82–83.

31. *Writings* 925–926.

32. *Writings* 943–950.

33. *Writings* 540–558.

34. *Writings* 556–557. I have left out a lot of moral bombast.

35. For a fascinating account of the politics of this situation, see Robert Middlekauff, *Benjamin Franklin and His Enemies* (Berkeley and Los Angeles: University of California Press, 1998), 77–85.

36. *Writings* 802–805.

37. *Writings* 367.

38. See Middlekauff, *Benjamin Franklin and His Enemies*, 82.

39. *Writings* 1426.

40. *Writings* 169.

41. *Writings* 1396.

42. *Writings* 1178–1180. Franklin was very frank about these doubts with his friend George Whitefield. See *Papers* 16: 192.

43. *Writings* 230–232.

44. *Papers* 30: 50–53.

45. The translation is from *Writings* 939–942.

46. *Papers* 3: 39–40.

47. As the editors of the *Papers* point out, "these words are inscribed on a picture of Thomas à Kempis at Zwolle, Holland. According to Heribert Rsweyde (preface to *Imita-*

tio Christi, 1617), the author wrote them in a copy of the *Imitatio*" (*Papers* 3: 39; translation is from *Writings* 1531).

48. Douglas Anderson, *The Radical Enlightenments of Benjamin Franklin* (Baltimore: Johns Hopkins University Press, 1997), 87, wants us to believe that Franklin really wanted to imitate Jesus and was a serious devotee of Thomas à Kempis. But to make this claim about Franklin's devotion to Thomas à Kempis stick, he reads the only textual evidence—the letter to James Read—as if the joke were merely a reflection of James's newly married status and not what it obviously is: an eye-popping and obscene blasphemy. Anderson says of the joke, "The line from Kempis that James apparently referred to is not, in fact, part of the *Imitation of Christ*. 'Pleasure,' as Franklin is well aware, is a very strained translation of 'requiem' (rest or peace) and '*in angulo puellae*' is at best clumsy anatomy." But if the joke is too indelicate to accept, then why does Franklin mention it at all, and why the coarse joke at the expense of Jesus' chastity? Only great devotion could see this obscene and blasphemous joke as clumsy anatomy.

49. See "Defense of Observations" (*Papers* 2: 114).

50. Too much realism often makes us unrealistic. No matter how nasty and selfish a political type might be, no real person of the kind really believes the following: "I'm nothing but a snake, do nothing good for others, and deserve nothing of the power that I have." Such human beings simply do not exist, and Franklin knew this perfectly well.

51. *Writings* 1308.

Chapter Five: The Metaphysical Follies

1. The copy in the Library of Congress is a facsimile reprint from the original in the possession of Henry Stevens. After publishing his edition of Franklin's writings in 1817–1818, the feckless William Franklin lost interest in the papers and left them to his widow, who abandoned them. They were discovered in 1840 in a London tailor shop, where they were being cut up and used as patterns. Stevens bought them in 1851, and in 1880 he saw that they came into the possession of the U.S. government. The facsimile was printed in London, probably in 1854. Franklin certainly wanted William to have the pamphlet, to be published with all else that he bequeathed his grandson. The boy published the letter to Vaughn, but just did not think to publish the *Dissertation*, perhaps because he believed what he read in the letter to Vaughn. At any rate, Franklin clearly intended the pamphlet to survive. See *Papers* 1: xxiii. See also Henry Stevens, *Recollections of Mr. James Lennox* (New York: New York Public Library, 1951), 174–175.

2. For an excellent discussion of the earliest editions of the *Autobiography*, see *The Autobiography of Benjamin Franklin: A Genetic Text*, ed. J. A. Leo Lemay and P. M. Zall (Knoxville: University of Tennessee Press, 1981), xlviii–lviii.

3. See *Papers* 31: 57–60.

4. *Writings* 1015–1017.

5. See also the similar remark in a 1746 letter to Thomas Hopkinson, *Writings* 435. See note 32 below.

6. Douglas Anderson, *The Radical Enlightenments of Benjamin Franklin* (Baltimore: Johns Hopkins University Press, 1997), 69, claims that the *Articles of Belief* continues in the same vein as the *Dissertation*: Its liturgical purpose is to excite Franklin to moral virtue in a metaphysical context in which to aim at "perfect innocence" and "good conscience" is to strive "to be the best of men in a world in which disinterested virtue is an

impossibility and from which human culpability as well as human liberty has been banished." The piece is metaphysical, to be sure. But Anderson's specific claims as to its content are just not supported by the textual evidence. In the *Articles*, there is no mention whatsoever of the absence of free will and culpability. On the contrary, the first petition explicitly appeals to *merited* divine reward for virtue and holiness; that is, it is an explicit appeal to free will and divine justice. But pass the salt, please. See Elizabeth E. Dunn, "From a Bold Youth to a Reflective Sage: A Reevaluation of Benjamin Franklin's Religion," *Pennsylvania Magazine of History and Biography* 111 (1987): 501–524.

7. *Writings* 163–168. J. A. Leo Lemay dates this piece to 1730, unlike the *Papers*' editors, who date it to 1732 on the grounds of its place in Franklin's commonplace book. Aldridge originally suggested changing the date, but not with great certainty; see his review of *The Papers of Benjamin Franklin*, ed. Leonard W. Larabee et al. (New Haven, CT: Yale University Press, 1959) in *American Literature* 32: 208–210. The evidence Aldridge cites is the letter from Vaughn referring to the piece on prayer written in 1730. He argues that this essay on providence is the one mentioned in the letter to Vaughn. Although it is true that the providence piece contains the argument about prayer, it is but a small part of the essay and definitely is not the "foundation" of the providence essay. I would come down on the side of Aldridge's doubt about changing the date to 1730, and I would further suggest that the essay is at least relevant to the topic of the piece referred to by the asterisk in the *Articles*, if it is not in fact the very piece referred to by that asterisk.

8. *Writings* 1359–1360, 1382.

9. *Writings* 1016.

10. Alfred Owen Aldridge, *Benjamin Franklin and Nature's God* (Durham, NC: Duke University Press, 1967), 17. To conclude that Franklin was subject to this confusion we would have to assume that he (1) knew what Deism is; (2) rejected scientific-metaphysical Deism because it cannot be proved; (3) was then, at the very latest by 1746, a moral-humanitarian Deist; and (4) when he wrote the *Autobiography* confused Deism and atheism. This alone would require us to think that by the time of the *Autobiography*, Franklin was well on his way to senility. And this is not to mention his having to have by then "forgotten" completely about the second section of the *Dissertation*, on the equality of pleasure and pain and the rule of divine justice. Melvin Buxbaum misrepresents Aldridge's position on this matter; see Buxbaum, *Benjamin Franklin and the Zealous Presbyterians* (University Park: Pennsylvania State University Press, 1975), 232n31.

Franklin's comment about charcoal occurred in his 1746 letter, probably to Thomas Hopkinson, on Andrew Baxter's doctrine of *Vis inertiae* (*Papers* 3: 84–89). In rejecting the "author's" claim to have put Deists in a desperate position by establishing the clear grounds for "the doctrines of the immateriality of the soul, and the existence of God, and of Divine Providence," Franklin says, "I oppose my *Theist* [Franklin's term here for "Deist"] to his Atheist, because I think they are diametrically opposite and not near of kin, as Mr. Whitefield seems to suppose where (in his Journal) he tells us, Mr. B. *was a Deist, I had almost said an Atheist*. That is, Chalk, I had almost said Charcoal." But if the case has not been made desperate for atheists, why would Franklin make the change from atheist to Deist, if in fact they were not at least akin? Moreover, the joke here is obvious: Chalk and charcoal are as different as white and black, but they are also just the same in being able to make marks. See also Aldridge, *Benjamin Franklin and Nature's God*, 75–77.

11. James Campbell, *Recovering Benjamin Franklin: An Exploration of a Life of Science and Service* (Chicago: Open Court, 1999), 132n84.

12. *Writings* 1359. Franklin's description here is complicated, but it is clear on this score.

13. Campbell tries to make sense of the "practical" rejection by saying that Franklin's "point was not that freethinking is 'true' but harmful. Rather, his point was that the conclusions at which he arrived in his freethinking were valid deductions—a point open to dispute, of course—from assumptions that he had made, and that since these conclusions had sanctioned conduct that was 'not very useful,' the original assumptions had to have been mistaken" (Campbell, *Recovering Benjamin Franklin*, 132). Aside from the patent absurdity of such an argument on Franklin's part, there is no evidence for it in the text. Moreover, to deny the original assumptions would be to deny (1) that there is a God, and (2) that he is all-wise, all-good, and all-powerful. How would these have to be changed? One thing is persuasive in this argument: that what we think about justice determines what we think about God. Franklin came to suspect just this fact—but it turned out not to be such good news for God.

14. Plato, *Apology*, 18c.

15. J. A. Leo Lemay is correct to note Franklin's caution on this matter. See Lemay, "Franklin and the *Autobiography*: An Essay on Recent Scholarship," *Eighteenth-Century Studies* 1, no. 2 (Winter 1967): 202. But for that reason, we cannot with ease conclude that Franklin was an atheist; we can only conclude that he "wanted religion." To get to Franklin's atheism, if indeed it exists, we have to understand its grounds in the critique of morality (and thus of metaphysics and Deism). This I do below.

16. Xenophon, *Memorabilia*, Book 1, chapter 1, paragraph 11; Book 4, chapter 7; see Plato, *Apology*, 19b–e and *Phaedo*, 96a–99d.

17. *Writings* 1321–1323.

18. John Dryden, "Oedipus," Act III, scene 1, lines 244–248.

19. *Writings* 57–71.

20. *Writings* 61. See Anderson, *Radical Enlightenments*, 41–42. Anderson sees this as expressive of Shaftesbury's notion of common sense. Cf. Anthony Ashley Cooper, third Earl of Shaftesbury, *Characteristics*, ed. Lawrence E. Klein (Cambridge: Cambridge University Press, 1999), 190–191, 433. If men have a natural inclination to altruism as part of the grand natural whole, and if altruism grows when tested by hardships, then even evil is part of the good.

21. *Writings* 62.

22. *Writings* 62–71.

23. *Writings* 64. So again, as with Shaftesbury, altruism and selfishness are equal parts of the divine moral order of the world; see Shaftesbury, *Characteristics*, 51, 54.

24. *Writings* 68.

25. *Writings* 69–71.

26. *Writings* 71.

27. *Writings* 59.

28. *Writings* 62.

29. *Writings* 70.

30. In describing the pamphlet in the *Autobiography* (*Writings* 1359), Franklin identifies the author of the motto as Dryden, but then misquotes it as:

Whatever is, is right
Tho' purblind Man / Sees but a Part of
The Chain, the nearest Link,
His Eyes not carrying to the equal Beam,
That poises all, above.

It is certainly possible that Franklin just made a mistake here, and if he did, the slight difference bears no likeness at all to the serious contradictions, problems, and obscurities in the moral saga. At the least (and as with variations in the "Speech of Miss Polly Baker"), it creates no problem that Franklin had to have been able to see. In identifying the author, Franklin clearly makes it possible for us to check up, and of course we have the text of the *Dissertation* as well. However, there is nevertheless a suggestive difference: By eliminating "is in its Causes" and the reference to "Fate," the quote is more directly related to God (rather than to some other power) and to the fact that things are just fine here and now, and not with regard to some abstract consideration of the justice of the whole. The replacement of "just" by "right" makes no difference at all here. In other words, in the *Autobiography* Franklin gives us the quote in a form that points even more directly than the original to the *Dissertation*'s absurd conclusion: The wretch on the rack is as well-off as the king of Siam.

31. *Writings* 57.

32. Franklin made the remark about the "great uncertainty" of the "metaphysical way" first in the 1746 letter (probably to Hopkinson) as a closing remark in his critique of Baxter's doctrine of *Vis inertiae*. Here too, Franklin also says that metaphysics led him as a youth into horrible errors. Vaughn had a copy of this letter and published this letter in his edition of Franklin's works in 1779. See *Papers* 3: 88–89.

33. *Writings* 57.

34. In *Poor Richard's Almanack* of 1749, Franklin noted and eulogized John Calvin just after doing so for Bacon. *Writings* 1252–1253.

35. John Calvin, *Institutes*, Book 1, chapter 16, section 3. Franklin did not like Calvinism, but in order to dislike it as he did, he had to have understood it well—and he did.

36. Douglas Anderson, in *Radical Enlightenments*, 41, is absolutely correct to see the moral dimension and egalitarianism of the second part of the *Dissertation*. But he just does not read Franklin carefully enough at this point. Anderson claims that here Franklin "affirms not human blindness and divine justice but human equality and divine esteem." But this claim is simply contrary to the evidence. When Franklin argues for equal divine esteem in the *Dissertation*, he appeals, as regards divine use, *precisely* to justice as human beings understand it and raises the crucial distinction between esteem as rational accordance with justice and esteem as the result of compliance with justice.

37. *Writings* 83–90.

38. *Writings* 85–88.

39. *Writings* 88–90.

40. See Plato, *Alcibiades II*. I thank David Leibowitz for reminding me of this.

41. *Writings* 90.

42. Such a thing is reason, that it tells us whatever we want to hear. See *Writings* 1339.

43. *Writings* 84.

44. Thomas Hobbes, *Leviathan*, ed. Richard Tuck (Cambridge: Cambridge University Press, 1996), 74–79, chapters 11 and 12.

45. Shaftesbury, *Characteristics*, 368.

46. Kerry S. Walters, in his *Benjamin Franklin and His Gods* (Chicago: University of Illinois Press, 1999), 8, 84–86, is persuasive in arguing against Aldridge's claim that Franklin was a real polytheist. But his explanation of Franklin's intention in writing the *Articles* is, it seems to me, strong additional evidence that the *Articles* simply cannot be taken seriously. The argument needed to make sense of the essay—according to Walters,

that Franklin was a believer in "theistic perspectivism"—is as far-fetched as the argument Franklin presents. Walters (following Aldridge) argues that Franklin rebelled against Calvinism and was first converted to a very dry Deism, expressed in the *Dissertation*, that denied both God (ultimately) and humanism. Especially as regards humanism, says Walters, Franklin was driven, in the heat of the rapid and enthusiastic composition of the *Dissertation*, to overstep his own intention. Unable then to tolerate the resulting nihilism, Franklin worked out "theistic perspectivism," which is expressed in the *Articles of Belief*. This combined the first-cause god of Deism—by its nature completely divorced from and indifferent to the affairs of men—with lesser, creator gods that are moved to particular providence. These gods are understood by the "theistic perspectivist" (though not the believers?) to be human projections or creations that serve for guidance, edification, and instruction and are "faltering attempts to represent the deity to finite minds in such a way as to overcome, at least to some extent, the alienating distance between them" (10–11).

Now, as interesting as Walters's book is, the stages and ways and means of Franklin's inner turmoil and wrestling with religion and arrival at an unconventional piety are all speculatively projected from the modern religious psychology of James W. Fowler. And the entire argument about what Franklin was "up to" in writing the *Articles* (Walters, *Benjamin Franklin and His Gods*, 83–95) is based on assimilating what Franklin must have been thinking to later theories of religion. But aside from the question of the evidence, we are asked to believe that Franklin really believed the following: The first-cause god really exists but is by its nature utterly indifferent to human affairs. The gods that are not indifferent and that engage providentially in human affairs are figments of our hopes and imaginations, and in Franklin's case, he knows this fact *but nevertheless* worships one of them. Repeat: Franklin really believed that the gods that matter as the absolute core of all religion (the gods that engage in particular providence) do not exist, but he worshipped one of them anyway. Walters assures us, however, that for Franklin, unlike for Hobbes and Hume, these projections are not merely fabrications: They are not illusory because they are "founded in and motivated by an intuition of the First Cause's reality, and they stand for and shed light on something." Walters provides not a shred of textual evidence for this claim, which he would surely need to do in order to make sense of the following: The first-cause god is real but does not move; lesser gods are psychological projections and thus are not real, and we only make up the fact that they move; the lesser gods are not unreal (or they are sort-of-real) because *we think* of them vaguely in some terms taken from the real one that does not move. That such a hard-nose as Franklin would actually be moved to spiritual enthusiasm (however heterodox) by a god he knew he had made up is, to my mind, hard to believe on its face. It is much easier to believe that Franklin was a believing polytheist (which he was not) or that his piece the *Articles of Religion* was a joke (which it was) than it is to think that he was a serious adherent of modern psychotheology.

Moreover, the entire argument depends on Franklin believing that "sincerity and integrity" are genuine moral virtues—something he clearly denied in the 1732 essay "On Simplicity," to mention just one instance. The move from the *Dissertation* to the *Articles* is, on Walters's account, a move from the denial of "any distinction between good and evil" and to the "reality" of virtue and a God who rewards us in proportion to our virtue (Walters, *Benjamin Franklin and His Gods*, 82–83). But the *Dissertation* does not deny "any distinction between good and evil." Rather, it depends on divine goodness and divine justice and is more morally conventional (though for that reason more goofy) than at first meets the eye. See Isaacson, *Benjamin Franklin: An American Life* (New York: Simon and Schuster, 2003), 84–88, 526–527n39.

47. *Writings* 163–168.

48. *Writings* 164.

49. *Writings* 165.

50. *Writings* 165–168.

51. *Writings* 165–166.

52. *Writings* 166–167.

53. *Writings* 167.

54. *Writings* 167–168.

55. *Writings* 57.

56. Even the hard-nosed Calvin maintained that although men can do nothing to deserve justification (salvation), those who do not get it deserve to be damned. See Calvin, *Institutes*, Book 3, chapter 23, sections 1–9.

57. Franklin parodies the conventional Shaftesbury. Shaftesbury knew of the ancients' and Bacon's ironic writing and practiced that writing himself, and it is almost certain that Franklin knew these facts about writers he knew so well. See Shaftesbury, *Characteristics*, 29–33, 87–88, 368; and *The Works of Francis Bacon*, ed. James Spedding, Robert Ellis, and Douglas Heath (Stuttgart: Friedrich Fromann Verlag, 1963), 3: 248, 404–405, 473–475; 4: 448–450; 5: 31–34, 111–119.

Chapter Six: Dialectics and the Critique of Morality

1. Aristophanes, *The Clouds*, lines 1105–1112, 1149–1177. See Anthony Ashley Cooper, third Earl of Shaftesbury, *Characteristics*, ed. Lawrence E. Klein (Cambridge: Cambridge University Press, 1999), 17, 110.

2. *Writings* 1321.

3. Anderson misrepresents Franklin's account of the Socratic refutations. According to Anderson, Franklin dropped Socratic refutation "once he discovered that it often brought him unmerited victories." Douglas Anderson, *The Radical Enlightenments of Benjamin Franklin* (Baltimore: Johns Hopkins University Press, 1997), 60. Anderson's clear implication is that Franklin dropped it because he came to see the victories as unmerited or, by further implication, wrong. But Franklin says nothing of the sort: He says only that these victories were "not always merited," which does *not* mean that they were often unmerited. There is no suggestion in the text that he dropped the refutations because they were unmerited or wrong. On Anderson's claim that Plato was probably more important for Franklin than Xenophon, see note 28 to chapter 2 above.

4. See Plato's *Euthydemus*. I thank David Leibowitz for reminding me of this.

5. *Writings* 1324–1326.

6. See the letter long thought to be from Franklin to Tom Paine, regarding one of Paine's writings, in which Franklin warns his correspondent that arguing against particular providence as he does is to unchain a tiger. Burning the essay, says Franklin, will "save yourself a great deal of the mortification from the enemies it will raise against you, and perhaps a great deal of regret and repentance" (*Writings* 748–740).

7. *Writings* 1321–1323.

8. Alexander Pope, *An Essay on Criticism* (1711), lines 574–575, substituting "should" for "must." See *Writings* 1554.

9. Pope, *An Essay on Criticism*, line 567, substituting "to" for "and." See *Writings* 1555.

10. Pope, *An Essay on Criticism*, lines 530–533.

11. Wentworth Dillon, Earl of Roscomon, *An Essay on Translated Verse* (1684). Franklin used the second and revised edition that was printed in 1685 and is reprinted in *Critical Essays of the Seventeenth Century*, ed. J. E. Spingarn (Bloomington: Indiana University Press, 1957), 2: 297–309. The quoted lines are at page 300. Franklin substitutes his "modesty" for Dillon's "decency."

12. Thanks again to David Leibowitz for this formulation, and for his comment that led me to clarify my thinking on this matter.

13. By looking to the *Spectator* on the other-obliging pleasure of conversation, rather than to the content of Franklin's text, Anderson (*Radical Enlightenments*, 60–61) explains Franklin's emendation of the lines from Pope as an example of this pleasure: "As if to underscore this expansion of verbal possibilities, Franklin follows his endorsement of the pleasures of conversation with a playful exercise in the emendation of two lines from Pope. The process of emendation is delightfully instructive, for it allows Franklin to dramatize his nondogmatic principles by surrendering to better judgments the very critical points that he so deftly makes." But the content of Franklin's emendation is crucial— and a real blockbuster. Of course it is appropriate to leave it to others—and those others are us—to follow it up and not to make the critical point explicitly, which would have been for Franklin an enormous expectoration into the wind. Franklin's artful clues provide just the means we need to conclude that he most certainly did not, by 1771, think that others had better judgment on this matter.

14. *Writings* 1398, 242–244.

15. *Writings* 244–248.

16. *Writings* 1398, 181–184. See Anderson, *Radical Enlightenments*, 229.

17. *Writings* 1385.

18. Francis Bacon, *Essays* (Amherst, NY: Prometheus Books, 1995), 60–63. For a different take on the issue of sincerity, see the fine essay by Steven Forde, "Benjamin Franklin's *Autobiography* and the Education of America," *American Political Science Review* 86, no. 2 (June 1992): 357–368.

19. Bacon, *Essays*, 17–20.

20. *Writings* 1322–1323.

21. So Aldridge is correct to say that the Deists (and most aggressive atheists, too, for that matter), for all their freethinking, were devotees of high moral principles. Alfred Owen Aldridge, *Benjamin Franklin and Nature's God* (Durham, NC: Duke University Press, 1967), 17. For Franklin, that was just their problem.

22. *Writings* 1016.

23. *Writings* 435.

24. It is obvious that I do not agree with Herbert W. Schneider's view of Franklin as an "austere" and "Puritan" though secular moralist. But my deeper disagreement with Schneider, one of the great Franklin scholars and one of the first to take Franklin seriously as a philosopher, concerns his claim that Franklin separated ethics from philosophy, metaphysics, and theology. As I hope to have shown, Franklin's philosophy consisted in his dialectical critique of morality and his startling discovery of the essential link between our moral opinions and intuitions and religious experience. See Schneider, *The Puritan Mind* (Ann Arbor: University of Michigan Press, 1958), 237, 241, 255; and Schneider, "The Significance of Benjamin Franklin's Moral Philosophy," in *Studies in the History of Ideas*, vol. 2 (New York: Columbia University Press, 1925), 300–301.

I have already had some critical things to say about Douglas Anderson's *The Radical Enlightenments of Benjamin Franklin*. This book is as important as it is impressive. Anderson presents Franklin as a rationalistic and religious moralist—a devotee of the "moral sublime" under the influence of Shaftesbury and Francis Hutcheson. Franklin's religious moralism took practical shape in his project for achieving moral perfection, which motivated his lifelong promotion of a universalistic party of virtue. According to Anderson, even the radical *Dissertation* reflected an important first moment in Franklin's quest for disinterested moral vocation and heroism. Far from defending atheism, the *Dissertation*, in Anderson's view, contains Franklin's critique of pride and grounds his egalitarianism. In its assertion of equal divine esteem for all the orders of creation (along with the denial of free will and vice and virtue), the *Dissertation* reveals Franklin's Hutchesonian "faith in a sublime moral harmony [that] sustains human consciousness against the 'casual evils' of earthly existence" (Anderson, 54). The later *Articles of Belief*, rather than being a spiritual and moral about-face, reflects Franklin's further spiritual development—in the lights of Newtonian polytheism, Milton's "exuberant pleasure in movement and in the participatory equality of all created matter," and "the shared moral nature of creator and created being that Francis Hutcheson emphasizes in his construction of the moral sense as the common basis of the natural design and of the unexhausted 'Delight' experienced by its human witnesses" (Anderson, 66–68).

Anderson's book is richly documented and passionately argued: He not only sees Franklin as a moralist and pursuer of moral heroism, but he also obviously admires him for it. Much of what Anderson sees in Franklin is extremely important. But obviously I disagree with his conclusion. In my view, the evidence just does not support such a rosy picture of Franklin as a religious moralist. Anderson is absolutely correct to see the common threads uniting the *Dissertation* and the *Articles*: Both are metaphysical treatises, and the *Dissertation*, despite first appearance to the contrary, combines the hard denial of free will, virtue and vice, and merit with a kind of cosmic moral harmony. So far, so good. But then things get fuzzy. As I noted above, Anderson then interprets the moral doctrines of the two texts—as regards the issue of divine justice and free will—in ways unsupported by the texts (Anderson, 41; see chapter 5, note 36, above). The issue at stake—which never becomes clear in Anderson's discussion—is the matter of particular providence. Franklin says over and over again that particular providence is the fundamental principle of all religion, and he meant what he said. Franklin's point is that even the most radical and hard-edged Deism—as expressed by the *Dissertation*—often cannot free itself from our moral intuitions (including particular providence, which sneaks in the back door) about justice. The most radical freethinking can be no less in the grip of these intuitions than are all forms of theism (including the most bizarre, dogmatic, and enthusiastic), and these intuitions are completely incoherent. That, I am arguing, is the position on these pieces to which Franklin directs us by the clues in the *Autobiography*.

When he wrote the *Autobiography*, he had a perfectly clear picture of the *Dissertation* in his mind, and he provides us with the clues by which we can think for ourselves about what was really wrong with the *Dissertation*, whether it was dangerous, and if it really was dangerous, then how and to whom and why. Of Franklin's counting the *Dissertation* as one of his moral errata, Anderson (33) tells us that a slip in Franklin's recall caused him to understate the "social origins" of the *Dissertation* (and hence to overstate its dangerousness). But Anderson makes no mention of the 1779 letter to Vaughn in which Franklin reports having burned the extant copies of the pamphlet because of its "ill tendency." Are we to believe that Franklin omitted this absolutely crucial and absolving fact from the *Autobiography* because he forgot it? Impossible. Franklin is giving us the clues: He both overstates and understates the pamphlet's dangerousness so that we will figure things out for ourselves.

The 1731 essay "On Simplicity" was written just *after* the "Observations on My Reading History in Library," in which Franklin says he first outlined his "great and extensive project" for a "party of virtue." It seems to me impossible that a man committed to "moral heroism" and who really believed, with the *Articles*, that hypocrisy is odious to him (Anderson, 68) could have written such a hard-boiled Baconian and Machiavellian essay. As I have shown, I hope convincingly, that piece is a defense precisely of well-used hypocrisy and lying for the sake of one's own happiness. It also shows why a clever liar should prefer a world in which most people do not lie and where a reputation for honesty is esteemed, and therefore useful (see Shaftesbury, *Characteristics*, 43–44). "On Simplicity" is a clear refutation of the busybody's moral hero, Cato. To make this evidence go away, we would have to believe that Franklin did not write this piece—but J. A. Leo Lemay has shown conclusively that he did (*The Canon of Benjamin Franklin, 1722–1776* [Newark: University of Delaware Press, 1986], 60–62). It is surprising that Anderson makes no reference to this essay.

Chapter Seven: The Political Principles of the Good Life

1. *Writings* 71, 1016, 1359.
2. Thomas Hobbes, *Leviathan*, ed. Richard Tuck (Cambridge: Cambridge University Press, 1996), 70–71; see also 46.
3. John Locke, *Essay Concerning Human Understanding*, Book 2, chapter 21, paragraphs 56, 61, 67; see Book 2, chapter 20, paragraph 6. See also Locke, *Second Treatise*, chapter 5, paragraphs 30, 32, 34, 37.
4. *Writings* 469–472.
5. *Poor Richard's Almanack* is full of advice about how to succeed at business, and the *Autobiography* is in considerable part the account of his own business career as a model for others to follow. And Franklin exerted considerable self-restraint and hard work to advance his business career. But for Franklin, business was a necessary means to other good things, and he worked hard in order to retire as soon as possible. At least for him, business was not choice-worthy in itself. What Franklin most desired was a life of independence and leisure for the activities he most enjoyed, and he was not indifferent to the charms of French aristocratic life. It must be remembered that Franklin was born to relative poverty and obscurity. To obtain those things he wanted, he had no alternative but to make it on his own by way of business and all of the discipline and sacrifices required. As soon as he became a rich man, however, he left business for other pursuits, and although it would be an exaggeration to say that he aspired to be an aristocrat, there is no doubt that he did wish to be, and succeeded in becoming, a gentleman. See Gordon S. Wood, *The Radicalism of the American Revolution* (New York: Random House, 1991), 77, 85–86, 199. See also Walter Isaacson, *Benjamin Franklin: An American Life* (New York: Simon and Schuster, 2003), 127–128, 532. Franklin would have loved to have been an aristocrat, but he could not have thought aristocracy somehow deserved its privileges or deserved to govern. There was no such thing as deserving in Franklin's mind. Thus, he would not have thought the "middle class" particularly deserving of privilege or power, either (or individual aristocrats, for that matter).
6. *Writings* 209–210.

7. *Writings* 210–211.

8. *Writings* 817.

9. *Writings* 816.

10. Carl Van Doren, *Benjamin Franklin* (New York: Penguin, 1991), 322.

11. That Franklin understood the folly and villainy of so many people in the world did not mean that he thought life in this world a bad thing, at least not for him or any clear-sighted person. J. A. Leo Lemay goes astray, I think, in suggesting that the "private Franklin" had a pessimistic take on life. The evidence—a line from *Poor Richard's Almanack* of 1753 ("He that best understands the world, likes it least") and a comment to his sister, Jane Mecom ("She is doubtless happy: which none of us are while in this life") (*Papers* 4: 405; 11: 253)—certainly allows no conclusion about the private Franklin's pessimism. The line in *Poor Richard* is not enough to infer that Franklin was pessimistic (and it is followed by one about the folly of most anger), and the line to Jane was to console her for the death of her daughter. See Lemay, *The Canon of Benjamin Franklin* (Newark: University of Delaware Press, 1986), 52–53.

12. *Writings* 1200.

13. *Writings* 1384–1385.

14. *Writings* 1385–1386.

15. *Writings* 1391.

16. *Writings* 1384–1386, 1391.

17. *Writings* 1392–1394.

18. John Calvin, *Institutes*, 2.2.11.

19. Calvin, *Institutes*, 3.18.1, 3.21.1.

20. See Anthony Ashley Cooper, third Earl of Shaftesbury, *Characteristics*, ed. Lawrence E. Klein (Cambridge: Cambridge University Press, 1999), 42–43. Shaftesbury gets a good whiff of Hobbes's rationalistic idealism.

21. See Denis Tilden Lynch, *"Boss" Tweed: The Story of a Grim Generation* (New York: Boni and Liveright, 1927), 51–66. And Franklin, like Tweed, rarely missed an opportunity to use public service for private gain. I thank Carey McWilliams for pointing out this delectable fact.

22. See Franklin's charming and witty letter of apology to Vergennes (*Writings* 1060–1061).

23. I thank Carey McWilliams for reminding me of this. See Max Farrand, ed., *The Records of the Federal Convention of 1787* (New Haven, CT: Yale University Press, 1966), 2: 204–205, 208, 210. See William G. Carr, *The Oldest Delegate* (Newark: University of Delaware Press, 1990), 109–110.

24. Robert Middlekauff, *Benjamin Franklin and His Enemies* (Berkeley and Los Angeles: University of California Press, 1998), 55–114; Gordon Wood, *The Americanization of Benjamin Franklin* (New York: Penguin, 2004), 91–101, 262n81.

25. Wood, *The Americanization of Benjamin Franklin*, 151, 158–166. See Cecil B. Curry, *Code Number 72: Ben Franklin Patriot or Spy?* (Englewood Cliffs, NJ: Prentice-Hall, 1972).

26. Wood, *The Americanization of Benjamin Franklin*, 66–67, 201–207.

27. In his wonderful and perceptive new book, *The Americanization of Benjamin Franklin*, Gordon Wood cites the following evidence for his view of an eventually angry Franklin. First, he notes (150–151), Franklin's "Proposed Memorial to Lord Dartmouth," written in heat after the final plan for reconciliation was dismissed contemptuously by the House of Lords; Franklin's description of the Houses of Lords and Commons in the

March 22, 1775, "Journal of Negotiations in London," written in the form of a letter to his Tory son William, the royalist governor of New Jersey; and Franklin's description in that same journal of the reaction of his friend, the banker Thomas Walpole, upon reading the Proposed Memorial, who "looked at it and at me several times alternately, as if he apprehended me a little out of my senses." Of course Franklin was irritated. But the evidence does not suggest that his anger got the best of him or lasted for too long. The "Proposed Memorial to Lord Dartmouth" was hot. But Franklin had the cool head to have Walpole take a look, and when the latter, catching up with Franklin in the House of Lords the next day, warned him that it "might be attended with dangerous consequences to your person, and contribute to exasperate the nation," Franklin, never one to be needlessly reckless with his person, thought the better of it. Then, again in the journal, he lambastes the Lords not just with a crack about their being unfit to rule swine but with a gibe to the effect that hereditary legislators were no more suited for their responsibilities than "hereditary professors of mathematics" were for theirs. He was mad at British stupidity, but he was, as always, able to be bemused as well. All this speaks of one who can and does reflect coolly on the passions of the moment. As he said in the journal about Walpole's warning: "I had no desire to make matters worse, and being grown cooler took the advice so kindly given me" (*Papers* 21: 508–510, 526–528, 528–529, 582–583, 598–599).

Second, Wood cites (160–163) Franklin's July 7, 1777, letter to his friend Jonathan Shipley, complaining about English military behavior, in which he admitted that he was "warm" and that "if a temper naturally cool and phlegmatic can, in old age, which often cools the warmest, be thus heated, you will judge by that of the general temper here, which is now little short of madness" (*Papers* 22: 96–98). And to this Wood adds the example of the 1782 hoax about the cargo of American scalps and the matter of Franklin's break with William, which I discuss in the conclusion below. The letter to Shipley does not allow us to conclude that Franklin was in some sense deeply and lastingly angry: The trope about his cool and phlegmatic character (which we will see again) has an ironic tone and is meant more to illustrate by contrast the Americans' madness than his own anger, and this fact is clear from the abrupt change of tone that follows: "I drop this disagreeable subject; and will take up one, that I know must afford you and the good family, as my friends, some pleasure." The topic is the good state of Franklin's family, and in a cheery tone he tells his friend that "were it not for our public troubles, and the being absent from so many that I love in England, my present felicity would be as perfect, as in this world one could well expect it." This is not the expression of a man consumed with anger. Nor is the scalp hoax, which can be seen as the work of an angry man only by ignoring its comic and ironic tone and its general reflection not simply on English barbarity but on the common folly and viciousness of all involved (see my discussion in the section "Not the Revolution" in chapter 4 above). See Isaacson, *Benjamin Franklin*, 557n27.

Third, Wood (190–191) mentions Franklin's uncontrollable anger during a meeting on January 6, 1775, with Paul Wentworth, emissary from England (and master spy), as described by Wentworth. Wood admits that Franklin was "no fool" in this secret meeting, which he knew would be revealed to Vergennes. Franklin used the meeting to goad Vergennes into making the treaties before reconciliation occurred between England and the colonies. But even though Franklin was no fool, Wood concludes this about Franklin *despite* the fact that Franklin was as "angry as he was." Perhaps. But Franklin had been cool as a cucumber just the day before in a meeting with the possibly freelancing emissary Sir Philip Gibbes, and he had good reason to let Wentworth think—and to let Vergennes find out—that if reconciliation were to occur, it would not be with a cowed but with an angry America, so that the French would harbor no hopes to regain their possessions. And for Franklin to have sucked up too much would have been transparent to Vergennes. But all this is speculation. What is not speculation is what Wentworth reports about Franklin's heated and personal remarks. When Franklin was warned not to mix personal quarrels with the business of his country, Wentworth says that Franklin "replied that his warmth did not proceed from a feeling of personal injuries, but that they, going all along with the barbarities inflicted on his country, the remembrance of these roused in an old man, constitutionally phlegmatic, the resentments of high mettled youth. And it should serve to convince me, of the resentments of those on the spot, seeing the regular system of devastation and cruelty which every general had pursued." Now, Franklin might have next really lost his breath in a paroxysm of anger, but not before plucking from his rhetorical quiver *the very same* trope he had used in the earlier letter to his friend Shipley. This was a very cool and effective move—and not one to be expected from someone in a foaming and breath-stopping wrath. It is far likelier that Franklin's behavior was pure theater (see *Papers* 25: 419–423, 435–440).

Fourth, Wood (222–225) discusses Franklin's December 1778 letter to Charles Thomson, to whom Franklin sent his letter to Congress requesting his unpaid salary. Franklin wanted the accounts settled in order to put an end to charges that he had pocketed public funds. And lest Congress forget what he was really owed, Franklin included with the letter to Thompson a "Sketch of the Services of B. Franklin to the United States of America." Alfred Henry Smyth, ed., *The Writings of Benjamin Franklin* (New York: Macmillan, 1907), 9: 691–697. Wood implies that Franklin's anger led him "to go too far" in his reproach of republics, so that, realizing the fact, he "would pass these reflections into oblivion." But Franklin did not go too far: His letter says no more than what was true about what had been done to him by Congress, and he comments that "this is all to yourself only as a private friend; for I have not, nor ever shall, make any public complaint" *before* he comments that he would have acted no differently had he anticipated congressional ingratitude and that he is well aware of the "nature of such changeable assemblies" that forget and that are worked on by "envious and malicious persons." When he then says that he will thus pass his reflections into oblivion, he follows the remark with a concluding comment that if his friend ever suffers from an ungrateful republic he should remember that he can "unbosom" himself "in communicating your griefs to your ancient friend." In other words and again, the "reproach" upon republics—"that *they are apt to be ungrateful*"—is just between them. The tone here is not anger but philosophical resignation in the face of the inevitable fickleness of life—the very same tone he used in the above-mentioned 1766 letter to Jane Mecom (written well before Franklin's hopes for the empire were dashed), in which he said that despite the ingratitude of those for whom one works, it is still a "pretty good sort of a world."

Finally, Wood (226–229) says that when Franklin signed the memorial to Congress, in February 1790, requesting the abolition of slavery, "this was a very different Franklin from the earlier pragmatic Franklin. No longer was he the tactful conciliator looking for the practical compromise between very diverse opinions." Rather, Franklin was eager to provoke Congress and his tormentors Richard Henry Lee and Ralph Izard. The implication is that Franklin's personal anger overwhelmed his pragmatism. Perhaps—and with one foot in the grave what did he have to lose? But one cannot read the hoax on slavery and conclude that he was finally capable of righteous indignation. That piece is a double-edged sword and entirely in keeping with the skeptical and philosophical Franklin whom I discuss in chapter 8 below.

Robert Middlekauff, in his wonderful book *Benjamin Franklin and His Enemies*, presents a spirited case for Franklin's having been driven to his reckless behavior, in his vain pursuit for royal government for Pennsylvania, by hatred for Thomas Penn. That hatred was "so powerful as to overcome his reason. The hatred of Penn was obsessive, uncontrollable, and almost without limits" (107). There is no doubt that there was bitterness between the two men, especially on Penn's part, and no doubt that in the course of the long affair, Franklin got hot under the collar. But the portrait of Franklin as nearly insane from anger is more inferred from the length of his project and the difficulties Franklin should easily have seen than it is from any of the textual evidence. That evidence is scarce, and what there is does not permit any firm conclusion about blinding and uncontrollable anger. Middlekauff himself says that Franklin really thought he could pull off the scheme and was used to getting his way and not above strategically baring sharp teeth (107–114). And the argument for an irrationally angry Franklin rests primarily on three pieces of evidence: (1) Franklin's letter to Robert Norris recounting Franklin's meeting with Penn in January 1758, in which Franklin, confronted with Penn's argument that it was the original colonists' own fault if they misunderstood the charter, expressed his "cordial and thorough contempt" for Penn and compared him to a "low jockey" (*Papers* 7: 360–362); (2) Franklin's later comment to Joseph Galloway that he did not regret the insult (*Papers* 8: 309–316); (3) Franklin's "anger" in his long-winded "Preface" to "The Speech of Joseph Galloway" (*Papers* 11: 267–311).

In the letter to Norris, Franklin leaves no doubt about his contempt for Penn and no doubt that he let his face reveal it during the exchange. But he also tells us that although he let his face speak, he held his tongue and answered with something of a joke: "However finding myself grow warm I made no other answer to this than that the poor people were no lawyers themselves and confiding in his father did not think it necessary to consult any" (*Papers* 7: 362). To Galloway, Franklin admits that he might not have included the insult in his letter (and that Fothergill had admonished him for his harshness), but he explains himself *reflectively*: "But indignation *extorted* it from me, and I cannot *yet* say that I much repent of it. It sticks in his liver, I find; and even let him bear what he so well deserves. By obtaining copies of our private correspondence, he has added another instance confirming the old adage, that listeners seldom hear any good of themselves" (my emphasis; *Papers* 8: 313). In other words, Penn had it coming, but Franklin's indignation (being irrational) got the better of him and eventually he will come to regret it. And in the "Preface," Franklin was clearly writing for rhetorical effect, as he very often did. And, also as he often did, he tells a nasty joke at Penn's expense: Referring to the assembly's praise of the first proprietor, Franklin says that the first one's sons heard "*the Father, the honored and honorable Father*" repeated so often that they "grew sick of it; and have been heard to say to each other with disgust, when told that A. B. and C. were come to wait upon them with addresses on some public occasion, '*Then I suppose we shall hear more about our Father*'" (*Papers* 11: 297).

There seems no doubt that Franklin got and stayed angry at Penn. But the evidence at hand simply does not bear the weight of an argument that Franklin's anger drove him clean out of his senses. Again, I do not mean to argue that Franklin was above all passion, including anger. But I do not think a case can be made that he was in character an angry man, such that anger was the wellspring (as it almost always is in others) of his political attachments. He was not, because his critique of morality showed him the incoherence of the opinions that work along with anger. Thus, when he did get mad, he was usually able to get over it, and, if he could not get over it because of the attachments of the heart, he was always able to reflect on its moral absurdity, as I discuss in the conclusion (again, on the matter of William).

28. Franklin knew that Poor Richard was understating the case when he said in 1753: "Anger is never without a reason, but seldom with a good one" (*Writings* 1277).

29. *Writings* 1342–1345.

30. *Writings* 1344.

31. Franklin never sent the famous letter to his longtime friend William Strahan, in which Franklin declared Strahan, as a member of Parliament, to have become his enemy (*Papers* 22: 85; see also 21: 526–529).

32. In arguing for the moral priority of public service in Franklin's view, Wood, *The Americanization of Benjamin Franklin*, 67, joins Edmund Morgan, *Benjamin Franklin* (New Haven, CT: Yale University Press, 2002), 26–29, in depending on a letter written by Franklin in 1750 to Cadwallader Colden, who was both a philosopher and lieutenant governor of New York. In the letter, Franklin praises public service over science and refers to Newton's obligation to take the helm of the ship in a storm, rather than just staying in his cabin. The letter is, however, double-edged, to say the least. For we cannot miss the fact that Newton would, should he stick selfishly to his cabin, drown with everyone else should the bark founder. Franklin began the letter by remarking on the "melancholy account of the declining nature of the English and increase of the French interest among the Six Nations. I hope the interview intended with them by your Government will be a means of securing their attachment to the English nation. Methinks a great deal depends on you in this important affair." And then follows the remark about Newton. Franklin was by this time interested in defense and in Indian affairs (along with electricity), and he wanted Colden, who had retired and who soon was offered but declined the office of secretary for Indian affairs, to help. From this letter we can infer no moral turn from philosophy to public service; Franklin simply did not think the two incompatible. It is much simpler to conclude here that Franklin thought Colden would be useful in the politics in which Franklin was interested and that he wanted to get Colden to leave private life for politics (see *Papers* 4: 68). Franklin continued with his scientific investigations throughout his life, even while in Paris.

33. *Writings* 927–931; see Smyth, *Writings*, 7: 357.

34. I thus agree with Gordon Wood that for Franklin the Revolution was a very private affair. But all politics was for Franklin ultimately a private affair (his), and he played political chess because he liked the game, not because he was compelled to it by the call of public duty. See Wood, *The Americanization of Benjamin Franklin*, 158, 201–202.

35. *Papers* 1: 259–264.

36. *Papers* 1: 263.

37. See the "Canada Pamphlet," *Papers* 9: 60–66; Gerald Stourzh, *Benjamin Franklin and American Foreign Policy* (Chicago: University of Chicago Press, 1969), 71–82.

38. See the discussion of moderation above.

39. Esmond Wright, *Franklin of Philadelphia* (Cambridge, MA: Harvard University Press, 1986), 245–247; cf. 173. See Morgan, *Benjamin Franklin*, 93–94, 143, 173.

40. I thus respectfully disagree with Ralph L. Ketcham's claim that "Franklin was confident of this progress because he was sure his age had discovered the eternal verities—natural rights—of enlightened politics." Nor do I agree that Franklin "took the natural

rights too much for granted to have spent much time trying to define them." Franklin thought deeply about natural rights and saw no need to define them because he did not think they exist. See Ketcham, *Benjamin Franklin* (New York: Washington Square Press, 1966), 198–200.

41. Compare the Declaration of Independence with Locke, *Second Treatise*, 19: 225. And then compare John Trenchard and Thomas Gordon's opinions about Hobbes and Locke in *Cato's Letters*, ed. Ronald Hamoway (Indianapolis, IN: Liberty Fund, 1995), 236, 370, 498, 743, 767.

42. *Writings* 1017.

43. *Papers* 2: 184–185; *Writings* 424–425. See also Lemay, *The Canon of Benjamin Franklin*, 74–75.

44. No wonder Logan was not one of the founding members of the Junto. Franklin must have thought him a highly learned dolt. See Morgan, *Benjamin Franklin*, 56.

45. Thomas Hobbes, *Leviathan*, ed. Richard Tuck (Cambridge: Cambridge University Press, 1996), 89.

46. Compare Jean-Jacques Rousseau, *Second Discourse*, trans. Victor Gourevitch (Cambridge: Cambridge University Press, 1997), 132, 152.

47. Hobbes, *Leviathan*, 89–90.

48. *Papers* 16: 305–306. David T. Morgan, in his excellent *The Devious Dr. Franklin, Colonial Agent* (Macon, GA: Mercer University Press, 1996) gives a clear and persuasive account of Franklin's increasingly radical position on American "rights" and representation. Morgan argues that Franklin's turn toward radicalism was "reluctant" and, as revealed by the marginalia, later (1769) than was claimed by Verner Crane (1766). The marginalia do indeed reveal Franklin's tougher position, but at the same time, as I hope I have shown, they demonstrate that Franklin's more "radical" position was not based on a doctrine of natural rights or moral republicanism. Cf. Morgan, *The Devious Dr. Franklin*, 164–177; and Verner Crane, *Benjamin Franklin and a Rising People* (Boston: Little, Brown, 1954), 127–128.

49. *Papers* 16: 279.

50. *Papers* 16: 307.

51. *Papers* 16: 305.

52. *Writings* 1081–82.

53. *Papers* 16: 309.

54. Hobbes, *Leviathan*, 91.

55. Hobbes, *Leviathan*, 101; Psalms 10: 13.

56. *Writings* 564.

57. *Papers* 15: 3; *Writings* 607–615.

58. *Writings* 611–612.

59. *Writings* 613; *Papers* 15: 8–9, 10.

60. *Papers* 16: 309–310.

61. *Writings* 387, 403, 405, 564, 572, 608, 1081.

62. *Papers* 22: 78–81.

63. *Papers* 22: 81.

64. Smyth, *Writings*, 10: 59.

65. Hobbes would point out to us that according to our Constitution, the majority of the people could, if they *really* wanted to, abolish the Bill of Rights and pass an amendment making all people with red hair second-class citizens. This would not be very smart, redheads would be free to take off if they could, and the government would be free to

prevent them from doing so if it could. And there would be no injustice involved on anyone's part.

66. Hobbes, *Leviathan*, 129–130.

67. Franklin's turn was indeed abrupt, since his view of the empire and the monarchy had become almost Tory. See Wood's excellent discussion, *The Americanization of Benjamin Franklin*, 120–124.

68. *Writings* 1140. See Farrand, *The Records of the Federal Convention of 1787*, 2: 642–643. It is surprising that Walter Isaacson, in quoting Franklin's speech, excises this theoretically most important and Hobbesian point (Isaacson, *Benjamin Franklin*, 457–458). If it was just "basic eighteenth-century wisdom," Franklin's understanding of it was certainly more than basic. See Barbara B. Oberg, "Plain, Insinuating, Persuasive," in *Reappraising Benjamin Franklin*, ed. J. A. Leo Lemay (Newark: University of Delaware Press, 1993), 175–192.

69. *Writings* 403.

70. I do not mean to argue for a second that Franklin always used political technology well or dispassionately. He seems clearly to have misjudged public opinion in Pennsylvania and the view of the British government in his machinations to move from proprietary to royal rule. He misjudged the American reaction to the Stamp Act, and the Hutchinson letters affair seems to have been a very serious blunder. Even so, when Franklin complained about the irrationality of the American response to the Stamp Act, he was not being naïve but was, rather, in error. It is easy to see how Franklin, himself a rationalist, could overestimate the rationality of others despite being so profoundly aware of the roots and degree of human folly.

71. *Papers* 16: 318.

72. *Writings* 709–710.

73. *Papers* 21: 582–583.

74. *Writings* 10–13.

75. *Writings* 1324.

76. Smyth, *Writings*, 10: 59–60. See also Farrand, *The Records of the Federal Convention of 1787*, 1: 48.

77. See Isaacson, *Benjamin Franklin*, 18–20, for the alternative explanation that Franklin's father withdrew him from the grammar school because he did not think the lad "suited for the clergy," and not for financial reasons.

78. Thomas Jefferson, *Writings* (New York: Library of America, 1984), 1004.

79. *Writings* 1073–1074.

80. See Joyce Appleby, "The Adams-Jefferson Rupture and the First French Translation of John Adams' *Defense*," *American Historical Review* 73 (April 1968): 1084–1091. See also *The Papers of Thomas Jefferson*, ed. Julian P. Boyd and Ruth W. Lester (Princeton, NJ: Princeton University Press, 1982), 20: 279n36. See also Franklin's 1788 letter to Louis-Guillaume le Veillard, Smyth, *Writings*, 9: 673–675.

81. *Writings* 49–50.

82. *Writings* 1043.

83. *Writings* 975–983.

84. *Writings* 1084–1089.

85. There is no contradiction between Franklin's view that private property is useful and essential for stability and prosperity and his belief that there is no natural right to it.

86. *Writings* 622–625.

87. *Writings* 367–374.

88. See Franklin's marginalia to Ramsay, *Papers* 16: 291–292.

89. *Writings* 874.

90. Locke, *Second Treatise*, 5: 41.

91. *Writings* 471.

92. *Writings* 371.

93. *Writings* 1017.

94. *Writings* 1047–1048.

95. As a deep reader of Shaftesbury and as a well-schooled Baconian, Franklin knew perfectly well what it meant to say that men are "badly constructed." I will say it yet again: According to Shaftesbury, when Bacon said this, it was only by good luck that he was not recognized as an atheist. See Shaftesbury, *Characteristics*, 368.

96. Franklin here refers to the ferocious Battle of the Saints Passage on April 12, 1782, between the French fleet commanded by Admiral François-Joseph-Paul de Grasse and the English fleet commanded by Admiral George Rodney. The battle, won by Rodney, was for control of the West Indies. Franklin was of course well aware that de Grasse's previous blockade of the Chesapeake Bay had been crucial for assuring victory at the decisive Battle of Yorktown, in 1781.

Chapter Eight: The Political Project of the Good Life

1. *Writings* 1252.

2. *Papers* 4: 17. Franklin's natural science is beyond the scope of this book. Without question, the best studies of Franklin's natural science are those by the late I. Bernard Cohen, especially *Benjamin Franklin's Science* (Cambridge, MA: Harvard University Press, 1990) and *Science and the Founding Fathers* (New York: Norton, 1995). Also excellent is Charles Tanford, *Franklin Stilled the Waves* (Durham, NC: Duke University Press, 1989). See also the fine articles by J. L. Heilbron, "Franklin as an Enlightened Natural Philosopher," in *Reappraising Benjamin Franklin*, ed. J. A. Leo Lemay (Newark: University of Delaware Press, 1993), 196–220, and Heinx Otto Sibum, "The Bookkeeper of Nature," in Lemay, *Reappraising*, 221–242.

3. In the 1784 spoof "An Economical Project," Franklin comments that "utility is, in my opinion the test of value in matters of invention, and that a discovery which can be applied to no use, or is not good for something, is good for nothing" (*Writings* 985). The reference is to invention, not discovery as such, and his comment does not imply that apparently useless discoveries may not turn out to be or lead to useful purposes. And "useful" can mean different things. What is useless to some men could well be most useful to others: for instance, the truth about the world of nature as it really is. Franklin was surely aware of Bacon's argument, in the *Novum Organum* (trans. Peter Urbach and John Gibson [Chicago: Open Court, 1994], 1: 129), that the light of knowledge is more valuable than all uses. Whether seeing clearly or providing for use is the better depends first on whether charity is the end of science and whether the use is for oneself or for others. This question, as Franklin surely knew along with Bacon, depends on whether God, revelation, and miracles exist. This is a matter that cannot be decided by science or metaphysics, according to Franklin.

4. *Writings* 1424.

5. *Writings* 1422–1424.

6. *Writings* 361–367.

7. *Writings* 364–367.

8. *Writings* 1017.

9. *Writings* 1074.

10. *Writings* 1167.

11. *Writings* 373.

12. Here I must again disagree with Edmund Morgan's argument that Franklin "underwent a new dedication to public service between 1748 and 1750," at least if we are to understand him to mean by "a new dedication" that Franklin came to see science as somehow selfish and public service as not. Morgan, *Benjamin Franklin* (New Haven, CT: Yale University Press, 2002), 25–30. Given Franklin's manifest Baconianism, it would be turning to public service that would be selfish, denying as it would Franklin's shoulder to the wheel of science and the amazing boons offered by that science to humanity. By moral comparison to that great project, the ship of state would look puny, just as Jefferson said it is. See chapter 7, note 32, above.

13. *Papers* 9: 78–79.

14. *Papers* 9: 7.

15. *Papers* 25: 100–102. Cf. Gordon Wood, *The Americanization of Benjamin Franklin* (New York: Penguin, 2004), 190.

16. *Writings* 367–374. See David Waldstreicher, *Runaway America: Benjamin Franklin, Slavery, and the American Revolution* (New York: Hill and Wang, 2004), for a superb and sensitive account of Franklin's hard-nosed and changing views on slavery. Waldstreicher is especially to be praised for his understanding of Franklin's artful slipperiness and belief in "above all . . . the virtue, and necessity, of silence" (239).

17. *Papers* 19: 112. See Melvin H. Buxbaum, *Benjamin Franklin and the Zealous Presbyterians* (University Park: Pennsylvania State University Press, 1975), 28–29. The charge still haunts Franklin. When I told a faculty member from another department that I was writing about Franklin, he said: "Oh Franklin, he was anti-immigrant and a language bigot." It is hard not to think that this charge was not also on the minds of those behind the "Prophecy" hoax, the prophecy being an anti-Semitic diatribe Franklin supposedly delivered at the Constitutional Convention. On a recent trip to a bookstore to get a book on Franklin, I encountered a clerk who said to me: "Oh Franklin, he was an anti-Semite, wasn't he?" See Claude-Anne Lopez, *My Life with Benjamin Franklin* (New Haven, CT: Yale University Press, 2000), 3–16. (Don't miss this wonderful and charming book.) See also the dispute between Buxbaum, *Benjamin Franklin and the Zealous Presbyterians*, 185–219, and the spirited Francis Jennings, *Benjamin Franklin, Politician* (New York: Norton, 1996), 158–159.

18. *Writings* 374. See Robert Middlekauff, *Benjamin Franklin and His Enemies* (Berkeley and Los Angeles: University of California Press, 1998), 98–99.

19. *Writings* 443–446.

20. See Douglas Anderson, *The Radical Enlightenments of Benjamin Franklin* (Baltimore: Johns Hopkins University Press, 1997), 163.

21. *Writings* 546.

22. Walter Isaacson, *Benjamin Franklin: An American Life* (New York: Simon and Schuster, 2003), 152–153, and Morgan, *Benjamin Franklin*, 77–79, but not H. W. Brands, *The First American* (New York: Doubleday, 2000), comment on the Boors remark. Isaac-

son sees the matter of the Indians but not the obvious Franklin sleight of hand. David Waldstreicher is a trifle (and uncharacteristically) heavy-handed in his treatment of the passage. The point isn't that anyone reading the essay "would have noticed that most people in America were, by the measure Franklin proposed, black, tawny, or swarthy." That ironic point is established by Franklin's comical recommendation that America be scoured in order to increase the numbers of whites and the tawny Indians. We can't, thus, well describe the passage simply as "frank, if strategic, racism." Frank and definitely strategic to be sure, but also undercut by the clever irony. Thus the "relativism" of the concluding comment about Franklin's partiality doesn't "mitigate" the racism of the final paragraph; the paragraph does that all by itself. I should note as well that given Franklin's understanding of morality, he could not have concluded that racial inferiority, even if it proved to be real, could *justify* slavery. I am also somewhat wary of drawing from Franklin's polemical writings his genuine philosophical thoughts on any matter. See Waldstreicher, *Runaway America*, 136–139.

23. See *The Interest of Great Britain Considered, Papers* 9: 49–100.

24. *Papers* 6: 75–82.

25. Cadwallader Colden saw immediately that Franklin had committed a rhetorical error in his last paragraph. So Colden suggested that the last paragraph was the only one liable to exception and that Franklin should move it to the middle of the piece because at the end of the discourse, the reader "should be most fully satisfied when you take leave of him" (*Papers* 5: 197).

26. *Writings* 843–844.

27. *Papers* 7: 98–101, 252, 356.

28. *Papers* 9: 12.

29. *Writings* 799–800.

30. *Papers* 10: 396.

31. See I. Bernard Cohen, "The Empirical Temper," in *Benjamin Franklin and the American Character*, ed. Charles L. Sanford (Boston: D. C. Heath, 1955), 91.

32. *Papers* 4: 229.

33. *Writings* 646–653.

34. *Writings* 876.

35. Abraham Lincoln, *Speeches and Writings, 1859–1865* (New York: Library of America, 1989), 116–117. See also Lopez, *My Life with Benjamin Franklin*, 196–205, on Franklin's changing views on slavery and on his late correspondence with Condorcet's Société des Amis du Noirs.

36. *Writings* 1154–1155.

37. Carl Van Doren, *Benjamin Franklin* (New York: Penguin, 1991), 550. I do not think that by the change Franklin meant to imply that the truths "cannot be made more plain and evident by demonstration, because 'tis its self much better known than any thing that can be brought to prove it." See Cohen, "The Empirical Temper," 89.

38. See *Writings* 645, 974.

39. *Writings* 371.

40. *Writings* 1157–1160.

41. See Anderson, *Radical Enlightenments*, 222.

42. *The Works of Francis Bacon*, ed. James Spedding, Robert Ellis, and Douglas Heath (Stuttgart: Friedrich Fromann Verlag, 1963), 6: 721–722.

43. Ibid.

44. See Francis Bacon, *Advancement of Learning*, in *Works of Bacon*, 3: 349–359.

45. Francis Bacon, *New Atlantis*, ed. Jerry Weinberger (Arlington Heights, IL: Crofts Classics, 1989). See my essay "On the Miracles in Bacon's *New Atlantis*," in *Francis Bacon's "New Atlantis*," ed. Bronwen Price (New York: Manchester University Press, 2002), 106–128.

46. See "The Antediluvians Were All Very Sober," *Writings* 303–304.

47. Thomas Hobbes, *Leviathan*, ed. Richard Tuck (Cambridge: Cambridge University Press, 1996), 86–90.

48. Compare Hobbes, *Leviathan*, 86–90 and 99–100.

49. Hobbes, *Leviathan*, 99.

50. Hobbes, *Leviathan*, 91.

51. Hobbes, *Leviathan*, 46.

52. Hobbes, *Leviathan*, 315, 431–434. I must respectfully disagree with J. A. Leo Lemay's comment that Franklin was, "concerning such topics as the nature of man and the state of nature," a "Hobbesian pessimist." This judgment simply gets Hobbes wrong. Hobbes is, as I have noted, denying the doctrine of original sin and is presenting human beings as by nature rational and capable of solving the problem of justice once and for all. Hobbes was an atheist, that is certain. But he was also an Enlightenment optimist, and that is where he and Franklin parted company. See J. A. Leo Lemay, "Franklin and the *Autobiography*: An Essay on Recent Scholarship," *Eighteenth-Century Studies* 1, no. 2 (Winter 1967): 208.

53. On his own grounds, and as a careful reader of Shaftesbury, Franklin could also have thought that Hobbes was moved, perhaps half-consciously, by the desire to merit praise, reward, and honor for his gift of enlightenment to the world—a gift that was free and not based on any covenant or mutual agreement with those who received it. See Anthony Ashley Cooper, third Earl of Shaftesbury, *Characteristics*, ed. Lawrence E. Klein (Cambridge: Cambridge University Press, 1999), 43–44. This could easily have resulted from Hobbes's failure to think through moral phenomena as they are actually and commonly and most deeply experienced. In favor of this latter thought is the lingering possibility that for Hobbes, a person in the state of nature would deserve what he has if there was no objectively determined necessity for another to take it, so that the concept of deserving is, for Hobbes, not an internally incoherent idea. See the discussion of Franklin and natural right in chapter 7.

54. *Papers* 16: 305–306.

55. *Papers* 16: 306.

56. *Writings* 971–972.

57. *Writings* 1047. If I am right about Franklin, then his claim about our poor construction is not metaphysical or deduced from some claim about the origins of nature.

58. That china breaker was, by the way, the Quaker Benjamin Lay, called by David Waldstreicher "the first modern abolitionist." Waldstreicher errs when, in describing Franklin's "engagement and distance from the dangers of anti-slavery," he says that Franklin indicated respect for Lay by calling him the "Pythagorean-cynical-christian Philosopher." That phrase occurs in Franklin's account of the attack on the china, in which Lay is comically presented as deranged. Waldstreicher, *Runaway America*, 81–82.

59. *Writings* 179–180, 1383, 1396.

60. See Isaacson, *Benjamin Franklin*, 491. See also James Campbell, *Recovering Benjamin Franklin: An Exploration of a Life of Science and Service* (Chicago: Open Court, 1999), 256.

61. *Writings* 1396. That effort included his published creeds, his "revision" of the Lord's Prayer, and his limited collaboration with Le Despencer in the abridgment of the Book of Common Prayer. *Writings* 638–641, 883; *Papers* 20: 343–352.

62. *Writings* 1382–1383. See Buxbaum, *Benjamin Franklin and the Zealous Presbyterians*, 76–152.

63. *Writings* 1399–1400.

64. *Writings* 256–261; *Papers* 2: 37–65, 65–88, 90–126.

65. *Papers* 2: 114.

66. *Papers* 2: 56.

67. *Writings* 257.

68. Buxbaum, *Benjamin Franklin and the Zealous Presbyterians*, chapters 3 and 4.

69. *Papers* 2: 67.

70. Letter to Roger C. Weightman in Thomas Jefferson, *Writings*, ed. Merrill D. Peterson (New York: Library of America, 1984), 1516–1517.

71. *Papers* 2: 259–260.

72. *Writings* 1406.

73. Given Franklin's earlier assault on the doctrines of original sin and justification by election and the righteousness of Christ, he surely knew from the get-go, and before 1740, what Whitefield believed. See Buxbaum, *Benjamin Franklin and the Zealous Presbyterians*, 139.

74. Hence Franklin's charge, in the defense of Hemphill, that the Presbyterians were antinomians. *Papers* 2: 108–109.

75. *Writings* 959.

76. *Writings* 969.

77. *Writings* 960.

78. *Writings* 1048. See *Papers* 34: 465–466; 35: 52–53, 64–66.

79. *Writings* 1157–1160.

80. Albert Henry Smyth, ed., *The Writings of Benjamin Franklin* (New York: Macmillan, 1907), 10: 85–86.

81. *Writings* 1178–1180.

82. *Writings* 475–477.

83. *Papers* 4: 504.

84. *Writings* 1179.

85. *Writings* 475.

86. The other letter Franklin sent to Stiles has not been identified, but Smyth and J. A. Leo Lemay both identify it as the one written in 1757 about the dangers of writing subtly and to some extent persuasively against particular providence. In that letter, Franklin warned his friend to burn his manuscript because it struck at the very "foundation of all religion," which is so essential for the practice of virtue. If this was the letter, then Stiles would indeed have gotten a nose full of Franklin's skepticism. See Smyth, *Writings*, 10: 85; *Writings* 1548. Smyth, who dates the letter to 1786, thinks the recipient of the letter was Tom Paine, but this is very unlikely according to the date established by the editors of the *Papers* (7: 293). See, however, Isaacson, *Benjamin Franklin*, 562n47.

87. Indeed, the famous epitaph, written by Franklin probably in 1728 and for years copied and given by Franklin to friends (including Stiles) and that spoke of a future appearance of his life as "a new and more perfect edition," was consciously not used by Franklin as his epitaph. See note 1 in the introduction, above.

Conclusion: Will the Real Ben Franklin Please Stand Up?

1. Walter Isaacson, *Benjamin Franklin: An American Life* (New York: Simon and Schuster, 2003), 480, 491; James Campbell, *Recovering Benjamin Franklin: An Exploration of a Life of Science and Service* (Chicago: Open Court, 1999), 256. See also J. A. Leo Lemay, "Franklin and the *Autobiography*: An Essay on Recent Scholarship," *Eighteenth-Century Studies* 1, no. 2 (Winter 1967): 203. To say, as does Lemay, that "Franklin's *Autobiography* argues directly and by example that virtue, that the moral responsibility of man, is in fact utilitarian" is, as Franklin knew perfectly well, to say that a square is round. Franklin knew that in a pinch (and there are lots of them in this life), virtue and utility do not jibe. But that is not his deepest point, which is, rather, that our common notions of "virtue" and "responsibility" simply do not make any sense.

2. Isaacson, *Benjamin Franklin*, 491.

3. See the excellent account of the matter in Gordon Wood, *The Americanization of Benjamin Franklin* (New York: Penguin, 2004), 162–163. See also Sheila Skemp, *William Franklin* (New York: Oxford University Press, 1990), 181; see also her *Benjamin and William Franklin* (Boston: Bedford Books, 1994), 126–146.

4. Albert Henry Smyth, ed., *The Writings of Benjamin Franklin* (New York: Macmillan, 1907), 10: 494. See Wood, *The Americanization of Benjamin Franklin*, 163nn24, 25.

5. The term is Wood's.

6. Smyth, *Writings*, 9: 232–233.

7. For those readers too young to know, I refer to the old TV celebrity game show *What's My Line?*

Index

Abolitionism, 13, 222, 263, 268, 272, 273, 316–317n27, 324n58
Abraham, Father. *See* "A Letter from Father Abraham, to His Beloved Son"
Absolute power, 235
Adams, John
  on BF, 1, 4, 290
  BF and, 13, 111
  defense of state constitutions, 243
  in France, 12
  negotiations with England, 13
  on "Speech of Miss Polly Baker," 85, 87, 91–92
Aging, 259–260
Albany Congress, 9
Albany Plan, 9, 220, 234, 236, 264
Aldridge, Alfred Owen, viii–ix, 2, 139, 140, 166, 300n13, 306n10, 308n46, 311n21
Alrihs, Harmanus, 115, 116–117, 118
American Philosophical Society, 8
Anderson, Douglas, 305n6, 310n3, 311n13, 311–313n24
Angels, 126–127, 133
Anger, 222–224, 290–292, 314–318n27, 318n28
Anti-Semitism, 322n17
"Appeal for the Hospital" (Franklin), 122, 257–258
Argument
  disputatious method, 17–18
  See also Socratic methods
Aristocracy
  BF's view of, 241, 290, 313n5
  emigrants to America, 244–246
  French, 244, 290
  hereditary, 247
  titles, 243–244
Aristophanes, *The Clouds*, 174
Arnauld, Antoine, *Port Royal Logic*, 18, 57, 201
Articles of Belief and Acts of Religion (Franklin), 162–166
  as metaphysical work, 138–139, 305–306n6
  scholarly views, 308–309n46, 311–312n24
  writing of, 27, 136

Articles of Confederation, 12
Artisans, 245, 246
"The Art of Virtue," 16, 28, 34, 53, 64–65
  See also Virtues
Atheism
  of Bacon, 299n39
  BF seen as atheist, 47–48, 58, 62, 142, 175
  confusion with Deism, 140, 306n10
  of Hobbes, 324n52
  seen in BF's writings, 140, 142, 307n15
Autobiography (Franklin)
  Abel and Vaughn letters, 3, 26, 34, 35, 41, 137
  addressed to posterity, 15
  as comic work, 36–37, 39, 40–41, 199–201
  contradictions, xii, 5, 7, 42, 48–50, 57, 59, 64, 65
  early life, 16–17
  honesty, 46–47
  image presented, 2
  irony, 35–36, 40, 41–42, 46, 65, 290
  message, 33–34
  method of discourse, 64–65
  modern opinion of, 4
  moral errata, 19–22, 24–25, 50, 51–53, 57, 241
  moral saga, 15–16, 35, 36–37, 45, 55, 65–66, 199
  motive for writing, 134
  Part One, 16–26
  Part Three, 29–33
  Part Two, 26–29
  publication, 136, 137
  stages of moral saga, 16–33, 144–145
  writing of, 2–3, 11, 13, 14, 26, 49
  See also Religious history in *Autobiography*

Bache, Sarah, letters to, 2, 246–248
Bacon, Francis
  atheism, 166, 299n39
  BF's differences from, 273–275
  BF's references to, 195–197, 199
  death marked in *Poor Richard's Almanack*, 255

Bacon, Francis, *continued*
  Essays, 255
  importance to science, 255
  moral reputation, 255
  on natural science, 113, 114
  New Atlantis, 274
  Novum Organum, 321n3
  "Of Cunning," 197–198
  "Of Simulation and Dissimulation," 197,
    198–199
  on religion, 274
  Wisdom of the Ancients, 273–274
Baconianism of Franklin
  in political career, 225, 234–236, 237, 254–261
  in scientific outlook, 112, 260
Baker, Polly. *See* "Speech of Miss Polly Baker"
Banks, Joseph, letters to, 242–243, 259
Bartram, John, letters to, 266
Battle of the Saints Passage, 321n96
Baxter, Andrew, 306n10
Beauty, 102, 105–106, 107–109
Benezet, Anthony, letter to, 268
Bentham, Jeremy, 12
Bible
  comparison of *Autobiography* to, 34–35, 36
  Luke, 257
  miracles, 71
"Bilked for Breakfast" (Franklin), 119
Bowdoin, James, 119
Braddock, Edward, 9
Brands, H. W., ix–x
Bray Associates, 266, 267
Brillon de Jouy, Anne-Louise, 13
British Empire, 220, 260–262
Bruce, Lenny, 100
Bunyan, John, 17
Burke, Edmund, 12
Business career of Franklin, 8, 313n5
  retirement, 9, 220, 313n5
  success, 25, 26, 30–31
Buxbaum, Melvin H., 280, 300n13

Cakes and wine, 125–127
Calvin, John, 160, 217, 310n56
Campbell, James, 289
Canada, 261–262, 265–266
Canada Pamphlet, 220, 261–262
Charity, 40
  BF's view, 34–35, 122
  care of sick, 122, 124, 257–258
  motives, 37
Chastity, 130–131, 213, 219
Chess, 225
Christianity
  BF's critique of, 264
  care of sick, 257–258
  mocking of, 128–131
  moral doctrine, 72
  views of Deists, 63
  See also Presbyterian Synod; Religion

Cincinnati, Order of the, 246–248
Civilization, 208–209, 251
Cleanliness, 213, 219
Clergy
  satire of, 240–241
  See also Hemphill, Samuel; Whitefield,
    George
Colden, Cadwallader, 323n25
  letter to, 318n32
Collins, Anthony, 7, 18, 57, 62, 200–201
Collins, John, 17–18, 20, 21, 23, 47, 57
Collinson, Peter, 8–9, 119
  letter to, 208–209
Comic pieces of Franklin, 66
  accounts of bizarre behavior, 68–72
  "Dialogue between the Gout and Mr. Franklin,"
    120
  "A Letter from Father Abraham, to His
    Beloved Son," 92–98, 133
  "Parody and Reply to a Religious Meditation,"
    125–127
  "Speech of Miss Polly Baker," 85–92, 132–133,
    301–302n28
  "The Trial and Reprieve of Prouse and
    Mitchel," 80–85, 132, 133
  See also Hoaxes
"Compassion and Regard for the Sick" (Franklin),
  124
Congress
  BF's message on slavery to, 268
  Connecticut compromise on representation,
    13–14, 221
  See also Continental Congress
Constitutional Convention
  BF as delegate, 13–14, 221, 241
  BF's concluding speech, 236
  Connecticut compromise on representation,
    13–14, 221
  suffrage issue, 113, 221
Constitutions, state
  Pennsylvania, 12, 241, 245
  publication in France, 243, 245
Continental Congress, 12, 237
  See also Declaration of Independence
Conversation
  humility in, 29
  pleasures of, 311n13
  unguarded expressions, 44–45
  See also Socratic methods
"Conversation on Slavery" (Franklin), 268
Cool Thoughts (Franklin), 10
Credulity, 111
  belief in spirits, 72–73, 74–75, 78
  interaction with reason, 79–85
Crito. *See* "A Man of Sense"
Cunning, 195–198
Cushing, Thomas, 11–12

Danby, John, 115, 116–117, 118
Deane, Silas, 12

Death
    condition of soul following, 151
    fear of, 274
    views of, 127
Declaration of Independence
    BF's role in writing, 12, 110, 226–227, 232, 269
    equal rights, 268–269
    unanimous vote, 237
Defense of Observations (Franklin), 72, 279–280
Defoe, Daniel, 17
Deism
    BF's arguments in favor of, 23, 57
    BF seen as Deist, 6, 139, 300n13
    BF's readings on, 7, 47
    claim in *Autobiography*, 23, 57, 62, 139
    confusion with atheism, 140, 306n10
    covert atheism and, 63
    defense in A *Dissertation*, 6, 8, 140
    distinction from BF's "want of religion," 63, 142
    dry and wet, 139, 293n4
    general providence, 125
    lack of evidence for BF's belief in, 6, 78–79, 290
    parodies, 173
    parody in *Dissertation*, 155, 157, 160–162, 166
    view of justice, 161–162
    views of Christians, 63
De la Freté, Madame, 119
Democracy
    representative government, 233, 234, 236
    See also Egalitarianism
Denham, Thomas, 8, 22, 23, 223
Dialectical writings
    discourse on self-denial, 136, 139, 182–188
    Socratic dialogue "A Man of Sense," 136, 139, 182, 188–195
"Dialogue between the Gout and Mr. Franklin," 120
"Dialogue between Two Presbyterians" (Franklin), 279, 280
Digestive gas, proposal to change odor, 112–114
Diplomatic career of Franklin
    attempts at reconciliation with England, 239–240
    in France, 12–13, 221, 244
    negotiations with England, 13, 221
    relationship to moral principles, 222
Disease
    gout, 120
    vulnerability to, 257–258
Dishonesty, 190–191, 194–195
    See also Honesty
Disputation. *See* Socratic methods
A *Dissertation on Liberty and Necessity, Pleasure and Pain* (Franklin), 145–157
    absurd conclusions, 206–207
    comedy in, 155, 166
    comparison to "On the Providence of God," 170–171
    contents, 145–152

defense of Deism, 6, 8, 140
    error insinuated in, 23, 47, 135–136, 139–140, 146, 159, 172–173
    first section, 146–149, 156–157
    hypothetical argument, 152, 159–160
    not taken seriously by BF, 145–146, 166
    parody of Deism, 155, 157, 160–162, 166
    publication, 8, 47, 137, 305n1
    publication described as error, 6, 21–22, 138, 157–159
    scholarly views, 140–141, 311–312n24
    second section, 149–151, 152–153
Douglas, Stephen, 268
"Drinker's Dictionary" (Franklin), 118
Dryden, John, 146, 157, 161

Eagles, bald, 248
"An Economical Project" (Franklin), 321n3
Education
    BF's support, 220
    of Franklin, 17, 242, 320n77
    of black children, 266–267
Egalitarianism
    of BF, 230, 234, 240–248, 251–253, 278
    equality of opportunity, 241, 248, 251, 263
    racial, 267–268
Electricity
    accidental electrocution, 119
    electrocution of turkeys, 119
    experiments with, 8–9, 119, 220, 256
    Spencer's lectures, 8
    treatment of paralysis, 284
Emigration
    BF's opposition to ban on, 238–239
    from Europe to America, 244–246
    See also Immigration
Enlightenment, 207–208, 212
Equality. *See* Egalitarianism
Evil
    choice of, 90, 181–182
    existence, 147, 151–152, 156
Experiments and Observations on Electricity (Franklin), 267

Faith
    interaction with reason, 79–80
    See also Credulity; Religion
Fothergill, John, 122
    letters to, 122–124
France
    aristocracy, 244, 290
    diplomatic mission in, 12–13, 221, 244
    financial support for Revolution, 221
    publication of U.S. state constitutions, 243, 245
    Terror, 242
Franklin, Benjamin
    critics of, vii–viii, 1–2
    death, 14
    education, 17, 27, 242, 320n77

Franklin, Benjamin, *continued*
  epitaph, 294n1, 325n86
  family, 7, 17–18
  as First American, 288–290
  flight from Boston, 7, 20, 57–58, 175,
    298–299n28
  intellectual journey, 199–205
  life, 7–14
  marriage, 8, 25, 106
  masks worn, x, xii–xiii, 4
  philosophical, 4, 5, 287–292
  popular image, 2
  "real," 287–292
Franklin, James
  BF's apprenticeship, 7, 17, 19, 20, 52, 57, 241
  newspaper, 7, 19, 240
  political problems, 57
  reconciliation with BF, 31–32
Franklin, John, 20
Franklin, Josiah, 7, 17–18, 19, 36, 223
Franklin, William
  Autobiography addressed to, 15
  BF's relationship with, 290–292, 315n27
  letters to, 239–240, 291–292, 315n27
Franklin, William Temple, 136, 137, 305n1
*Franklin's Political, Miscellaneous, and Philosophical
  Pieces*, 136, 137
Freemasons. *See* Masons
Free trade, 246
Free will
  choice of evil, 90, 181–182
  existence, 95, 148, 156, 160, 206
French and Indian Wars, 9, 265–266
French Revolution, 242
Frugality, 213, 214, 217, 218, 219

Galloway, Joseph, 317n27
Gas pill, proposal for, 112–114
Germans
  immigrants, 264, 266
  Palatine Boors comment, 9, 10, 263–265
Godfrey, Thomas, 25
"Good Humor" (anonymous pamphlet), 229
Good things in life
  for BF, 288
  BF's view, 209, 212
  perfection, 209–211
  securing, 212–220
  See also Virtues
Gout, 120
Government
  best forms, 236–237
  BF's view of, 236–237
  conflicts with governed, 238–240
  Hobbes on forms of, 235–236, 237
  monarchy, 235–236
  origins, 227
  purpose, 237
  representative, 233, 234, 236
Grand Ohio Company, 222

Grasse, François-Joseph-Paul de, 273, 279, 282,
  321n96
Grenville, George, 11

Hamilton, Alexander, 268
Hamilton, Andrew, 24
Happiness
  BF on, 211–213
  Enlightenment view, 207–208
  knowledge and, 219
  virtue as means to, 55, 163, 164–165, 214, 216,
    217, 219
  See also Good things in life
Harvard College, satire of, 240–241
Helvétius, Anne-Catherine, 119
  BF's marriage proposal, 13, 106
  letters to, 109–110
Hemphill, Samuel, 8, 31, 72, 279–281, 300n13
Hillsborough, Lord, 11, 12
Hoaxes
  Masonic initiation, 114–118
  scalps article, 110–112, 282, 315n27
  "Sidi Mehemet Ibrahim on the Slave Trade,"
    270–273, 282
Hobbes, Thomas
  argument against spirits, 75–76, 78, 165–166
  atheism, 324n52
  BF's differences from, 228, 273, 275–278,
    324nn52,53
  BF's reading of, 201, 227–228
  on forms of government, 235–236, 237
  influence on BF, 228–234
  Leviathan, 75, 165–166, 207, 227–228, 232,
    235, 275–277, 278
  optimism, 324n52
  political theory, 276–277
  rationalism, 278
  on religion, 275–278
  on state of nature, 228–229, 231, 232, 275–276,
    277, 278
Home, Henry, Lord Kames, letter to, 261–262
Honesty
  in *Autobiography*, 46–47
  Bacon on, 199
  dishonesty, 190–191, 194–195
  simplicity and, 195
  utility and, 36, 41, 141–142, 194
  See also Sincerity
Honor, 247
Hopkinson, Thomas
  letter to, 6, 306n10
  reaction to Whitefield sermon, 37–38
Hospitals. *See* Pennsylvania Hospital
Huey, Joseph, letter to, 284–285
Hume, David, 10, 11, 12
Humility, 28–29, 35, 59, 128–129, 213, 216–217,
  289
Humor
  of BF, xi–xii, 67–68
  blasphemous, 71–72

political implications, 134
scatological, 92–98
shamelessness, 100–101, 132
vulgar, 68
See also Comic pieces of Franklin; Hoaxes;
    Satires
Hutchinson, Thomas, 11–12
Hutchinson letters affair, 11–12, 221

Ignorance, 94–95, 180–181
Imitation of Christ (Kempis), 129, 305n48
Immigration
    dangers of, 9, 10
    of Germans, 264, 266
    See also Emigration
Immodesty, 177–179
Immorality, 51–53, 55
    See also Morality
Indians
    attacks on settlers, 120–121
    carefree lifestyles, 208–209, 251, 277–278
    defense against, 9, 121
    European settlers and, 120–121, 249
    manners, 112
    murders by Paxton Boys, 120–124
    scalps hoax, 110–112, 282, 315n27
    skin color, 265
    in state of nature, 229, 230, 277–278
Indignation, moral, 269–270, 278–279, 282–283
Industry, as virtue, 213, 214, 217, 218, 219
"Information to Those Who Would Remove to
    America" (Franklin), 244–246
Integrity, 141–142, 194–195
"The Interest of Great Britain Reconsidered"
    (Franklin), 220, 261–262
Invention
    benefits, 250
    BF's activities, 8, 10
    refusal to profit from, 35
    utility of, 321n3
Ireland, poverty in, 250, 251
Irony, BF's use of, xii–xiii, 4-7, 294n12. See also
    Autobiography: irony
Isaacson, Walter, ix, 289, 322–323n22
Islam
    Koran, 271, 272
    Purist sect, 270, 272–273, 282
Izard, Ralph, 12, 316n27

Jackson, James, 270
Jackson, Richard, 266
James (apostle), 34, 36
James, Abel, letter to Franklin included in
    Autobiography, 3, 26, 35, 41
Jay, John, 13
Jefferson, Thomas
    on BF's role in writing of Declaration of
        Independence, 110
    defense of Terror, 242
    in France, 13, 243

negotiations with England, 13
on rights, 280–281
writing of Declaration of Independence,
    226–227, 232, 269
Jesus
    BF's view of, 45
    divinity, 36, 45, 283, 284
    imitating, 129, 216, 305n48
    satires of, 128–131
Jones, Evan, 115, 116
Junto
    formation, 8
    library, 25, 26
    papers written for, 138–139, 143, 166–170, 209
Justice
    biblical principle, 91
    claims, 269–270
    Deists' view of, 161–162
    divine, 85, 97–98, 152, 171–172, 173, 204
    earthly, and divine anger, 85–92, 132–133
    existence, 229
    God's equal treatment of all, 149–151, 153–155
    hope for, 172, 173
    of horse theft, 147–148, 158
    as virtue, 213, 214, 219
    See also Punishments; Rewards

Keimer, Samuel, 7, 8, 20, 21, 23, 24
Keith, William, 7–8, 20, 21, 63, 223–224
Kempis, Thomas à, *Imitation of Christ,* 129, 305n48
Ketcham, Ralph L., 318n40
Kinnersly, Ebenezer, 281
Knowledge, 188–190
    acquiring, 217–218
    silence and, 217, 218–219
    of true interest, 191–192, 193
Koran, 271, 272

La Sabliere de la Condamine, letter to, 79
Lathrop, John, letter to, 259
Laurens, Henry, 13
Lawrence, D. H., vii–viii, 1, 4, 39–40, 42, 212
Lay, Benjamin, 70, 324n58
Lee, Arthur, 12, 262–263
Lee, Richard Henry, 316n27
Lee, William, 12
Lemay, J. A. Leo, 314n11, 324n52
Lerner, Ralph, 5
"A Letter from Father Abraham, to His Beloved
    Son" (Franklin), 92–98, 133
"Letter of the Drum" (Franklin), 72–73, 78
    response of Philoclerus, 72, 73–77, 100
Letter to a Friend in the Country (Franklin), 279–280
Leviathan (Hobbes), 75, 165–166, 207, 227–228,
    232, 235, 275–277, 278
Levin, David, viii
Liberty, 148, 263, 268
Libraries
    of Junto, 25, 26
    Philadelphia public, 25, 26

Lincoln, Abraham
  address at Cooper Institute, 268
  second inaugural address, 273
Lind, John, *Remarks on the Principal Acts of the Thirteenth Parliament*, 234
Livingston, Robert R., letter to, 244
Locke, John
  BF's reading of, 18, 57, 201
  Essay Concerning Human Understanding, 18, 207–208
  Second Treatise of Government, 227
Logan, James, letter to, 228
Love. *See* Marriage; Sexual desire
Luke, Gospel according to, 257
Lyons, William, 22

Madison, James, 222
Mandeville, Bernard, 8, 22, 159
"A Man of Sense" (Socratic dialogue; Franklin), 136, 139, 182, 188–195
Manufacturing, 245–246, 250, 265
Marriage
  advantages, 101, 104
  to beautiful woman, 107–108
  of Franklin, 8, 25, 106
  satires of, 101–106, 107, 109, 130
Masons
  BF's letter to parents, 117, 118, 224
  BF's membership, 8, 115
  oaths, 115, 116, 117, 118
  phony initiation, 114–118, 224
Masturbation, 105, 108
Mather, Cotton, 7, 17
Mecom, Jane, letter to, 211–212, 218
Mercantilism, 246
Mercury, 115–116
Meredith, Hugh, 23, 24
Merit, 184–185, 186–187, 285
Mesmer, Franz, 79
Metaphysical writings, 143
  abandonment, 139–140, 143
  differences from Socratic refutations, 143–144, 201–202
  on prayer, 138, 139, 165
  "On the Providence of God in the Government of the World," 139, 143, 166–171, 306n7
  See also Articles of Belief and Acts of Religion; A Dissertation on Liberty and Necessity, Pleasure and Pain
Metaphysics
  dogmatism, 202
  errors, 172–173, 204
  rejection of, 166
  uncertainty, 308n32
Middlekauff, Robert, 222, 317n27
Militia, 9, 121, 220
Milton, John, *Hymn to the Creator*, 163
Miracles, 71, 78, 160, 165–166
Mitchel, James, 80–85, 132, 133

Moderation, 213, 215–216, 219
Modernity
  BF's view, 288
  new possibilities, 254–255
  project, 260–263
  religion and, 40
Monarchy
  BF's view of, 225, 236
  Hobbes on, 235–236
Moral errata, 19–22, 24–25, 50, 51–53, 57, 241
Morality
  Christian, 72
  critique of, 203–204, 205, 288
  positive doctrine, 212–220
  reasons for bad choices, 95
  relationship to religion, 203-205, 282–284
Moral perfection project, 15–16, 27–28, 29–30
The Morals of Chess (Franklin), 225
Moral virtues. *See* Virtues
Morellet, Abbé, 127–128
Morgan, David T., 319n48
Morgan, Edmund, x, 40, 322n12
Morris, Gouverneur, 268
Morris, Robert, letter to, 230–231

Narrative of the Late Massacres (Franklin), 120–122, 124
Natural rights. *See* Rights
Natural science
  Bacon's importance, 255
  BF's activities, 8–9, 254
  BF's interest, 112, 212
  experimental, 112, 255, 256, 274
  future progress, 259–260
  goals, 256–260, 273–274
  satires, 112–114
  See also Electricity
Nature, state of, 226
  Hobbes on, 228–229, 231, 232, 275–276, 277, 278
  Indians in, 229, 230, 277–278
  origins of government, 227
Negro School, Philadelphia, 266–267
New England Courant, 7, 19, 240
Newton, Isaac, 22, 318n32
Nicole, Pierre, *Port Royal Logic*, 18, 57, 201
Norris, Robert, letter to, 317n27

"Observations Concerning the Increase of Mankind, Peopling of Countries, etc." (Franklin), 9, 249, 263–266, 322–323n22
  Palatine Boors comment, 9, 10, 263–264
  reprinting, 267–268
"Observations on my Reading History in Library" (Franklin), 29
Observations on the Proceedings against Mr. Hemphill (Franklin), 279–280
Old Mistress Apologue (Franklin), 101–106, 107, 109, 130
Oliver, Andrew, 11–12

"On a Proposed Act to Prevent Emigration" (Franklin), 238–239
"On Simplicity" (Franklin), 195–197, 254, 255, 311–313n24
"On the Labouring Poor" (Franklin), 249
"On the Providence of God in the Government of the World" (Franklin), 139, 143, 166–171, 306n7
"On Titles of Honour" (Franklin), 243–244
Opinions and Conjectures (Franklin), 256
Order, as virtue, 213, 219
Order of the Cincinnati, 246–248
Original sin, 130–131, 275, 280, 281, 324n52
Orpheus, 273–274

Pain and pleasure, 149–151, 153
Paine, Tom, letters to, 71, 310n6
Palatine Boors, 9, 10, 263–265
Palmer, Samuel, 8, 21, 22
Parker, James, 9
    letter to, 264
"Parody and Reply to a Religious Meditation" (Franklin), 125–127
Patriotism, 186
Paxton Boys, 120–124
Pemberton, Henry, 22
Penn, John, 121, 122, 123
Penn, Richard, 10
Penn, Thomas
    BF's relationship with, 9, 122, 220, 222, 317n27
    taxes on property of, 10
Penn, William, *No Cross, No Crown*, 243
Pennsylvania
    Constitution, 12, 241, 245
    Indian attacks, 120–121
    politics, 121
    proprietary government, 10, 122, 123, 220, 222, 317n27
Pennsylvania Assembly
    BF as agent in London, 9–12
    BF as clerk, 8
    BF as member, 9, 10, 220
    matching grant bill for hospital, 9, 36, 257
Pennsylvania Gazette, 8, 31, 72, 115, 118, 125, 195, 256
Pennsylvania Hospital, 9, 36, 122, 220, 256–258
Pennsylvania Society for Promoting the Abolition of Slavery and the Relief of Free Negroes Unlawfully Held in Bondage, 13, 268
Perfection
    in life, 209–211
    moral, 15–16, 27–28, 29–30, 212–220
Pessimism, 314n11, 324n52
Philadelphia
    BF as postmaster, 8
    City Council, 220
    defense, 220
    fire company, 8, 9, 220
    library, 25, 26

Negro School, 266–267
religious politics, 8, 31, 72, 279–281, 300n13
Philadelphia Academy, 220
Philoclerus. *See* "Letter of the Drum"
Pitt, William (Lord Chatham), 239
"Plain Truth" (Franklin), 9
Plato, 298–299n28
    Republic, 96–97
Political career of Franklin, 9
    abolition issue, 13, 222, 263
    activities in London, 9–12
    Baconianism, 225, 234–236, 237, 254–261
    compatibility with philosophical life, 134
    Constitutional Convention, 13–14
    defense issue, 9, 10, 220
    efforts to replace proprietary with royal government in Pennsylvania, 10, 122, 123, 220, 222, 317n27
    elective offices, 9, 10, 13, 220
    enemies, 10
    hospital project, 9, 36, 122, 220, 256–258
    modernity and, 260–263
    motives, 131–132, 222–223, 224–225, 260–261
    as political fixer, 131, 220–222
    projects, 254
    scholarship on, 222–223
    seen as game, 225
    support of British Empire, 220–221, 222, 225, 260–262, 287
    support of Revolutionary War, 222, 262–263, 287
Political principles, 225–226
    Baconian, 225, 234–236
    Hobbesian, 228–234, 237
    liberty, 148, 263, 268
    See also Egalitarianism; Rights
Poor Richard's Almanack, 8, 30–31, 71, 92, 98–99, 212, 255, 313n5
Pope, Alexander, 19, 143, 311n13
    An Essay on Criticism, 176–178
Port Royal Logic, 18, 57, 201
Poverty, 249–251
Power
    absolute, 235
    arbitrary, 241
    sovereign, 235
Pragmatism, 288–289
Prayer
    existence of, 137–138
    writings on, 138, 139, 306n7
Presbyterian Synod
    BF's education, 27
    BF's relationship with, 31, 220, 280, 281
    Hemphill controversy, 8, 31, 72, 279–281, 300n13
Pride, 59, 61, 216–217
Priestley, Joseph, 12
    BF's relationship with, 10
    letters to, 227–228, 251–253, 258–259, 260

Property
   private, 234
   rights, 230–231
"Proposals and Queries to be asked in the Junto"
   (Franklin), 209
"Proposed Memorial to Lord Dartmouth"
   (Franklin), 314–315n27
Proprietary Party, 121, 122, 220
Prouse, James, 80–85, 132
Providence
   arguments against, 325n86
   arguments for, 139, 143, 166–170, 202–203
   BF's claim to have believed in, 6, 48
   BF's contradictory account of belief in, 7, 27,
      48–50, 54, 65, 142, 145–146
   Deist view, 125
   denial of particular, 202, 204, 206, 284–286
   general, 125
   mocking of, 124–128
   particular, 168–170
   writings on, 139, 143, 144, 166–170, 306n7
Prudence, 178–180
Public service
   BF's view, x, 134, 222, 224–225, 318n32,
      322n12
   Philadelphia public library, 25, 26
   realistic view of, 41, 42
   See also Diplomatic career of Franklin; Political
      career of Franklin
Punishments
   as deterrents, 91
   divine, 53, 97–98, 153, 154–155, 278
   necessity for righteousness, 54, 55–56
   secular, 54–55, 91
   for vice, 171–172
   vice as own, 96, 179, 180

Quaker Party, 10, 121

Race
   BF's reputation as racist, 322n17
   BF's view of, 263–266, 267–268
   skin colors and, 264–265, 267–268,
      322–323n22
Ralph, James, 8, 21, 22, 23, 47, 157–158
Ramsay, Allan, "Thoughts on the Origin and
   Nature of Government," 229–230, 231,
   233–234, 238
Raynal, Guillaume-Thomas-François de, 85
Read, Deborah
   appearance in dream, 109–110
   assistance in printing business, 26
   courtship, 21
   death, 11
   disagreement with cousin James, 129
   family, 7
   marriage, 8, 25, 106
   mob threats against, 11
   moral erratum concerning, 21, 52
   Waring letter and, 266

Read, James, letter to, 129–130, 305n48
Read, John, 7
Reason
   interaction with credulity, 79–85
   rationalism of Hobbes, 278
Rees, Daniel, 115–117
Religion
   Bacon on, 274
   BF's comic pieces ridiculing, 71–72, 78–79, 132
   BF's differences with Bacon and Hobbes,
      274–278
   BF's "want of," 47, 63, 142, 204, 284–286,
      307n15
   critique of, 288
   frauds, 45
   Hobbes on, 275–278
   origins, 277
   relationship to morality, 203–205, 282–284
   as restraint on vice, 281–282
   warning against ridiculing, 73–74
   See also Atheism; Christianity; Deism
Religious history in *Autobiography*, 26–29, 40
   adolescent fall from religion, 17
   as comedy, 36–37, 199
   contradictions, 7, 27, 48–50, 64, 65, 199
   creed, 29–30, 44, 47–48
   Deism, 23
   moral reformation, 22–24, 50–51, 54, 64, 136
   moral saga, 47–48
   scholarly views, viii–x, xii, 145
   skepticism, 56
   thought of as atheist, 47–48, 58, 62, 142, 175
   tolerance, 71
"Remarks Concerning the Savages of North
   America" (Franklin), 112, 278
Remington, John, 115, 116
Resolution, 213–214, 219
Revolutionary War
   BF's support, 222, 262–263
   French support, 221
   natural rights doctrine in, 227
   officers, 246–248
   scalpings by Indians, 111
Rewards
   divine, 53, 54, 55–56
   secular, 54–55
   for virtue, 97–98, 171–172, 186
   See also Justice
Rights
   American views, 233
   BF's understanding, 226–227, 230, 232–234,
      263, 269–270, 318–319n40, 319n48
   in Declaration of Independence, 268–269
   of emigration, 238–239
   Jefferson on, 280–281
   natural, 226–227, 229, 232–234, 263
   property, 230–231
Rodney, George, 273, 279, 282, 321n96
Royal Society, 8, 9
Russel, Phillips, 101

Satires
  of Deism, 155, 157, 160–162, 166, 173
  of Harvard College, 240–241
  of marriage, 101–106, 107, 109, 130
  of providence, 124–128
  of religion, 71–72, 78–79, 132
  scalps hoax, 110–112, 282, 315n27
  of self, 118–124
  shamelessness, 100–101
  "To the Royal Academy of *****," 112–114
  of William Penn, 243–244
Scalps hoax, 110–112, 282, 315n27
Schneider, Herbert W., 311n24
Science
  knowledge of, 188–190
  quackery, 79
  See also Natural science
Scotland, poverty in, 250, 251
Second Continental Congress, 12
Secrecy, Bacon on, 198–199
Self-denial
  discourse on, 136, 139, 182–188
  relationship to virtue, 182–188
Sexual desire
  advice for managing, 101, 103–105, 108
  affairs with old women, 102–104, 105, 107,
    108, 109, 130
  chastity and, 130–131
  satisfying with masturbation, 105, 108
  sinfulness, 87–90
Shaftesbury, Earl of (Anthony Ashley Cooper)
  on Bacon, 166, 299n39
  BF's reading of, 7, 18, 53, 57, 62, 200–201
  influence, 148
  parodies of, 173
  on Xenophon, 298–299n28
Shipley, Jonathan, 234
  letter to, 315n27
Shirley, William, letter to, 234, 236
"Sidi Mehemet Ibrahim on the Slave Trade"
    (Franklin), 270–273, 282
Silence, 213, 217, 218–219
Silence Dogood essays, 7, 19, 240–241, 298n28
Simplicity, 195–197
Simulation and dissimulation, 198–199
Sincerity, 141–142, 194–195, 197, 213, 214, 219
Slavery
  abolitionism, 13, 222, 263, 268, 272, 273,
    316–317n27, 324n58
  BF's view of, 263, 266–267, 268–273
  economic disadvantages, 265, 268, 269
  education of children, 266–267
  "Sidi Mehemet Ibrahim on the Slave Trade"
    (Franklin), 270–273, 282
  slaves owned by BF, 263
Smith, Adam, 10
Smith, Joshua, 125
Smyth, Albert Henry, 67–68, 101, 110
Socrates, 129, 130, 142, 174, 266
Socratic dialogue. *See* "A Man of Sense"

Socratic method number one (dialectical
    refutations)
  consequences of use, 58, 60–61, 175
  differences from metaphysical reasoning,
    201–202
  learning from, 175, 204–205
  learning of, 18, 57
  period of time used, 60, 62, 143, 158–159,
    174–175, 203
  risks, 176
  use in nonreligious discussions, 61, 62, 142
  use in religious discussions, 58, 61, 62, 63
Socratic method number two (diffident)
  contradictions in account of transition to,
    59–64
  learning of, 18–19
  transition to, 58, 143, 174, 200
  usefulness, 58–59, 175–176
  use in religious discussions, 62
Sovereign power, 235
"Speech of Miss Polly Baker" (Franklin), 85–92,
    132–133, 301–302n28
Spencer, Archibald, 8
Spinoza, Baruch, 147, 201
Spirits
  belief in, 72–73, 74–75, 78
  Hobbes's argument against, 75–76
Stamp Act, 10–11, 211, 212, 221, 222, 229, 320n70
Stevenson, Margaret, letter to, 106–107
Stiles, Ezra
  letter from, 283
  letters to, 124, 283–284, 285–286, 325n86
Sturgeon, William, 266, 267
Supreme Executive Council of Pennsylvania, 13,
    14

T., Mrs., 22, 52, 53
Tackerbury, John, 115
Taxes, 230–231, 233–234, 238, 249
Technology. *See* Invention
Temperance, 213, 214, 219
"That Self-Denial is not the Essence of Virtue"
    (Franklin), 136, 139, 182–188
Thomson, Charles, letter to, 212, 316n27
Tolerance, religious, 71
"To the Royal Academy of *****" (Franklin),
    112–114
Townshend Acts, 11, 233
Tranquility, 213, 219
"The Trial and Reprieve of Prouse and Mitchel"
    (Franklin), 80–85, 132, 133
Turkeys, 119, 248
Twain, Mark, 2, 4, 290

Unicameralism, 13, 221, 241
Updike, John, xii
Utilitarianism, 289

Van Doren, Carl, 212
Vanity, 35, 118, 133–134

Vaughn, Benjamin
   letter to, 6, 137–138, 139, 140, 143
   letter to Franklin included in *Autobiography*, 3,
      26, 34, 35, 41, 137
   publication of BF's writings, 136, 137
Vegetarianism, 21, 35–36, 113
Vergennes, Charles Gravier de, 13, 221,
      315–316n27
Vernon, Mr., 20, 21, 23, 24, 52
Vice
   existence, 55, 56, 65, 153, 158, 206
   hidden, 92, 97
   human nature and, 251–253
   ignorance and, 94–95, 180–181
   immodesty, 177–179
   as own punishment, 96, 179, 180
   prudent use, 192
   punishments, 171–172
   responsibility for, 94
   restraints of religion, 281–282
   scatological comparisons, 92
Virtue
   apparent, 92, 94
   challenge, 95
   distinction from prudence, 179–180
   existence, 55, 56, 65, 153, 158, 206
   as means to happiness, 55, 163, 164–165, 214,
      216, 217, 219
   natural, 185–186
   need for, 92
   as own reward, 179, 180
   project for party of, 29–30, 43, 44, 64–65
   relationship to self-denial, 182–188
   rewards, 97–98, 171–172, 186
   sacrificial nobility, 96–97, 133, 179–180,
      181–182
   writings on, 136
Virtues
   BF's list of thirteen, 28, 34–35, 212–220
   charity, 34–35, 37, 40, 122, 124, 257–258
   chastity, 213, 219
   cleanliness, 213, 219
   contribution to felicity, 214, 216, 217, 219
   frugality, 213, 214, 217, 218, 219
   happiness and, 163, 164–165
   humility, 28–29, 35, 59, 128–129, 213,
      216–217, 289
   industry, 213, 214, 217, 218, 219
   justice, 213, 214, 219
   moderation, 213, 215–216, 219
   moral, 214
   order, 213, 219
   resolution, 213–214, 219
   silence, 213, 217, 218–219
   sincerity, 197, 213, 214, 219
   temperance, 213, 214, 219
   tranquility, 213, 219
   utility of, 52–53
   See also Honesty

Wagstaff, Timothy, 5
Waldstreicher, David, 322–323n22, 324n58
Walpole, Richard, 222
Walpole, Thomas, 222, 315n27
Walters, Kerry S., 308–309n46
War, BF on, 242–243
Ward, John William, viii
Waring, John, 266
   letter to, 267
The Way to Wealth, 98–99
Wedderburn, Alexander, 12
Wentworth Dillon, Earl of, 177–178, 200
Whatley, George, letter to, 301n19
Whatley, Thomas, 11
Whitefield, George
   comparison to BF, 43–44
   enthusiasm, 281
   friendship with BF, 32–33, 37–38, 43, 45–46,
      281
   imagined excellences, 43–44, 45, 46, 50
   orphanage project, 32, 37–39
   prayers for BF's conversion, 36
   preaching, 281
   rhetorical skill, 32, 37–39
   sermons published by BF, 8
   writings, 4–5, 33, 43, 44
Wickedness. *See* Evil
Williams, Ted, 260
Wine, 125–128
Witch trials, 69–70, 77–78
Wollaston, William, 21–22, 147, 153
Women
   beauty, 102, 105, 106
   gratitude of old, 102–103, 130
   preferences for old, 102–104, 105, 109, 130
Wood, Gordon, x, 4, 13, 222, 314–316n27,
      318n32
Wright, Esmond, 226–227
Written word, dangers of, 4–5

Xenophon, 266
   BF's reading of, 18, 57, 62, 201, 205,
      298–299n28
   Memorabilia, 18, 142

Yale College, 283